Boubacar Barry is one of the leading figures in West African historiography. His authoritative study of 400 years of Senegambian history is unrivalled in its detailed grasp of published and unpublished materials. Taking as its subject the vast area covering the Senegal and Gambia river basins, this book explores the changing dynamics of regional and Atlantic trade, clashes between traditional African and emergent Muslim authorities, the slave trade and the colonial system, and current obstacles to the integration of the region's modern states. Professor Barry argues cogently for the integrity of the Senegambian region as a historical subject, and he forges a coherent narrative from the dismemberment and unification which characterized Senegambia's development from the fifteenth to the nineteenth century. This newly translated study is a vital tool in our understanding of West African history.

# Senegambia and the Atlantic slave trade

*African Studies Series 92*

*A list of books in this series will be found at the end of this volume*

# Senegambia and the Atlantic slave trade

Boubacar Barry

*University Cheikh Anta Diop de Dakar*
*Translated from the French by Ayi Kwei Armah*

**CAMBRIDGE**
UNIVERSITY PRESS

PUBLISHED BY THE PRESS SYNDICATE OF THE UNIVERSITY OF CAMBRIDGE
The Pitt Building, Trumpington Street, Cambridge CB2 1RP, United Kingdom

CAMBRIDGE UNIVERSITY PRESS
The Edinburgh Building, Cambridge CB2 2RU, United Kingdom
40 West 20th Street, New York, NY 10011-4211, USA
10 Stamford Road, Oakleigh, Melbourne 3166, Australia

Originally published in French as *La Sénégambie du xvᵉ au xixᵉ
siècle: traite négrière, Islam et Conquête coloniale*
by Editions L'Harmattan, Paris 1988
and © L'Harmattan, 1988
First published in English by Cambridge University Press 1998 as *Senegambia
and the Atlantic slave trade*

English translation © Cambridge University Press 1998

Printed in the United States of America

Typeset in 10/12pt Times NR  [SE]

*A catalogue record for this book is available from the British Library*

*Library of Congress cataloguing in publication data*

Barry, Boubacar.
    [Sénégambie du XVe au XIXe siècle. English]
    Senegambia and the Atlantic slave trade
    /Boubacar Barry; translated from the
    French by Ayi Kwei Armah.
        p.  cm. – (African studies series; 92)
    Includes bibliographical references.
    ISBN 0 521 59226 7. – ISBN 0 521 59760 9 (pbk.)
    1. Senegambia – History.  I. Title.  II. Series.
    DT532.25.B37  1997
    966.305–dc21                                    97-6026
                                                    CIP

ISBN 0 521 59226 7 hardback
ISBN 0 521 59760 9 paperback

For
Aïda, Sow-Pullo.

To the People of Senegal, cordial hosts to thousands of
Guineans looking forward to the coming of a Greater
Senegambia, Land of Peoples without frontiers.

# Contents

# Preface

This book is not about the Senegambian Confederation that brought present-day Senegal and Gambia together after the Kaur Conference of 1981. It is about the Greater Senegambia region, that vast stretch of territory covering the two great river basins, the Senegal and the Gambia River valleys, understood as an inclusive region beginning at the sources of the two rivers high on the Futa Jallon plateau, and ending at their mouths on the Atlantic coast. It comprises a West African region bordered by the Atlantic Ocean, the Sahara desert, the Savanna grasslands and the Equatorial forest.

In times past this region embraced all the states that now share the area: Senegal, Gambia, Guinea Bissau, as well as parts of Mauritania, Mali, and Guinea Conakry. Each of these six nation-states falls, wholly or in part, within the Greater Senegambian zone. All are now confronted, after a quarter century of independence, with a serious teething crisis threatening, in the long run, to block all likelihood of the region's population ever freeing itself from chronic underdevelopment and its grotesque sequel, negative development. Responses to the impasse, sad to say, have been unimaginative: a proliferation of such white elephants as the Senegal River Valley Development Authority (OMVS), the Gambia River Valley Development Authority (OMVG), the Sahel Region Inter-State Anti-Drought Committee (CILSS), the West African Economic Community (CEAO), and the Economic Community of West African States (ECOWAS). This is a mere sample from the long roster of regional and sub-regional organizations of which the six Senegambian States are members, full or associate. Each also belongs, under OAU auspices, to several continental organizations. Finally, each belongs to the hydra-headed United Nations system. Levels of involvement differ, but the goal is constant. The region's states, having failed to achieve political union, are groping, through these multiple memberships, at meaningful economic integration. For they see integration as a way to ensure the survival of the population within frameworks less stifling than the frontiers of our artificial states.

Each such regional or sub-regional agency was born long on hope. All have come up short on achievement. The cause is an original flaw: each of these states left over from the nineteenth-century colonial order clings to its sovereignty. And that divisive heritage frustrates progress toward future union. It was this impasse that moved me to undertake this study on the geopolitical dismemberment – past and present – of Greater Senegambia.

My initial plan was to highlight the insight that in the same period (from the fifteenth to the twentieth century) which saw the region's dismemberment, there was also an opposite movement toward political and economic unification in Greater Senegambia. An awareness of this countervailing process, I think, is necessary for the accurate understanding of regional trends toward unity and fragmentation. It is an understanding indispensable now, if we are to break free of the futureless political and economic straitjackets into which our nation-states have double-locked the Senegambian people behind artificial frontiers. I do not intend to parrot the insincere slogans mouthed by officials singing our peoples' common cultural and ethnic identity even as they themselves busily harden barriers between states, blocking the free movement of people, goods, ideas. My aim is different. While I have no intention of obscuring differences and contrasts between the region's diverse component parts, the main thrust of my work will be to highlight their complementarity. For that is the factor that points most clearly to the region's potential unity. And that potential needs to become reality if the region's peoples are to survive. My aim, in short, is to contribute to a spirit of unity, much as Kwame Nkrumah, Cheikh Anta Diop and, more recently, Edem Kodjo have done. I hope to do this by giving our present generations the historical consciousness needed for coping with life in these ceaselessly challenging times.

Our artificial frontiers have a clear function: to legitimize each nation-state's claim to sovereignty. They are also grounded in a peculiar history. Whoever wishes to understand the active hostility of our nation-states to the creation of a Greater Senegambia – a union of the region's peoples – must first understand that history. Today we cannot sidestep the issue of political unity in a federal framework within which all member states will give up their international sovereignty. That is the prerequisite for the creation of a viable regional space. The point is not to modify existing frontiers. It is to unify existing states in ways that enable the zone's people and natural regions to rediscover their homogeneity within a vast supranational framework. Only such a framework, capacious enough to nurture grassroots initiatives and autonomy, can help us solve the crucial problems of industrialization, agricultural modernization, education, and the development of our cultural identity through the promotion of African languages. It makes no sense to redraw existing boundaries. We must abolish them. That is the way to expand our economic and political system, in an internally driven process of integrated development based on precise knowledge of active, complementary relationships between the zone's different natural regions and the diversity of its resources and populations.

The six states in this one region have a total population of fewer than thirty million inhabitants. This small population is burdened with six presidents, hundreds of ministers and ambassadors, and thousands of civil servants and parliamentary representatives, all clinging resolutely to their national privileges. This top-heavy state apparatus is now the main obstacle to regional integration policies designed to end our common misery, requiring us to pool our energies to achieve a better future.

A reading of our history, recent and remote, shows that unity is the only way forward. We do have a history: of that there is no doubt now. The problem is that we still live outside our history. That is because in the abundance of political rhetoric flowing from our states, and in all their activities, serious thinking about the experience of our societies is rare. Our ruling elite seems scared to face its history, afraid to face its present. It cannot look into the mirror of reality because it is terrified of the image awaiting it. On those rare occasions when history is invoked, the talk is merely about great empires in Ghana, Mali, and Songhai. Our elite seems content to recall vaguely that in the past most of West Africa was united under the Mansas or the Askias. Then comes the invocation of heroes from the period of resistance to colonial rule. The names of Samori, Lat Joor, Shaykh Umar, and other chieftains are pressed into service, to underpin the legitimizing ideology of our new charismatic leaders amid choruses of national unanimity. Beyond these two poles of our history, beyond dirges on the Slave Trade and denunciations of apartheid, all is emptiness.

We are afraid, perhaps, to focus on this long history, to look into the many phases of our mass population movements. We fear to evaluate the causes of conflicts that made our peoples clash against each other in the past. We dread knowledge of the mechanisms of our social and economic inequalities, the role of violence in our societies, our technological adaptations, the revolutions our societies have undergone. Above all, we have not had the nerve to contemplate the unending procession of our failed dreams.

The time has come to shed our fear, to look at our history with open eyes. It is time for us to study with constant clarity all aspects of our variegated history, from the most glorious to the most abject.

I have chosen to focus on that long stretch of our history from the fifteenth to the nineteenth century. In sad truth, that period saw our societies regress on every level. In a steady slide, we lost our autonomy. Worse, we lost the capacity to take initiatives. If today we have fallen to a negligible quantity in the sum of human affairs, a great part of the explanation lies in our decline during that period. That is why we need to project a fresh vision of history, a vision which sheds critical light on our own past, from the viewpoint of a present situation that constitutes a constant challenge. In this situation, in this context of political and economic dismemberment under the rule of our *de facto* one-party states, the historian's challenge is inseparable from the general struggle for democracy, for unity and for fundamental human freedoms. If we aspire to take charge of our own future, we have to meet a prerequisite challenge: the development of a clear historical consciousness.

When, in 1980, I outlined this project, my intention was to write a historical overview of the Senegambian zone from the fifteenth to the twentieth century. I thought such a study would provide opportunities for discussing current issues of regional integration embracing the six nation-states of Senegal, Gambia, Mauritania, Mali, Guinea Bissau, and Guinea Conakry. Four years' sustained research and drafting made it clear that a single volume could not contain a study of such vast scope. I therefore decided to write two volumes. This book, covering the period from the fifteenth to the nineteenth century, is the first. The four centuries covered here provided enough of a challenge. Beyond that, the main difficulty came from the double ambition that inspired this project. I wanted to produce a comprehensive historical overview of this vast region for the general public. At the same time, I was determined to offer scholars specializing in Senegambian studies an update on research over the past quarter century.

The growing body of new research on Senegambia made it particularly necessary to take the time to conduct a comprehensive state of the art assessment. This, as usual, entailed considerable risk of potential career damage. I took that risk. The result, I dare hope, will prove essential to the advancement of research in the field. Further, I trust it will help to liberate our historical studies from the straitjacket fad of discrete case studies.

For, in substance, this work is a synthesis, in a regional framework, of monographs on parts of Senegambia produced over the past quarter century by a legion of researchers from all fields. My previous research on the kingdom of Waalo, at the mouth of the Senegal River, and on the kingdom of Futa Jallon, at the sources of the Senegal and Gambia Rivers, gave me a key advantage, in that it put me in touch with all researchers in the region. This helped me to make direct use of research findings, some published, some unpublished, available in the form of academic dissertations or scholarly articles in French, English or Portuguese journals. All these studies helped me greatly in the challenging task of establishing an overall framework. To their authors I am deeply grateful. As for the flaws in the resulting work, they are mine alone, the outcome of my limitations and my personal vision of the future.

In the drafting of this general work, I made a deliberate attempt to emphasize points of agreement with the various authors to whose works I referred. My aim was to steer clear of academic polemics likely to add unnecessary freight to the text. The reason is that, from my perspective, the key objective is to achieve a regional historiography within the framework of a coherent vision of the Senegambian zone. That vision should give undue importance neither to the boundaries of precolonial kingdoms nor to the present frontiers of the hand-me-down states left over from the era of colonial partition.

That is the only framework within which we can understand the dynamics of regional and inter-regional trade, the impact of the Atlantic trading system, the upshot of clashes between traditional *ceddo* African rulers and emergent Muslim authorities, the processes of dismemberment and consolidation within Senegambia, the steady loss of autonomy in all domains, the colonial system, and current obstacles to the regional integration of the six states left over from the dismemberment of the Senegambian zone over the centuries.

What I present here, then, is not a simple accretion of separate histories of individual states, the typical offering of current historiography. In my view, the multiple forms taken by these states resulted from a long process of political dismemberment from the fifteenth to the nineteenth century. What I intend to focus on, instead, is the twin process of dismemberment and unification subtending the period's history. The time was one of pervasive violence and the regression of society in all domains in a crucial phase of contact with Europe, which to this day dominates our continent. Only a regional orientation can provide an adequate framework for understanding the total experience of our societies on this vast scale.

The example of Maba Jaakhu provides an excellent illustration. Several scholars have conducted fine monographic studies on Maba Jaakhu's itinerary in various parts of the region: Charlotte Quinn in Gambia, Martin Klein in Siin and Saloum, Lucie Colvin and Mamadou Diouf in Kajor, Eunice Charles in Jolof, and David Robinson in Futa Toro. What such studies also illustrate, unintentionally no doubt, is the kind of artificial dismemberment to which the single historical character Maba Jaakhu has been subjected. For once relevant information contained in these monographs is brought together in a coherent framework, the real dimensions of this great Muslim activist emerge: his field of action stretched from the Gambia River all the way to the waters of the Senegal.

From such an integrative viewpoint, Maba Jaakhu stands out as the figure who, on the eve of the colonial conquest, nearly unified the entire region between the Gambia and the Senegal rivers. He was in effect the only leader working within a dynamic of unity, the indispensable antidote to the divisive relationships between the legitimist sovereigns of the Rip, Siin,

Saloum, Kajor, Jolof, Futa Toro, etc., all of whom proved incapable of pooling their forces to fight the invader. Seen against the background of the heroic but suicidal resistance of such individualistic rulers as Lat Joor, Alburi, or Abdul Bokar Kane, who to the bitter end clung to their legitimistic privileges as national sovereigns, the unifying efforts of Maba Jaakhu take on a different meaning.

The point is that the Senegambian zone, whether in the fragmented configuration of its pre-colonial kingdoms, or in the form of its current states, looks like a historical jigsaw puzzle. Viewed separately, the pieces make little sense. But when brought together, the bits of shredded data, from vignettes of personalities to social sketches and political snapshots, reveal new meanings. In saying this, I have no wish to belittle the contribution made by all the individual monographs I consulted. It was their inestimable content, after all, that helped me write this overview of Senegambian history. I owe a great deal to the numerous authors of these monographs. My debt extends even to those authors whose viewpoints I may not share. Such is the case with regard to Philip Curtin, whose first comprehensive work on the history of the Senegambian region, remarkable in several aspects, had a profound impact on my own work, if only through the challenges it posed to African historiography.

Throughout this book, citations and references to the numerous works of all these authors are legion. I might therefore be forgiven for not mentioning here all the researchers from all disciplines and continents who came to do their fieldwork in Senegambia, this zone at the crossways of the Savanna grasslands, the Sahara desert, the Equatorial forest, and the Atlantic ocean. In this special position, the region has come under particularly decisive influences from the Atlantic connection since the fifteenth century. The impact of external pressures has been correspondingly important. All this is probably why the region now plays such a key role as a meeting ground for European and American researchers, on the one hand, and Senegambian researchers, as represented by the Dakar group, on the other. True, there is an imbalance between the considerable volume of work produced by European and American schools, and that produced by the Dakar group. The latter, strapped for resources, can hardly afford to be competitive. This imbalance is principally a consequence of our dependent status in all domains. As citizens ambitious to confront our own destiny in this new world that treats the weak and the poor with such pitiless indifference, it is our increasingly urgent responsibility to face this situation, and to assume complete responsibility for changing it.

The progress achieved in all fields over the past quarter century owes a great deal to the pioneering work of my secondary school teacher, Jean Suret-Canale, who sparked my interest in history as a profession from the earliest days. Another of my teachers, the late Yves Person, author of the monumental study on Samori, supervised my advanced training in research. The efforts of Vincent Monteil to infuse fresh ideas into Islamic studies; the achievement of Jean Boulègue in producing the first historical overview of the Senegambian zone in the fifteenth and sixteenth centuries as a frontierless whole; the endeavors of Guy Thilmans to unearth buried European sources; the efforts of Charles Becker to overhaul Senegambian studies in all domains; the magnificent achievement of Claude Meillassoux, Adrian Adams and Jean Copans in bringing economic anthropology into the limelight, the success of Catherine Coquery Vidrovitch in breathing new life into economic history; the achievement of Christian Roche in his history of the Casamance region, may justly be regarded, to some extent, as the prime contribution of French researchers in this period of the decolonization of African history.

Anglophone scholars (I include British and – especially – American researchers in this group) have achieved clear dominance in Senegambian historiography, mainly through the impressive volume of their output. A notable characteristic of their work is the systematic use of oral traditions. Among them the leading scholar is undoubtedly Philip Curtin, the first to produce a historical overview of the Senegambian zone – a remarkable achievement – even if the area he covered was geographically smaller than my Greater Senegambia. Curtin's work, quite apart from its other merits, inspired a series of other outstanding studies. Of these, Martin Klein's work on Siin, Saloum and slavery, David Robinson's on Futa Toro and Sheikh Umar Tal, Lucie Colvin's on Kajor and migrations in Senegambia, Charlotte Quinn's on the Manding chiefdoms in Gambia, George Brooks's on Yankee traders and the history of the Southern Rivers, Joye Hawkins's on the Forria, and Charles Stewart's on the Moorish emirates, among others, deserve special mention.

British-based scholarship in this field is dominated by John Hargreaves, with his work on the partition of West Africa. Special mention should be made of such diasporan Senegambians as my late friend Walter Rodney, who produced a ground-breaking study of the Guinea Coast; Franklin McGowan, author of a monumental work on Futa Jallon, and Lamine Sanneh, with his detailed study of the Jakhanke.

Pitched between the English and French schools we have the Portuguese school, under the undisputed domination of the late Texeira Da Mota, whose work has achieved a singular dominance of Senegambian historiography.

And finally there is the Dakar group. In scholarly terms, it is not necessarily opposed to the French or Anglophone groups. What distinguishes it is its straightforward determination to link historiography with the struggle for the liberation of the Senegambian peoples. Its work is characterized by on-site case studies, hemmed in by the various intellectual, moral, and material constraints exercised by our society, and from which as scholars we are impotent to break free. This kind of research is necessarily interdisciplinary. Pioneered by Cheikh Anta Diop, Abdoulaye Ly, Joseph Ki-Zerbo, and Assane Seck, it was continued by Abdoulaye Bara Diop, Boubacar Ly, Djibril Tamsir Niane, Pathé Diagne, Amady Aly Dieng, Bakary Traoré, Samir Amin and Cheikh Ba in the 1960s. The Dakar group developed considerably in the 1970s in the field of history, owing to works by Sékéné Mody Cissoko on the Manding world, Thierno Diallo on Futa Jallon, Mbaye Guèye on the Atlantic trade, Oumar Kane on the Futa Toro, Abdoulaye Bathily on the Soninke, Mamadou Diouf on Kajor, and Rokhaya Fall on Baol. The Dakar researchers cover a field far wider than the spatial and temporal limits of our Senegambia. It ranges from prehistoric times to contemporary history, embracing ancient Egypt and the medieval era in the process.

The Dakar group, while much indebted to the French and Anglo-Saxon schools, is known for its open-mindedness. Above all, it is famous for its determination to bring greater depth to social science research in the effort to change the destiny of our societies. Still, despite the dynamic excellence of its output, the Dakar School remains on the fringes of the intellectual world, dependent on external forces, its intellectual autonomy limited by the weight of the French academic tradition coupled with a policy out of sync with the needs and aspirations of the African university of our dreams. In the drafting of economic projects, for instance, Dakar researchers are marginalized because foreign experts automatically receive preferential treatment in the conduct of feasibility studies as well as in implementational work. They are further marginalized in practical matters because of their opposition to current political trends. For official political behavior makes any dissident historical discussion of our political, economic, and social realities taboo. The pitiful state of our research establishment is, as a consequence, an accurate reflection of our inability to find independent solutions to our problems. This parlous situation also reflects the degree of political despotism and ideological terror, factors which considerably limit the potential role of scholarly debate in bringing about change.

With research thus reduced to the status of an underdeveloped craft, with attempts actually being made to strangle the enterprise of scholarly investigation outright, it is hardly surprising that the Dakar group remains relatively uncompetitive, incapable of playing its optimal policy role, that of catalyst in our economic and social development. There lies the entire meaning of our historiographical work, and, beyond that, the purpose of our struggle for intellectual autonomy. Every historical or cultural debate,

however, presupposes a political debate. That is what we need now, if we are
to break out of the dead ends to which a quarter century of bungling despotism have misled us.

Destitute though our research establishment may be, its very indigence
gives me the pleasant opportunity of paying homage to all those who, in the
course of these many long years, gave me the moral and material support I
needed for the completion of this task. Considerations of space make it
impossible, unfortunately, for me to name all of them.

The African American Scholars' Council awarded me a fellowship in
1974 to enable me to collect in Dakar, Paris and London the archival documentation on which my research on the Senegambian zone was based. In
1981, the IDRC awarded me their Pearson Fellowship, freeing me for
fifteen months from my heavy teaching responsibilitites, and enabling me
to devote time and energy to researching and writing this book. It was
during the eight months spent as a Fellow of the prestigious Woodrow
Wilson International Center for Scholars in Washington, followed by a
short stay at the Carter Woodson Institute for Afro-American and African
Studies of the University of Virginia, that I completed this study on
Senegambia. I take this opportunity to say thanks again to all these institutions which, by giving me the support that freed me from the gritty constraints of underdeveloped research – the daily fate, alas, of scholars
trapped in our University – enabled me to finish this work.

Above all, I owe an inestimable debt of gratitude to numerous friends
and colleagues for the hospitality, help and moral support they gave me in
the long years devoted to this study of Senegambia. In France, England, the
United States and Canada, many were the members of the Senegambian
diaspora who extended the hand of hospitality to me. Some were born in
the zone; others adopted it. All gave me a heartfelt welcome as I paused a
moment during my endless Senegambian quest. Ibrahima Sory Barry and
Marie Jeanne Poiret, Elias and Françoise Barry, Lucie G. Colvin, Lansiné
Kaba, David Robinson, Martin Klein, Georges Brooks, Angela and
Abdoulaye Barry, Youssouf Sylla, Chezia B. Thompson, Charlotte Quinn,
Han Astrid Van Broekman, Prosser Gifford, Thierno Oussou Barry,
Aïssatou and Ousseynou Diop, Julia Hotton, Abdoulaye Baldé, Habib
and Yacine Sy, Catherine Coquery-Vidrovitch, Yves Benot, Claude
Meillassoux, Alfa Ibrahima Sow, Ibrahima Baba Kaké, Jean-Pierre
Chrétien, Joye Hawkins, Kandjura Dramé, Robert Fatton, Joseph Harris,
Lamine Sanneh, Charles de la Roncière, Léonie Gordon and others; let
each accept here my profound thanks for their hospitality and for the scholarly help they gave by reading over the manuscript numberless times, and
giving me the benefit of their critical insights. I would like to give special
thanks to Lucie G. Colvin for her friendship, more meaningful than any

frontier, dating from our first meeting, twenty years ago, on the border between the old Waalo and Kajor kingdoms.

Nor shall I forget all those, more numerous still, who gave me their friendship and support in the long years of so-called exile before I returned to my native "village", Guinea, after twenty-one years of absence, in May 1984. At that point I had just finished writing this study of Senegambia. For me this book is a symbol, the intersection of my twin experience, evenly divided between my native "village" of Guinea, and Senegal, my adoptive "village" in this interval before the union of our peoples in a Greater Senegambia.

In the course of my long "exile" I came to understand fully the deadly absurdity of our artificial frontiers. Further, we came to appreciate the long-term threat that this myopic proto-nationalism poses to the necessary unification of our various states. I came to understand even more deeply how necessary it is, at the present juncture in our destiny, for us to reach out to each other and to acknowledge the necessity of sharing all our resources, problems, and projects from now on, if we are to ensure our survival and our future prosperity. The way forward lies through unity and the observance of democratic freedoms; there just is no alternative. This is the theme of the second volume of this work, focused on Senegambia in the twentieth century. In the interval, it is my pleasure to express my appreciation to those many Senegalese friends from all walks of life who have so generously extended to me the loving hospitality that is such a familiar staple where we too come from. It is humanly impossible to name all of them here, since behind every individual name stretches the entire African extended family. From deep in my heart I thank them all: the Sow, Diallo, Kane, Mbaye, Ndir, Doukouré, Camara, Diagne, Sané, Wane, Diop, Fall, Fati, Niang, Goudiaby, Sy, Bathily, Dieng, Ly, Thiam, Guèye, Becker, Vaz, Mendy, Senghor, Sarr, Touré, Gassama, Diouf, Bâ, Sall, Boye, Mbodj, Ndiaye, Traoré, Dramé, Mbacke and Bassene families. All made me feel at home in Senegal, in this time of waiting for the Greater Senegambia. Among them I would like to express particular thanks to my father-in-law, Alioune Sow Dembel, Father to us all, for his generosity. He made me welcome to his home, offering a wife and beyond that, a family to the orphan I had become, apparently so far from home, so close in reality.

I took the exile road along with thousands of my compatriots. In all these years of hardship their moral and material support never failed me. To all my companions on this great adventure I here express my appreciation: Idrissa Barry, Diawo Bâ, Thierno Diallo, the late Diouma Barry, Tidiane Barry, Jacques Fowler, Moussa Soumah, Ibrahima Diallo, Thierno Mouctar Bâ, Mody Bokar Barry and others. I sincerely hope that our rich and painful experience will help to strengthen bonds between the various peoples of Senegambia, banishing from this region all forms of tyranny and oppression.

My heartfelt thanks go, without exception, to those colleagues who worked with us to found the Pan-African Association of Historians, established to enhance our continental unity and, by the same token, our intellectual autonomy.

To my colleagues in the History Department at the University of Dakar I owe an inestimable debt of gratitude. In the course of the years spent together, they worked together with me to create a congenial family atmosphere. In effect, this overview of Senegambian history is primarily the outcome of a common quests with the Dakar School, as it gropes its way toward unity in diversity, for a greater Senegambia. I owe a special word of thanks to my secretary Rosalie Da Sylva, who typed out with unfailing intelligence the successive drafts of this homage to Senegambia.

I take this opportunity to thank all my relatives, especially my father and mother, who waited so patiently for my return. I thank my brothers Almamy Ibrahima Sory and Bademba, my sisters Kanny, Hassatu, Hadjatu, Aminata, Yaye Aï and Yaye Tahiru, along with my sister-in-law Aimée Diallo, all scattered like wind-blown seed throughout the world, tasting the bitterness of exile.

Lastly, and most surely, I give my wife Aïda Sow the thanks she so fully deserves for so much love, so much comfort over these many long years spent in the writing of this study, my homage to a frontier-free land of Peoples, Senegambia.

Fann-Résidence, 31 December 1986

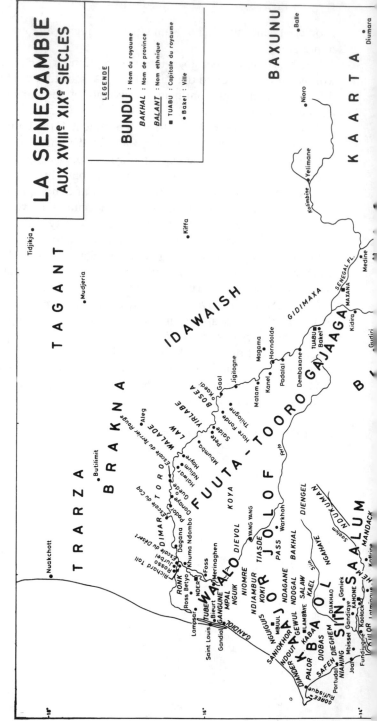

LA SENEGAMBIE
AUX XVIIIᵉ XIXᵉ SIECLES

LEGENDE

**BUNDU** : Nom du royaume
*BAKHAL* : Nom de province
*BALANT* : Nom ethnique
■ TUABU : Capitale du royaume
● Bakel : Ville

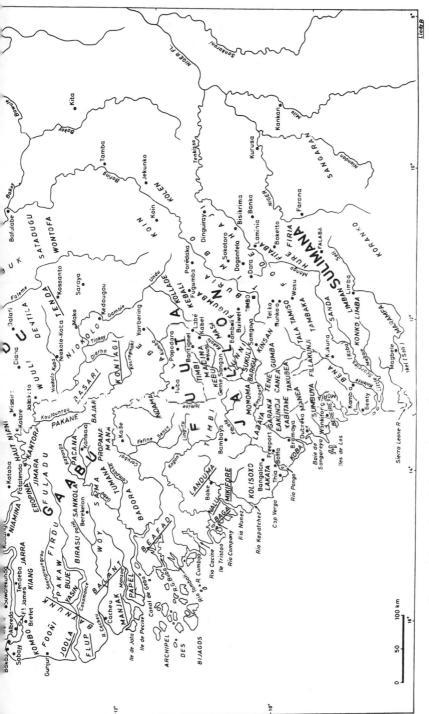

Senegambia in the eighteenth and nineteenth centuries

*Part I*

Senegambia from the fifteenth to the seventeenth century: a haven for incoming populations, a station for migrants on the move

Senegambia, bordered by the Senegal River in the north, the Kolonté in the south, and the foothills of the Futa Jallon plateau to the east, has a natural geographical coherence. The region is wide open to the Atlantic ocean and the west.[1] Geographically, its features are remarkably diverse. Still, beneath the surface diversity, the population possesses a profound cultural cohesiveness. On account of this unity, the Senegambian zone has played a special role in West African history since the fifteenth century. For it has been the confluence of all the area's migratory streams, from the watersheds of the Upper Niger valley in the east to the Atlantic ocean in the west; from the Adrar highlands in the north to the Futa Jallon plateau in the south. The resulting mixture blends demographic and cultural traits dating back to the medieval empires of Western Sudan with influences brought in by Berber nomads from the Sahara desert.

A historical cohesiveness parallels this geographical unity. Senegambia was dependent on western Sudan and the Sahara almost until the fifteenth century. Then, with the arrival of the Europeans, old continental influences began yielding to new maritime currents.

Senegambia deserves its reputation as both a terminus for incoming populations and a point of departure for migrants on the move. Here, influences from the medieval empire of Mali merged first with Islamic influences introduced by the trans-Saharan Trade, then with the European impact of the Atlantic trading system. By the fifteenth century, Senegambia had acquired an identifiable form as a demographic, economic unit, as well as in all aspects of political organization. It kept that identity, broadly speaking, until the onset of colonial conquest in the late nineteenth century.

The fifteenth century was a watershed in the formation of Senegambia. The region steadily loosened its ancient dependence on the Sudanese sahel and the Sahara desert, while increasingly yoking its future to the Atlantic ocean. Internally, its states underwent major restructuring at a time when the last but one wave of mass immigration before colonial conquest was entering the region. The Senegal and Gambia rivers, along with the Southern Rivers, made Senegambia accessible to the Atlantic trading

3

system. The region thus became the main route for penetration into the Sudan, cradle of the great empires of Ghana, Mali and Songhai.

Before the fifteenth century, the main communications artery of the Sudan, the Niger River, flowing first toward the Sahara, had been the center of gravity for all of West Africa. But from the fifteenth century on, the dominant trends in Senegambian history became the Atlantic trading system, the re-formation of states, and the spread of Islam. And the gradual but steady triumph of the caravel over the caravan left an impact visible in every aspect of life to this day. In Yoro Fall's apt phrase, this was when Europe began to encircle Africa.

# 1    Senegambia in the fifteenth and sixteenth centuries: dependence on the Sudan and the Sahara

A defining feature of the Senegambian zone is its geographical location between the Senegal and the Gambia Rivers, far from the Niger Bend. A second is its position between the Sahara desert and the tropical forest zone. This dual intermediary location made Senegambia dependent on the states of the Sudan and the Sahara until the fifteenth century. Only later, with its opening out onto the Atlantic seaboard, did the region begin to play its pivotal geographical role in full. To this day it continues to play that role, serving the West as a gateway for economic and political penetration into the African hinterland.

The zone is home to a great diversity of peoples: these include Wolof, Peul, Tukulor, Manding, Sereer, Soninke, Susu, Joola, Nalu, Baga, Beafada, Bainuk, and Basari. The cultural unity underlying this diversity comes from centuries spent living together. The organization of economic, political, and social life here bears strong traces of influence from old Mali and the Muslim religion. These influences were decisive in the transition of Senegambia's societies from kin-based political forms such as the *lumunal* or the *kafu* to the organization of monarchical states.

Geographically, Senegambia lies wholly within the tropical zone between the Sahel and the forests of Guinea. Two rivers, the Senegal and the Gambia, both underpin and symbolize the region's geographical unity. Both spring from the same upland mass, the Futa Jallon plateau. They flow through similar geological formations, tectonic structures, and climatic zones. And they flow into identical tidal regimes in the same Atlantic ocean, a few hundred kilometers apart.

The countryside presents a richly varied aspect that in no way detracts from its overall unity.[1] Lifestyles here often reflect regional variations due to local geographical conditions. This gives northern and southern Senegambia discernibly different flavors. The Gambia River, the main route of penetration into the Sudan, is the divide between northern and southern Senegambia. It is also a magnet for all the zone's populations. In former ages the Gambia, given its central location, symbolized the diversity and unity of Senegambia's civilization, the reality that connected it to, but also distinguished the region from, the Sudan to the east, the Sahara to the north, and the forest zone to the south. In time, the Atlantic added its pull to the sum of influences.

## A.     The states of Senegambia

Seen from the Sudanese sahel, Senegambia before the fifteenth century was a dead end. Starting to the east, in the Manding heartland, waves of cultural influence radiated into the zone. Westward lay the ocean, leading, apparently, nowhere. As early as the eighth century, influences from the Sudan encountered reinforcing currents from the Sahara. The desert caravan trade opened up Senegambia's northern reaches (Tekrur and Silla) to the Mediterranean, while facilitating Islamic penetration. Sudanese influences were felt mainly in the Upper Valley region under the Ghana empire, while on the Futa Jallon plateau and in the southern river valleys, they came through the Mali empire. At its peak that empire dominated most of Senegambia.[2]

In the eighth century the Upper Senegal valley was part of the Ghana empire. Ghana was ruled by a Soninke dynasty that drew its power from the trans-Saharan gold trade centered in Bambuk and Bure, linked to the Sahara towns of Awdagost. Alongside the influence of Ghana, radiating over a large part of the Sahel, the region faced pressure from the Sanhaja Berber confederations, controllers of the market at Awdagost. This is the context that, with hindsight, explains the migrations of Sereer, Wolof, Peul, and Tukulor populations from Adrar in the north into the Senegal valley, at a time of steady desertification in the Sahel. The migrants settled down or moved farther south, where they displaced or overran the Socé, considered the oldest inhabitants of northern Senegambia.

Given its special geographical location at the edge of the tropical world, the Senegal valley became the site of two cities, Tekrur and Silla, oriented toward the trans-Saharan trade, at a very early date. As early as the tenth century, the king War Jaabi converted to Islam, creating the first political center known as Tekrur, whose sphere of influence extended over the greater part of the Senegal valley. Here also were the origins of the eleventh-century Almoravid movement. In its passage, this movement left a lasting imprint on the banks of the Senegal River in the form of a militant strain of Islam, on its way north to conquer Morocco and the Iberian peninsula.

From the twelfth century onward, after the fall of Ghana, the entire Senegambian zone fell increasingly into the direct orbit of the Mali Empire, which exerted a decisive influence until the fifteenth century and even beyond. It was Mali's impact that catalyzed the transformation of the region's kinship-based societies into states. It also helped to integrate the whole of Senegambia into the long-distance trading system reaching northward across the Sahara, eastward along the Niger Bend, and southward through the mangrove belt skirting the forest zone. For the Manding, who already controlled the gold mines at Bure and Bambuk, also tried very early on to gain control over the salt-producing regions of the coast. At the height of its power, Mali undertook nothing less than a westward colonizing mission, thrusting past the Futa Jallon plateau, then following the river Gambia and the upper valleys of the Casamance, the Rio Cacheu, and the Rio Geba. In the process, the Manding founded the Kaabu kingdom in the south, along with the principalities of Noomi, Badibu, Niani, Wuli, and Kantora, on both banks of the Gambia River. They did this by displacing or absorbing indigenous populations from the Bajar group, together with Jola, Beafada, Papel, Balante, Bainuk, Baga, Nalu, Landuma, and others, whose descendants today live in the Southern Rivers area between Gambia and Sierra Leone.

The Manding were also the ancestors of the Gelwaar, who founded the Siin and Saloum kingdoms in the Sereer regions. In northern Senegambia, however, the influence of the Mali Empire seems to have been less solid. For that reason, as from the mid-fourteenth century, the succession crisis that followed the death of Mansa Suleiman in 1360 facilitated the creation of the Jolof Confederation, which brought together the Wolof provinces of Waalo, Kajoor, and Baol. Within a context of decentralized political institutions, the Jolof kingdom, founded by Njajaan Njaay, thus dominated northern Senegambia, forcing the waning Mali Empire to retreat toward southern Gambia.

Jolof hegemony was shaken quite early, before its final break-up in the sixteenth century, by an invasion led by Koli Tengela. The invasion began as a spillover from events in western Sudan, and ended up entirely upsetting the balance of political power in Senegambia.[3]

For, beginning in 1450, Peul populations from the Sahel, crisscrossing Senegambia, settled temporarily on the high plateaux of the Futa Jallon range. From there, in 1490, the Peul, led by Tengela and his son Koli Tengela, crossed the Gambia River, making their way back north. On their way they ravaged the Manding of Wuuli and other satellites of the Mali Empire before going on to conquer Gajaaga and the middle valley of the Senegal River, which then became known as Futa Toro. This was one of the largest internal population shifts in Senegambian history after the fifteenth century. Alvares de Almada has left a vivid description of this "Peul invasion crossing the Gambia from north to south, destroying everything up to the Rio Grande, where the Beafada defeated the Peul. So numerous were the invaders that at one point on the Gambia River, twelve leagues above Lamé, they filled the riverbed with stones so as to cross over. The place is now called 'the Peul Ford'."[4] The fact that Koli had an impressively large following, further swollen at each stage by people from the areas they marched through, is confirmed by Lemas Coelho and Barros. The sheer size of this invasion changed the population map of Senegambia. For, beginning in the Sahel and the upper Niger valley, it flowed successively over the Falémé, Bundu, Futa Jallon, the Rio Grande, the Gambia, the Ferlo, and the Senegal valley. At every stopping-place it left behind many of Koli's followers.

By the end of the fifteenth century, then, Senegambia was home to several political units of varying sizes. The Denyanke kingdom dominated the middle and upper valleys of the Senegal River, while the rivermouth along with the entire region between the Senegal and Gambia Rivers remained within the Jolof Confederation. The area from the Gambia valley past the Southern Rivers all the way to the foothills of the Futa Jallon mountains was still under the influence of the Mali Empire. Here, the Kaabu constituted the biggest of the major political units that coexisted with kinship-based states forming a patchwork of population groups: Joola, Tenda, Bajaranke, Nalu, Baga, Jallonke, plus the Cocoli south of the Gambia.

The only major changes in the configuration of the area's states during the sixteenth century were the decline of Malian influence and the break-up of the Jolof confederation. These changes were related to the influence of the Atlantic trade. The gradual withdrawal of Mali's authority gave back their autonomy to the expansionist Manding states. Kaabu was particularly successful in taking advantage of the changing situation: it extended its authority over the principalities on both banks of the Gambia River, and gradually gained control over the Southern Rivers. The break-up of the Jolof confederation resulted from the rebellion of the Kajor, Waalo and Baol provinces against the authority of the Jolof *Buurba* in the mid-sixteenth century. Each province then became an independent kingdom. Kajoor was ruled by the *Damel*, Waalo by the *Brak*, and Baol by the *Teeñ*. The new configuration restricted the *Buurba's* authority to the Jolof kingdom. By the same token, Jolof authority over the Sereer kingdoms of Siin and Saalum was loosened. Henceforth, each of these kingdoms was ruled by its own *Buur*.[5]

Up until the mid-fifteenth century, Senegambia lived under the influence of the Sahara and the Sudan. Then came the invading Portuguese traders, bringing a new factor into the regional equation. Before moving on to a study of this decisive stage in which the Atlantic trading system became dominant, let us pause to describe the landscape and its inhabitants, providing a profile of the economic, political, and social structures of the

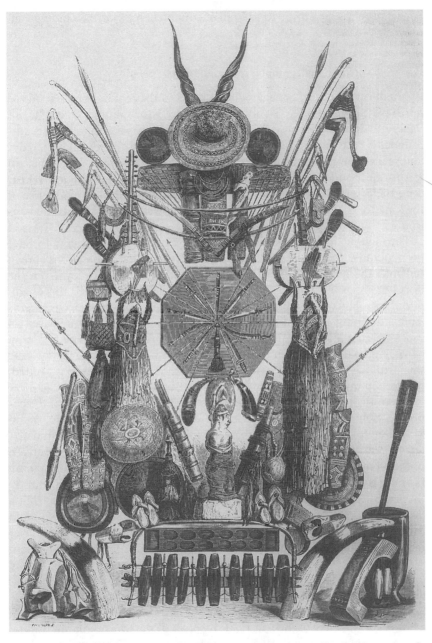

Plate 1 Battle trophy comprising weapons and utensils of the peoples of Senegal

Senegambian states prior to the far-reaching changes of the coming centuries.

## B.     Northern Senegambia: the land and the people

By the term Northern Senegambia we refer to the region bounded on the north by the Senegal River and on the south by the Gambia River. In this Sahelo-Sudanese area, the Senegal valley forms a sort of vast oasis surrounded by the western lowlands of the West African corridor. The flat, dry landscape is suited to the large-scale use of horses, the principal vehicle of territorial conquest before the introduction of firearms. Ghana and Tekrur were the original rulers of this land. Their fall was followed by the rise of the kingdoms of Futa Toro and Gajaaga, followed by the Jolof confederation.

Throughout its pre-modern history, the Senegal valley seems to have been a cradle, or at least an antechamber, from which populations spread out into the rest of northern Senegambia. The Senegal valley, from the upper through the middle valley down to the delta, has played this exceptional role thanks to annual floods which make it a vast oasis.[6] The river is a life-sustaining gift in this region of single-crop cereal agriculture based on two staples, millet and sorghum, yielding two crops a year. The first crop comes in the dry season on the alluvial plains known as *waalo* land, where the farm belt can stretch as wide as 20–30 km. The second crop is rainfed, planted on higher *jeeri* land in the rainy season.

Given the importance of flood recession farming, land is central to economic, political, and social life in the delta, cradle of the future Waalo kingdom, following the break-up of the Jolof confederation in the mid-sixteenth century. Land is equally important in the middle valley, the domain of the Denyanke kingdom of Futa Toro. In the *waalo* areas, flood-recession farming is dominated by different varieties of large-grained millet. But on the *jeeri* highlands, fine-grained millet takes over as the staple. Farming cycles here are closely intertwined with a major livestock cycle. Peul and Moorish herdsmen range over the area, grazing their herds on the river banks in the dry season, heading north and south during the rainy season.

On account of this dual agricultural activity, supplemented with fishing and animal husbandry, the region grew to be a kind of granary, a permanent relay station bringing together sedentary black populations from the Senegal River valley and Berber or Peul nomads from the Chemama-Ferlo areas on both banks of the River. At the peak of the trans-Saharan trading system, Berber middlemen plied between the Senegal River valley and the trans-Saharan trade routes. Mostly, they traded horses for slaves. On occasion they also traded manufactured goods from the Maghreb and the

Mediterranean for gold. In the time of the Mali Empire, the Senegal valley lay somewhat remote from the main routes of the trans-Saharan trade. Nevertheless, the river remained a significant trading avenue all along its course. For the delta dwellers traded salt from the rich salt flats of Ganjoole (Awlil), along with salted fish, for millet sold by people from Futa Toro and the Upper Valley as far as Kayes.

Demographically, and from the viewpoint of political and social institutions, the delta was part of the great Wolof grouping of the Jolof confederation, of which Waalo remained a province until the mid-sixteenth century. Here, however, the Waalo ruler, a descendant of the foreign conqueror Njajaan Njaay, was not of *Lamanal* origin – a circumstance that set him apart from other Wolof kings. So with the establishment of the monarchy, the *Brak* paid tribute to the principal *Lamans* on the day of his enthronement.[7]

Land was a crucial political and economic resource, even if competition for it was not as acute as it always was in Futa Toro, given the low density of the Waalo population and the shrinkage of arable land due to saltwater infiltration in the delta area.

Njajaan Njay's ascension introduced an elective monarchical system into the Waalo area, as indeed into all the Wolof kingdoms. At the time of the break-up of the Jolof confederation, the political power of the *Laman Dyaw*, formerly the landholder, shifted to the *Brak*. The *Brak* was elected from among three matrilineal kin groups known as *meen* (*Loggar*, *Joos*, and *Teejek*), by members of a Council of Electors called the *Jogomay*, the *Jawdin*, and the *Maalo*.[8] The system was originally an oligarchic compromise between different communal chiefs or *Lamans*, who as a result became either members of the Grand Council of Electors or provincial chiefs, leaving paramount power in the hands of the *Brak*. But the *Brak* also had the power to make new appointments, thus consolidating his personal support base to the disadvantage of hereditary officeholders.[9]

In Futa Toro, on the other hand, the Denyanke dynasty, having incorporated Tekrur and the state named after War Jaabi, gave the middle Senegal valley its political unity and laid a lasting foundation for the area's economic and social organization. For example, it consolidated land ownership structures, especially in the rich alluvial plains, by letting the aristocracy distribute holdings among their most faithful entourage. The result was the creation of extensive landholdings side by side with small family plots. Such a system indicates the existence of a class of major landowners, with Denyankobe taking the lion's share. The history of Futa Toro is principally a record of the continual reconstitution of landholdings to the benefit of the ruling class.[10]

Futa Toro is the prime heartland of the Peul and the Tukulor. Nomadic peoples by inveterate custom, their goings and comings have made the middle Senegal valley not only a gathering place, but also a point of departure for their many migratory movements throughout West Africa. On account of the great extent of *waalo* land, Futa Toro is incontestably the millet-producing granary of this whole region bordering on the Sahel.

It was after the conquest of the Futa region by Koli that the regime of *Satigis* was created. This system kept selected local chiefs in office after their defeat. One example was the *Lam Tooro*. Nevertheless, the *Satigi* himself appointed several of his own companions as local chiefs. These appointees were especially numerous among *Sebbe* chiefs, leading generals in his army. In this way, right from the beginning, the system strengthened the role of the military in the Denyanke dynasty.[11]

The history of Futa Toro also bears the imprint of the geographical configuration of the area. This is a narrow corridor of land, stretching for over 400 km along the Senegal River, but scarcely ever exceeding 20 km in width on either bank. Futa thus comprises three main territories: Toro in the west; Central Futa, including Haïlabe, Law, Yirlabe Hebbyabe, and Bosea provinces; and lastly the eastern Futa, with Ngenar and Damga on its remote eastern borders. Each of these provinces was governed by one or more kin-group families whose political rights were based mainly on their control over the fertile *waalo* flood plains. Thus, the Toro region was ruled by the Ardo Gede, the Ardo Edi, and the Farba Walalde; the Law was ruled by Saïbobe Peul bearing the title of *Kamalinku* in Gollere, *Joom* in Mbumba, and *Ardo* in Meri. Saïbobe dominance reached all the way into Yirlabe Hebbyabe. After that came Futa proper. The area was marked by the presence of numerous *Sebbe* from the Koli line in Orefonde and Cilone. Here also was the site of Godo, one of the spiritual capitals of the Denyankobe. Lastly, out in the east, Ngenar and Damga was the traditional settlement zone of Denyankobe and Kolyabe *Sebbe*. Here, Jowol served as the political capital of most of the *Satigi*.[12]

But the excessive length of the territory considerably curtailed the power of the *Satigi*, who held their hereditary power by virtue of their status as Denyankobe descendants of Koli Tengela. Gerontocracy was the order of the day, with power going to the eldest relative of the deceased sovereign, be he brother, nephew, uncle or son. The legitimate heir was known officially as *Kamalinku*. The fact that the succession was accessible to so many qualified candidates led to numerous political crises. It was also at the root of the weakness of the central authority.

Direct control over the entire country was also limited by the autonomy of provincial chiefs led by the *Ardo* from the Saïbobe, Denyankobe, and Yalalbe Rangale lines, or by the *Farba* of *Sebbe* origin. Political power was considerably decentralized. It was based on the landed property rights of kin-groups controlling rich alluvial *waalo* land, as distinct from the rainfed lands in the *jeeri* areas. On account of the relative overpopulation of this region, still the millet granary of the Sahel zone, the history of Futa Toro is characterized by a series of territorial amputations followed by migratory waves known as *fergo*, in reaction to increasing population pressure.[13]

In the upper Senegal valley, around Bakel and Selibabi, the alluvial valley becomes increasingly narrow. With so little prime alluvial land available, the farming populations here have to fall back on rainfed *jeeri* land, which is more plentiful. Because of its geographical location at the entrance to the Sudanese hinterland, the upper Senegal valley contains a layered series of populations who moved into the area in successive waves: Soninke, Manding, Khasonke. This is an area where, due to the small amount of *waalo* land, land rights are not a crucial factor in political life. Extensive cereal farming on *jeeri* land is practiced in close association with trade and mining.

Directly connected to the long-distance trade routes of the Niger Bend and the Sahara, the upper Senegal valley played a strategic role in the economic history of Senegambia. This was the terminus of different trade routes: from the east by horseback; from the south on donkeys; from the north on camelback. At the same time, it was a distribution entrepôt for trade along the entire length of the Senegal River. The proximity of the Bambuk and Bure gold mines gave the area a commercial boost under the monopoly of the Soninke and the Jakhanke, the precise equivalent in western Senegambia of the trading Juulas.[14]

There is conclusive evidence that the Gajaaga regime, sited in the upper Senegal valley, was the successor state of the Ghana empire, reduced to a rudimentary vestige in the shadow of an ascendant Mali. Quite clearly, it was in the eleventh century that the Bacili Sempera migrated from Wagadu, after the fall of that kingdom, on their way to Suela (Sokolo). In their flight they preserved the ritual veneration of Biida, the sacred snake of the Wago.[15] Admittedly, the Soninke had lived in Gajaaga for a long time. But the *Tunka* regime did not become consolidated until the thirteenth century, through a series of military campaigns combined with diplomatic initiatives among the local peoples.[16] Among the descendants of the three brave sons of Khasan Mariyam, it was the eldest Bacili selected from among the royal families of the provinces of Guey and Kammera who took the title of *Tunka Nyaaye*; the title given to the second was *Tunka Seega*. In all provinces, the *Tunkas* were assisted in their official functions by *Mangus* appointed from the Bacili Sononne, Gunjamu or Jaguraga, Jallo, Siima, Fade, and Timmera lineages, who functioned as military chiefs or *Kuru nimu*. This society was stratified along rigid hierarchical lines. At the top were free men, known as *hooro*. Below them came castes, called *namakhala*. At the bottom were slaves, called *komo*.[17]

The basic division here was between the ruling military class and a sub-

Plate 2 Inhabitants of Lower Senegal

jugated peasantry. But the social system was complicated by the existence, from a long way back, of old families of Muslim clergy such as the Sakho, Darame, Siise, Ture and Silla. These constituted powerful groups in religious and economic affairs. Gajaaga owed all its importance to its strategic location at the intersection of the Sudan, the Sahel, and Senegambia. And the proximity of the Bambuk and Bure gold mines reinforced the commercial power of the Soninke throughout West Africa.

It should be pointed out, at this juncture, that before colonialism, indeed until the independence process in 1960, states on both banks of the Senegal River did not consider the river a political frontier. For example, Juurbel, capital of the Waalo kingdom, remained on the right bank until the eighteenth century. And Futa Toro and Gajaaga, like Tekrur and Ghana, were very much involved in the Sahel regions to the north. By historical tradition, the sedentary populations of northern Senegambia originated from the Sahel. Adrar, in present-day Mauritania, was their gathering site before their southward migration. Reacting to climatic changes, especially the desertification of the Sahel, combined with the political pressure of nomadic Berber encroachments, settled Sereer, Wolof, Peul and Tukulor communities gradually began moving south. Their north–south migratory movement has continued to this day.

Economic and political control over the towns of the Sahara, trading centers linking North Africa and the Sudan, was from time immemorial an important prize for kingdoms on both sides of the Sahara, this sea of sand misleadingly called the desert. Strictly speaking, the Sahara did not really become a desert until Atlantic fleets supplanted its camel caravans. This vast turnabout totally ruined the trans-Saharan trading system as from the fifteenth century. The steady rise of the trans-Atlantic system, increasingly dominant in the Senegal River valley, hastened the southward movement of Berbers from the Mauritanian Sahel through the absorption of Chemama into Senegambia.

Southward from the Senegal River, the valley merges into the western plains of southern Senegambia. This is the veritable homeland of the Wolofs, whose political and social structures were shaped in the framework of the Jolof confederation. From the northern margins of the delta to the outskirts of the Saalum valley, the Wolof countryside is dotted with an uninterrupted network of villages. Rainy-season cereal farming is the traditional basis of economic production here. Millet and sorghum reign supreme over the productive economy and all rural life.[18] Prior to the beginning of the Atlantic trade, this region of subsistence farming, rather remote from the major trade routes of Senegambia, does not seem to have played an important commercial role. Nevertheless, the Jolof confederation, founded in the late thirteenth and early fourteenth centuries, during the decline of the Mali Empire, at its peak occupied most of Senegambia between the Senegal and the Gambia rivers.[19]

Originally, the Wolofs were divided into kin-based communities or clans. But very early in their history, these chiefs came to be known as *Lamans*, and their former functions of patriarchal heads and managers of landed property evolved into political status roles, making them clearly superior to clan or family heads. It was from this new political class that a new set of paramount *Lamans* rose to head the territorial units of Kajoor, Baol, and Jolof, before becoming vassal chiefs within the Jolof confederation founded by Njajaan Njay. The Wolofs, then, were familiar from the start with a land tenure system of the *lamanal* type, in which land rights belonged to kin-based communities and were managed by the community head or *Laman*. Farms were worked individually by families paying land rent to the *Laman*. Lastly, it was possible for outsiders to settle on such land with their families, provided they paid settlement duties to the *Laman* along with regular rent, in return for permanent, inheritable farming rights.

Once the Jolof Empire fell apart, monarchy became the rule in the remnant units. This did not change the *lamanal* land tenure system fundamentally. But management functions shifted from the *Laman* to the *Borom lew*, responsible for land tenure appointments. Furthermore, despite the importance of landed property as a basis of monarchical authority, land did not play a crucial role in political relationships within Wolof society, because fallow land was plentiful and farming techniques remained stagnant, except in the delta.[20]

As from the thirteenth century, Njajaan Njay provided all the Wolof kingdoms in the Jolof confederation with the foundations of their monarchical institutions on the basis of an extremely hierarchical society. For example, the kingdom of Kajoor, an offshoot of the territorial break-up of the Jolof Empire, was from that point on ruled by the *Damel*, appointed from among matrilineal royal families known as *Garmi*, which included the Seno, Wagadu, Gelwaar, Bey and Gej, provided they also belonged by patrilineal descent to the Faal clan. In central government affairs, the *Damel* was assisted by the *Jawrin Mbul*, who acted as Prime Minister, superseding the *Laman Jamatil*, selected by his peers to defend the interests of the *Jambur*, the social category of notables. Local power remained in the hands of the *Laman*, who enjoyed considerable autonomy before the *Damel* imposed his royal agents, the *Jaaraf* or *Jawrin*. At the regional or provincial level, these agents were administratively and politically subordinate to the *Kangam* as well as to a large retinue of appointees and officials. In later centuries, indeed, the monarchy relied much more on the *Jaami-buur*, royal slaves, to force through the regime's plans.

Wolof society remained rigidly hierarchical. At its top sat the royal families, the *garmi*. Next came the *Jambur* or notables, then the *Badoolo*, the mass of ordinary people with no particular power. Below them came the *Ñeeño*, the group of handicraft castes. At the bottom of the social pyramid came the *jaam*, slaves.[21] This political and social structure was duplicated in the Baol kingdom, whose rulers, bearing the title of *Damel Teeñ*, were often linked to those of Kajoor. The same was true of the rump Jolof state left over from the shrinkage of the confederation. There the ruler was known as the *Buurba*. However, succession to the Jolof throne continued to be decided by patrilineal descent from the line of Njajaan Njaay's royal family. But in the sixteenth century, the Jolof kingdom, landlocked as it was, no longer played an important role in the history of Senegambia, a region undergoing full-scale transformation.

Farther south, the Wolof region shades into territory inhabited by the Sereer. The Sereer are a peasant people, originally from the Senegal River valley, where records indicate their presence up until the eleventh century. Having rejected both Islam and the domination of the Jolof, the Sereer gradually settled on the wooded highlands of Siin and Saalum, traveling in successive waves of large family movements each led by a *Laman* or Master of the Fire (Hearth). These *Laman*, who thus became the first to take possession of the woodlands, took on the functions of community heads and territorial rulers until the fourteenth century, when the Gelwaar aristocracy of Manding origin arrived among them from Kaabu. Thus Maïsa Wali Jon, founder of the kingdom of Siin, whose capital was Diakhaw, established the state organization needed to maintain Sereer autonomy. This was the situation in which Mbegaan Nduur, grand-nephew of Maïsa Wali Jon, founded the kingdom of Saalum in the late fifteenth century.[22]

As in the Wolof areas, here too the agricultural economy was based solely on rainfed farming on dry land. The staple was millet, both large-grained and fine. There was a difference, however. Sereer peasants very early on established a production system in which animal husbandry was closely and permanently yoked to farming. Sereer peasants, in effect, had an agrarian civilization in which millet farming and cattle rearing were indispensable components. Furthermore, Sereer peasants made judicious use of stands of *Acacia albida* and animal manure, making long fallow periods unnecessary, thus facilitating year-round farming on the humus-poor sandy and sandy–clay soils of their environment.[23] Meanwhile, on the borders of the Siin kingdom, the Sereer, the Ndut, and the Saafen maintained their egalitarian social structures. But they continued to experience pressure from Kajoor and Baol, since they were, in principle, integral parts of these kingdoms.

The Sereer area stretches southward between the mouths of the Saalum and the Gambia rivers in a series of islands in the wide creeks or *bolons* whose inhabitants practice a mixture of farming and fishing. These Niominka people, subject to Sereer influences from the north and to Manding influences from the south, are real peasant sailors. The egalitarian nature of their society, structured around the limited village environment, puts them in a transitional zone between northern and southern Senegambia, right on the border between the rice-based and the millet-based civilizations. Economic life here is intense, a reflection, primarily, of this situation. The main commodities are salt, from the Saalum flats, traded for riverland rice, and fish.[24]

## C.    Southern Senegambia: the land and the people

Southern Senegambia stretches from the Gambia River to the forests of Guinea. It includes the Southern Rivers region and the Futa Jallon plateau. The coast is marked by mangrove swamps watered by numerous streams feeding onto the Casamance, the Rio Cacheu, the Rio Grande, the Rio Ceba, the Rio Nunez, the Rio Pongo, and the Mellakure, all with their sources in the Futa Jallon high plateau, a veritable West African water tower. Southern Senegambia is much more humid than northern Senegambia. The region's mangrove swamps, and the difficulty of communications in Futa Jallon, account largely for its isolation and its lack of large-scale political structures up until the fifteenth and sixteenth centuries.

Like the Senegal River, the Gambia River was not a political frontier at any time in Senegambian history before colonial conquest. It did mark the geographical divide between the sandy plains of northern Senegambia and the mangrove swamps of the Southern Rivers area. In this western bulge of the African continent, the Gambia River gives the easiest access into the interior from the Atlantic ocean. That was why the Mali Empire used it as a key route in its westward expansion. But the Manding principalities strung out along the valley inhabited only a narrow strip of land along the river's banks.

For, unlike the Senegal valley where flood-recession farming was conducive to very dense settlement patterns, the Gambia valley owes its importance to its geographical location, excellent for traders heading south into the forest belt along the Southern Rivers waterways, north to the Senegal River, and east toward the Niger Bend. Indeed, at the time of its decline under the assaults of a new power, Songhai, combined with a Moroccan invasion, the Mali Empire managed to hang on for a while to its Gambian province, where it came into contact with Portuguese traders at a very early date. It is therefore no accident that the Manding principalities established by trading communities consolidated themselves on both sides of the Gambia River. It should also be remembered that the river was navigable from its mouth all the way to the Barrakunda Falls, in the remote hinterland.

The principalities of Wuli, Niani, Badibu, and Niomi occupied the north bank of the Gambia River, moving westward. Because these were larger, they were more stable and more autonomous than most of the others – Kantora, Jimara, Jaara, Kiang and Kombo – established on the south bank, from east to west. Indeed, the south bank principalities were very rapidly absorbed by the powerful kingdom of Kaabu which, after the final eclipse of the Mali Empire, grew to dominate southern Senegambia from the Gambia River all the way to the Futa Jallon plateau.[25]

The Gambia River was commercially important. Downstream, Wuli was a terminus for trade routes ranging east into the Manding heartland, and north to the Upper Senegal River valley, in turn linked with the Soninke network. A major reason for its importance was the trade in cola and cotton cloth, key commodities in exchanges between the forest belt to the south and the savanna to the east and north.

Cola, like salt, was a strategic commodity then. It grows only in the southern forest regions below southern Senegambia. It is widely used as a medicinal stimulant, but its chief function is symbolic: it is consumed or exchanged in rituals and ceremonies throughout the savanna. Its juice is also used as a dye in the cotton dye industry throughout the savanna. There was an important cola trade network centered on the Gambia and directly linked with trade routes in the Rio Grande, the Rio Geba, and the Rio Cacheu valleys, plied by Baïnuk, Beafada, and Manding traders.[26] All this made the Gambia River a major trading link, dotted along its entire bank with Juula trading communities of Manding, Soninke, or Jakhanke origin.

South of the Gambia, mangrove swamps become increasingly frequent and extensive. Behind them lie palm groves. The mangrove swamps are part of a dense network of creeks, on account of which this southern reach of Senegambia came to be known as the Southern Rivers.[27] This region from the Gambia to the Kolonte River, on the frontier of the cola growing zone, is inhabited by a diverse population. Yet it has a degree of unity that sets it off from other parts of the Rivers area, jumbled into a series of enclaves by the large number of rivers. They flow into the Atlantic down wide estuaries, the mouths of the Casamance, the Rio Cacheu, the Rio Geba, the Rio Grande, the Rio Nunez, and the Rio Pongo.

Unlike the millet growers to the north, people in the Southern Rivers region excel in rice farming. Here Joola, Baïnuk, Beafada, Balante, Felupe, Cocoli, Landuma, Nalu, and Baga populations share an environment of mangrove swamps, on land crisscrossed by streams which often serve as refuges, however precarious. For centuries, people in this area faced pressure from incoming Manding migrants. This goes a long way towards explaining the extreme political fragmentation of the Southern Rivers area.

In this area without large-scale political units, the level of the people's adaptation to their natural environment was remarkably high. These peasant societies were egalitarian in outlook. The village was their basic unit, but the collective consciousness was reinforced by the importance of religion. Socialization worked through a system of initiation. Known among the Joola *Bookin* as *Ata Eumitt*, and among the Baga or Landuma as *Simo*, it created potent social bonds as well as precious links between humans and nature.[28]

The outstanding feature of life here, however, was undoubtedly the creation of a rice-centered civilization by these populations. For they perfected rice farming techniques on flood plains, using the *kayando*, a long spade marvelously effective for working wet soils. In addition to rice farming, people here also made use of forest produce, especially from the graceful stands of palm trees that yielded two key staples: palm oil and palm wine.[29]

Paradoxically for a region without large-scale political units, economic and trading activities were extraordinarily dynamic. While horses, donkeys, and camels were the indispensable means of transport in the vast open spaces of the savanna and the Sahel, here the prime vehicle was the canoe, popularly known as *almadies*. These vessels helped give the Southern

Rivers an important strategic role between the forest belt to the south and the savanna to the north.[30] Clearly, at that time, it was much more profitable to transport cola, indigo dye, and iron goods produced in the forest regions for sale in the savanna to the north by canoe along the coasts and up the Southern Rivers, than to have headporters haul them overland across the Futa Jallon plateau.[31]

Thanks to these advantages, several trading networks developed in the area, dominated by the Baïnuk, the Beafada, and the Manding. The Baïnuk network, for instance, connected the lower Cacheu, Casamance, Sungrugru, Bintang, and Gambia valleys. A parallel Manding network running east connected the Rios Grande, Corubal, upper Geba, Cacheu, and Casamance with the Senegalese middle and upper valleys as well as the upper Niger valley. These Baïnuk and Manding networks converged with the Beafada network, which freighted in cola, malaguette, indigo, ironware, and other products by canoe from the forest belt beyond present-day Sierra Leone.[32]

So despite their political division into tiny enclaves, Southern Rivers people were, for the most part, active players in the north–south trade. The only group that seems to have been excluded from these various trading networks was the Joola. The reason was that traffic passed through Bintang valley, down the Sungrugru and Cacheu through Baïnuk country. So trade between the Gambia and the Cacheu flowed along inland corridors just outside the eastern borders of Joola settlements.[33]

Understandably, then, the Baïnuk in those times played economic and political roles infinitely greater than in later centuries when pressure from the Manding of Kaabu and from the Joola reduced them to a shadow of their former status. In the fifteenth century there were at least five small Baïnuk states strategically located along the trading network linking the Rio Cacheu, the Casamance, and the Gambia; the most important are Bichangor, Jase, Foni, and Buguando. The last was the center from which the Baïnuk extended their commercial network northward, merging it with that of the Nyominka, the peasant river navigators of the Saalum islands.[34] The second commercial center was dominated by the Beafada. Their principal state was Guinea, situated between upper Rio Grande and the Corubal river. They monopolized the southern trade in cola, indigo, and iron bars. So great was their prowess that the Beafada were the only people to have defeated Koli Tengela's great army between 1480 and 1490.[35]

The gigantic invasion mounted by Koli Tengela and his Peul followers, crisscrossing Senegambia from the Futa Jallon plateau through Gambia to the Senegal River, marks a major historical break in Senegambian history. Koli Tengela made Futa Jallon a major player in the overall demographic dynamics of Senegambia. He thus erased the perception of the plateau as an obstacle to population movements, and a refuge for people settled there. And he stimulated the expansion of Kaabu into the Southern Rivers area from the fifteenth century onwards.

Kaabu, situated above most of the Southern Rivers, occupied a central strategic location between the coast and the Futa Jallon plateau. In this country of forests and savanna woodlands, the sheer abundance of rivers descending from Futa Jallon is a striking feature. Alternating dry and rainy seasons gave a pleasant cadence to agricultural life in this area where millet and rice were the dominant staples. The Kaabu region was mainly populated by successive waves of Manding immigrants who, beginning in the twelfth century, intermixed with the indigenous Joola, Baïnuk, and Balantes.[36] Only in the twelfth century did Mali, at the peak of its power, organize the famous Tiramagan expedition to conquer Kaabu and to consolidate its imperial influence westward, with a view to gaining access to the coastal salt flats and the cola trade network along the Southern Rivers.

Mali dominated its western province of Kaabu well into the fifteenth century. But the province, which from a very early date enjoyed a great deal of autonomy, took advantage of Koli Tengela's invasion to affirm its independence and to impose its authority throughout southern Senegambia, from the Futa Jallon foothills to the Southern Rivers. Senegambia at the time was divided between the zones of influence of the Denyanke kingdom to the north, the royal Jolof Confederation in the center, and Kaabu to the south. Meanwhile, Portuguese traders were gaining dominance on the Atlantic coast.

Kaabu was originally conquered by Sundiata's warrior lieutenants. For the remainder of its history it retained its traditional martial character. This gave it power over the Manding principalities along the Gambia River, more focused on trade than on war. Kaabu wielded effective influence over all the western Manding. Sometimes it achieved this through military pressure. Sometimes it did it through placing members of its *Nyaanco* aristocracy, the Maane and the Saane, within royal lineages. That was the case in the neighboring states of Noomi, Birasu, Woy and Kasa. This system reached as far as the Sereer areas, where the Gelwar dynasty ruled in Siin and Saalum.[37]

Kaabu was a confederation of sorts. It contained some thirty provinces, the number sometimes changing according to circumstance. The most important provinces included Sama, Jimara, Pacana, Mana, Sankolla, Cana, Kantora, Nampoyo, Kolla, Propana and Bajar. Royal power rotated among the three chief *Nyaanco* provinces, Sama, Jimara, and Pacana, under the two royal lineages, Maane and Saane. The *Mansa*, chosen to head the confederation, was required by tradition to leave his original province and to take up residence in the capital, Kansala, in Propana province. Each royal province maintained special ties with one or more other provinces or *Korin*, whose lineages provided the central authority with its principal dignitaries. Of these the most important was the Prime Minister.[38]

The monarchical power that rotated among the three leading provinces was essentially matrilineal. The transmission mechanism was bilinear. The rule was that successors had, in Sékéné Mody Cissoko's apt phrase, to be *Nyaanco* "by both beard and breast." For that reason, princes whose mothers were not *Nyaanco* were excluded from royal succession. They became second-class nobles, just above the *Korin*, chiefs of the non-royal provinces within the confederation. The existence of a matrilineal system here is, above all, proof of the influence of the native Baïnuk populations on the western Manding. In Kaabu, the Manding created an original civilization different from that of the Niger Bend, the heartland of the Manding people. The first migrants were hunters by profession. After them came the conquering soldiers who moved in with the famous army of Tiramagan Trawore. The combined traditions gave Kaabu a distinctive militaristic character, in a culture where the spirits of sacred forests or *Jalan* also played a key role in political and social institutions.[39]

The prevalence of warrior values was typified by the status of the Soninke, a group whose role in Kaabu society was like that of the *ceddo* in Wolof society. Kaabu, unlike the original societies of the Southern Rivers area, was highly hierarchical. At the apex stood the military aristocracy, the *Nyaanco*. Below them came the *Korin* nobility, ruling over the ordinary mass of free peasants. Here too there were castes of craftspeople called *namaalo*, equivalent to the Wolof *ñeeño*. They included leather-working *Karanke*, *Numoo* ironsmiths, and griots, the class of public spokespersons and traditional historians, known as *Jali*. All were forbidden to marry free persons, those born outside caste limits. At the bottom of the social pyramid came the slaves. And among them, royal slaves were considered a cut above slaves bought on the open market.[40]

Kaabu society was the product of a long process of intermixture between native populations and successive waves of Manding conquerors or migrants who imposed their language and culture on the region. It was, on the whole, extremely cosmopolitan. Kaabu civilization, symbolized by the *kora*, the large *jun jun* drum and the *bala* xylophone, was an original synthesis of old Manding culture from the Niger valley and the civilization of all the native populations of the Southern Rivers. Islam, brought by communities of Soninke, Jakhanke and Manding traders, had an active presence here too, especially along the banks of the Gambia. However, the families of Muslim clergy, the Kote, Daabo, Tuure, Saano, and Jaane, known as Kaabu *Sula*, lived in segregated quarters called *Morikunda*. They had no political power. That was entirely in the hands of the *Nyaanco* aristocracy. In Kaabu, as in fundamentally *ceddo* Wolof areas, Soninke ideology did not tolerate Islam as a basis for political power.[41]

Before reaching the Futa Jallon plateau, the Kaabu countryside was bordered from north to south by a series of plains and plateaux, transition zones between the Southern Rivers and the Futa mountains. In the southwest, the region was dominated by the Susu, a people of Manding origin very close to the Jallonke of Futa Jallon. While the kinship of the Susu and the Jallonke is indisputable, traditions among both peoples indicate knowledge of origins antedating the Peul invasion. Portuguese sources say the Susu were already settled on the coast when they arrived. The Jallonke, on the other hand, lived in the hinterland, on the Futa Jallon plateau. Quite probably, then, the Susu came from the middle valleys of the Bafing and the Gambia, before traveling toward the coast, their main mass skirting the Futa Jallon plateau by going down the Cognon valley in really ancient times. Some Jallonke, driven out by Koli's Peul invaders, and others who moved out in the wake of the Muslim revolution, encountered the coastal Susu, with whom they very quickly merged. Incidentally, it was a habit of the Susu to keep absorbing members of the Nalu, Baga, Landuma, and Mikhifore minorities who traveled to the coast from the Futa plateau in successive waves.[42] As with the *Kafu* Manding, their political organization was based on collections of several villages, called *Ta*, under partriarchal families known as *Fookhe*. Farming was based on shifting cultivation. The dominant crops were rainfed rice and fonio in the uplands, flood-basin rice on the swampy plain.

In the north-east, the middle valleys of the Bafing and the Gambia cross uneven, hilly land. The region around the Basari mountains is difficult of access and very sparsely populated. Beyond it lies Jallonkadugu, another depopulated region between the Gambia and the Niger basins. There the kingdom of Tamba was established with the participation of Jallonke from Sangalan, driven out of the Labé region.

Housing patterns here resembled those of the Manding. Farming methods, however, were similar to those used in Susu areas. The region suffered from chronic instability caused by frequent migrations of whole villages over vast distances under pressure from Manding attackers from Kaabu, as well as from Peul migrants moving in from Futa Jallon.

In the north-west lie the extensive Konyagi plateau country and the cliffs of Bajar. Low-lying areas, flooded in the rainy season because of poor drainage, were often intensively farmed, along with sandy soils in other parts of the area. The inhabitants of the Konyagi area practiced a three-year fallow system based on millet and fonio. They shifted their mobile straw houses as they moved from used to fallow land. In contrast to the agglomerations of unified villages typical of the Konyagi, the hill-dwelling

Basari lived in widely spaced, mobile huts. Their communities, organized in matrilineal lineages, were fiercely warlike, constantly forced as they were to resist their neighbors' assaults. On account of such harassment, they could not develop a political organization transcending their villages.[43] Lastly, above the Konyagi plains lay the Bajar. Its inhabitants, the Bajaranke, were farmers of Manding culture, related to the Konyagi-Basari and the Fulakunda, a Peul people combining farming with animal husbandry. The Bajaranke, skilled producers of strip-woven cotton cloth, preserved, like the Fulakunda, a highly patriarchal organization. They were politically influenced by the Manding of Kaabu.[44] This region was crisscrossed by nomadic Peul ranging from the Senegal River past the Ferlo and Bundu regions all the way to Futa Jallon. For a long time they were subjugated in this region by sedentary groups, especially the Manding of Kaabu, who enslaved most of the rural Peul (*Fulbe Burure*). That practice resulted in the distinction between *Fula forro* (free Peul) and *Fula jon* (Peul slave).[45]

All of Senegambia is bordered on the east, from north to south, by the foothills of the Futa Jallon plateau. Sometimes these upland areas were a refuge for populations under pressure, at other times they served as an outlet. The Futa Jallon plateau provided a passageway for all migrations from the hinterland to the coast. At the same time, they were a crucial transition zone between the Sudan and the western reaches of Senegambia.[46] Jean Suret-Canale has, incidentally, given a fine definition of the historical role of the Futa Jallon plateau as both refuge and barrier. This is typical hill country, with ranges of hills and plateaux intercut by abrupt canyons, almost all above 750 m.

The Niger, the Gambia and the Senegal, all springing from this mountain range, make it West Africa's prime watershed. In addition, the area's relief features and climatic characteristics help to give it a varied range of landscapes and ecosystems dominated by extrusions of hard rock known as *bowe*. All this makes arable land extremely scarce.

Soil types here include the friable *hansanere*, found piled up at the foot of escarpments; this is the best soil for growing rainfed rice. Next come the dark, acid soils of the swampy lowlands. Together with the *hollande* soils that become flooded in the rainy season, they are also suitable for rice farming. In the steep-sided valleys, *dunkire* and *parawol* soils along the river banks, periodically flooded, are also useful for growing swamp rice. Lastly, more gently sloping land on the central plateau, known as *dantari*, is covered with light, friable soil, excellent for fonio cultivation. As a rule, the extensive cultivation practiced here quickly exhausts the soil. The agricultural system, based on the old-fashioned hoe, produces incredibly low yields. Farmers regularly supplement their produce with crops from home gardens protected by makeshift fences. Thanks to the use of household manure, these gardens produce crops all the year round.[47]

Because the area is abundantly supplied with permanent waterways and pasture ranges that remain useable in the dry season, the Futa Jallon plateau very early became a key cattle-rearing area. In sum, the area, already attractive as refuge and barrier, enjoys a third advantage: it is good grazing territory.

Jallonke of Manding origin have coexisted here for long periods with the Baga-Timne, Landuma. and Nalu peoples, pushed toward the coast by incursions of new groups: the Susu, kin to the Jallonke; the Pulli, nomads who immigrated between the thirteenth and fifteenth centuries from the Sahel, the Senegal River Valley, and Massina with their enormous herds of cattle. All these populations were already settled on the coast before the Portuguese arrived.

The invasion of Koli Tengela, who dominated the entire north and west of the range toward the end of the fifteenth century, was the main event that produced lasting changes in the region centered around the capital, Geme Sangan. When Koli and his lieutenants moved on to conquer the Senegal valley, the northern *Kafu* Jallonke regained their independence for a while, under the *Manga* Labé as paramount chief.[48] The *Kafu* Jallonke, however, were unable to set up a powerful, centralized state capable of resisting pressure from Kaabu in the sixteenth and seventeenth centuries, prior to the success of the Muslim revolution in the early eighteenth century.

Meanwhile, the Futa Jallon continued admirably to play its role as a refuge for all populations streaming out of the Sudan and Senegambia. At the same time, it remained the principal obstacle blocking the way from the Niger Bend to the Atlantic ocean. Despite their increasing numbers, the Peul, still a nomadic people, retained an organizational structure based on lineages. This system had a pronounced tendency to break up the population into tiny groups seldom larger than a single family. Beginning in the late fifteenth century, however, the coastal trade in leather and cattle strengthened the pastoral potential of the Futa Jallon plateau and boosted the economic status of the livestock-owning Peul.

Given its geographical position as a window so close to Europe, Senegambia was the first West African region to come into contact with the Atlantic trading system. This contact developed in the latter half of the fifteenth century, when the European commercial system was entering an expansionist phase. As we shall see, that period radically changed the course of Senegambian history. Before examining it and the changes it brought, however, we need first to study the internal dynamics of the societies then inhabiting the area, the better to understand the impact of the Atlantic trading system.

# 2    Social dynamics in Senegambia

The scarcity of documents makes it hard to outline the dynamics of political, social, and economic life in Senegambia in the fifteenth and sixteenth
centuries. At that time the region was coming into direct contact with
Europe by way of the Atlantic. Senegambian societies shared a common
civilization in which political and social systems were closely knit, and both
were based on an autonomous subsistence economy.

Politically, societies here were initially organized along kinship lines.
Later they shifted to a monarchical system based on violence and inequality. The caste system which supported the hierarchical ordering of social life
served to rationalize this inequality. On the whole, however, the self-
sufficient domestic subsistence economy did much to attenuate peasant
exploitation by an aristocracy often excluded from long-distance trade.

## A.    Political and social organization: the system of castes and orders

Senegambia contained two types of societies. The first, egalitarian in
outlook, derived political power from lineage. The second, hierarchical in
outlook, imposed monarchical power upon the lineage-based system. This
was done within the rigid framework of *Kafu* or *Lamanat* authority, or
under the authority of the *Ardo*. Under the *Kafu* and *Lamanat* systems,
land rights were linked to political or religious power under the authority
of a territorial chief. That same chief functioned as a community head. For
nomadic peoples like the Peul, or for populations forced into migration, the
*Ardo* was primarily the head of a community on the move, prior to its settlement on a given territory.

Lineage-based societies were prevalent in the Southern Rivers area,
where, because of the geographical isolation of communities, or because of
pressure from neighboring groups, the state was often a mere collection of
villages. But even where external pressure turned communities into
refugees, and the state was reduced to its simplest expression, Joola,
Baïnuk, Balante, Felupe, Beafada, Nalu, Landuma, and Baga communities
did have a system of state organization.[1]

Communities in this region very early came under pressure from the Kaabu Manding in their drive toward the coast. And with the arrival of the Portuguese, they became victims in organized, large-scale manhunts. These states, already reduced through loss of territory, often regressed to community-based organizational systems. At the same time, their refugee status reinforced tendencies toward egalitarian and isolationist values. This tended to simplify social organization. The result was that, for the most part, these rice-growing peasant societies had nothing to do with the system of handicraft castes and hierarchies distinguishing free classes from slaves.

The odds of any one of these societies being matrilineal or patrilineal were even. Social organization was generally based on age-groups. Education was through initiation, a process that underlined the essential role of religion in social bonding. The *Simo* among the Baga, Nalu, or Landuma, like the *Bookin* among the Joola, ensured cohesion and survival among the coastal populations of the Southern Rivers. Ethnic or lineage-based families were close-knit. Land tenure rules, clearly defined, had governed the use of precisely allocated rice plots for centuries. Still, one result was that available land was cut up into tiny plots. Further, these small plots of riceland were very unevenly distributed from village to village, as well as among peasants in the same village.[2]

Understandably, therefore, conflicts over possession of ricelands and over control of waterways, natural inter-regional trade routes, were the driving force of history in the Southern Rivers area. Meanwhile, the area came increasingly under the influence of the Kaabu Manding, attempting to subjugate the Baïnuk, Beafada, and Joola populations from the Rio Cacheu all the way to the Gambia River. Pressure also came from the Susu, slowly assimilating the Baga, Nalu, and Landuma in the basins of the Rio Nunez and the Rio Pongo. This combined Manding and Susu pressure, however, was not sufficient to erase the egalitarian outlook of this patchwork of rice-growing societies.

Political and social organization was more complex in the savanna lands of northern Senegambia. To begin with, the wide open spaces did not offer the Wolof, Peul, Tukulor, Soninke, and Manding populations the same protection as the Southern Rivers or, to a lesser extent, the Futa Jallon plateau. This meant that, quite early in their history, people here had to adopt territory-wide organizational methods to ensure their protection. They achieved this by creating kingdoms or royal confederations. Here horses were a powerful means of transport. They were also highly useful for the military conquest of territory, the basis of most of the region's monarchies. So horse trading for slaves or gold was a key factor in the growing relationship between North Africa and Senegambia. Here in the Senegambian savanna, the Manding chief or Soninke *kafu*, the Wolof or Sereer *laman*, the Peul *ardo* or the Tukulor *farba*, was originally a community head responsible, among sedentary populations, for land management. Among nomadic herdspeople he administered pasture ranges. It was he who, using fire and instruments of war to establish his rights, set up the first territorially based political entities while managing land rights for various lineages.

The second stage saw the emergence, on a larger territorial scale, of more powerful *lamans* at the head of the *kafu*, or of *farbas* rising to become sovereigns in the Denyanke kingdom of Futa Toro, the Jolof confederation, the kingdom of Kaabu, or that of Gajaaga. The monarchical system, imposed through conquest as in Kaabu and Futa Toro, through persuasion as in the Jolof confederation, or through secession as in Kajoor and Waalo, was often a foreign import. As such, it allowed community chiefs to retain selected prerogatives, especially their power to manage land. Often, though, local chiefs lost their political power. Even so, they became members of an Electoral Council. Sometimes they also served as executives under various sovereign monarchs.[3]

The monarchical system, in short, acknowledged the rights of former chiefs, while simply placing them under the authority of royal appointees. In the Wolof kingdoms, for instance, the *lamanal* mode of production might be defined as a transitional stage between the patriarchal mode, which involved no fees or tribute, and the tributary mode, which did. The latter system flourished under the monarchical system. At this level, however, there was already in place a dual structural arrangement in which land was held in common but worked on an individual basis. From that point on, the payment of fees by heads of families owning plots of land (*boorom ngajj*) to the *laman* as manager of collective property helped to create the basis for social classes and a state.[4] However, the king, while acknowledging the rights of the *laman* as land administrator, had more and more vacant land to distribute among relatives and allies, including warriors, notables, and religious leaders in his entourage. On occasion, he even felt tempted to encroach on land under the *laman*'s control. This custom was the origin of the system of appointments. In short order, it brought about the "feudalization" of the land tenure system.[5]

In most kingdoms, the monarchical system was oligarchical, and succession was bilineal. Bilineal kinship became necessary because Wolof kinship structures required that the social legacy of political power as seized and exercised by men be handed down through males, while biological heredity (blood-based pedigree, for instance) was transmitted through females.[6] A further reason probably applied in other kingdoms: bilineal descent could also be a compromise between a defeated ruling class and a conquering military class of foreign origin. By giving its daughters in marriage, the old aristocracy managed to retain a measure of authority while legitimizing the new political regime. This was true of the *Nyaanco* dynasty in Kaabu, as well as of the *Gelewar* in Siin and Saalum.

Power was vested in the royal aristocracy. The king was chosen from among two or three families vested with hereditary eligibility. Selection was by an electoral council appointed either from among former community chiefs or by a council of elders. Royal power was hedged around by a wide range of rights accruing to different social groups, including slaves.

The monarchical system was the logical outcome of the hierarchical ordering of Senegambian society that began with the rule of the *laman* or the *kafu*. Senegambian societies were quintessentially non-egalitarian. The epitome of inequality was the caste system, on which rode a system of subsidiary social divisions, or orders. Indeed, caste, established under Malian influence, was among the most ancient features of social stratification in most Senegambian societies. Castes comprised hereditary, endogamous groups specializing in particular professions. They implied hierarchical relationships between *gëër* and *ñeeño* among the Wolof,[7] between *riimbe* (singular: *diimo*) and *nyeënbe* among the Peul, between *proro* and *namakala* among the Manding, and between *jambuurini* and *nakhmala* among the Soninke. Persons in the first-named groups were all free. They differed from those in the second by virtue of their professional status. Their work was taboo to people outside the caste group. Those who broke the rule lost status. Thus, among the Wolof, there were distinctions between *jëf lekk*, a handicraft category that included the *tëg* or ironsmiths, *wude* or leatherworkers, *seen* or woodcarvers, and *rabb* or weavers, on the one hand, and *sab lekk*, including *gewël* or griots, and *noole* or courtesans. The same caste system existed in other Senegambian societies, except that the *cubaalo* or fisherfolk belonged to the category of *ñeeño*. In all cases, the caste system, based on a division of labor, was perpetuated through a biological and racial ideology that imposed hereditary rules and endogamous practices.[8] Incidentally, in each specific society, caste members were assigned foreign origins – a further rationale for imposed endogamy.

On top of the caste system, there was also a system of hierarchical orders. This was established by a political regime which divided society into hereditary and hierarchical strata, thus maintaining political domination and economic exploitation. Orders involved aspects of freedom and servitude. Among the Wolof, for instance, they created a major duality between the free *gor* or *jambur* and the slave *jaam* in social life, along with a division between *buur* and *baadoolo* in political affairs. *Buur* held political power or had access to it. *Baadoolo* were subjects. They had no political power; neither could they aspire to it. It was the relationship of each social category to the royal regime which determined its position in the system of orders, defined its status and functions, and fixed its social and economic relationships with others.[9] As with the caste system, the system of orders existed among the Soninke, the Manding, the Peul, and the Tukulor, though the names used varied from kingdom to kingdom.

The Soninke called free men *hooro*; slaves *komo*. The Manding called them *fooro* and *joon*. The Peul and the Tukulor called free men *riimbe* and slaves *maccube*. Throughout Senegambia, established monarchical regimes also legitimized, in addition to the division between free and slave, a political hierarchy that divided society into three classes: the upper, royal nobility; the notables; and lastly the ordinary mass of free persons. These last were excluded from power through the hereditary system which restricted political eligibility to selected family lineages.

## B.    The domestic economy and the social hierarchy

It is the region's political and social institutions that most clearly reflect the fundamental cultural unity of Senegambian societies in general. This unity was primarily based on similar economic conditions in a context of self-sufficient domestic subsistence economies. These societies were essentially agricultural. The only exceptions were certain Peul groups on their nomadic journeys from the Futa Jallon plateau to the borders of the Ferlo on the banks of the Senegal River, as well as a sprinking of Berbers from Chamana.

According to Claude Meillassoux, the basic features of this domestic economy were

sufficient knowledge of agricultural and craft techniques to run a farm system productive enough to yield adequate food for members and seed for the next farming season; the use of human labor as the prime energy source in agricultural and craft work; and the use of individual farm tools whose manufacture required no investment beyond individual labor.[10]

Production was based on a degree of collectivism supported by lineage and extended family ties. Land ownership was tied to production and reproduction relationships. It could not be acquired as a simple commodity. Neither could it be traded or transferred in such a way as to divorce it from the social context that gave it economic and use value.[11]

In this domestic economy, land was certainly the basis of political power. But it was not, in any fundamental way, the basis of all production relations within the community. For fees were low and land was plentiful. Exceptions were the flood recession basins of the Senegal valley and the developed rice fields of the Southern Rivers area. In most cases, extensive cultivation was the rule on account of technical stagnation and the two-season cycle in this tropical zone.

The fact that free land was available also accounted in large measure for the capacity of the different Senegambian communities to absorb newcomers. Population settlement patterns became gradually stable in the fifteenth and sixteenth centuries. Most often, conflicts arose among distinct communities when a massive invasion of a neighboring people directly threatened the property rights of the original population. The considerable diminution of such Southern Rivers populations as the Baïnuk was related to the seizure of rice lands by Manding or Joola invaders, apart from the hemorrhage caused by the slave trade. Strictly speaking, however, territorial conquest was not the basis of political affairs in the Senegambian states, because the dual system of community heads and territorial rulers was maintained even within monarchical institutions. The practice of vesting land management in territorial rulers did a great deal to frustrate the development of a strong central authority within the kingdoms. It was also, in part, the reason why confederal systems were so popular in Senegambia.

A key feature of political institutions in Senegambian states during the fifteenth and sixteenth centuries was the decentralization of power. Royal regimes administered persons without always necessarily managing the land. For that reason, monarchical power, often imposed by violence, initiated the prevalence of political relationships over land relations. In this way it hampered the emergence of a feudal mode of production in which peasants were bonded to the soil. The dominant mode of production might be described as tributary. Typically, it involved the existence of patriarchal communities with collective ownership rights over the land they tilled. By these means, from a combination of agriculture and handicrafts, they generated a surplus which a dominant class representing the state appropriated.[12] This exploitation practiced by the dominant class took the form of fees and dues on land collected in kind, along with a vast array of other duties and taxes. On the whole, however, the low population density, made even lower by the slave trade, the resulting abundance of land, and, last of all, the stagnation of agricultural technology, kept Senegambia locked into a subsistence economy. This resulted in low tax revenues for political regimes which, though centralized at the level of the monarchical system, had to rely on a local land tenure system without the basic features of the feudal system.[13] Indeed, from the fifteenth and sixteenth centuries onward, the trend toward feudalization of the land tenure system was checked by a series of political and social institutions peculiar to Senegambia, together with external factors related to the arrival of Europeans. The latter, in a sense, froze this state of stalled feudalization over several centuries.

Similarly, slavery was an ancient institution in the domestic economy of Senegambia, with the exception of the egalitarian Southern Rivers societies. The practice legitimized the division between free persons and slaves.

But slavery does not seem to have played a key role in the mode of production, which remained tributary even within the monarchical context. Still, for centuries, slaves were sent in small numbers to the northern markets for sale. Slaves were used as currency in arms deals. During the time of the trans-Saharan trade, they were also used to buy salt, horses, and luxury goods – the aristocratic status symbols of the day. Aristocrats sold some slaves, obtained through inter-state warfare, in the inter-regional trading system. Others were turned into domestic slaves, kept to work on family farms or to produce handicraft goods. House slaves were more or less integrated into their masters' families after one, two, or three generations.

There is little evidence for the argument that slavery was the dominant mode of production in Senegambian societies during the fifteenth and sixteenth centuries. Trends that could have made it so stalled in the face of the subsistence economy and the tributary mode of production, in which political rulers siphoned off production surpluses in a system of patriarchal exploitation.[14] Above all, from the sixteenth century on, such a development was blocked by the slave trade, which favored the massive export of labor as opposed to its use at home in the context of a classic slaveholding economy.

Meanwhile, Senegambian societies, made up of domestic communities ranging from villages to states, were by no means autarchic, even if the subsistence economy played a very important role. As a whole, Senegambia was integrated into a regional and a long-distance inter-regional trading system. To start with, there was the exchange of agricultural products for dairy products, fish and handicraft products. The complementary interactions of these economic sectors was a permanent reality that determined the operations of local or inter-regional trading circuits. Cereal trading between the sedentary populations of the Senegal River valley and the Berbers of present-day Mauritania was particularly important. At the same time, there was a lively trade in fish, mainly from the mouth of the Senegal River to the upper Valley, where it was traded for millet. A second circuit led to the rice-producing Southern Rivers. There was also the inter-regional trade in cola, cloth, indigo dye, and iron bars, transported through the Southern Rivers toward the savanna and the Sahel.

As a rule, trade in agricultural and handicraft products, as well as in produce gathered wild, went on between zones producing and zones needing them. The result was a complementary economy involving the varied exchange of produce from the savanna, the Sahel, the mangrove swamps, and the forest. This inter-regional trading system linked Senegambia with three major trading zones: to the north with the trans-Sahara trade; to the east with the Sudanese trade along the Niger Bend; and finally to the south, with the forest trading circuits of Sierra Leone.

Long-distance trade, however, remained restricted to luxury items such as salt, gold, cola, horses, cloth, and, occasionally, slaves. Trading circuits were monopolized by communities of specialized traders often identified with their ethnic groups: Zawaya Berbers, Jakhanke, Soninke, and so forth. Trade and Islam went together. Politico-military ruling groups and communities of Muslim traders were not particularly close. The latter formed a series of interconnected enclaves strung out through the states of Senegambia and beyond.[15]

This system was a legacy of the trade-oriented Islam of the medieval Sudanese empires. Because only a minority of the population was actively involved, it could not effect fundamental changes in the political and social structures of the kingdoms of Senegambia. In the absence of a large, dynamic merchant class, then, production relationships within the domestic economy were slow to change. Subsistence needs continued to dominate the economy, especially since land, the sole measure of wealth, remained the common property of different home communities under the management of family lineages with typically low production levels. In short, possibilities of radical political and social change were limited by economic conditions peculiar to the pre-capitalist societies of Senegambia.

At this juncture, then, the development of Senegambian societies was stalled in two ways. They could not move on to a Western-style feudal mode of production. Neither could they develop toward a slave-based mode of the ancient Greek or later American type. This stagnation implied a serious potential of regression from the tributary mode of production toward more archaic forms similar to the communal mode. Thus, while in the fifteenth and sixteenth centuries most Senegambian states were at the level of the tributary mode of production, certain population groups such as the Tenda Basari and Konyaagi in the interior, or the Baïnuk and Felup in the Southern Rivers area, threatened with extermination by the combined impact of neighboring populations and the manhunts of the slave trading era, turned inward and developed a form of social and political egalitarianism in the narrow context of kin-based "democracies" isolated from the world at large.

Whatever the nuances, structural change in the area's political and social systems was generally slow, given the overall characteristics of the domestic subsistence economy. The political and social hierarchy remained intact. Hence the close linkage between political and social systems in Senegambia. As Pathé Diagne has aptly pointed out,

Relationships were not between individuals but between families and lineages. Their hierarchical bonds affected the degree of freedom allowed in segregated relationships. These in turn were based on occupational and social status considerations, complicated by varied rationales, straightforward contractual connections of the *laman* type, as well as relationships involving sovereignty, dominance and subordination. All this had more or less far-reaching economic implications.[16]

We should remember, however, that even such closely knit political and social institutions could accommodate changes in the political status of given social groups. Such changes could happen as part of the society's own development, or in the context of a revolution.[17]

Throughout Senegambia, the exercise of specified functions by given family lineages as a hereditary right remained a fundamental principle. From the outset, monarchical power was doubly insulated against threats of succession breakdowns or revolutions. And this was the juncture at which Islam became a functional ideology capable of changing the bases of political and social structures in the states of Senegambia. By the fifteenth century, Senegambia already had a secular experience of Islam, thanks to influences coming from both the Sudan and the Sahara. From the Sahara, it was the Zawaya families of Berber marabouts who converted populations in northern Senegambia to Islam. The impact of the Almoravid movement was the measure of their success.

From the Sudan it was the Jakhanke, led by Al Hadj Salimu Suware, who propagated Islam in southern Senegambia and Futa Jallon. The Jakhanke, a Muslim elite from Diakha in Massina, first settled in Jafunu and later in Bambuk on the Bafing. There they created a marabout community dedicated to teaching the Koran. Their religious center, Bambukhu, acquired a reputation for piety. From there, the Jakhanke fanned out throughout Senegambia, founding Muslim enclaves along the trading routes as from the fifteenth century. The Suware, Silla, Fofana, Girassi, Darame, and Jakhite Kabba families were the leading Muslim clerics. Throughout the ensuing centuries they worked peacefully to convert the populations of Senegambia.[18]

Alongside their religious vocation, the Jakhanke, ethnic kin to the Soninke and the Manding, were also deeply involved in trade – a circumstance that made them the western equivalent of Juula traders. In the beginning, however, these Muslim trading communities were simply tiny enclaves in an environment of political structures peculiar to Senegambia. For even though a few sovereigns had been converted to Islam, nowhere in Senegambia did Islam constitute the ruling ideology. It was tolerated and accepted in royal courts. But political power was regulated by institutional principles peculiar to Senegambia. Islam emerged clearly as an ideology of political change around the time when Europe was imposing its mode of capitalist production on the domestic societies of Senegambia.

Senegambia is a transitional zone between the Sahara, the Sudan, and the forest belt. The region exhibits a measure of economic, political, and social unity symbolized by the millet and milk diet of the north, the related rice and palm oil culture of the Southern Rivers, and the fonio and milk diet of the Futa Jallon plateau. This peasant culture runs parallel to the cultural influence of the *khalam*, the *kora*, and the *jun-jun*, musical instruments imparting a characteristic beat to the daily lives of these societies situated at the junction of so many diverse influences from the Sahara, the Sudan, and the forest. Though economically rather independent of each other, each with its subsistence economy, these societies were by no means isolated from each other. Individuals and groups did a great deal of traveling in all directions. When they reached a different community, they intermingled according to the rules of their host communities, in a region where there was still plenty of space for incoming migrants.

In the process, people switched ethnic groups and languages. There were Toures, originally Manding, who became Tukulor or Wolof; Jallos, originally Peul, became Khaasonke; Moors turned into Naari Kajor; Mane and Sane, originally Joola surnames, were taken by the Manding royalty of Kaabu. There was, in short, a constant mixture of peoples in Senegambia, destined for centuries to share a common space. Senegambia, in some respects, functioned like a vast reserve into which populations in the Sudan and the Sahel habitually poured surplus members. In their new home the immigrants created a civilization of constant flux, in which ethnic identities were primarily a result of the mutual isolation of domestic communities caused by the subsistence economy. Nowhere in this Senegambia, where population settlement patterns assumed stable outlines as early as the end of the fifteenth century, did any Wolof, Manding, Peul, Tukulor, Sereer, Joola, or other ethnic group feel they were strangers.

But from the late fifteenth century, this common destiny, related to Senegambia's role as a transition zone, or even as an outlet for the Sahel and the Sudan, changed profoundly. Up until then, Senegambia's Atlantic coast was of little significance. Then contact with the European maritime powers gave it unprecedented importance. That contact brought about deep economic, political, and social transformations. From now on the pre-capitalist societies of Senegambia came under pressure from a Europe in the full force of its capitalist expansion. The encounter took place under conditions of thoroughgoing economic and political domination that radically altered the destiny of Senegambia. From that point on, it becomes impossible to understand the development of Senegambia without factoring in the impact of the European trading system, an external factor which monopolized exchanges between Africa, America and Asia by conquering the international market.

# 3 The Atlantic trading system and the reformation of Senegambian states from the fifteenth to the seventeenth century

The course of Senegambian history was radically changed with the arrival of Europeans on the coast. The Portuguese impact was the most spectacular. The seacoast became, from then on, the leading front for acculturation. The settlement of the Portuguese at Arguin around 1445 was the first victory of the caravel over the caravan. Its consequence was the rerouting of trade circuits toward the Atlantic.

Portuguese seeking gold attempted to penetrate into the Sudan along the Senegal River and, more energetically, along the Gambia. But the Felu Falls made navigation up the Senegal River difficult. Along the Gambia, too, the Portuguese faced problems from the dominant Manding. When, in 1488, their attempts to build a fort on the banks of the Senegal River failed, the Portuguese resorted to trading along the coast and up the estuaries of the Senegal and the Gambia, using boats shuttling in from the Cape Verde islands. They established a solid foothold in the Southern Rivers region and in the Gambia because the region was important in the inter-regional trade of Senegambia.

Portuguese traders, dealing in gold, ivory, hides, spices, and – right from the start – slaves, used the old inter-regional trade circuit for cola, salt, cotton cloth, and iron. Under the Portuguese monopoly, this trade produced profound changes as early as the mid-sixteenth century. In particular, it reshaped the political map of Senegambia.

In southern Senegambia, the kingdom of Kaabu dominated the Southern Rivers and Futa Jallon. In northern Senegambia, the Jolof confederation broke up, yielding place to the tiny kingdoms of Waalo, Kajoor, Baol, Siin, and Saalum. Meanwhile, in the Senegal valley, the Denyanke kingdom of Futa Toro consolidated its hold. Everywhere in the region, the process of the political dismemberment of the Senegambian states, reeling under the impact of the Atlantic trading system, got under way.

## A.    The Portuguese trading monopoly

From the start, the Portuguese, the first Europeans to explore the African coast, settled at Arguin and up the estuaries of the Senegal and Gambia

Rivers. Their aim was to divert the gold trade from the Sudan toward the Atlantic. After occupying Arguin around 1445 in a bid to take advantage of the trans-Saharan gold trade from the Sudan, the Portuguese went up the Senegal valley, and made even more strenuous efforts to go up the Gambia River. In Gambia, they very quickly invaded the key commercial center of Wuli, the starting point for caravans linking the Gambia northward with upper Senegal and eastward with the Niger Bend. The Gambia thus became the principal outlet for the waning Mali Empire. Caravans went down the river, a waterway dotted with numerous Manding principalities, all trading centers in direct contact with the Portuguese trading establishment, obsessed with its search for Sudanese gold.

It is difficult to estimate the quantity of gold traded by Senegambia then. At the time, the region's main supplies came from the mines at Bure and Bambuk. Philip Curtin has estimated that, in the sixteenth and seventeenth centuries, the quantity of gold exported from Senegambia was no more than 35 kg in a good year.[1] On this point, however, there is no reason for leaving out of the Senegambian market total the trade from Arguin. For that trading post, using camel-riding nomadic middlemen, certainly got its supplies through Bambuk, mainly from the gold mines between the Falémé and Bafing rivers. In effect, the main consequence of the Atlantic trading system was to expand Senegambia into the Sahelian zone. This pattern became clearer in the eighteenth century, with the development of the gum trade, which irresistibly drew the Berber nomads toward the Senegal River, the center of the Atlantic trading system. Because of the steady decline of the trans-Saharan trade, the entire southern region of the country now known as Mauritania, beginning from Arguin, came within the orbit of Senegambia, attracted by the Atlantic trading system. For that reason, the region came to play an increasingly important role in the evolution of states along the Senegal valley.

A study by Victorino Magalhàes Godinho shows that the factory at Arguin reported trading an annual average of 4,709 gold doubloons between 1499 and 1501. In 1513, a single ship carried off 2,000 gold doubloons.[2] Furthermore, on the basis of data culled from books kept at the Lisbon Currency Exchange, Godinho has estimated the annual intake ceiling during the last quarter of the fifteenth and the first quarter of the sixteenth century, a time when the Arguin factory was in decline, at something between 20 and 25 kg, the equivalent of 5,500 to 7,000 cruzados. He adds that, as from 1542, the factory was ruined by smuggling, the turnover of which it was hard to estimate. A second ruinous factor was the circumstance that, from then on, Portuguese traders could trade directly along the estuaries of the Senegal and Gambia Rivers.[3]

The arrival of Portuguese boats in the Upper Gambia valley, at stations not far from the Futa Jallon foothills, was a turning point in the history of the Sudanese gold trade. From then on, gold from the Sudan found its way to the fairs of Wuli and Kantora. This new trade route, which provided access to the coast from the Senegal River all the way to Sierra Leone, was largely influential in diverting trade from Bambuk and Bure away from the old Niger Basin and Sahara connections, thus definitively integrating the zone into Senegambia.

In Gambia, the Portuguese purchased between 5,000 and 6,000 gold doubloons a year from 1456. From 1510 to 1517, when trade franchises were farmed out from Kantora and the Gambia, acquiring companies paid out 45,400 reals a year to the state. Incidentally, the account books at the Royal Lisbon Currency Exchange registered the sum of 5,000 cruzados and 35 grains as the value traded on 12 May 1532.[4] According to Walter Rodney, in 1551 the captain of a trading vessel, the *Santiago,* traded nearly 20 pounds of gold at Kantora. And according to a source dating from 1581, Gambian gold could be estimated at 10,000 to 12,000 cruzados.[5] Lastly, it must not be forgotten that part of the gold taken from Senegambia (Bambuk, Bure) was sold as far off as on the Sierra Leonean coast, where its value rose as high as 12,000 to 20,000 doubloons. This gold traffic stretched farther afield, all the way to the Gold Coast, with annual production exceeding 410 kg (over 100,000 cruzados) during the first twenty years of the sixteenth century.[6] All this shows the relative importance of Senegambian gold in Portuguese commerce before it was superseded by the trade in slaves. The data also show what a major problem the quantitative evaluation of the gold trade poses.

The leather trade was also important. Senegambia exported 6,000 to 7,000 hides annually. In 1660, in response to high European demand, the area produced 150,000 hides – a record total.[7] According to Coelho, the trading post of Rufisque alone exported 35,000 to 40,000 hides around 1660.[8] The leather trade very quickly boosted the importance of the Futa Jallon plateau, an area suitable for animal husbandry. This in turn speeded up the process of social differentiation there. From 1606, the Futa region exported nearly 40,000 hides annually along the Southern Rivers circuits, a sign of steady settlement by nomadic Peul looking for fresh pastures.

There was, in addition, the wax trade and, above all, the ivory trade. The Southern Rivers area, together with the Cokoli and Landuma areas, were particularly renowned for their ivory. A single cargo sometimes contained as many as 28,000 elephant tusks.[9] The Rio Nunez alone exported 300 quintals of ivory, and, again according to Coelho, it was known that the Dutch took delivery of approximately 1,500 to 2,000 quintals of wax and ivory through Afro-Portuguese middlemen trading between Cacheu and Gorée. In 1673, apart from Portugal whose monopoly was under steady attack, other European countries traded 3,000 quintals of wax and ivory.

After 1658, the French became extremely active in the wax and ivory trades, centered on Bissao. But it was the English companies which soon took command of the export trade, loading 20–30 tonnes of wax or ivory per cargo.[10] The destruction of elephant herds, prevalent throughout Senegambia at that time, was to continue inexorably throughout the ensuing centuries. In the beginning, Portuguese traders were primarily interested in produce. Gold and spices were leading items. They were obtained south of Senegambia, on the Malaguetta Coast located in what is now Liberia.

But even then the Portuguese were already involved in the slave trade, the importance of which in Senegambia during the fifteenth, sixteenth and seventeenth centuries is often overlooked. Philip Curtin thinks Senegambia was certainly the first source of slaves taken to Europe by sea, and during the sixteenth century it remained the main exporter. However, Curtin estimates the number of slaves taken between 1526 and 1550 at 250 to 1,000 annually; two centuries later, practically the same figure is advanced for 'just' the coastal region, including Wolof, Peul, Sereer and Gambian Manding populations. Thus, as the slave trade feeding the New World developed, there was a relative drop in the importance of slave exports from Senegambia, with the region's percentage dropping from 20 percent to 1 percent of the overall total.[11] I have no intention of challenging the fact that the supply of slaves from Senegambia declined as exports from the gulf of Guinea and Angola, which became the principal sources of slaves as from the seventeenth century, increased. Clearly, though, Philip Curtin unjustifiably underestimates the population drain caused by the slave trade in Africa as a whole.

In the precise case of Senegambia, Laranzo Coelho has provided estimates of the number of slaves shipped on a single vessel at Arguin in 1513. Arguin was only a remote trading post on the edge of the Sahara, set up expressly to divert trade from the desert caravan route toward the Portuguese Atlantic circuit. Even so, Godinho thinks Arguin accounted for the export of 800 to 1,000 slaves annually.[12] Unfortunately, there are no statistical data with which to evaluate the size of the slave trade at the time the Cape Verde and the Madeira islands were being developed, and later, at the start of the sugar economy in the New World. In effect, Senegambia, given its advantageous position between Europe and America, was alone the source of 50 percent of total slave exports from 1526 to 1550.[13]

Slave trading became even more important following the development of the trans-Atlantic slave trade supplying the Spanish possessions. Senegambia as a whole, and the Southern Rivers and Cape Verde islands in particular, became busy havens for slaving vessels, on the evidence of permits issued in 1562 and 1595. The area remained the prime slave exporting zone for the Spanish possessions until the break between Portugal and Spain in 1640. Not surprisingly, then, Guinea alone exported more than 3,000 slaves, and the Portuguese *Conselho Ultramarino* estimated the number of slaves exported annually from Cacheu at 3,000. Walter Rodney estimates the annual rate of exports from the Southern Rivers alone from 1562 to 1640 at 5,000, on the basis of records antedating both the expansion of slave plantations in the Americas and the full development of the Asiento.[14]

For northern Senegambia, unfortunately there is a shortage of statistical data. Still, it is known that Wolofs made up nearly 20 percent of slaves exported from Senegambia.[15] Lavanha reports that in 1600 slaves accounted for the bulk of Portuguese trade along the Senegal River.[16]

What the people of Senegambia received in exchange was, in the early stages, horses, each horse being valued at between eight and fifteen slaves. The horses, reared in North Africa, were brought mainly by the Portuguese, who thus emptied the old trans-Saharan supply source. A 1606 account left by Baltasar Barreira gives a good idea of the scope of the horse trade. For instance, the Grand Fulo or *Satigi* of Futa Toro alone possessed hundreds of carefully selected horses, kept saddled and harnessed in a permanent state of readiness.[17] Silver coins were used as currency among the populations of the Gambia, Rio Cacheu, and Rio Geba. Iron was also used as currency. It was the main Senegambian import, followed by textiles, alcohol, arms, and, finally, trinkets. In 1683, for instance, the market at Cacheu was reported to have an annual import capacity of 122 tonnes of iron.[18]

The Portuguese, the first to discover this part of the African coastline, were the principal beneficiaries of the Atlantic trading system up until the mid-seventeenth century. They were integrated into the Senegambian market, ensuring exchanges with Portugal, and they were particularly active in Senegambia's own inter-regional commerce. For, after the failure of their attempts to build a fort in the Senegal River estuary, and after equally unsuccessful attempts to establish a permanent foothold in the Gambia, where powerful Manding kingdoms jealously protected their territories, the Portuguese fell back on the Cape Verde islands, where they built a permanent settlement. From that point, economic and social ties developed between the Cape Verde archipelago and Senegambia, expanding seaward.

Portuguese settlers in the islands traded intensely with the continent, at the same time developing a system of plantation agriculture at Santiago and Fuego based on the massive use of slave labor drawn mainly from Senegambia. Thus, in 1582, the population of Fogo and Santiago included 1,608 whites, 400 freed slaves and 13,700 slaves producing sugar, cotton, and indigo dye.[19] Miscegenation soon produced a category of Afro-

Portuguese, known as *Lançados* or *Tangomaos,* who carved out a niche for themselves in Senegambia's inter-regional trade as indispensable middlemen between European traders and the Senegambian kingdoms. Using small boats called *pinnaces* and *lanches*, Portuguese from Santiago traded salt for gold, ivory and, above all, cola, in Sierra Leone. Philip Curtin estimates, on the basis of figures culled from Coelho's narrative, that about 225 tonnes of cola were shipped northward every year in the mid-seventeenth century.[20]

From Sierra Leone, the Portuguese plied up the coast all the way to Portudal and Joal, where they traded part of their cola cargo for cotton goods. They also traded ivory for textiles from Cape Verde, from where they set off on the return trip to Cacheu, to sell the remaining cola and cotton goods for slaves.[21] Similarly, in 1526, they traded iron bars bought in the Great Scarcies in Sierra Leone for slaves and ivory all along the Rio Cacheu valley. They thus obtained fifty to sixty slaves in exchange for products bought directly during their trading trips along the Senegambian coast from Cape Verde to Sierra Leone. The cost price of each slave amounted to 150 reals, yielding profits of 9,000 to 10,000 reals for just a small initial investment.[22]

Henceforth, Senegambia would be directly linked by sea with ecological zones as remote as the Gold Coast on the Gulf of Guinea. Thus the Portuguese settled down to a lucrative trade in the Senegambian environment, supplying increasing quantities of textiles made in the Cape Verde islands. These textiles edged out cotton goods made in the savanna lands of West Africa, formerly traded in the Southern Rivers and in the forest regions of Sierra Leone. The Portuguese also sold textiles along the Rio Nunez for indigo dye, needed by the cotton-weaving industries of the northern countries. Meanwhile, cotton plantations using slave labor enabled the Afro-Portuguese of Cape Verde to continue playing an important role in the slave trade until the late eighteenth century. They were in a position to trade their cotton goods directly on the continent for slaves; alternatively, they could buy slaves directly from European slavers with their local products, since the *Barafula* was practically used as legal tender in the region.[23]

So advantageously placed was Cape Verde that the *lançados*, with support from the middleman populations (Lebu, Papel, Beafada) ended up threatening the metropolitan Portuguese as trading competitors. In response, the Edict of 1508 imposed substantial restrictions on *lançado* traders. Another Edict, in 1514, signed by Manuel I, codified conditions for overseas trade while strengthening the monopoly system to the exclusive advantage of the metropole. Despite this real conflict, the *lançados*, like Afro-Europeans at all European trading posts in the area, henceforth made up a class of compradors in this proto-colonial situation. They exploited the Senegambian population to the maximum for their personal profit, their key role being to serve the major interests of European commercial capitalism.[24]

The first direct contact between Senegambia and Europe resulted from initiatives taken by a European commercial system in full expansion. It tended to dominate various levels of the African economy, assigning it specific roles within the global production system of emergent capitalism. From that point on, all internal transformations within Senegambia's societies would be governed by this context of increasing subordination to the capitalist system.[25] This would be the cause of future economic changes in the Southern Rivers area. It would also reshape the political landscape in northern Senegambia from the second half of the sixteenth century.

## B.    Reshaping the political landscape of the Senegambian states

Though still relatively modest in scope, Portuguese trade had a significant impact on the development of Senegambia's societies and states as early as the sixteenth century. The main consequences of this trade were discernible in the Southern Rivers region by the end of the fifteenth century, when the Portuguese seized control of the zone, a strategic area as far as interregional trade in Senegambia was concerned.

Critical changes occurred very early in the region between the Casamance River and the Rio Cacheu, a section with a heavy influx of Cape Verdian traders. Here they found highly skilled Baïnuk and Kasanga weavers and dyers, who quickly became the principal buyers of cotton from Cape Verde. The Baïnuk also prospered from their agricultural work, producing food for resident Europeans as well as for slaving vessels. Their lucrative niche provoked a conflict with the *lançados*, and in 1570 the latter appealed to the *Mansa* Tamba, king of Kasanga, for help. Rivalries between the Baïnuk of Buguendo and Bishangor, on the one hand, and the Kasanga states, instigated by Portuguese interests, on the other, did not end until around 1590, with the death of the *Mansa* Tamba of Kasa.[26]

But right from the onset, slave trading, the central business of Portuguese traders, began to exert a more durable pull on the economic, political, and social situation of the Southern Rivers. For the Manding took to specializing in large-scale slave raiding, strengthening the position of Kaabu which thus controlled the entire territory between the Gambia River and Futa Jallon. Kaabu took advantage of the passage of Koli Tengela's troops through the territories of the Baïnuk, Papel, Kasanga, and Beafada peoples, to assert its dominance over most of the Southern Rivers area, the better to profit from the maritime trade.

Similarly, the inhabitants of the Bijagos Islands systematically organized themselves to participate in manhunts on the mainland. The system was as follows: while women concentrated on agriculture, fishing, and home-building, men built the boats that became notorious as *almadies*. These they then turned into fleets of war canoes with which they spread terror throughout the Southern Rivers. Thus the varied populations of the Southern Rivers, Baïnuk, Joola, Papel, Balante, Nalu, Landuma and Baga, became the first victims of the slave trade. Isolationist tendencies intensified among people in the mangrove areas, a region of natural refuges. This was especially true among the Joola. Meanwhile, minority groups in the Tenda areas, such as the Basari, the Konagi, and the Bajaranke, who lived between Futa Jallon and the Southern Rivers, suffered most heavily from the slave trade.[27]

An economic, political, and social crisis thus arose quite early in the Southern Rivers. It pushed some coastal groups into isolated positions, leaving the advantage to the continental power, Kaabu. The political evolution of lineage-based states in the Southern Rivers toward more complex monarchical systems was blocked by pressure from neighboring peoples as well as by violent manhunts. This stagnation worsened steadily until the nineteenth century, the time of colonial conquest.

Kaabu became the dominant regional power after the fall of the Mali Empire. Kaabu was a genuine military power. Taking control of the Baïnuk and Beafada trading networks and exploiting them, it also gained control of Manding principalities along the Gambia River. The *Farim* of Kaabu was the region's most energetic slave hunter. The Mane and Sane families, who made up the sovereign *Nyaanco* dynasty in Kansala, consolidated their warrior status, and from the start symbolized the reign of *ceddo* warlords, political masters of Senegambia in the era of the slave trade. One telling testimony to the power of this kingdom was the conquest of Siin and Saalum by the Gelwaar dynasty, originally from Kaabu.

Kaabu reached the peak of its power in the sixteenth and seventeenth centuries. All along the Southern Rivers, it superseded Mali. This was the situation until the theocratic revolution of Futa Jallon, which halted Kaabu's expansion into the hinterland in the early eighteenth century. That expansion concided with the development of the slave trade, and, above all, with the European takeover of trade in the Southern Rivers area. The initiative in inter-regional trade in the Southern Rivers, of vital importance to all of Senegambia, slipped from the indigenous population to the Portuguese, who settled solidly along the old north–south coastal circuit, relegating the Beafada, the Baïnuk, and, above all, the Manding and the Bijagos to the lowly work of hunting slaves or hustling as intermediaries in the Atlantic trading system with the hinterland.

Northern Senegambia between the Gambia and the Senegal Rivers also underwent a profound and lasting reshaping of its political landscape from the second half of the sixteenth century.

The Jolof Confederation, already shaken by Koli Tengela's massive invasion, disintegrated under the impact of Portuguese trade which, by giving the coastal provinces an advantage, speeded up the political dismemberment of Senegambia. Thus, Amari Ngone, after his victory over the *Buurba* Jolof at Danki, proclaimed the independence of the coastal province of Kajoor, becoming its first *Damel*. The provinces of Waalo, at the mouth of the Senegal River, and Baol, in the south-west, followed suit. This left the original Jolof with only the hinterland to rule. The shrinkage was due in part to Jolof's lack of direct contact with the newly dominant Atlantic trade. Another reason was that to the north it was cut off from the trans-Saharan trade by the powerful Denyanke kingdom of Futa Toro.[28]

The Jolof confederation collapsed after a long series of battles that signaled the beginning of the violent age of warlords. *Ceddo* monarchies established violence as the determinant value, not only in relations between Senegambia's states, but also in political and social relations within each state. The same process, incidentally, led to the foundation of the kingdoms of Siin and Saalum, both of which definitively liberated themselves from the Jolof empire during the sixteenth century.

Following the breakup of the Jolof confederation, the *Damel* of Kajoor, Amari Ngone, tried for a while to impose his hegemony by annexing the Baol and part of Waalo, especially the mouth of the Senegal River, in contact with the Atlantic trading system. He took the title of *Damel-Teeñ*, thus initiating a long series of temporary unions between the kingdoms of Kajoor and Baol. For every *Damel* of Kajoor dreamed of becoming the *Teeñ* of Baol, just as every *Teeñ* also wanted to be a *Damel*. Very soon, however, the rivalry between Kajoor and Baol prevented the *Damel* from going on to unify the provinces of the former Jolof Confederation under his authority. Instead, this failure proved beneficial to the rising Denyanke kingdom in Futa Toro.

The *Satigi*, nicknamed the "Grand Ful" by European sources, in turn took advantage of the disintegration of the Jolof confederation to extend his rule over most of northern Senegambia. Thus the Denyanke dynasty reached its zenith at the beginning of the seventeenth century, in the reign of Samba Lamu. Futa Toro, by occupying the mouth of the Senegal River along with part of the Malian and Mauritanian Sahel, henceforth played a double role: it controlled trade routes linking the Sudan with the Sahara, as well as the European maritime trade.[29]

From the end of the sixteenth century the impact of the Atlantic trading system began to dominate all aspects of Senegambian development. Trade circuits were increasingly oriented from the hinterland toward the coast.

The main beneficiaries were the Portuguese, controllers of Senegambia's inter-regional trade with the Sudan, the forest belt, and the Sahara. The preponderance of the Atlantic trading system led to the rise of Kaabu in southern Senegambia, and to the breakup of the Jolof confederation in northern Senegambia. But the Atlantic trading system was increasingly dominated by the slave trade, far and away the main factor in the regression of Senegambia's societies, now bowed under the rule of violence.

# 4 The partition of the Senegambian coast in the seventeenth century

Right from the start of the seventeenth century, the Portuguese monopoly was challenged by the arrival, one after the other, of the Dutch, the English, and the French. These new European powers invaded the African coast, beginning the grand adventure that was to become the encirclement of Africa.

European powers began a lively competition, establishing their domination in Senegambia by setting up zones of influence jealously guarded by fortified trading posts along the coast. The entire Senegambian coastline was thus garrisoned with forts at Arguin, Saint Louis, Gorée, Fort Saint James, Cacheu, and Bissao.

The principal business of these trading posts was to hold slaves in transit. For, as from the second half of the seventeenth century, the slave trade became the principal business of the European powers on the African coast. Intense slave trading necessarily required manhunts. These caused profound economic, political, and social crises. The slave trade, for example, engendered violence in inter-state relationships, the militarization of regimes, and the advancement of militant Islam. And from the end of the seventeenth century, Senegambia became the venue for a vast marabout-led movement intent on unifying the states of the Senegal valley in order to combat the negative effects of the slave trade, already manifest in the region.

## A.    Trading posts and the partition of coastal Senegambia

The reshaping of the political landscape went hand in hand with resurgent violence between states and the development of the slave trade, which accelerated the political dismemberment of Senegambia. This coincided with the arrival of the Dutch, the English, and the French, who consolidated their presence on the Senegambian coast from the second half of the seventeenth century, cracking the Portuguese monopoly. Indeed, the slave trade, which had become the cornerstone of colonial mercantilism following the development of the sugar industry in the New World, hastened the partition of Senegambia into zones of influence through the construction of fortified trading posts all along the coast.

In 1621, the Dutch settled on Gorée island. They were followed in 1659 by the French at Saint-Louis, across from the mouth of the Senegal River. Meanwhile, in 1651, the English built Fort Saint James at the mouth of the Gambia River. The Portuguese, gradually pushed out of northern Senegambia, restricted their activities to Cacheu and Bissao, working out of their permanent base on the Cape Verde islands. But they were already being forced to share the rich market of the Southern Rivers with the new powers. In any case, the construction of a string of fortified trading posts along the coast completed the redirection of Senegambian trade toward the Atlantic seaboard.

The fort of Saint-Louis, at the mouth of the Senegal River, gave the French control over trade on the Senegal river during the annual trading season from February to May, at different desert trading posts in Waalo, including the Escale du Coq and the Terrier Rouge in Futa Toro. The construction of Fort Saint-Joseph in the late seventeenth century in Gajaaga gave the French a monopoly on the Senegal River, from its mouth to the Upper Valley, gateway to Sudanese commerce. France now tried to make the Senegal River the commercial center of gravity for northern Senegambia, by drawing trade from Arguin and Portendick on the Mauritanian coast, as well as from central Sudan around the Niger Bend, to its trading posts.[1]

Gorée Island was first occupied by the Dutch, then retaken by the Portuguese in 1629 and 1645, before passing into English hands in 1667. The French finally took it over in 1677. The island controlled the trading monopoly on the Petite Côte. From their base in Gorée, the French traded with Kajoor at Rufisque, with Baol at Portudal, and with Siin at Joal. Gorée also tried to spread its influence southward, into Gambia, with the Albreda factory, and into the Southern Rivers with Bissao and Cacheu. But here the French ran into competition from the Portuguese, and into especially stiff rivalry from the British, with their solid foothold in Gambia. Fort Saint James, initially built by the British, effectively controlled all trade along the Gambia River, with trading posts at Jufure, Bintang, and all the way to the falls at Barakunda, with trading posts at Sutuko and Fatadenda in Wuuli.

The Gambia River had one enormous advantage: it was navigable all year round. Each Manding principality along it was a potential trading post the dominant English could use. The British were thus well positioned to conquer the trading posts along the Petite Côte to the north and those in the Southern Rivers region. And they were excellently placed to pose a dangerous threat to French trade in the upper Senegal Valley.[2] The Gambia offered many more facilities that could draw trade from the Sudan into its orbit. The Portuguese, eliminated from the north, retreated to the Southern Rivers, where they established trading posts at Bissao and Cacheu. But by now Portugal's economic weight in Europe was no longer a match for the competitive English, French, and Dutch. It was the *lançados* from the Cape Verde islands who now represented Portuguese commerce.

The entire Senegambian coast, then, was dotted with a series of fortified posts. The favorite sites were on islands, and the principal task of these posts was to draw the regional trade toward the ocean. Permanent constructions, the fortified trading posts had a double purpose. First, they protected each zone of influence within their range from the competition of other European powers. Secondly, they guarded against the danger of any Senegambian state opposing the monopoly enoyed by European trade in general.

Following the Portuguese, there was a massive influx of Dutch, French, and English traders into Senegambia. At that time, the only other area on the West African coast so densely occupied by Europeans was the Gold Coast. This large-scale influx was directly related to the rise of colonial mercantilism. For, in the wake of Portugal and Spain, the fevered accumulation of wealth – money – took hold of other Atlantic powers such as Holland, France, and Britain. And they set out to conquer markets in Africa, Asia, and the New World.

The occupation of Senegambia coincided with the development of the sugar industry in north-eastern Brazil and the Caribbean. Sugar, cultivated on a large scale on New World plantations using slave labor, led to the the trans-Atlantic slave trade, which became the keystone of the triangular trade between Europe, Africa, and America.

Each of the European powers, while constructing fortified trading posts on the African coast, also created chartered companies, intended to monopolize maritime trade. The spheres of influence of these companies often went beyond Senegambia. They were: the Dutch West India Company (1625); the French West India Company (1664); and, finally, the Royal African Company, created by the British in 1672. These chartered companies, created with the blessings of reigning monarchs, symbolized the rise of nation-states in Europe. They also reflected the new spirit of competition between European powers for the conquest of markets.

In metropolitan Europe, the nobility had been losing economic clout to the rising bourgeoisie. By creating chartered companies, they could con-centrate on overseas trading ventures without losing social status at home. For all these reasons, rivalries in Europe had immediate repercussions in Senegambia, where trading posts changed hands in accordance with the local or metropolitan balance of power.

The Dutch were the first to threaten the Portuguese monopoly. But, beginning in 1677, they were rapidly driven off the Senegambian coast by the British and the French. Their only remaining footholds were Arguin and Portendick. There, on account of the growing significance of the gum trade, they remained, on the Mauritanian coast, until the first half of the eighteenth century. Senegambia remained divided, with the French zone of influence from Saint-Louis to Gorée, and the British zone in Gambia. Meanwhile, both the French and the British struggled with the Portuguese for control of the Southern Rivers. Possession of Senegambia remained vitally important because of the region's closeness to Europe and America. This was a time when the accelerated development of plantations caused a sudden threefold increase in the demand for black slaves, to be used in the French and English West Indies between 1651 and 1700.[3]

The fashion for building forts on the coast, preferably on islands, was primarily a response to the need for slave labor. For by this time, slave procurement had become the main business of the Atlantic trading system. Saint-Louis, Gorée, Cacheu, and Bissau were transformed into full-scale entrepôts for slaves brought from markets in the hinterland to the coast, there to await slaving vessels headed for the New World. At the height of the slave trade, captives from raids in the hinterland were routinely marched from the Niger Bend to the coast. Before then, it was the coastal populations, especially those of Senegambia, who supplied the bulk of the captives.

The fact that Senegambia was close both to Europe and to America, coupled with the fact that the opening of major slave markets in the Gulf of Guinea and Angola was a late development, explains why Senegambia was so important in the slave trade at its inception in the sixteenth and seventeenth centuries. It seems quite obvious that Philip Curtin underestimates this region's role in the trade when he reduces it to less than 10 percent after 1640, the absence of dependable statistical data notwithstanding.[4] At any rate, the importance of Senegambia's participation in this trade is no myth, as evidenced by the testimony of a witness from 1682, Lemaire:

In exchange for these negroes we trade cotton baft, copper, tin, iron, spirits and a few glass trinkets. From such trading we make a profit of 800%. Hides, ivory and gum go to France. As for the slaves, they are sent to the French islands in America to work on sugar plantations. Good quality slaves can be had for ten francs apiece, to be resold for over a hundred écus. Often enough, you can get a pretty good slave for four or five jars of alcohol. So one spends less on purchases than on transport, since outfitting the ships costs a great deal.[5]

Admittedly, there is no way to make accurate quantitative evaluations of Senegambian exports then. It is necessary, however, to underline the relationships of unequal exchange that became established from this early date between Europeans and Senegambians. Above all, the consequences of this dominant Atlantic trade for the historical evolution of the region must be made clear. Besides, evidence of the scope of the slave trade exists in the form of a profound political and social crisis that sparked a widespread marabout-led movement in the Senegal River valley, a few years after the construction of the fort at Saint-Louis.

## B.    The war of the marabouts

The Senegambian states were reshaped in the sixteenth century under the influence of Portuguese commerce. Now, in the second half of the seventeenth century, they underwent a profound economic, political, and social crisis. The crisis was most obvious in northern Senegambia. It was connected both to the intensification of the slave trade and to the impact of the Atlantic trading system as a whole on the economic, political, and social evolution of Senegambian societies.

The Islamic movement led by the Moorish marabout Nasir Al Din was a clear indication of the serious crisis created at the time by the European presence in Senegambia.[6] The movement, under the banner of a puritan version of Islam, began in the southern part of what is now Mauritania. The Berber population in that area, on the whole, had been subjected to a profound economic upheaval caused by the decline of the trans-Saharan trade. That decline was aggravated after the French settled at Saint-Louis in 1659.

The island of Saint-Louis, owing to its strategic location at the mouth of the Senegal River, had begun diverting all trade from the valley toward the Atlantic. This development shattered a centuries-old system of economic complementarity between the nomadic Berbers of Chemama and the sedentary farmers of the Senegal valley. The commercial monopoly exercised by Saint-Louis not only denied the Moors access to the slave labor they had relied on for centuries for both production and trade with North Africa; it also cut off cereal supplies from the valley, the bread-basket feeding Sahelian lands north of the Senegal river. The development of slave entrepôts on the coast redirected the cereal trade toward trading posts on the Atlantic seaboard, to meet increasing demand from cargo vessels both during the long loading wait and during the Atlantic crossing. This economic crisis exacerbated the political and social enmity between the Banu Maghaf, Hassani Arab warriors, and Sanhadja marabouts of Berber origin.

Berber society was, in effect, caught in a closing vice. From the north, Arab warriors were pressing southward. To the south, Saint-Louis had established a monopoly that diverted trade from the Senegal valley to the advantage of the new trading posts. To save disintegrating Berber society, then, Nasir Al Din started a religious movement based on puritan Islamic values. The movement's objective was to conquer the Senegal valley, an area vitally important to the Sahelian economy. The struggle between Hassani

Arab warriors and *Zawaya* Berber marabouts thus erupted in the proclamation of a holy war in the kingdoms of the Senegal valley. In the Berber country where it started, Nasir Al Din's movement was an attempt to regulate political and social life by the application of hyper-orthodox, purist *Sharia* or Koranic law. The ideal was to end the arbitrary power of Hassani Arab warriors and to establish a thoroughgoing Muslim theocracy.

The proclamation of holy war in the Senegal River valley had twin motives. Economically, the motive was to reconquer lost cereal and slave markets. Ideologically, the motive was to convert the population and to purify Islamic practice. Beginning in 1677, the success of the holy war in Waalo, Futa Toro, Kajoor, and Jolof was considerably facilitated by the profound crisis ravaging northern Senegambia following the intensification of the slave trade in the second half of the seventeenth century. In the main, it was the consequences of organized, large-scale manhunts that gave Nasir Al Din's movement the main principles for its creed.

This was a puritan, arguably reformist movement. To begin with, it opposed the slave trade and vigorously denounced the tyranny of kings who took an active part in the manhunts it entailed.[7] The absence of statistical data does not constitute sufficient reason for denying the disastrous economic, political and social consequences of the slave trade.[8] It needs pointing out, however, that, right from its onset, this marabout movement, originating in Mauritania, was primarily a defensive reaction mounted by trans-Saharan traders against the increasingly powerful monopoly of the Saint-Louis trading post. As such, it did not simply oppose the Saint-Louis monopoly over the Senegal valley; it was also particularly hostile to the continuation of the slave trade – that is to say, the large-scale export of the labor force, a development that disturbed the region in decisive ways.

This opposition to the slave trade did not by any means imply that the movement wanted to abolish domestic slavery or petty slave trading. In the context of the old trans-Saharan trade, the latter was a centuries-old practice that had never brought about a crisis as serious as that provoked by the trans-Atlantic trade. It needs to be said further that Islam, the ideological excuse for the religious movement, underwent a change in the process. For, starting out as the religion of a minority caste of traders and hangers-on at the royal courts, Islam became a reaction of popular resistance against the arbitrary rule of the reigning aristocracies, combating the negative impact of the Atlantic trading system in general.

In the last analysis, it was the crisis created by the oppressive behavior of the ruling aristocracies, selling their own subjects at whim to buy European commodities, which gave Nasir Al Din's movement its revolutionary impetus. Helped by indigenous Muslims and supported by the masses, the marabout movement overthrew reigning aristocracies one after another in a tidal wave that swept through Futa Toro, Waalo, Kajoor, and Jolof, never meeting any determined resistance. Having defeated the four kingdoms, Nasir Al Din went on to replace the fallen aristocracies with religious leaders loyal to his cause. Chambonneau called them *Buur Jullit* (Muslim rulers) or Chief Prayer Leaders. This was the triumph, throughout northern Senegambia, of Muslim theocracies under the political and spiritual authority of Nasir Al Din. The process took on specific features in each of the kingdoms thus occupied by the marabout movement.

Detailed information on the process as it unfolded in Futa Toro is lacking. Nevertheless, it is clear that the marabouts achieved a devastatingly rapid victory. In particular, the population participated massively and violently in the overthrow of *Satigi* rule. In Walo, the *Brak* Fara Kumba Mbodj put up a lively resistance. But he was overwhelmed by the sheer number of partisans of the religious movement recruited in Futa Toro. With the death of the *Brak* Fara Kumba on the field of battle, the marabout movement came to power. It appointed a puppet *Brak*, Yerim Kode, a member of the royal family, who agreed to the conditions imposed by the theocratic system set up by Nasir Al Din.[9]

Oral traditions in Kajoor are much more explicit about the circumstances leading to the success of the marabout-led movement, which gained enormously from the political crisis within the aristocracy.

Traditional accounts indicate that the movement, led by the *Xaadi*, rallied to the cause of the *Linger* Yaasin Bubu, who had been deposed by the new *Damel*, Decce Maram Ngalgu, who replaced her with her own mother. Yaasin Bubu converted to Islam, taking with her part of the *garmi* ruling aristocracy and her entourage. She married the marabout Njaay Sall, who killed the *Damel*, Decce Maram Ngalgu, and replaced him with another king, Mafaali Gey, who had also converted to Islam through political ambition. But some time later, the marabout Njaay Sall killed Mafaali in his turn for disobeying Koranic precepts. The marabout then declared himself viceroy within the structure of Nasir Al Din's *Tubenan* movement. The assassination of Mafaali caused a rift between the religious movement and the *garmi* aristocracy. The latter, seeing that they had lost their privileged hold on the throne of Kajoor, appealed to the *Buur Saalum*, Makhureja Joojo Juuf, to intervene on their behalf.[10]

In 1674, however, the Muslim leader Nasir Al Din died while fighting Hassani Arab warriors in Mauritania. His death forced his movement into retreat. At the same time, conflicts broke out in the viceroyalties established in the states along the Senegal River. This retreat gave the French at Saint-Louis an opportunity to intervene directly, offering military support to the dethroned aristocracies in Futa Toro, Waalo, Kajoor, and Jolof. Up until the total defeat of the marabout movement in 1677, business at the Saint-Louis trading post came practically to a halt. That circumstance was more than enough reason for the reaction from Saint-Louis. Moreover, Saint-Louis wanted to resume the slave trading so necessary for the prosperity of New World plantations and, by the same token, of the triangular trade. In other words, the Saint-Louis trading post was perfectly aware that the marabout movement directly threatened its interests. In giving military and financial aid to various dethroned aristocracies, Saint-Louis wanted to help them to regain power.[11]

The clarity of Chambonneau's testimony notwithstanding, Philip Curtin, claiming to "decolonize African history," tends to deny any connection between the European presence and the evolution of Senegambian societies, which he examines in a vacuum.[12] It was in line with their own interests, clearly understood, that the French provided logistical aid to the *Brak* of Waalo, Yerim Kode. At the first opportunity the latter left the marabout movement in the lurch, going on to play a key role in its annihilation in Futa Toro, Jolof, and Kajoor. Thus the movement was practically eliminated from 1677, with help from Saint-Louis and to the benefit of the old aristocracies, who saw their privileges re-established. The failure of this first reaction against the slave trade and the arbitrary impositions of the established regimes had a lasting impact on the evolution of the Senegambian kingdoms. In Mauritania, where the movement originated, the defeat of the *Zawiya* Berber marabouts entrenched the political power of the military Hassani Arab rulers, who formed the Emirates of Trarza and Brakna. From the eighteenth century, they exerted constant military pressure on states on the left bank of the Senegal River, as the gum trade grew in importance, enabling the Moors to become advantageously integrated into the Atlantic trading system. The war of the marabouts, known to European sources as the *Toubenan* movement, and in Berber chronicles as *Shurbuba*, had longer-lasting consequences than the eleventh-century Almoravid movement, which also started in the same region.

The Almoravid movement had turned its conquering impetus northward; Nasir Al Din's movement drove south. Even though it failed, this movement signaled what was thenceforth to become the inevitable direction of the Chamama Berbers. Drawn by the Atlantic trading system, they gravitated toward the Senegal River valley. They took an increasingly active part in the political, economic, and religious history of Senegambia. On the one hand, the Emirates of Trarza and Brakna were full-time players in the generalized use of violence as arbiter in inter-state relationships in the Senegal valley. On the other hand, *Zawiya* marabouts continued developing close bonds with marabout groups established in the Senegambian kingdoms. In this way they participated in the Islamic challenge to military regimes. From all points of view, then, the Chamama was an integral part of Senegambia from the late seventeenth century.

The long war of the marabouts led to a series of famines throughout the region. Above all, it provoked reprisals against Muslims, thus considerably swelling the slave trade, to the profit of the Saint-Louis trading post and the triumphant aristocracy. The defeat of the marabouts thus ensured a continued commercial boom in Saint-Louis with the complicity of the regional aristocracy, the only part of the local population to benefit from the Atlantic trading system. Saint-Louis thus definitively exorcised the danger of the formation of a vast political unit capable of imposing its own conditions for continued trading in the Senegal River valley.

The political dismemberment of the region was intensified on account of internal crises related to power struggles and internecine wars between different kingdoms bent on supplying slaves to the Atlantic trading system. The massive use of firearms became common. In all kingdoms, autocratic military regimes took power, using *ceddo* warriors or royal slaves to do the capricious bidding of reigning aristocracies. Still, the victory of Saint-Louis widened the chasm between the aristocracy and the people, who turned increasingly toward Islam. From then on, the Muslim religion became the main oppositional force facing established regimes throughout Senegambia.

Beginning in this era, numerous families of marabouts migrated from the coastal regions and the Senegal valley, seeking refuge in the hinterland, especially in Bundu and Futa Jallon. There they attempted to consolidate the autonomy of Muslim communities. Muslim revolutions in Bundu at the end of the seventeenth century and in Futa Jallon in the early eighteenth century thus signaled the triumph of militant Islam as a reaction to the impact of the slave trade. Conflicts between Muslim theocracies and *ceddo* regimes thus dominated the history of Senegambia in the eighteenth century, absolutely the worst century of the slave trade.

*Part II*

Senegambia in the eighteenth century: the slave trade, *ceddo* regimes and Muslim revolutions

Beginning in the second half of the seventeenth century, the development of sugar cane, cotton, and tobacco plantations in the New World led to an expansion of the slave trade. So from the eighteenth century to the first half of the nineteenth, slave trading became the center of Europe's trade with Africa. To use Samir Amin's expression, America became the European periphery, and Africa became the periphery of the American periphery. In this slaving era, the continent of Africa went through "one of the most massive processes of human transportation ever to have taken place by sea."[1] Throughout the fifteenth, sixteenth and part of the seventeenth centuries, Senegambia had been the main source of slaves. After that, it was superseded by other regions, especially the Gulf of Guinea and Angola. Still, on account of its geographical position, Senegambia continued to supply the sugar-growing islands on a permanent basis.

Senegambia, conquered by the Portuguese, the French, the Dutch, and the British, expanded eastward toward the Sudan and northward toward Mauritania, thus bringing the Bambara states of the Niger Bend and the Moorish emirates of Chamama into the orbit of the Atlantic trade. From this time on, Senegambia became the natural outlet from most of western Sudan toward the Atlantic. This redirection of trade routes toward the sea signaled the final victory of the caravel over the caravan. It also marked the definitive decline of the trans-Saharan trade.

The slave trade was a permanent reality of the time. Alongside it, however, there was a brisk commodity trade, especially in gum, a key item in northern Senegambian commerce. This gum trade, conducted along the Mauritanian coast and the Senegal valley, was the main reason behind the southward push of the Berbers, followed by their profitable integration into the Atlantic trading circuit. The nomadic Berbers, under the authority of the emirates of Trarza and Brakna, and, beyond those, of the Sultan of Morocco, took an increasingly active part in the political, economic, and religious affairs of the states of Gajaaga, Futa Toro, and Waalo. In this development, the Saint-Louis trading post was the gravitational center of a northern Senegambia that now included Chamama, the land of the Moors.

On the whole, it was the negative consequences of slave raids that mainly determined the political, economic and social evolution of Senegambian states. The militaristic states of Waalo, Futa Toro, Gajaaga, Kajoor, Baol, Siin, Saalum, and Kaabu consolidated themselves, each within the narrow framework of frontiers left after the dismemberment of the Jolof confederation in the second half of the sixteenth century. Internally, the Atlantic trading system everywhere reinforced arbitrary rule and the centralization of monarchical power. It was this centralization of power in the hands of warlords that hardened social orders into antagonistic forces. In the first place, the political crisis within the monarchy took the form of conflicts between various royal families in each kingdom. From this point on, the history of these kingdoms was dominated by a long series of civil wars. The new atmosphere of generalized violence gave the class of royal slaves a new role in political power struggles. They became a dominant force, superseding elected assemblies or chiefs who had formerly held hereditary responsibilities in central or local government. Under the rule of the warlords, the monarchy robbed political and social institutions of their meaning. It also alienated the majority of the population, who turned to Islam as the only recourse against the arbitrary impositions of the ruling aristocracy.

While resisting the power of the warlords, Muslim adherents grew into increasingly autonomous communities within the various kingdoms. And they placed themselves under the authority of marabouts for protection against the arbitrary exactions of the aristocracies and the effects of slave raids. Islam thus served at the time as a catalyst for a series of internal revolutions. In Bundu, Futa Jallon, and Futa Toro, movements headed by Muslim religious leaders took power, establishing Muslim theocracies. To begin with, these Muslim revolutions tried to broaden the political arena. To a certain extent, they also ensured the security of Muslim citizens within each state. But in short order, political power became concentrated around descendants of the marabouts who had led the holy war. The result was the formation of a new aristocracy of warlords, who behaved exactly like their predecessors.

As a matter of fact, the Muslim theocracies ended up taking an active part in the slave trade, the main business of European traders on the coast. As a consequence, domestic slavery developed on a large scale, to become an extension of the trans-Atlantic trading system. Social conflicts in Senegambia were seriously aggravated as a result. Ethnic minorities came under intensifying pressure from powerful states, some ruled by warlords, others by armed marabouts, heirs to recent Muslim revolutions. Everywhere, productive forces regressed and social conflicts flared up. All this worked to undermine the resistance of Senegambian societies under the Western onslaught. Meanwhile, the struggle between warlords and marabouts provided a background for the history of Senegambia as the region was subjected to the disastrous consequences of the slave trade.

# 5    The slave trade in the eighteenth century

The slave trade had a tremendous impact on Senegambian societies. To understand their development, therefore, we need to examine more closely this complex process during which, as Jean Copans has pointed out, primary producers themselves, as potential slaves, became the main product.[1] Whatever else might be said about it, the slave trade, with its logical corollary of slave raids, became between the second half of the seventeenth century and the first half of the eighteenth the main business of the British, French, Portuguese, and Dutch settled on the Senegambian coast and elsewhere.

Slave trading was a key element in the colonial mercantile system. Furthermore, it was a sort of imperative in international competition. For at the time, all conflicts over control of the sugar trade were primarily about possession of captive African labor and trading outlets.[2] To satisfy its "hunger for Negroes," Europe imposed the slave trade as a permanent reality, with the complicity of the region's reigning aristocracies. In this way Europe created conditions for the economic, political, and cultural takeover of Africa in the second half of the nineteenth century. Senegambia may have been a supplier of secondary importance. But this region too suffered from the slave trade, and its progress continues to be hampered by the longterm effects of the slaving era. So attempts by historians like Philip D. Curtin to minimize the number of slaves exported and the impact of slave raids on Africa's evolution run a high risk of becoming exercises in absurdity.

## A.    The population drain

Given the current state of documentary evidence, it is regrettably difficult not only to get an accurate idea of the population of Senegambia during the period in question, but also to establish precise statistical data on slave exports – a necessary procedure if we are to evaluate correctly the scope of the population drain in this region caused by the slave trade. Except for the

Table 5.1 *Estimate of slave-exporting capacity of Senegambia. Distribution of slaves according to loading port*

| Date of estimate | Saint-Louis | Gajaaga | Gorée | Gambia (French) | Gambia (British) | Annual total | Years | Periodic total |
|---|---|---|---|---|---|---|---|---|
| 1687 | 100 | | 500 | | 750 | 1,350 | 1681–9 | 12,150 |
| 1693 | 200 | | 200 | | 500 | 900 | 1690–1704 | 13,500 |
| 1716 | | | 2,380 | | 750 | 3,130 | 1705–16 | 32,160 |
| 1718 | 50 | 600 | 470 | 400 | 750 | 2,270 | 1717–23 | 15,890 |
| 1730 | | 1,090 | | | 3,000 | 4,090 | 1724–35 | 49,080 |
| 1741 | | 900 | | | 2,140 | 3,040 | 1736–46 | 33,440 |
| 1753 | 500 | 550 | | 540 | 1,000 | 2,590 | 1747–60 | 36,260 |
| 1766 | 1,110 | | | 425 | 1,511 | 3,050 | 1761–67 | 21,350 |
| 1769–78 | 1,500 | | | 300 | 1,500 | 3,300 | 1768–78 | 36,300 |
| 1779–88 | | 1,716 | | | 1,050 | 2,800 | 1779–92 | 39,200 |
| 1795 | | | | | 1,000 | 1,000 | 1793–1800 | 8,000 |
| 1802–10 | | | 700 | | | 700 | 1801–10 | 7,000 |

Total 304,330

Total for the period 1711–1810 only 259,900

attempts of Philip D. Curtin and Mbaye Guèye, and recent updates from Charles Becker and Victor Martin, there is no systematic study of the slave trade offering an account of the number of slaves exported from the Senegambian region as a whole.[3] So far, Philip Curtin is undoubtedly the one who has come up with the most detailed study on the number of slaves, even if his conclusions are compromised by the omission of several sources, and above all by his penchant for whittling down available figures by substantial amounts. Worse still, he does this without taking into account the contraband trade, which figures nowhere among official statistics. As is well known, the slaving era was above all that of freebooters captained by adventurers of all varieties challenging the monopoly of chartered companies in the second half of the seventeenth century.

In Table 5.1, Curtin estimates that the export capacity of Senegambia from 1681 to 1810 was 304,330 slaves. For the period between 1711 and 1810, this leaves the low figure of 259,900 slaves.[4]

According to Curtin, then, throughout the eighteenth century the annual level of Senegambia's slave exporting capacity (the figures apply in fact to northern Senegambia) varies from 1,000 for the period 1793–1800, the lowest, to 4,090 for the period 1724–35, the highest.[5]

Curtin then gives the figures shown in Table 5.2 for slave exports from 1711 to 1819, on the basis of calculations from real data. His conclusion is

Table 5.2 *Slave exports from Senegambia: 1711–1810*

| Dates | French exports | British exports | Total |
|-------|----------------|-----------------|-------|
| 1711–20 | 10,300 | 20,600 | 30,900 |
| 1721–30 | 13,400 | 9,100 | 22,500 |
| 1731–40 | 12,300 | 13,900 | 26,200 |
| 1741–50 | 7,700 | 17,300 | 25,000 |
| 1751–60 | 6,300 | 16,200 | 22,500 |
| 1761–70 | 2,300 | 11,800 | 14,100 |
| 1771–80 | 4,000 | 8,100 | 12,100 |
| 1781–90 | 17,400 | 2,900 | 20,300 |
| 1791–1800 | 3,400 | 2,800 | 6,200 |
| 1801–10 | 500 | 1,500 | 2,000 |
| Total | 77,600 | 104,200 | 181,800 |

that the total export figure was 181,800 slaves, of which the French accounted for 77,600 and the British 104,200.[6]

Under these conditions, a comparison of Tables 5.1 and 5.2 reveals a decrease from 259,900 to 181,800, a difference of 78,100 slaves between estimates and data for the period 1711–1810. Incidentally, the annual average from 1721 to 1730, given a total of 22,500 slaves according to Table 5.2, was supposedly 2,250 slaves. This would almost cut in half the first estimate of 4,090 slaves per year for 1730.

Jean Suret-Canale does a good job of highlighting Curtin's positive contributions. But he also takes him to task for his complicit silence on the impact of the slave trade on Senegambian societies.[7] Better still, Charles Becker clearly shows the arbitrary nature of figures advanced by Curtin on the basis of shipments for selected years. He therefore proposes a tentative estimate of 500,000 slaves in place of Curtin's estimate of 304,330. Becker uses alternative data sources to arrive at that estimate. Pending the publication of findings from detailed studies on the slave trade based on naval archives that would make it possible to advance definitive statistics, his estimates seem to be the most accurate to date.[8]

Meanwhile, it seems quite clear that Curtin's estimates – arrived at by arbitrarily selecting figures for slaves exported, relying on estimates based on the lowest figures, then cutting them almost by half – cannot, for the time being, contribute in any serious sense to the evaluation of the population drain caused by the slave trade. The fact is that numerous sources enable us even now to rethink Curtin's estimates and conclusions. For instance, according to the *Journal Historique et suite du Journal Historique*, 1,350 slaves were loaded in Saint-Louis and Gorée in 1730 on the following vessels:

| Vessel | Number of slaves loaded | Date of departure |
| --- | --- | --- |
| La Diane | 300 | January 1730 |
| La Vierge de Grâce | 304 | April 1730 |
| Le Saint-Louis | 350 | October 1730 |
| La Néreide | 200 | November 1730 |

Adding the considerable figures from British trade along the Gambia, far in excess of the volume of French trade and estimated by Francis Moore at 3,000 slaves annually,[9] we get a total of 4,350 for the year. That figure covers only northern Senegambia, that is to say, the region between the Senegal and Gambia rivers. Against this background, it is hard to understand how Philip Curtin manages not only to pare his own estimates for the same year down to 4,090 slaves, but also to reduce this estimate almost by half, to arrive at an estimate of 2,250 for the real number of slaves traded. Now if we compare Curtin's annual average of 2,250 slaves, for both French and British slave shipments from 1721 to 1730, to the figure given by the Mémoire, a trade register dated 23 April 1723, for French shipments alone, we are entitled to entertain serious doubts about the scholarly quality of Curtin's estimates. Moreover, Pruneau de Pommegorge confirms the fact that French shipments could easily exceed 2,000 slaves per year, as the following table shows:[10]

| Date | Number of slaves shipped |
| --- | --- |
| 1736 | 1,985 |
| 1737 | 1,995 |
| 1738 | 2,353 |
| 1739 | 2,207 |

Walter Rodney gives estimates of slaves shipped in the Southern Rivers area, which remained the main market for British, French, and Portuguese slave traders operating in Senegambia. From 1754 on, Bissao and Cacheu became the principal entrepôts for the large scale export of slaves, fed by the revival of manhunts and warfare in the hinterland. In 1789, the Southern Rivers easily exported over 4,000 slaves.[11] In 1788, French naval intelligence reports estimated the number of slaves exported by the British at 3,000 from Gambia, 2,000 from Casamance, Cacheu, and Bissao, and 4,000 from Sierra Leone.[12]

The critical evaluation conducted by Jean Mettas on Portuguese commerce at Bissao and Cacheu between 1758 and 1797, under the near-total monopoly of the Companhia General do Grâo Parâ e Maranhâo, gives a good idea of Senegambia's contribution to the development of certain parts of Brazil. The turnover of slaving vessels owned by the C.G.G.P.M. at Cacheu and Bissao was exceptionally rapid. Between 1756 and 1778, the total number of voyages was as high as 105.[13] Jean Mettas estimates that the Portuguese shipped an annual average of 420 captives from Cacheu between 1758 and 1777, while Bissao, more open to the inflow of French or British slavers, shipped an annual average of 620 slaves from 1767 to 1773.[14] It is a remarkable fact that in the second half of the eighteenth century the number of slaves exported averaged slightly over 1,000 per year. The uninterrupted drain caused by Portuguese traders was particularly devastating for the inhabitants of the Southern Rivers: the Balante, Bijago, Joola, Manjak, Baïnuk, Papel, Nalu, Beafada, and, to a lesser extent Manding and Peul from the hinterland. The Portuguese monopoly belonged to the C.G.G.P.M., a chartered company whose slaving business was part of a vast enterprise of interconnected activities in Portugal and Brazil. Its profits were impressive: starting with a capital base of 465,600,000 réis, the company succeeded in paying out 917,396,000 réis to its shareholders between 1759 and 1777, with a rate of profit running at 11.50 percent from 1768 to 1774.[15]

Jean Mettas, alas, left his work unfinished. Fortunately, though, it has been complemented by the studies of Charles Becker and Victor Martin, whose estimates for the second half of the eighteenth century certainly show the large scale of the slave trade in Senegambia. As can be seen clearly in their table, reproduced here as Table 5.3, for 1775 and 1786, the years for which data on all slave shipment ports are available, figures for Senegambia as a whole were 6,300 slaves for the first year, 8,000 for the second.[16]

It would be reasonable to estimate that, on average, Senegambia as a whole exported 6,000 slaves annually throughout the eighteenth century. This figure would not factor in the 10 percent to 15 percent mortality rate suffered during slave raids and at the coastal transit entrepôts. What all this indicates is that the issue of the slave trade is complex, and that the work remaining to be done in order to obtain the complete records of trading vessels – work begun by Jean Mettas – with a view to arriving at an objective assessment of the ensuing population drain requires finely honed scholarly skills indeed.[17] Statistics on slave shipments are, needless to say, of uncertain accuracy. One reason is that the sources themselves cultivated secrecy; another is that there were so many outlets, each country maintaining its own network. None of this, however, justifies the reduction by half of already available figures on the number of slaves exported from Senegambia.

One of the most dubious assertions Philip Curtin advances in his work is the notion that in the eighteenth century the trans-Saharan slave trade was still larger in volume than the Atlantic trade. In this regard, Curtin declares

Table 5.3 *Slave shipment statistics for the second half of the eighteenth century*

| | St. Louis, R. Galam | Gorée, Petite Côte | Saalum | Subtotal* | Gambie | | Total |
|---|---|---|---|---|---|---|---|
| Year | | | | | French | English | |
| 1750–8 | | | | 1,500–2,000 | | | |
| 1750–8 | | | | 800–900 | | 400 | 1,200–1,300 |
| 1753 | | | | 500 | | | |
| 1762 | 2,550 | | | 450 | | ? | |
| c. 1766 | | | 800 | | | | 15,000 |
| 1769 | | 60–300 | | | | | |
| 1773 | | 200 | | | 300 | 300+ | |
| 1775 | 8,000 | | | | | | |
| c. 1775 | 2,800 | 300 | 200 | | 3,000 | | 6,300 |
| 177 | | 300 | 100–200 | | 800–900 | 800+ | |
| 1776 | | 250–300 | | | 800 | 800+ | |
| c. 1777 | 2,400 | | | | | 2,000 | |
| c. 1780 | | | | | | | 3,000 |
| c. 1780 | | | | | 1,740 | | |
| 1782 | | | | 4,000 | | 1,000 | 5,000 |
| 1783 | | 200–220 | | | | | |
| 1783 | | | | | | | 2,000+ |
| c. 1783 | 1,300–1,500 | | | 4,500 | | | |
| c. 1783 | | | | 1,200–1,500 | | ? | |
| 1784 | | | | 2,500–3,000 | | 1,000 | 3,500–4,000 |
| pre-1779 | | | | | | | 3,000 |
| 1784 | | | | 1,071 | | ? | |
| 1784 | | 600 | | | | | |
| 1786 | 2,200 | 300 | 1,800 | 700 | | 3,000 | 8,000 |
| pre-1789 | | | | 1,200–1,500 | | ? | |
| pre-1794 | 1,000–1,200 | | | 2,000–3,000 | | | |
| 1784–1799 | 1,500 | | | | | | |

*Note:*
*This column contains totals given by some authors for shipments from a range of areas. In our table, these areas are combined. For example, some figures (b) represent shipments from the Senegal River, Gorée, the Petite Côte, and Saalum, as well as French shipments from the Gambia. Similarly, figures placed between the two columns under Gambia (one for French shipments, the other for British shipments) represent the total of shipments from the Gambia under both French and British flags.

that "most of the time the weight of the trans-Saharan trade is hard to assess." In his opinion, the trade seems to have been particularly massive from the failure of the holy war led by Nasir Al Din in 1670 up until the end of the threat from Morocco toward the middle of the eighteenth century. The zenith was between 1710 and 1720, when Mulai Ismail's black army numbered 180,000 men. At the time of his death, in 1727, the total included 120,000 recruits. Such a large army implies the import into Morocco of at least 200,000 slaves in fifty years, at an average rate of 4,000 a year. That would be the equivalent of double the number of slaves exported from Senegambia by sea in the same period. Morocco also imported slaves from throughout the Sahel all the way to Timbuctoo in the east. Senegambia might have contributed nearly half the total.[18]

Further, in his discussion of the middle Senegal valley, Curtin adds that states in this region, namely Futa Toro, Gajaaga, Bundu, and even the Manding states of Bambuk, constantly resisted the sale of their own subjects, but that

the raids of the Ormankoobe from 1680 to 1750 constituted the great exception. They probably directed an inestimable number of tens of thousands of slaves northward. Even later, the Sahelian Moors continued mounting slave raids into the Senegal River valley and southward, into Bundu and Bambuk. A number of slaves captured from there were transported westward in desert caravans and sold at Saint-Louis, but at no point did such sales constitute a major source of sea-borne exports from Senegal. Most of these slaves captured by the Moors were absorbed by Mauritanian society or sent north across the Sahara.[19]

It is rather paradoxical that Curtin, so punctilious when it comes to debunking statistics relating to slave shipments toward the New World, scarcely spares a single page to ground his sweeping hypothesis on the greater volume of the trans-Saharan slave trade as compared to the trans-Atlantic trade. The most noteworthy instance is his refutation of the information that 8,000 slaves were taken from Waalo in 1775 following Moorish raids organized with the complicity of the British Governor O'Hara. Curtin's argument is that the source, being French, is suspect. He adds that the information, dated 1783, was recorded after the actual date of the event. Yet Curtin's sole source, when it comes to supporting his assertions on the size of Mulai Ismail's army in 1727, is a diplomatic source dated 1789. That does not stop him putting forward the colossal figure of 200,000 slaves as the sum of Morocco's imports over a fifty-year period.[20]

It seems quite clear that if Curtin denies the evidence about the population drain suffered by Waalo and confirmed by numerous sources, it is because he is predisposed to minimize the importance of the trans-Atlantic slave trade. The fact remains that in a letter dated 18 August 1775, O'Hara himself wrote that the Moors have totally submerged all nations of Blacks inhabiting the banks of this stream near the Senegal. They have killed and sold several thousands of persons and forced others to flee the country. By these means the Moors are becoming masters of both banks of the Senegal. For several leagues around Podor, the countryside is in the same distress and the Moors pose a constant threat to Saint-Louis, obliging the British to abandon the Fort at Podor.[21]

Clearly, the animosity of the Moors at Podor toward the British originated from the Brakna Moors, their immediate neighbors, pressure from whom led to the Toorodo revolution of 1776 in Futa Toro. This does not preclude the possibility that O'Hara acted in connivance with the Trarza Moors, next-door neighbors to Waalo. Such complicity was all the more likely because he was personally involved in the slave trade. On 22 August 1775, the inhabitants of Senegal sent a petition deploring the personal business activities of the Governor, arguing that he was ruining trade. In effect, O'Hara, who took part personally in slaving expeditions into the hinterland, set fire to all the Brak's villages on the banks of the Senegal River.[22] A second petition, dated 10 June 1776, repeated these accusations, further confirmed by a communication sent from Gorée by Armeny de Paradis.[23] In April 1777 he predicted that the French would obtain 3,000 slaves and the British 6,000 in less than two years, if the "Moors who have just devastated the kingdom of the *Brak*, turning it into the most desolate countryside, decide to dethrone the *Damel*, with arms supplied them by the French."[24]

O'Hara's activities were also confirmed by Lamiral, who lived in Senegal from 1779.[25] Other corroborating testimony came from the 1783 memoir, the veracity of which Curtin so heatedly disputes.[26] Lastly, confirmation also comes from Maxwell, who was Governor in 1811, during the second period of British occupation – a source surely beyond dispute.[27] Quite apart from O'Hara's connivance with the Moors, he left such a grim reputation that up until the beginning of the nineteenth century people in Waalo still used his name to scare crying children into silence.

As a matter of fact, the domination exercised by the Moors on both banks of the Senegal River during the second half of the eighteenth century was linked to a process that Philip Curtin misses entirely. That process was the gradual and profitable integration of Moors into the Atlantic trading system as from the early seventeenth century, thanks to the growth in volume of the gum trade. Economically stronger, militarily better armed with guns bought with proceeds from gum trading, and with the advantage of the mobility given them by camels and horses, the nomadic Berbers were well equipped to play an active role in the slave trade by organizing ceaseless raids against the sedentary peoples of the Senegal valley. Under these conditions, the trans-Saharan slave trade could certainly survive indefinitely as in the past; but it was no longer so great in volume as to surpass the trans-Atlantic slave trade. But we need not waste more time quibbling about statistics. The main point, once again, is the impact of the slave trade – the centerpiece of the trans-Atlantic trading system – on the evolution of Senegambian societies.

## B.      The Atlantic trading system in the eighteenth century

The case of the Companhia General do Grâo Parâ e Maranhâo, whose monopoly over slave trading at Bissao and Cacheu from 1755 to 1778 was linked to its ownership of salt works and plantations in Brazil as well as to manufacturing industries in Portugal, shows that the slave trade was an integral part of a vast commercial system linking Europe, Africa, and America. In this triangular system, trade in produce from the period before the heyday of the slave trade (hides, gold, ivory, wax, spices, etc.) remained substantial though secondary, aiding directly in the accumulation of financial capital in Europe, which remained at the center of the trans-Atlantic trading system.[28]

As far as northern Senegambia, bordering on the Sahara, was concerned, in addition to traditional produce there was also the trade in gum, which remained a key commodity throughout the eighteenth century and for a considerable part of the nineteenth. Given the importance of the gum trade during the first half of the eighteenth century, control over the stretch of the Mauritanian coast between Cape Blanc and the mouth of the Senegal River was one of the major African colonial policy objectives of France, Britain, and Holland, who at that time jointly controlled the main maritime trading circuits and the textile industry.[29]

Gum was a strategic raw material for the booming textile industry. It held a key position on the Senegambian market at the time, though it did not definitively supplant slaves, increasingly purchased in the Galam area of the upper Senegal valley. Gum, a vegetable resin, was indispensable for practically all dyeing operations and the manufacture of colored fabrics. It was also used in "the conditioning of silk materials, ribbons, gauze, cambric and hats. Paint factories used it. So did gilders. It had several other uses. And it was also a healthy and very satisfying foodstuff."[30] Trying to monopolize the gum trade, France, from 1713 to 1763, applied "the doctrine of exclusive rights, the most extreme form of the so-called colonial pact." The aim of the exercise was to counter other European interests on the Mauritanian coast.[31]

Inter-European rivalry was at the root of the Gum War. The first phase lasted from 1717 to 1727, a period during which the French sought by all possible means to keep British and – above all – Dutch freebooters out of Arguin and Portendick. For example, on 28 July 1717 André Brüe signed a friendship treaty with Alichandora, the Emir of Trarza, confirming that the *Compagnie du Sénégal* was entitled to a monopoly of the gum trade on the

Plate 3 Moors pursuing Negroes to enslave them (from D.-H. Lamiral, *L'Afrique et le peuple africain considérés sous tous les rapports avec notre commerce et nos colonies.* Paris, Dessene, 1789)

Mauritanian coast. Brüe had to start a series of cruiser patrols on the Mauritanian coast to keep off British and Dutch competitors. The campaign failed, because even though Salvert captured Arguin in February 1721, the intense activity of the freebooters did not stop.

The French expedition of La Rigaudière, which again besieged Arguin

Table 5.4 French trading profits in the colony of Senegal as of 23 April 1723

| Quantity of goods | Unit price | Cost price in Senegal (Senegal pounds) | Unit selling price (francs) | Selling price in France (francs) | Profit |
|---|---|---|---|---|---|
| 8,000 quintals gum | 6/quintal | 48,000 | 35/quintal | – | 232,000 |
| 2,000 Captives | 120 | 240,000 | 800 | 1,600,000 | 1,360,000 |
| 400 quintals Ivory | 72 | 28,800 | 150/quintal | 60,000 | 31,200 |
| 1,000 quintals Wax | 64/quintal | 64,000 | – | 200,000 | 136,000 |
| 10,000 Rawhides | 10 each | 5,000 | 3/10 each | 35,000 | 300,000 |
| 50 marcs. Gold | 512/marc | 25,600 | 100/marc | 50,000 | 24,400 |
| TOTAL | | 411,400 | | 2,225,000 | 1,813,600 |

*Notes:*
The balance sheet shows that the company could make 1,813,600 francs a year from trade in Senegal. Out of this sum, costs would be deducted as follows:
– Food and salaries for company employees in the colony, estimated at an annual rate of 200,000 lt (Senegal pounds);
– Loading and maintenance costs for seven vessels used year round for company business at 60,000 lt per vessel, a total of 420,000 lt. These two items amount to 620,000 lt. Deducted from 1,813,600 lt, this would normally leave the Indies Company with a net annual profit of 1,193,600 francs.

from 17 to 22 February 1723 with five gunboats, cost nearly one million pounds. It showed how important the gum trade was in colonial rivalries in Senegambia. After the failure of their attempts to control the Mauritanian coast, Brüe and his successors mounted a full scale political and miltary campaign aimed at the rulers of Waalo and Trarza, with the aim of diverting the gum trade to the banks of the Senegal River.[32] From 1743 to 1746, the West Indies Company loaded more than 1,000 tonnes of gum.[33] Statistical data do not give an adequate idea of the commercial importance of gum, because slave trading was such a dominant business then.

In this connection, Table 5.4 provides a statistical overview of French trading profits in the colony of Senegal as of 23 April 1723.[34] These estimates, covering only French trade, clearly show the preponderance of slave trading. Furthermore, Golberry, as quoted by Becker and Martin, gives the following overall estimates for Senegambian trade in 1786:

| | |
|---|---|
| Captives | 4,560,000 francs |
| Gum | 3,000,000 francs |
| Gold | 94,000 francs |
| Miscellaneous | 451,000 francs |

Plate 4 Government Square and market, Gorée

These figures give a good idea of the long-term status of slave trading as the main business of the trans-Atlantic system. The trade lasted until the end of the eighteenth century. In that time, British and French exports, taken together, might easily have totaled about 8,000 slaves a year.[35]

In the eighteenth century, spheres of influence established earlier generally remained unchanged. Senegambia remained under French, British, and Portuguese control, with the Dutch mounting sporadic incursions on the Mauritanian coast. The Portuguese sought to maintain their monopoly in Cacheu and Bissao in the Southern Rivers area. Meanwhile, the French and the British divided up the remainder of Senegambia, the former occupying the Senegal valley, the latter the Gambia valley. Thus, working from Gambia and Senegal, the British and the French competed with each other for control over lucrative east–west trading circuits along the two rivers.

From the beginning of the eighteenth century, the French signed treaties with states in the Upper Senegal valley, especially Bundu. Their aim was to stop caravans from traveling to the Gambia, then in British hands. To that end, the Indies Company adopted a policy calling for the construction of a series of small forts along the Falémé, in Bundu, and in Bambuk, with a view to taking over the gold trade in that region. From 1710 until the 1750s, this colonial policy produced no significant results. The reason was that the British, from their strategic position in the Gambia, offered much more competitive prices to traders from the upper Senegal valley. Unlike the

Plate 5 Interior of a house, Gorée

Senegal River, blocked in places by sand bars, the Gambia River was navigable all the year round by ocean-going vessels all the way up to the Barakunda Falls.[36] Senegambia's economy was now entirely under European control. The British, French and Portuguese continued to compete to maintain their old spheres of influence or to acquire new ones. Following the Gum War in the first half of the eighteenth century, the Dutch were eliminated with the signature of the Treaty of the Hague in 1727. That left the British and the French in direct confrontation. The high cost of French gum caused a crisis in the British textile industry, worsening ill feeling between the French and British. The new Company of Merchants Trading to Africa, created in 1752, obtained support from the British government right from the beginning of the Seven Years' War, and in 1758 the British occupied the trading posts of Saint-Louis and Gorée with ease. The 1763 Paris Treaty confirmed British control over the Senegal valley by ratifying the occupation of Saint-Louis, along with the forts of Podor and Saint-Joseph. Britain gave Gorée back to France, which also retained the right to trade along the Mauritanian coast.[37]

The British occupation of Saint-Louis lasted until 1783. For the first time, Senegambia as a geo-political unit appeared in official documents as a sphere of influence under direct control of the British Crown, in the same sense as the American colonies.[38] On the whole, however, there was no fundamental change in British commercial priorities. The British tended to neglect trade in the remote trading posts of the Senegal River valley such as Galam, in favor of the much more profitable Gambian circuit. British traders also showed a preference for the Mauritanian coast, on account of the importance of gum. The French, cooped up on the island of Gorée, struggled unsuccessfully to break through the omnipresent British cordon in Senegambia.

An examination of the trading activities of the European commercial powers in Senegambia raises one principal question: how profitable was this trade, generally dominated by the slave trade, from the eighteenth to the first half of the nineteenth century? On this point, colonial history presents a long string of camouflaged bankruptcies, in which nothing is said about profits made by the chartered companies or by private individuals who often triggered the bankruptcies involved. From the seventeenth century onward, company after company went bankrupt only to be re-established under a new name, all the while hungrily demanding support from the metropolis as well as an outright monopoly over trade in Senegambia or some other region. In all these cases, the only way to understand how these different chartered companies remained in business, and why the various European powers were so ferociously determined to secure trading monopolies for their nationals, is to look at their bottom lines. All the documents routinely condemn the dishonesty of company directors for being more interested in feathering their own nests than in managing the companies efficiently, while arguing energetically for the continued support of this or that company whenever the State refused to underwrite rigged company budgets.[39]

These camouflaged bankruptcies of chartered companies were caused in part by mismanagement on the part of directors. But another, even greater reason was the problems they confronted in their attempts to achieve monopoly control in the face of foreign competition on the one hand, and competition from indigenous traders committed to free trade, on the other.

For monopolies enjoyed by the charter companies were very rapidly punctured by free-trade enthusiasts who became a dominant force on the African coast in general and in Senegambia in particular as from the War of Spanish Succession. In 1713, France obtained legal access to Senegalese trade for French vessels. This freedom to trade was partially compromised from 1720 to 1725 and again from 1789 to 1791.[40] Apart from the effective control exercised by French and British chartered companies in the Senegal and Gambia River valleys, the remainder of Senegambia was dominated by a disparate crowd of slaving privateers who crisscrossed the seaboard from north to south. Worse still, around the forts and at most of the trading posts full-scale trading communities sprang into being, made up of Europeans

Plate 6 *Signare* and black attendants, Saint-Louis

from various national backgrounds, with even larger numbers of new Euro-Africans adding to the numbers of Afro-Europeans left behind from the heyday of Portuguese commerce.

What came into being was nothing less than a diaspora of European or Afro-European traders of French, British and Portuguese origin. They were later joined by Americans, and despite shifts of sovereignty from one colonial power to another involving the forts of Saint-Louis, Gorée, Fort Saint James, or Cacheu, the new communities thrived on the coast. Moreover, from 1750 to the end of the Imperial Wars, the British and French presence in Senegambia was considerably reduced on account of conflicts in Europe. This long absence encouraged the reinforcement of the class of Euro-African traders, who smashed the trade monopoly of the chartered companies. The Euro-Africans thus ended up creating their own trading diaspora along the coast from the forts of Saint-Louis, Gorée, and Fort Saint James all the way to the Southern Rivers as well as along the Senegal and Gambia River valleys. This complex network of European or Euro-African traders, some linked to chartered companies, others tied directly to European trading houses, teamed up with the Soninke, Manding and Peul network of *Juula* traders coming from the Senegambian hinterland.

By 1755 Saint-Louis already had a population of 3,000 inhabitants. A partial census conducted at the time shows that of that number, there were 15 naval captains, 15 lieutenants, 36 sailors, 3 translators or linguists, 36 day laborers, 98 company slaves, and 550 slaves belonging to the inhabitants. Thus, the annual trip that took the *Gajaaga* to the Upper Senegal valley kept between 300 and 400 persons busy. Because the merchants were so numerous and economically so powerful, they eventually gained control of the post of mayor, which after the French Revolution of 1789 became an elective office. From 1764 to 1778, Charles Thévenot was mayor. After him, it was the Euro-African families of Le Juge, Blondin, Pellegrin, or Charles Cornier (1780–90) who dominated political and commercial life in Saint-Louis. The rise of this powerful class of Euro-Africans was greatly facilitated by marriage arrangements in vogue in the region at the time. This was the system that produced the famed *signares*. These were wives of company personnel who accumulated colossal personal fortunes and rose to play important roles in the economic and social lives of such colonial enclaves as Saint-Louis, Gorée and Fort Saint James.[41]

In 1767, Gorée, for its part, had a population of 1,044, including 718 captives. From there, Euro-Africans of Dutch, Portuguese, British, and French descent controlled trade on the Petite Côte at the trading posts of Rufisque, Portudal, and Joal. They regularly sent their agents to Albreda in Gambia and the Southern Rivers.[42] In Gambia, the number of Euro-Africans was considerably lower, since ocean-going vessels could easily sail up the Gambia all year round, using wharfs and jetties at Jufure, Gereeja, Kaur, and Naaniman, Base, Sutuko, and Fatta-Tenda. The community of traders there, dominated by people like Robert Aynsley, was closely linked to that of Gorée, with which it indeed shared the market of the Petite Côte. On the whole, however, French and British chartered companies dominated the economic lives of trading posts at Saint-Louis, Gorée and Fort Saint James. In this northern part of Senegambia, their permanent presence and, above all, their role as a defense establishment, considerably curtailed the leeway enjoyed by the merchant communities. On the other hand, European and Euro-African traders were especially powerful in the Southern Rivers area, where chartered companies were feebly represented because there were no permanent forts, and the climate was unhealthy.

In the Southern Rivers area, particularly in Rio Cacheu and Bissao, it was the old *lançados* and *tangomaos* of Portuguese descent who, from the sixteenth century onward, dominated trading circuits from Casamance to Rio Grande. They were active as far as Gambia in the north and Rio Pongo in the south. Throughout their history these Euro-Africans maintained close social and economic ties with the Cape Verde islands. The Afro-Portuguese frequently employed members of the local Papel, Beafada, and Baïnuk communities as sailors, the so-called *grumetes*, equivalent to the *laptots* of the Senegal River valley. Despite the hostility of the Joola, Balante, and Bisago, the Portuguese and Afro-Portuguese had a much greater impact on the societies of the Southern Rivers area of Guinea Bissao than did the Manding of Kaabu and the Peul of Futa Jallon, isolated in their hinterland homelands and reduced to supplying slaves for the coastal slave trade.[43]

In close relationship with Portuguese trading circuits on the Cape Verde islands, the Afro-Portuguese settled securely in the Southern Rivers area, marrying into local society and producing a powerful diaspora. Among them, for instance, the famous Signara, Bibiana Vaz, built up a veritable trading empire from the Gambia to Sierra Leone from 1670 to 1680. Afro-Portuguese traders took effective control of the Ziguinchor zone as from 1760. This was when the Carvalho Alvarenga family not only provided commanding officers at the fort, but also wielded decisive influence in the Lower Casamance trading system. After 1780, this influence was more pronounced at Cacheu. From 1810 the couple Rosa Carvalho Alvarenga and João Pereira Barreto dominated both commercial life and administrative affairs at the fort. Incidentally, their son Honorio Pereira Barreto served as commanding officer at Cacheu before going on to the post of Governor of Guinea Bissao from 1830 to 1859. Apart from the short-lived monopoly of the Companhia General do Grâo Parâ e Maranhâo in Guinea Bissau from

1755 to 1778, it was generally the Afro-Portuguese, particularly such Cape Verdians as the Caetano family, who continued the Portuguese presence in the zone.[44] Serving British, French, or Portuguese trading interests, they operated as middlemen in the interval before they switched to serving Portuguese territorial interests, out of nationalistic commitment, in the nineteenth century. Ultimately, it was Rio Pongo and Rio Nunez, farther south, which rapidly became havens for new families of slave traders, who built up prosperous businesses dealing in slaves outside the monopoly control of the chartered companies, and free of interference from the European powers.

By the second half of the eighteenth century, Rio Pongo and Rio Nunez had become the main markets for slaves supplied by the new theocratic regime of Futa Jallon, continually at war with the Solimana. Because of the unhealthy climate, Europeans and Americans regarded life in this region as a high-risk gamble. It was therefore the more adventurous fortune-hunters among them who settled in the Rivers area as mavericks, often after careers serving as captains or ordinary sailors on slaving vessels. They settled in Rio Pongo or Rio Nunez under the protection of a landlord. In time they produced several generations of European and Euro-African slave traders perfectly integrated into local political and social life, on account of their multiple marriages with aristocrats in the Rivers region.

In Rio Pongo, under the rule of Kumba Bali, chief of Dominguia, an African-American from Boston, Benjamin Curtis (1774–1820), settled in Kissing before 1795 as an agent of an American trader, Gaffery. Similarly, the Englishman John Irving (1780–1807), married to a Baga woman, and the American William Skelton (1780–1804) established factories very early on at Kissing. At Bangalan, the second trading center on the Rio Pongo, on the other hand, the dominant slave trader was one Ferrie (1750–1804). There was also an Englishman from Liverpool, John Ormond (1750–91). Ormond was the most notorious slaver of the second half of the eighteenth century. Known as *Mange* (or chief) John, Ormond married into the families of most Susu and Baga chiefs in the area and became the dominant slave trader from the Loos Islands right up to the Rio Grande. The British contingent also included Sam Perry and Wilkinson. Together with the Portuguese Louis Gomez, they settled between Bashia and Karara on the Fatala Stream. They shared the market with the Euro-African Samuel Holman, son of John Holman (1750–90) and a Baga woman from the left bank. The last trading center, situated on the Bakia River, was under the control of Emmanuel Gomez Jr., who became chief of Bakia. Gomez (1769–1816) was the son of a Portuguese slave trader who settled in the area in the mid-eighteenth century.[45]

In Rio Nunez, one Doctor Walker (1750–96), settled at Kakandy since the mid-eighteenth century, dominated commerce. He shared his trading monopoly with John Pearce (1775–1818), Fortune (1750–1817), and especially with the Euro-African David James Lawrence (1775–1812), who lived at Kissassi.

The economic prosperity of these slave-trading families was indisputable. It enabled them to send their children to the best British schools. From 1794–5, however, slave traders began experiencing difficulties with the Sierra Leone Company, established in Rio Pongo to combat the slave trade. When Kumba Bali Demba agreed to the establishment of a company factory at Freeport in return for 100 bars a year, he drew vigorous protests from the slave traders. In November 1795, the slave traders agreed to lower the price of slaves, hoping this would make sellers from Futa Jallon hold back their trade from Rio Pongo, thus pressuring the company to leave. They obtained support from John Tilley, the agent for John and Alexander Anderson of London, ship's chandlers for slaving vessels in Rio Pongo, who also sold livestock and rice in Freetown. The alliance with the company turned out to be disastrous for Kumba Bali, who formerly recieved an annual payment from each resident slave dealer, plus a tax on each slave exported from the valley. Furthermore, the business of selling rice to slaving vessels naturally tied him to the interests of slave traders hostile to the company, which was interested in legitimate trade. In any case, the consequences of the French–British war curtailed company business potential considerably. As a result, the slave traders achieved a temporary victory. They also succeeded in blocking an attempt by the Edinburgh Missionary Society to set up a mission in Rio Pongo.[46]

One major reason for the dominant presence of European and Euro-African traders all along the Senegambian coast, as opposed to that of chartered companies endowed with state monopolies, was the gradual triumph of legitimate trade in the Atlantic trading system. Another reason was the numerous British–French wars, which seriously diminished the effectiveness of the presence of the European powers in Senegambia. For these reasons, this transitional period from the slave trade to legitimate trade saw the partial eclipse of Britain, France, and Portugal. Taking advantage of the situation, and making particularly profitable use of their neutrality in the Napoleonic wars, Americans infiltrated trading circuits on the African coast in general and on the Senegambian coast in particular. Beginning in 1780, Americans became the leading slave traders. They kept that status for decades, helped by the ability of their ships, as a rule, to slip through embargoes occasioned by the naval war between France and Britain. American traders dominated the Senegambian market for rum and tobacco, since American vessels trading directly on the coast charged lower prices than European traders charged for the same products imported via Europe.[47]

African commerce at the end of the eighteenth century was dominated by slave trading. Then followed a long transitional period in which attempts were made to replace slave trading with legitimate trade. That transitional period coincided with the entry of American traders. Still, the slave trade remained the basis of all commerce throughout the eighteenth century and well past the middle of the nineteenth century. This predatory business, which reduced the producer to an export commodity, pushed Senegambian societies into a state of regression. Henceforth, violence became the dominant motive force of their history. Violence determined relationships between states. Violence was also the arbiter within each state. Rampant violence led to the emergence of autocratic *ceddo* regimes under which monarchical power, originally elective, was confiscated by royal families whose power base was closely tied to slave trading. The royal monopoly on slave trading thus reinforced the centralization of royal *ceddo* power. It also sharpened animosities between the military aristocracy and the peasantry. The latter fell back increasingly upon Islam in their efforts to resist reigning regimes, and in the hope of creating a new order in the framework of the Muslim theocracies.

# 6 The strengthening of *ceddo* regimes in the eighteenth century

The Atlantic trading system in general, and the slave trading aspect of it in particular, gave the evolution of economic, political, and social structures in Senegambia during the eighteenth century a peculiar spin. Each state, depending on how close it was to the coast and the influences of the Atlantic trading system, went through a pattern of internal development which tended to reflect various aspects of the quasi-permanent economic, political and social crisis ravaging the territory in this time of generalized violence. In northern Senegambia, following the failure of the marabout movement at the end of the eighteenth century, the aristocracies of Kajoor, Waalo, Futa Toro, and Gajaaga, who had a stake in the Atlantic trading system, became even more warlike. They reinforced their centralizing authority, all the while enduring the pressure of the emirates of Trarza and Brakna, which were every bit as warlike.

In southern Senegambia, the kingdom of Kaabu decimated the population divided into a patchwork of small states in the Southern Rivers area, using a powerful war machine devoted exclusively to manhunts.

*Ceddo* regimes emerged during the eighteenth century in most of the Senegambian states. They came to symbolize the reign of violence in political relationships between and within states. Organized, massive manhunts created objective conditions for this violence. Violence became self-perpetuating in an infernal spiral of civil strife and inter-state wars that wasted the country and brought profits to European markets along the Senegambian coast.

The use of firearms encouraged the creation of standing armies. Made up of royal slaves, these armies grew into deadly instruments of centralized authority and arbitrary monarchical power. They thus robbed traditional institutional forms of all meaning. *Ceddo* power reached its peak under Lat Sukaabe Faal of Kajoor and Samba Gelaajo Jeegi of Futa Toro, leading stars in this firmament of warlords.

## A.    Ceddo regimes in the Wolof and Sereer kingdoms

The kingdoms of Waalo, Kajoor, Baol, Siin, and Saalum were remnants of the dismembered Jolof confederation. Generally speaking, all went through a similar evolutionary pattern in which *ceddo* regimes became centralized and strengthened. This growth of autocratic central power was linked to the consequences of the Atlantic trading system, a system dominated by the slave trade during the eighteenth century.

In this context of ubiquitous violence, the kingdom of Kajoor, under Lat Sukaabe Faal, was a perfect example of *ceddo* power in its progress toward the triumph of an autocratic monarchical regime. From 1677, the crisis that followed the failure of the War of the Marabouts and the intervention of the *Buur Saalum* considerably weakened the Kajoor aristocracy, paving the way for the rise of Lat Sukaabe Faal, symbol of the triumph of warlords in Senegambia. Considered a usurper, Lat Sukaabe Faal, originally the *Teeñ* of Baol, intervened in Kajoor in 1693 in answer to an appeal from the aristocracy, under threat from the *Buur Saalum*. Later he took the title of *Damel-Teeñ*, thus once more unifying the two kingdoms. Lat Sukaabe (1695–1720) imposed the hegemony of his maternal family line, the Geej, supplanting the Dorobe and the Gelwaar. He consolidated the centralizing regime of the *Damels* of Kajoor on new foundations. This dual royal power enabled him to reinforce central authority. He did this by finding support from the Atlantic trading system, taking full advantage of it to obtain the weapons that would thenceforth be necessary for the maintenance of his power. His technique was to advance his partisans within lineages with hereditary responsibilities. Simultaneously, he multiplied matrimonial alliances, creating a vast network of dependents in a system that became a permanent feature of Senegambian political life.

He also contracted matrimonial alliances with marabouts. The marabouts had indeed been defeated. Nevertheless, they remained a significant force in the political system of Kajoor. To win them over, Lat Sukaabe Faal initiated institutional reforms designed to bring them into the political establishment. The memory of Nasir Al Din's movement had taught him that such a movement could again shake the monarchical regime to its foundations. Now the marabout partisans split into two branches, one known as the *Seriñ Fakk Tall*, the other as the *Seriñ Lamb*. Lat Sukaabe Faal gave both of them new territorial responsibilities designed to coopt their younger branches. The new appointees were agents of the central regime responsible for the defense of the frontiers. Quite frequently, they were recruited from the *Naari Kajoor*, or Kajoor Moors, either in the region of Baol or among the *Seriñ* of Kokki, Mpal, Ñomre, or Pir. Of *Garmi* or *Doomi Buur* stock, and often having converted to Islam to make up for their lack of real clout within the royal nobility, the *Seriñ Lamb* generally behaved just like members of the ruling *ceddo* regime. Because of their double allegiance (to traditional political rulers on the one hand and to the religious leadership on the other), certain *Seriñ Lamb* were often tempted to exploit Islam in their attempts to regain power, especially in the latter half of the eighteenth century and in the nineteenth century. By contrast, the *Seriñ Fakk Tall*, like those of Langor in the Mbakol area, refused any compromise with the *ceddo* regime, focusing on their religious activities, especially teaching. In so doing, they often served as a rallying point for the aggrieved masses suffering under the impositions of the *ceddo* regime.[1]

Lat Sukaabe Faal had some real success implementing his policy of reinforcing central authority. Nevertheless, in the final years of his reign he ran into opposition from Muslims. He faced even fiercer hostility from French settlers at Saint-Louis and Gorée. To begin with, he confronted a Muslim rebellion at Njambur provoked by his own utterly violent ruling style. The Muslims called in the Emir of Trarza, with help from fellow Muslims in neighboring Waalo. The rebellion was crushed at the decisive battle of Ngangaram.[2] Following their defeat, Muslim partisans began an irreversible process of political separation by forming a new grouping based on the ideal of a Muslim community far wider than the Wolof ethnic environment in which Lat Sukaabe Faal had imposed his Geej solution.[3]

Meanwhile, Lat Sukaabe Faal achieved his objective of turning his matrilineal Geej clan into the dominant political force in Kajoor. For over a century the Geej monopolized power in the country, underlining the triumph of the matrilineal system. There is no doubt that this was, in a sense, a reaction to the patrilineal system of succession advocated by Islam.[4]

Throughout the eighteenth century, however, Lat Sukaabe Faal's project of reinforcing central authority to the advantage of the matrilineal Geej clan drew a reaction from the trading posts of Saint-Louis and Gorée. The unification of Kajoor and Baol under the Geej dynasty gave the *Damel-Teeñ*, Lat Sukaabe Faal, enough power to tempt him to impose his own terms in business dealings with Europeans at the trading posts of Gorée, Rufisque, and Portudal. Gorée had been in the hands of the Dutch. But as soon as the French captured it in 1677, they tried to set up a full scale commercial monopoly in the zone that would exclude all other Europeans. On the local scene, they also set up a system of fixed customary dues to be paid to the rulers of Kajoor and Baol.

In 1697, the energetic Director-General of the *Compagnie du Sénégal*, André Brüe, found himself in conflict with the *Damel-Teeñ,* Lat Sukaabe Faal. The latter was against both the French trading monopoly and the amount of customary duty payments the French were willing to pay – at a rate imposed by the French company. What Lat Sukaabe Faal wanted was to open his territory to free trade with all European nations. Free trade was all the more attractive to him because the British in Gambia were paying double the French rates. After the French seized the British ship *William*

Plate 7 The arrest of M. Bruë on instructions from the *Damel*, King of Cayor, June 1701

*and Jane* on 15 March 1699, Lat Sukaabe Faal ordered a commercial blockade against them. He took advantage of the weakened position of the French in the War of Spanish Succession to get André Brüe arrested, keeping him incommunicado in May and June of 1701. He also organized the sack of Gorée.

André Brüe was freed on 17 June 1701, but that did not restore calm between the trading post and Lat Sukaabe Faal. The dispute continued under the new director, Louis Lemaître, from 1702 to 1706. Right up to the death of Lat Sukaabe Faal around 1720, the conflict continued, with successive company directors having to deal with numerous anti-French blockades. In addition, there were continual incursions from British privateers bringing in smuggled goods, a constant threat to the French monopoly.[5]

For these reasons, the reign of Lat Sukaabe Faal is of particular interest. It signaled the definite rise to power of warlords in the Wolof kingdoms. One basis of his power was his skill in turning the resolution of internal conflicts to his own advantage. Another was his determination to profit fully from the Atlantic trading system. It was that determination that inspired him to wangle a monopoly on the importation of firearms – key weapons for slave raids and therefore elevated to the status of essential commodities in trade with Europeans on the coast. At this time he already owned 200 guns and two grape-shot cannon. Thus equipped, Lat Sukaabe Faal's army, according to a contemporary report, was capable of bringing back from a raid nearly "two thousand slaves – men, women and little children."[6]

The reign of violence characteristic of daily life in Kajoor certainly justified the still-remembered comments of the famous Wolof philosopher Cocc Barma, who described the regime as wily and utterly unscrupulous. In the conflict between the king of Kajoor and the trading company at Gorée, the king's effectiveness was considerably compromised by the fact that he was chronically in debt to the company. Relationships with Europeans on the coast were determined by power equations, and neither side challenged the primacy of the slave trade. That was the chief concern of both the African warlords and the European chartered companies. In defense of their interests, the two parties shared a common front.

Following the death of Lat Sukaabe Faal, a series of succession crises opened the way for constant French interference in the political affairs of the united kingdoms of Kajoor and Baol. The trigger for such interventions was the practice of customary payments to the rulers; henceforth, they became an important stake in all political conflicts. The French had learned to their cost, under Lat Sukaabe Faal, how inconvenient it could be for them to have the kingdoms of Kajoor and Baol united under a single sovereign. From now on they did their best to keep the two kingdoms apart. Thus, when in 1736 the *Damel-Teeñ* Maysa Tend Wejj reunited the two crowns, the Board at Gorée went into action to tear the two kingdoms apart.

It is essential for the good of company business that the kingdom of the *Thin*, recently conquered by the *Damel*, be in someone else's possession. One could find a way to drive him out of the country of the *Thin* by supplying arms and ammunition to his rival, a man reported to be exceedingly keen to restart the war, if only he had the means.[7]

Succession disputes between these two kingdoms were the main supply source for the slave trade. By the same token, they provided the chief motive for the purchase of arms supplies by the new warlords who now reigned unchallenged over the Wolof kingdoms on the coast.[8]

The Waalo kingdom was another striking case. There, too, the French trading company at Saint-Louis intervened constantly in a series of succession disputes that pitted three royal families, the Teejekk, the Loggar, and the Joos, against each other. The result was a chronic political and social crisis. The French adopted this interventionist policy at a time of major economic changes in the region due to the increasing importance of the gum trade. For, right from the beginning of the eighteenth century, spurred by demand from the European textile industry, the gum trade, monopolized by the Moorish emirates of Trarza and Brakna, helped them not only to cope with the economic crisis at the end of the seventeenth century, but also to put the kingdoms of the Senegal valley under constant pressure. Thus Waalo, Kajoor, Jolof, and Futa Toro suffered the long-term consequences of this new contradiction born of the determination of the French to divert the gum trade toward trading posts in the Senegal valley, where the profits would be all theirs. This determination was a reaction to the fierce competition the French faced at the trading posts of Arguin and Portendick on the Mauritanian coast. And it was this competition that sparked the first Gum War. Lasting from 1717 to 1727, it had particularly far-reaching consequences for the evolution of the kingdom of Waalo.[9]

After the failure of the expedition of La Rigaudière, intended to recapture the Mauritanian trading posts from the Dutch, Brüe, commanding officer in Saint-Louis, sought an alliance with the *Beecio* Malikhuri, provincial chief of Roos Beecio, whose other title was *Kangam*. The aim of this alliance was to pressure Alichandora, the Emir of Trarza, to restore the fort of Arguin to the French. He was also expected to counterbalance the hostility of the *Brak* of Waalo and the *Damel* of Kajoor toward the Saint-Louis trading post. In 1724, emboldened by the support of Saint-Louis, the *Beecio* Malikhuri rebelled against the *Brak* of Waalo, Yerim Mbanyik. This attempted secession was typical of the policy of Saint-Louis. That policy was now aimed at the territorial dismemberment of the region's states, as a way of protecting the company's interests.[10]

Once mediation efforts between Saint-Louis and Alichandora had failed, the company withdrew its support from the *Beecio* Malikhuri. As a result, Yerim Mbanyik defeated him. Under these circumstances, it was to be expected that Yerim Mbanyik, who had an army of two to three hundred horsemen and three thousand foot soldiers, half of them carrying firearms, would by 1734 become one of the region's most powerful kings. That was what enabled his successors, his two brothers, Njaak Aram Bakar

(1733–56) and in particular Naatago (1757–66), to dominate the neighboring kingdoms. Their dominance was especially tight over Kajoor, weakened by famine and seven years of civil war. These kings demanded overlordship of all land near the mouth of the Senegal River. They also demanded the delivery to them of all customary dues formerly paid to the *Damel* by Saint-Louis.

Waalo hegemony came under attack from the British, who occupied Saint-Louis from 1758, following numerous exactions by the *Brak*, Naatago Aram. The *Brak* had grown powerful enough to dictate terms to French traders in Saint-Louis, since he controlled trade routes along the Senegal River. Taking advantage of his role as gateman of the river, he increased customary dues and the price of slaves several times. In 1764, he twice blocked all trading at Saint-Louis, and stopped traders voyaging upriver through Waalo territory. In reaction, the British threw their support behind the *Damel* of Kajoor, Makodu Kumba Joaring, who, from August 1765, won back most of the territory he had lost to the Waalo.

For a while, O'Hara, the British governor, had considered building a fort on the mainland to protect trade at Saint-Louis. On the death of Naatago Aram, he saw his opportunity to shatter the power of Waalo for ever. Openly keen to drain the maximum number of slaves from the region to his own plantations in the Caribbean islands, O'Hara supplied arms to Moors, who reduced the entire Senegal valley to a killing field. In 1775, the British took more than 8,000 slaves from Waalo alone in less than six months. Such was the glut of slaves on the market that in the streets of Saint-Louis a slave could be bought for a simple piece of cloth.[11]

This tremendous human drain coincided with the start of a civil war that raged for almost twenty-nine years. While it lasted, the two other royal families, the Loggar and the Joos, tried to grab back the power monopolized since the beginning of the eighteenth century by the Teejekk family. For the rule of the three brothers Yerim Mbanyik, Njak Aram Bakar and Naatago Aram Bakar symbolized the victory of the Teejekk over the two other matrilineal clans. The pattern was the same as that which led to the Geej monopoly in Kajoor.

However, it was not long before Waalo came under the Moors of Trarza, made powerful by the gum trade. They intervened constantly in succession disputes which completely sapped the power of Waalo. Thus debilitated, the kingdom could no longer project an independent policy. Nor did it have sufficient energy left to produce another generation of serious warlords of the caliber of Lat Sukaabe Faal.

The Sereer kingdoms of Siin and Saalum went through developments similar to those in the Wolof kingdoms. But since the history of Siin was shaped by the narrowness of its boundaries, the context of generalized violence forced it to grow even more isolationist, and to develop an agricultural system of shifting cultivation in a bid to maintain internal cohesion. Still, the *Buur Siin* established a very well developed central administrative system working through the supervision of village heads, known as *Sakh-sakh*, appointed by the central regime. Here the exercise of power seemed less arbitrary than in the Wolof, Denyanke, or Kaabu kingdoms. This was part of the reason why new Islamic forces, on the rise throughout the other parts of Senegambia, played only a minor role in the Sereer kingdoms.[12] The impact of the trans-Atlantic trading system was considerably muted by the absence of permanent wharves in Joal and Portudal. These posts, as a consequence, did not play a major part in the slave trade.[13]

The kingdom of Saalum, given its greater land area and its cosmopolitan mix of Sereer, Wolof, Peul, and Manding, as well, especially, as its profitable commercial situation, developed differently. The Saalum River, running through the entire countryside between the Ferlo and the Gambia, was an extremely important trade route. Kawoon, the capital, remained a busy port on account of the highly productive salt works in the neighboring estuaries, which brought in very substantial revenues to the *Buur*. He could therefore participate in the slave trade, taking advantage of the weakness of neighboring states (namely, the Manding principalities from the Saalum to the Gambia) and the decline of Jolof to ensure the expansion of Saalum, which reached its peak in the eighteenth century. On the other hand, royal power in Saalum was weaker than in Siin, and cohesion within Saalum was constantly threatened by centrifugal local authorities. Drawn by the commercial pull of both Bathurst and Gorée, the *Buur Saalum* was as deeply involved in the violence of the region's *ceddo* regimes as the other kings, on account of the predominance of slave trading on the Senegambian market.[14] The control exercised by the central authority over families vested with the hereditary local offices of *Bummi*, *Buur*, and *Belup*, however, was less overt than in the Saalum. The Saalum was more open to Wolof migrants from Jolof and to Futanke migrants from Futa Toro, who brought their old Muslim traditions with them. Their immigration therefore strengthened the Muslim religious element, which now posed an increasing threat to *ceddo* regimes in Saalum.[15]

**B.    Ceddo regimes in the Denyanke kingdoms of Futa Toro and the Soninke kingdoms of Gajaaga and Kaabu**

Under the Denyanke dynasty from the time of Koli Tengela, Futa Toro developed along the same lines as the Wolof kingdoms. There, too, succession disputes, the recourse to violence as arbiter, and the massive use of firearms became permanent facts of life. Right from the start, the absence of precise rules governing succession in the *Satigi* regimes opened the way to wars between rival claimants. In addition, there were numerous usurpations engineered by powerful *ceddo* warlords. In this context where violence was the royal road to power, Bubakar Sire called in the Moroccans in 1716. This gave the Moroccans the opportunity to interfere in the affairs of Futa Toro. For from that date, the kingdom was put under an obligation to pay the *Mudo Horma*, a seed tax.[16] Furthermore, Futa Toro participated directly in the war between Alichandora, the Emir of Trarza, and the Brakna. This situation laid the groundwork for increasingly massive intervention by Morocco, through its troops, the so-called Ormans, in the affairs of the Senegal valley from Waalo all the way to Gajaaga.

The crisis began in 1720 when Alichandora, the Emir of Trarza, driven from his seat by his powerful northern neighbors, the Ulad Dellim, and despoiled of his property, petitioned the Sultan of Morocco for help. Alichandora wanted to end Brakna hegemony over what is now southern Mauritania. The real interest of the Moroccan Cherif, on the other hand, was to gain recognition as sovereign over the Moorish emirates south of Morocco. The Sultan sent 5,000 troops, by Saint-Robert's account. But, their mission once accomplished, these troops then turned to a completely independent agenda, ravaging all states on both sides of the Senegal River. Eventually, the Ormans split into two factions. One sided with Trarza, the other with Brakna. Alichandora, defeated in 1722 by the faction allied to Brakna, sought refuge with the *Beecio* Malikhuri in Waalo. The Ormans intervened actively in numerous succession crises during the first half of the eighteenth century in Futa Toro. For instance, total confusion reigned from 1721 to 1724, with Bubakar Sire and Bubu Musa each frequently dethroning the other and installing himself as *Satigi* or king. This went on until the legendary Samba Gelaajo Jeegi seized power in 1725 with help from the Ormans of Gaïdy and the commanding officer of Fort Saint Joseph.[17]

Samba Gelaajo Jeegi (1725–31) was the prototypical warlord. Futa Toro griots to this day tell legendary stories of his exploits, his delight in risk-taking, and his dauntless courage.

*Sambayel mo Lamotako*, little Samba who did not reign (because he usurped power through violence and was not enthroned according to custom), the warrior on his famous mare *Umulatum*, armed with his celebrated gun *Bubu Lowake*, Bubu the gun that needs no loading, was in all respects a perfect symbol for the reign of violence in the political life of Futa Toro. Samba Gelaajo Jeegi was the quintessential *ceddo* chieftain, a man who, with his army of gun-toting *sebbe*, fought forty-five battles in his short reign, spurred on by the sound of war drums, the so-called *bawdi peyya yiyam* or blood drums, to the accompaniment of martial music, the *dadde yiyam* or blood songs.[18]

The epic of Samba Gelaajo Jeegi is still chanted with marvelous grace in the Futa Toro. The two translations published by Amadou Ly and Amadou Abel Sy are excellent renderings of the original.[19] This poetic invocation of the *ceddo* saga which highlights the deeds of Samba Gelaajo Jeegi is still chanted by *sebbe* in their war chants known as *Gumbala* or *Lenngi*, to the accompaniment of bloodstained drums and bloody songs. The *Gumbala* is a hymn to fearless courage, an epic salute to death, in which the *ceddo* embraces the warrior's responsibility, his fidelity to his ancestors, and the ethos of his caste. The outstanding feature of *Gumbala* poetry is its focus on the virile themes of death and violence, fantastic rides and larger-than-life exploits. *Gumbala* poetry is a celebration of the macabre, a hymn to the warrior and his horse, his gun and his spear.

> That was the man who said:
> By my mother's prayers,
> By my father's prayers,
> God, let me not die a shameful death
> Lying in my bed
> Drowned in children's tears
> Deafened by old men's groans.[20]

*Lenngi* chants come from the same tradition. Sung exclusively by *ceddo* women during marriage and circumcision ceremonies, their theme is contempt in the face of death, and the commitment to uphold honor. The aim was to enact a great communion in which young men entering married life were reminded that they belonged to the warrior *ceddo* caste, and enjoined to revivify values that it was their duty to perpetuate.[21] Sadly, these days the epic of Samba Gelaajo Jeegi is recalled with no awareness of its real historical context. That context was dominated by the violent slave trade, which was the real reason behind the emergence of this type of warlord, steeped in the *ceddo* ethos.

In Samba Gelaajo Jeegi's time, Futa Toro was dominated by the interaction of several factors leading to a situation of permanent violence. Morocco, using its Orman army, was bent on controlling the Moorish Emirates participating in the Atlantic trading system through the gum trade and slave trading. As for the trading post at Saint-Louis, its French agents were present in the Senegal valley from its mouth all the way to the upper valley. Their main objective was to obtain as many slaves as possible from the region. All these external factors created a situation of chronic instability in Futa, where the Denyanke military aristocracy was engaged in a constant struggle for power with the *Satigi* in which their key tactic was to appeal for help from the Moors, their Orman allies, or from the French. Thus, Samba Gelaajo Jeegi, originally an ally of the Moors, later tried to get closer to the French at Saint-Louis, hoping to use them to shake off

Moroccan dominance. In 1725, Samba asked to trade about a hundred captives for guns, bullets, and powder. At the same time, he requested that the company build a fort in his capital at Jowol. Furthermore, in July of the same year, when the French were threatened with pillage by the Moors, Samba Gelaajo Jeegi tried to protect French interests. It was possibly this alliance that enabled him to rule uninterruptedly in Futa Toro from 1725 to 1731, despite the claims of two rivals, Bubu Musa and Konko Bubu Musa.[22]

The French, however, had little firepower so far from their base at Saint-Louis. They could therefore not end Moorish harassment. From now on, therefore, the Moors "held the land of the Blacks prostrate under them."[23] As a matter of fact, the French themselves ended up using certain factions in Futa Toro to weaken Konko Bubu Musa so as to help their ally Samba Gelaajo Geeji, once more driven into exile in Bundu. The background to this episode was that Samba, whose army included Orman troops brought to him by Saint Adou in exchange for 2,000 bars of trade goods, regained power from Bubu Musa, the ally of Tunka of Gajaaga, between 1738 and 1741. But Samba remained a hostage of his Orman and Moorish allies. His efforts to get the French to build a fort at Jowol, a move which might have enabled him to throw off the dominance of his Moroccan and Moorish allies, failed. A short while later, Samba Gelaajo Geeji died. To this day the circumstances of his death remain obscure. Tradition has it that he died a death befitting the courageous *ceddo* ideal – murdered by a treacherous wife corrupted by his enemies while he was in exile in Bundu.

You put *lalo* in my food, and this after the conversation we had the other day. I know this food will kill me; I will eat it all the same. Never shall it be said that I was afraid of death. Only before dishonor do I draw back. Never do I retreat before death.[24]

In the long run the circumstances surrounding the death of Samba Gelaajo Jeegi, this legendary hero of violence sacralized in a Futa Toro sapped by war, are of little consequence. For in 1752 the new *Satigi*, Sule Njaay, who made his capital in Galam, was in turn driven out by Yaye Hoola and his warriors, who pillaged Bundu with help from Khaaso and some Orman troops. Futa Toro seemed to have settled at the bottom of the abyss. *Satigi* after *Satigi* mounted and fell from the throne in rapid succession. In this confusion the winners were the Moors, masters of this region in which all factors now pointed to a Muslim revolution. It happened in 1776.[25]

Gajaaga, in the upper Senegal River valley, was also integrated from the seventeenth century into the Atlantic trading system. This considerably increased the business of Soninke traders, situated at the intersection of the three ecological regions of Senegambia: the Coast, the Savanna, and the

Sahel. Soninke traders were the main suppliers of salt and European goods to countries in the Niger Bend. They also supplied cotton goods to western Senegambia. Despite this commercial dynamism of the Soninke, however, Gajaaga experienced the same situation of political and social crisis related to the slave trade and the Orman invasion. The political crisis began around 1700 with a struggle between the *Tunka*, Naame of Makhanna, and his cousin, Makhan of Tamboukane in the province of Kammera. It extended into 1730 in a war between Gwey and Kammera. The conflict broke out after the deposition of the *Tunka*, Muusa Jaabe of Ciaabu, and his replacement with Bukari Sette of Makhanna, who was appointed head of the Gajaaga federation.

Tensions multiplied, peaking in a series of civil wars from 1744 to 1745, which forever destroyed the unity of the Soninke federation. The country was thus laid open to an invasion by Khaaso in alliance with the Bambara of Kaarta. The Khaasonke invaders were repulsed, but Gwey and Kammera were weakened by endless disputes which for a long time compromised the future of the Gajaaga confederation.[26]

Information on the kingdom of Kaabu, dominant in southern Senegambia until the triumph of the Muslim revolution in the Futa Jallon, is scarce. It is known, however, that the power of Kaabu, which lasted beyond the eighteenth century, was based on slave trading, a circumstance which considerably reinforced the warlike nature of the *Nyaanco* royal clan. Thus, around 1738, the *Mansa* of Kaabu had the capacity to deliver six hundred slaves a year to the Portuguese alone, quite apart from the fact that the Southern Rivers region under Kaabunke control habitually exported thousands of slaves.[27] Kaabu reinforced its hold over the coastal provinces while conducting slave raids on its Bajaranke, Fulakunda, Konyagi, and Basari neighbors in the hinterland. It seems to have reached the peak of its power under the *Nyaanco* aristocracy during the reign of Biram Mansa, who died around 1705. However, the state of permanent warfare also strengthened the positions of the provincial generals known as *Korin*, along with the power of Soninke warriors, notorious for their excessive drinking of *doolo*, alcohol. Here too, as in the political crisis of the nineteenth century, disputes between three royal lineages (Sama, Pacana and Jimara) were at the root of numerous civil wars aimed at imposing a unified central authority throughout the kingdom. This situation, more abundantly documented in the nineteenth century, sowed the seeds for the success of subsequent holy wars originating from the Futa Jallon and Bundu, as well as for internal Muslim revolutions against the Soninke state of Kaabu.

The development of *ceddo* or *Soninke* kingdoms throughout Senegambia during the eighteenth century bore the brand of the slave trade. It was symbolized by the rule of violence in all aspects of political and social life.

Trying to cope, Muslim communities organized themselves, sometimes to gain political and territorial autonomy from *ceddo* regimes, at other times to wage outright revolutionary struggles of the kind that led to the creation of theocratic states in Bundu, Futa Toro, and Futa Jallon.

The military defeat of the marabout movement led by Nasir Al Din in the latter half of the seventeenth century led, in many areas, to the development of underground Islamic movements opposed to *ceddo* regimes and the disastrous slave trade throughout Senegambia.

In various states controlled by powerul military aristocracies, Muslim communities under the leadership of highly influential families of marabouts built up their forces. They aimed, in gradual stages, to wrest political and social autonomy from existing regimes. Increasingly, at the same time, these Muslim communities, interlinked through far-reaching networks of religious, political, and economic solidarity that transcended state frontiers to cover the whole of Senegambia, tried either to create new states outright or to organize the violent seizure of established power by proclaiming a holy war.

Thus, right at the end of the seventeenth century, Malik Sy founded the Muslim theocracy of Bundu. This was followed, at the beginning of the eighteenth century, by the Muslim revolution in Futa Jallon led by Karamoko Alfa. Following Muslim successes in this borderline region of Senegambia, there was a lull until the second half of the eighteenth century before the triumph of the *Toorodo* group of Muslims led by the marabout Suleyman Bal in Futa Toro, the bastion of the Denyanke regime. This triple success testifies to both the continuity and the solidarity of the marabout movement throughout Senegambia. From this time on, the region's history would be dominated by the struggle between Muslim theocracies and *ceddo* regimes.

## A.    The Muslim revolution in Bundu

Reprisals against the Muslim leadership after the defeat of Nasir Al Din caused a mass exodus of Muslims from Futa Toro into Bundu, where around 1690 Maalik Sy founded the first Muslim theocracy in the Senegambian region. Needless to say, Maalik Sy's movement continued the work of the previous marabout movement. He himself was one of a group of brilliant Muslim leaders educated at institutions in the Kajoor centers of Pir and Kokki, closely connected with the *Zawaya* Berbers.

Born at Suyuma near Podor, Malik Sy, after his education, traveled all over Senegambia before settling down in the area of Gajaaga with the permission of the *Tunka* of Ciaabu. In keeping with the custom know as *Jonnu*, the *Tunka* gave Malik Sy land to settle on. The alliance between them was sealed. In short order, however, the pact was broken. The reason had to do with the strategic location of Bundu at the terminus of the Gambian trade routes.[1] For, once settled in this cosmopolitan area where Bajaranke, Konyagi, Basari, Jakhanke, and Soninke populations all lived together, Malik Sy took advantage of the weakness of Gajaaga to declare a holy war. The result was the theocratic state of Bundu, founded partly on his religious charisma, partly on the military organization he created with help from Muslim immigrants, most of them from Futa Toro, who had moved into the area after the defeat of the Marabout movement.[2]

The fact is that Malik Sy was furthering the interests of Jakhanke marabouts, whose trading business was under constant threat from the pillaging military aristocrats of Gajaaga. Once he made his move, the Muslim movement took control of the Falémé, a region whose commercial importance and agricultural wealth were to constitute the basis of the power of the Sisibe dynasty in centuries to come.[3] Malik Sy then took the title of *Almamy*, the Peul mispronunciation of *El Imam*, a title previously taken by Nasir Al Din.

Philip Curtin does a good job of elucidating religious and family linkages between Nasir Al Din's movement and the revolution in Bundu. Malik Sy may not have taken a direct part in the War of the Marabouts. But from every point of view he was a fervent disciple who achieved some of the political and religious objectives of the marabout movement.[4]

Given the dearth of documentary data, it is difficult to pinpoint the reasons behind the success of this first Muslim revolution. But with it, a pattern was already discernible: Muslim communities, gathering within the Senegambian region but far from the coast, the better to escape the oppressive policies of *ceddo* regimes, sought to consolidate their own power. Under these circumstances, since Bundu was the transitional zone between Muslim communities in Futa Toro and Futa Jallon, its destiny was henceforth linked with theirs. At its extraordinary location on trade routes connecting the Niger Bend with trading posts in the Gambia valley, Bundu grew gradually stronger under the Sisibe dynasty while the power of Gajaaga declined.[5]

## B.     The Muslim revolution in Futa Jallon

The Muslim revolution in Bundu was followed a few years later by a similar revolution in Futa Jallon. The conditions were practically identical. The Futa Jallon plateau, originally a natural barrier, became, over the passage of centuries, a refuge for the Jallonke, the Susu, and the Peul. In the six-teenth and seventeenth centuries, the region underwent a tremendous upheaval. Koli Tengela's invasion, and to an even greater extent the development of the Atlantic trading system, soon created conditions for a powerful process of acculturation. The new situation accelerated migra-tions from the Sudan to the forest belt and the coast. In these movements, the Futa Jallon plateau was a key transit area. It experienced a new eco-nomic boom thanks to substantial livestock herds brought in by large scale immigrations of Peul herdsmen attracted, after the fifteenth century, by the region's abundant pasturelands.

Now integrated into the Atlantic trading system, Futa Jallon underwent a profound economic, political, and social transformation which led to a Muslim revolution at the start of the eighteenth century. Walter Rodney's explanation of the economic, political and social context of the 1725 revolution, ending with the creation of a theocratic state in Futa Jallon by the marabout movement, is remarkably precise. He demonstrates that the hypothesis which boils the revolution down to a crude struggle between a downtrodden Peul population and their exploitative Jallonke masters is simple-minded.

The fact is that in the seventeenth century, favored by a combination of three factors, the Peul became probably the richest, most powerful social group in the region. The first factor was the large influx of Peul migrants from the Bundu, Futa Toro, Massina, and Sahel regions, attracted by good pasture. Second, the expanding Atlantic trading system stimulated large scale trade in livestock and hides. So the cattle-owning Peul became richer. The third factor was the introduction into this situation of militant Muslim thinking, an ideology geared to the construction of a new economic, polit-ical and social order.[6]

On this point, it is becoming incresingly clear that the Muslim revolution in Futa Jallon, like the one in Bundu, was a reaction against the general-ized violence and chaos caused by the slave trade. For one thing, the leaders of the Muslim revolution in Futa Jallon were not all from Massina. Some came from the Senegal valley, where they had been in direct contact with Nasir Al Din's marabout movement.

Philip Curtin and Levtzion have done a good job of highlighting reli-gious, political, and matrimonial ties linking the various families of mar-abouts in Futa Toro, Bundu, and Futa Jallon.[7] The road linking the Senegal valley to the Futa Jallon plateau through the Falémé has always been important in the demographic history of Senegambia. The nineteenth-century itinerary of Shaykh Umar illustrates the point. The marabout movement of the late seventeenth century had been defeated in Futa Toro. Bundu provided a transitory phase, before it triumphed in Futa Jallon at the beginning of the eighteenth century, supported by the region's Peul, Manding, and Jakhanke populations. This was a period of massive man-hunts organized by the powerful state of Kaabu. In that context, the Muslim revolution in Futa Jallon presents the hallmarks of a victory for the marabout movement, whose main objective was to ensure the security of the Muslim community.

This Muslim revolution was, in essence, a far cry from being an inter-ethnic war between Peul herdsmen and Jallonke farmers. Oral traditions make it quite clear that the revolution, originally led by twelve Peul and ten Manding marabouts, the latter doubtless of Jakhanke origin, was multi-ethnic. Indeed, it ran into opposition from the Kafu chiefs, Jallonke them-selves, as well as from Peul pagans, the Pulli, living in the rural areas with their cattle. There is no doubt that the Muslim Peul, who wanted to abolish taxes on livestock, made common cause for the moment with Manding or Jakhanke traders, the *Juula*, who invariably linked their trading activities with the practice of Islam. Both wanted to create a vast political unit in place of the tiny Jallonke chiefdoms, grown incapable, under the circum-stances of the slave trade, of ensuring the security of their populations.

There is no way the Muslim revolution could ever have been accom-plished by a disparate band of herdsmen roaming the savanna grasslands, owing allegiance to none. It was brought about, instead, by Muslims of diverse origins who had settled down in the sanctuary of the Futa Jallon plateau, putting down deep roots. The marabout leadership was mostly trained at the well-known Jakhanke school of Jakhaba on the Bafing. It was reinforced by numerous Peul, poised to develop their lucrative livestock economy under conditions of gradual sedentarization. Trading livestock and hides in the coastal markets, they built up their economic muscle. Meanwhile, Islam provided the ideology they needed for the construction of a new political and social order.

After the victory of the marabout movement in the holy war waged against various aristocratic Jallonke regimes, the Muslim leaders set up the Futa Jallon confederation under the leadership of Ibrahima Sambegu, alias Karamoko Alfa, head of the Sediyanke lineage of the Barry family of Timbo. His official title was the *Almami*. The confederation was divided into nine provinces (known as *diwe*, singular: *diwal*). Each provincial chief was given the title *Alfa*. All were appointed generals in the holy war. Thus, initial territorial divisions coincided with the territory liberated by each leader of the Muslim revolution. So the *Almami* Karamoko Alfa, head of the Futa Jallon confederation, was in the first place the *Alfa* of Timbo province. Right from the start, the power of the *Almami*, with his head-quarters in the capital at Timbo, was substantially limited. The provincial chiefs of Labé, Buriya, Timbi, Kebaali, Kollade, Koyin, Fugumba, and

Fode Haaji enjoyed considerable autonomy. A further check on central power was the Council of Elders, based in the religious capital Fugumba. Its functions were parliamentary.[8]

The Muslim theocracy of Futa Jallon was the outcome of a series of military campaigns between the marabout movement and the Jallonke *Kafu* chiefs, whose primary interest was the defense of their sovereignty. The main campaign of the holy war ended with the victory of the marabout movement at the famous battle of Talansan. However, hostilities smoldered on because of attempts to convert pagan populations in the hinterland to Islam. In these conflicts, Muslims confronted more resistance from the Pulli, nomadic herdsmen who had wandered over the region for centuries, and who were opposed to Islam, a religion that symbolized sedentarization, along with political and economic control. The Pulli were a rural Peul group that subsequently gravitated to the bottom of the social order, where they were exploited by the ruling class of marabout leaders. The very fact of their opposition should put to rest any simplistic race-based interpretation seeking to present the Muslim revolution as an invasion of Peul masters descending on indigenous Jallonke to enslave them. The real record indicates that opposition was long-lasting, and that the consolidation of the Muslim theocratic regime was a slow development. In the process, the regime was forced to create a new political structure to replace the Jallonke *Kafu*. The changes continued throughout the entire first half of the eighteenth century.[9]

When, around 1751, Karamoko Alfa died, his succession fell to Ibrahima Sory, popularly known as Sori Mawdo (Sori the Great). The religious leader of the *jihad*, in other words, was replaced by the Commander-in-Chief of the army. The military leader hurled Futa Jallon into an aggressive policy targeting neighboring countries, under the guise of a holy war. This type of campaign became the main form of slave raiding. Captives were used to meet the domestic needs of the ruling aristocracy as well as to satisfy the booming demand for slaves on the coast.

As in the case of the kingdom of Dahomey or that of the Asante Confederation, the historical development of Futa Jallon makes sense only when placed in the global context of the slave trade. At the time, slave trading was the dominant commercial activity on the African coast. These kingdoms were originally founded to combat the deleterious effects of slave raids. Once consolidated, however, they too made slave trading their exclusive business. Sometimes the reason was the need for self defense against neighboring states. But there were instances where the initiative came from the new states themselves, eager as they were to share in profits from the slave trade. In such cases, Islam was simply another opportune ideology that served to maintain and consolidate the power of the incumbent aristocracy.

Following this pattern, Ibrahima Sory Mawdo threw his forces into a series of wars against neighboring states. He wanted slaves and booty, and he was helped by the king of the Jallonke kingdom of Solimana. The coalition, however, was defeated in 1762 by Konde Burama, king of Sankaran, who from that date on was poised to occupy Timbo thanks to the defection of Solimana. The coalition had to dig deep into its reserves of patriotic fervor to stop Konde Burama's army outside the gates of Fugumba. It was only in 1776 that Ibrahima Sory definitively eliminated the threat. The defeat of Sankaran marked the beginning of a long period of Futa Jallon domination over the Solimana kingdom east of Timbo. This victory considerably reinforced the power of the *Almami* Ibrahima Sori Mawdo, and, until his death in 1791, he imposed the authority of the military faction over the religious faction.

When Sori Mawdo died, a period of political confusion followed. His son Sadu was assassinated in 1797 or 1798 by followers of Abdoulaye Bademba, son of the first *Almami*, Karamoko Alfa. No doubt, it was during this period that the system of alternate succession between the two families (the *Alfaya*, descendants of Karamoko Alfa, and the *Soriya*, descendants of Ibrahima Sori Mawdo) was adopted. This dual regime, modeled on the political structures of *ceddo* regimes ruled by two or more royal lineages, weakened the central authority considerably and allowed the Council of Elders, responsible for overseeing the observance of Muslim *Sharia* law, to control the *Almami*'s power. Above all, it enabled provincial chiefs to build up their autonomy.

Despite the inherent weakness of the political system right from its beginnings, Futa was able to protect its independence and even to expand its territory up until the colonial conquest. The new regime, however, gradually lost its revolutionary energy. For the marabout movement, once it had achieved security within the Futa Jallon region, turned into a religious and military aristocracy actively engaged in slave trading. As in other areas, slave trading became a monopoly of the state, which controlled trade routes and organized caravans heading for the coast. Because European traders were less interested in such products as gold, ivory and hides than in slaves, the predominance of the slave trade became a permanent feature of life in the eighteenth century. Thomas Watt, visiting Timbo in 1794, gave a good account of the dynamics of the trading system. Under it, the *Almami* had to wage war in order to obtain slaves, all he could trade for European commodities.

Under these circumstances, holy warfare dropped its religious mask. Islam became an excuse for slave raiding. The victims were pagan neighbors of Futa Jallon. The fact that slaves were the dominant commodity exchanged for European merchandise made the new regime particularly oppressive toward non-Muslims. Enslaved in large numbers, they were either taken to the coast for sale, or rounded up in slave villages called *runde*. The creation of these slave villages was the most typical institutional innovation of the new regime in Futa Jallon during the eighteenth century.[10]

Futa Jallon, situated between the Bambara states and the coast, was able to conduct slave raids or to buy slaves for domestic use. It sold surplus captives on the coast for European commodities and the salt needed for its livestock-based economy. In the eighteenth and nineteenth centuries, the slave trade brought countless slaves of various origins – Bambara, Kissi, Jallonke, Peul, Basari, Konyagi – to Futa Jallon.

The massive influx of slaves can only be understood when situated within the broader context of the slave trade. Taken outside that context, it has tended to distort our understanding of the internal historical evolution of Futa Jallon. For numerous historians, indeed, Futa Jallon history is no more than the massive invasion of Peul flowing in to enslave indigenous Jallonke. This hypothesis of conquering invaders enslaving conquered natives sets up a racial vision of Futa Jallon history. The pattern is neat and simplistic: it pits two ethnic groups, one Peul, the other Jallonke, against each other. Now it is an incontrovertible fact that the entire process of internal historical evolution in Futa Jallon was dominated by the creation of a hierarchical society, thoroughly committed to inequality, with Islam the ruling ideology. But in that framework, the primary distinction was between Muslims and non-Muslims. Muslims enjoyed all rights pertaining to free men. Non-Muslims were by definition consigned to slave status in the new society governed by Muslim law, the *Sharia*. The dominant status of Peul language and culture should not obscure our understanding of the real dynamics of the society's internal development. That evolution was typified by the existence of perfectly distinct social classes based on Muslim ideology.

Beyond the basic distinction between free men (*rimbe*), and slaves (*maccube*), the dominant society of free men also recognized a hierarchical system based primarily on unequal, exploitative relationships. Among free men the top group was the *Lasli*. It included the military aristocracy of sword and spear, and the intellectual aristocracy of the book and the writing tablet. Members of this class were descendants of major marabout leaders in the holy war. Their monopoly of power was absolute. They constituted the summit of the political and religious ruling class. They commanded numerous hangers-on and dependents who lived off the exploitation of large numbers of slaves penned up in the *runde*.

Below the aristocracy came the mass of free people. Their status and well-being depended on their relationship to the ruling political class, or to the marabout leadership, holders of power. Thus, at the bottom of this class of free persons, there were the rural Peul, most of them descendants of Pulli, late converts to Islam after the holy war. Their sole source of wealth was livestock. Beyond that, they were open to merciless exploitation by all members of the ruling political and religious class. Practically none of these rural Peul owned slaves. They therefore tilled the soil themselves – an occupation the aristocracy despised as impure. It was this mass of ordinary persons, in fact, who bore the brunt of exploitation in the form of fees and taxes collected by the ruling class. Meanwhile domestic slavery, closely linked to the Atlantic trading system, became the principal feature of the evolution of Senegambian societies during the eighteenth century. So massive was the concentration of slaves in *runde* situated in Futa Jallon and the Southern Rivers area that, towards the end of the eighteenth century, a series of slave revolts broke out in the region.

There is no doubt that the practice of domestic slavery was a root cause of cultural revolution in Futa Jallon. In that region, the marabout and political leadership, freed from the constraints of farm labor, had leisure to devote themselves to education. According to a report left by Winterbottom, who visited Timbo in 1794, the new regime was liberal in its endowment of Koranic schools throughout the country. From then on, Futa Jallon was organized solidly along political and social lines based on the *Sharia*. The sale of fellow-Muslims was forbidden. This saved the region from the sorry spectacle of anarchy and human decimation.[11] That was why, resource-poor though the Futa Jallon plateau was, it was so over-populated. The theocratic kingdom benefited from a stable, secure unity guaranteed by the Muslim ruling class.

Limited as it was, the Muslim revolution was followed by a genuine cultural revolution in the sense that quite early in their rule the marabouts translated the Koran into the Peul language, to facilitate the religious instruction of the population. This cultural revolution was speeded up by the Muslim popularizer Cerno Samba Mombeya. In his famous book, *The Way to Eternal Bliss*, he issued a manifesto for the use of the Peul language as a vehicle for the religious education of the people:

I shall quote the Authentic Ones in the Peul language, to make it easier for you to understand them. When you hear their words, believe them. To each person, only the mother tongue opens the gate to the understanding of the words of the Authentic Ones.

Many Peul, not understanding what is taught them in Arabic, stay trapped in doubt. It is not enough, in the works of Duty, to let doubt guide one's words or deeds.

Let whoever seeks Clarity, shorn of doubt, read here in the Peul language these verses of the common man![12]

The result was not only the birth of a rich, abundant literature in the Peul language but also a deeper Islamization of the ordinary masses. Thus, thanks to the Muslim revolution in the Futa Jallon, the Islam of such medieval cities as Timbuktu and Djenne flowered in Futa Jallon into a popular brand of Islam which later inspired the creation of a chain of theocratic states throughout West Africa. In this respect, Futa Toro was the third link in a long chain of triumphant Muslim revolutions throughout Senegambia in the eighteenth century.

### C.    The Muslim revolution in Futa Toro

After Bundu and Futa Jallon, Islam triumphed in Futa Toro during the second half of the eighteenth century under the leadership of the *Toorodo* marabout movement. This success owed much to the work of Suleyman Bal and Abdul Kader Kan. Here, more than in Bundu and Futa Jallon, the linkage between the *Toorodo* movement and the late seventeenth-century marabout movement of Nasir Al Din was clear. In practice, the *Toorodo* movement was a direct extension of Nasir Al Din's movement. Its basic objectives were also the same. Closely linked with the *Zawaya* Moors, it was substantially modeled on the successful holy war in Bundu and Futa Jallon in the early eighteenth century. For example, Suleyman Bal and Abdul Kader, leaders of the *Toorodo* movement, were alumni of the Muslim schools of Pir and Kokki in the kingdom of Kajoor. These schools were connected with the Daimani *Zawaya* of Mauritania. Spiritual heirs of Nasir Al Din's movement, they settled for a while in Futa Jallon and Bundu, consolidating their faith and installing a theocratic regime in Futa Toro, where the latent crisis of the Denyanke regime cleared the way for the triumph of the *Toorodo* revolution.

Because Saint-Louis was close to the scene, European sources of the time afford a more accurate perception of the political, economic, and social conditions behind the success of Islam in Futa Toro than in Bundu or Futa Jallon. Clearly, the crisis in the delta region during the eighteenth century also ravaged the Futa region of the middle Senegal valley, because of the magnitude of the Atlantic slave trade and the closeness of the Emirates of Brakna and Trarza.

In 1716, Bubakar Sire initiated a succession crisis that lasted throughout the eighteenth century, plunging Futa Toro into insecurity and civil strife. In the second half of the eighteenth century, this situation worsened as a result of a resumption of slave trading organized by the British Governor O'Hara. To facilitate his scheme, O'Hara encouraged the occupation of Futa Toro by Moors from Brakna and Trarza. Under these conditions, the *Toorodo* revolution was directed not only against the Denyanke regime that had lost its ability to ensure security throughout the country, but also against domination by Brakna Moors and the practice of selling Muslims as slaves. Right from the start, then, the *Toorodo* movement led by Suleyman Bal won a military victory against the Ulad Abdallah at Mboya. That ended the payment of the *Mudo Horma*, the annual seed tribute demanded by the Moors. Having imposed its authority in the central Futa region, the *Toorodo* movement ended several centuries of Denyanke rule. From July 1776, it forbade all trade between the British and the Galam area, as a reaction to pillaging raids organized in 1775 by O'Hara in his hunt for slaves.[13]

The victory of the *Toorodo* movement coincided with the death of its prestigious leader, Suleyman Bal. He was succeeded by Abdul Kader Kane, selected, on account of his religious learning, as someone capable of consolidating the new theocratic regime. Once elected *Almami*, Abdul Kader adopted several ceremonial customs from Futa Jallon ritual. At the same time, he maintained selected traditions of the Denyanke regime. Indeed, some Denyanke chiefs who crossed over to the *Toorodo* movement were allowed to keep their domains. Abdul Kader set about redistributing unoccupied land, known as *bayti*, while confirming the rights of the powerful *Toorodo* families over most of central Futa, controlled by three clans: the Bosseyabe, the Yirlabe, and the Hebbyabe. From the start, the powers of the *Almami* Abdul Kader were limited by those of these three clans, from whom the majority of the senior college of Electors, known as *Jaggorde*, came. Among these the best known were the *Ac de Rindiaw*, the family of Ali Dundu, dominant in Bosea, that of Ali Sidi of the Yirlabe, and that of Ali Mamadu. In the face of all these constraints, Abdul Kader still managed to consolidate the new regime, extending his religious influence beyond the borders of Futa Toro, into areas where his success raised great hopes for change among Muslim communities that already constituted powerful minorities within the Wolof and Sereer states. In short, Futa Toro served as a model that heightened tensions between Muslim reformers and the *ceddo* ruling classes of Waalo, Jolof, Kajoor, and Baol. Numerous peasants migrated in this period to Futa Toro, in search of the safety offered by the new regime, which absolutely forbade the sale of Muslims. Furthermore, Abdul Kader encouraged religious instruction in each village along with the construction of a mosque, under the management of an *imam* responsible for the observance of Koranic law in the new theocratic state.

By this time the French had returned, in a weakened position after a long eclipse, to Saint-Louis. Taking advantage of their weakness, Abdul Kader in 1785 imposed his conditions on them. These included a ban on sales of Muslims, payment of annual dues amounting to £900 sterling, plus fees on each vessel passing in transit through the upper Senegal valley. Like the *ceddo* kings, the *Almami* Abdul Kader thought the French ought to have to pay tribute in return for the protection of the Muslim regime, at that time reaching beyond the Futa frontiers in an attempt to impose Islam on its neighbors as the ruling ideology.

The *Toorodo* regime, having consolidated its hold on Futa, set out in 1786 to conquer Trarza. There, too, as he had already done in Brakna, Abdul Kader wished to impose his authority and to exact tribute. Using help from the already conquered Brakna, he defeated the Emir of Trarza, Ely Kowri, who died on the battlefield. Abdul Kader's victory was commemorated in a *qasida* by Mukhtar wuld Buna, a disciple of the Moorish *Zawaya* of the Daimani. It gave practical substance to the brand of Islam conceived a century earlier by Nasir Al Din as a weapon against the highway robbers, the warlike Hassani. For that reason, Abdul Kader considered himself, quite justifiably, the Commander of the Faithful, legitimate heir to Nasir Al Din. In that capacity, he dreamed of imposing Muslim law on the kings of Waalo, Jolof, and Kajoor, whilst expanding his authority over the Upper Senegal valley.

In 1790, however, the new *Damel* of Kajoor, Amari Ngoone Ndeela, rejecting his predecessors' submission to Futa, took severe reprisals against secessionist-minded reformers in the Muslim enclaves of Njambur province. The *Damel* killed the *Almami*'s messenger, Tapsir Hammadi Ibra, and the survivors of this massacre, led by a son of the marabout of Kokki, appealed to Abdul Kader to save the Islamic cause. In response, the *Almami* organized a huge military expedition made up of nearly 30,000 men, women, and children, for the purpose of colonizing Kajoor.

The expedition ended disastrously at Bungoy. The great army was defeated by the *Damel*, Amari Ngoone Ndeela, who very skillfully applied a scorched-earth strategy. Numerous Futanke were sold to slave traders; Abdul Kader was imprisoned in Kajoor, before being transferred to the Futa. Now the *Damel* Amari Ndeela could rest assured that the threat of invasion was definitively over. Oral traditions still recall the magnanimous behavior of the *Damel* Amari Ndeela, who defended with conviction the concept of the *ceddo* state as a secular polity, against the religious proselytization advocated by Abdul Kader in his desire to impose a theocratic state through holy war.[14] Baron Roger suggests, however, that the *ceddo* partisans owed their victory to the support the *Damel* Amari Ngoone obtained from the slave traders of Saint-Louis and Gorée, against the *Almami* Abdul Kader.[15] One reason for such support was the *Almami*'s hostility to the sale of Muslims and to the multiple conflicts between Futa and Saint-Louis from 1787 to 1790, which prevented boats sailing up the upper Senegal valley, and made the supply of millet to the island particularly problematic.[16]

The defeat at Bungoy was the beginning of the decline of the authority of Abdul Kader. Now his rule was challenged in the Futa region itself by

Ali Sidi of the Yirlabé clan and Ali Dundu of the Boséa clan, two influential members of the *Jaggorde* or Electoral Council. The powerful *Toorodo* family of Thierno Molle, hostile to the religious puritanism of Abdul Kader, forced the *Almami* to leave the capital and to settle on his own estate at Kobbilo. Meanwhile, Ali Sidi and Ali Dundu, upstart illiterate princes, pushed their way into power as the only intermediaries between the central regime and the eastern and western provinces of Futa.

This internal challenge to the regime came at a time of worsening hostility between Futa and the Saint-Louis trading post, whose business on the Senegal River had been interrupted from 1801 to 1803. Saint-Louis had refused to pay customary duties at the usual rate. Furthermore, it had sent an expedition of twelve boats upstream to burn some ten villages in western Futa and to take 600 captives, most of them members of the *Toorodo* ruling class. In 1805, Futa took its revenge, and, the following year, a new agreement was arrived at confirming the 1785 treaty. The break in business had hurt both sides.

For several years Abdul Kader had been without supplies of arms and trade goods needed to shore up his authority. That authority had thus come under increasing challenge from within the regime itself. Now he chose to mount an expedition in the upper Senegal valley to stop the raids of the *Almami* Séga, who was pillaging the Bundu marabouts. Abdul Kader had Séga executed, appointing in his place his own protégé Hammadi Pate in preference to another contender, the popular Hammadi Aïssata. In reaction, the latter concluded an alliance with the king of Kaarta.

The growing hostility of Saint-Louis, coupled with increasing opposition from members of the *Jaggorde* electoral council, prevented Abdul Kader taking part in the alliance between Kaarta and Bundu led by Hammadi Aïssata. Deposed by the *Jaggorde*, Abdul Kader formed an alliance with Gajaaga and Khaaso. In 1807 he was defeated by the combined forces of Bundu and Kaarta, aided by second-generation members of the *Toorodo* movement. Thus the death of Abdul Kader set the scene for the triumph of the Electoral Council, the *Jaggorde*. From now on they were free to impose an *Almami* devoted to their interests, and to retain substantial autonomy in their various fiefdoms.[17]

As in Bundu and in Futa Jallon, the leadership of the marabout movement had originally been made up of scholars. The generation to which they bequeathed political power was a military aristocracy with no pretensions whatsoever to religious erudition. The situation, in short, was similar to that of the old *ceddo* regimes. Power now became the exclusive property of hereditary clans locked in a ruthless power struggle. A new *Toorodo* oligarchy emerged that had nothing to do with the ideals of the 1776 revolution. Still, the revolution had confirmed for good the Muslim nature of state and society in Futa Toro, as distinct from the *ceddo* regimes still in power in the Wolof and Sereer kingdoms as well as in southern Senegambia.

Abdul Kader had failed in his attempts to impose Islam as the state ideology in the Wolof kingdoms. But his failure was considerably offset by substantial progress made by home-grown marabout movements in the region. Muslims had gained increasing numbers of adherents, and were trying to oppose the violent *ceddo* regimes from within. Kajoor was an outstanding example. There, the defeat of Abdul Kader at Bungoy was followed by a mass exodus of Muslims from Njambur province. They moved to the Cape Verde peninsula, where they helped found a theocracy under Jal Joop. These exiles from Njambur joined forces with Lebu opponents of the regime to resist the exactions of the *Damel*'s law enforcement officers. In the process, they also reinforced secessionist tendencies working against the central regime in the kingdom of Kajoor. The secessionists, after several years of resistance by the marabout movement, won their independence, marking the first territorial breakup and the triumph of Islam in the kingdom of Kajoor.[18]

The *ceddo* kingdoms, just like the theocratic kingdoms of Senegambia, felt the impact of the slave trade. That trade continued to be the principal cause of economic stagnation and chronic political and social crisis in the region.

# 8    The impact of the slave trade: economic regression and social strife

There is no doubt that the slave trade was the basic business of the Atlantic trading system from the seventeenth century to the nineteenth. Throughout this long period, the selling and buying of human beings, direct producers of goods, determined relations between Senegambia and the European powers. It also determined the nexus of economic, political, and social relationships within the region's various states.

The slave trade and its corollary, warfare between the Senegambian states, were a permanent part of a situation of chronic violence imposed within each state by the existence of a military aristocracy reigning above peasant populations, potential victims of slave raids. Slave trading became a royal monopoly based on violence. As such, it prevented the peasant population working productively under secure conditions.

The result was economic regression. Evidence that this was the state of affairs in all domains can be deduced from the innumerable famines punctuating the history of Senegambia throughout the long slaving era. The famines were caused sometimes by warfare, at other times by natural disasters, the consequences of which aggravated the population drain caused by the massive export of producers as slaves. On the domestic level, the slave trade deepened habits of servility in relationships between free men and slaves. Domestic slavery became an integral complement to the Atlantic slave trade.

In northern Senegambia, royal slaves became instruments serving the arbitrary power of *ceddo* regimes. The region also suffered from slaving raids organized by the Moorish emirates of Trarza and Brakna, and, beyond these, by the Sultanate of Morocco. The combination produced a situation of chronic upheaval that blocked the emergence of a classic slave-based production system. Domestic slaves could be sold off at any time. So could peasants. In southern Senegambia, especially in the Muslim theocracy of Futa Jallon, a region long sheltered from foreign invasions, domestic slavery developed in close tandem with the slave trade. The proliferation of *runde*, slave villages segregated from villages of free persons, was intended both to meet the food needs of the aristocracy and to grow food

107

for supplying slave-trading vessels plying the coast. The massive concentration of slaves at collection points in the Southern Rivers area, under the control of slave traders, was devised to meet food production needs in the rainy season and during the human export period in the dry season. Slaves also served as head porters for trade produce from the remote Senegambian hinterland to the coast – an essential aspect of the slave trade.

The violence of slave-holding relationships, and above all the tremendous exploitation of slaves, led to frequent slave revolts in the *runde* situated along roads leading to the coast, as well as in slave pens at the trading posts and factories. Lastly, the slave trade bound Senegambia definitively to the New World. Thousands of slaves exported there remembered their homelands. By the eighteenth and nineteenth centuries, they had already begun to establish indissoluble links between Africans in the diaspora and those on the African continent.

## A.     Natural disasters, warfare and famine

European sources, like oral traditions, confirm the occurrence of innumerable famines. Some were due to natural disasters, but others were the result of wars attendant on inter-state conflicts within Senegambia. Like natural disasters, warfare ended up providing major opportunities for meeting the chronic demand for export labor. The population drain was a key reason for the regression of productive forces in Senegambian societies, whose ability to resist the impact of natural calamities was reduced to zero. Despite a long series of famines caused by drought, floods, or locust invasions, Charles Becker provides solid evidence showing correlations between outbreaks of famine and the development of the slave trade. Correlations were especially close in times of war, which often coincided with the farming season.[1]

Senegambia's climatological history is still at an embryonic stage. Even so, various sources agree that the inter-tropical front shifted northward from the fifteenth to the sixteenth century, and that the change made agriculture possible in what is now southern Mauritania. The rise in relative humidity after that change led to the settlement, over appreciably wide stretches of land north of the Senegal River, of populations of Wolof, Tukulor, or Soninke. In the late sixteenth century the climate became drier. By the mid-eighteenth century it had reached its peak of aridity. As a result, all of northern Senegambia became exposed to the risk of drought, now a cyclical factor in the history of the Sahel. Curtin, the first scholar to draw up a balance sheet of the resulting series of natural disasters, analyses climatic data as though they were independent realities. In so doing, he overlooks the role played by human agents in the modification of the environment. Above all, he plays down correlations between warfare caused by slave trading, and droughts and famines.[2] Correlations between natural disasters and the devastating wars that fed the slave trade were so obvious that European sources, typically sparing of detail in their descriptions, mentioned them only when they had an impact on the trans-Atlantic trading system. The invaluable documentary collection put together by Charles Becker, notwithstanding the geographically and historically fragmentary nature of the European sources, clearly shows how frequently famines related to wars or natural calamities occurred.[3]

As early as 1606, Van Den Broeke reported that a locust invasion at Portudal had forced parents into selling their children to meet subsistence needs. A second locust invasion, between 1639 and 1641, caused the death of numerous inhabitants and pushed survivors into selling themselves as slaves to save their lives, according to a report by Dapper. In 1676, Chambonneau gave a detailed account of the consequences of the War of the Marabouts in the Senegal valley. He said some inhabitants of Futa Toro were obliged to offer themselves up as slaves in times of famine following periods of warfare. Chambonneau did a good job of picking out a striking correlation: periods of famine coincided with gluts on the slave market. Beyond that, he explained the enduring paradox of the slave trade: the fact that despite the glut, trade still tended to slump considerably after famines. For shortages of millet or rice meant that slave dealers could not feed the slaves in their prisons along the coast or on ships during the Atlantic crossing. To quote Chambonneau,

Throughout the year 1676, [the new ruling *Brak* of Waalo] spent all his time killing, taking captives, pillaging and burning the Toubenan region. He went as far as the very residence of Bourguli, devastating millet farms, cutting down seedlings. So complete was the destruction he caused that people were forced to eat boiled grass, carrion and bits of leather. This I saw in my travels in Futa during the month of July 1676. Moreover, entire familes asked me to take them captive, saying they would thereby have something to eat. So low had they sunk that they were reduced to killing each other to steal food. I did not wish to take any of them without first paying their price to some third party or to the captive himself, who transferred the goods paid for him to whomever he chose. It was necessary to go through these motions to forestall the very dangerous consequences that could arise. Thus, had we not run out of trade goods, we could this year have bought more than six hundred. As matters stood, some ships, mine in particular, could take on no more slaves.[4]

From 1719 to 1724, all of northern Senegambia was ravaged by pillaging Orman warriors, who tightened the domination of the Trarza and Brakna emirates over the sedentary populations of the Senegal valley. In general, from then on the people became victims of the Atlantic slave trade quite as much as of the trans-Saharan slave trade, in which they were used for gathering gum. The development of a slave-holding mode of production based on the use of thousands of black slaves, known as *Haratin*, was the key feature of the evolution of Berber societies to the north of Senegambia. Invariably, periods of woe caused by Orman pillagers were times of multiple natural disasters which worsened the food crisis. For instance, according to Morin, the great drought of 1720 caused a famine, with the result that in May 1721, 133 captives died for lack of millet to feed them.[5] A 1724 letter from Duballay described a situation of widespread famine that forced three-quarters of the population to feed on soil and roots, following an Orman invasion in Futa Toro coupled with a drought.[6] There are numerous eyewitness accounts of Orman raids and food shortages affecting all of northern Senegambia and lasting until 1744, except for a few years' brief reprieve.

From 1747 to 1754, a long cycle of drought occurred throughout Senegambia, causing mortality rates to peak. Wars and the Atlantic slave trade aggravated the situation. Apart from poor harvests in 1750–1, famines also resulted from succession wars in Kajoor from 1751 to 1754. In addition, there were civil wars in Futa and Galam, instigated by Orman agents. Evidence of a general famine in Senegambia in 1752–53 comes from numerous sources, all emphasizing the unusual harshness of the 1752 drought. On this point a letter from the High Council was quite explicit:

The general wretchedness of the country has made the ruling *Brak*, our neighbor, along with everyone in the Walo area, more demanding, and our fear of offending him has made us more easy-going. Never before in this territory has there been such widespread famine. It rages from Bissau all the way to Galam, and we are having a difficult time indeed finding food for nearly 600 captives.[7]

In 1753, 164 captives died in Saint-Louis, after the last ship had cast off, from lack of food. In 1754, famines still raging in the kingdoms of Kajoor and Baol drove destitute refugees into Waalo; there the ruling *Brak* sold them.

They knew for certain they would be captured. But that did not stop them from going to the only place where they could find relief from their misery. Since the only choices open to them were death or captivity, one can assume that the trade in slaves will not end until the off-season millet harvest comes in. That means waiting until the end of September.[8]

Wars between Kajoor and Baol, on the one hand, and between Kajoor and Jolof on the other, devastated the entire region, considerably increasing the number of captives. Sales were limited only by the shortage of food. Traders in Gorée had to raise the price of millet tenfold to persuade mainlanders to sell their own vital subsistence reserves. In any case, nearly a quarter of the population died following the notorious famine of 1751–4. War, pillage, and natural disasters combined to reduce considerably the productive capacity of the population. The following remarks, made about Kajoor in 1758, held true for all Senegambia in the era of the slave traders:

Kajoor is poor, uncultured. Kings in this country are bandits living only from pillage. As such, they destroy absolutely every possibility of their nation ever being motivated to work their lands.[9]

From 1764 until 1776, available documents indicate that the Moors, who monopolized the millet and gum markets, played a leading role in pillaging the land. The pillaging expeditions of Irarza Moors into Waalo in 1775, with help from O'Hara, typified the desolation to which the region's sedentary population were reduced by the highly mobile Berbers.[10] In 1786, drought and a locust invasion caused famine in the Gambia. People there were reduced to the awful necessity of selling each other to survive. For example, Manding from Kaabu used their grain reserves to ensnare and sell thousands of Felupe in the area between Cape Sainte-Marie and Cape Roxo as slaves.[11]

Oral traditions from different periods testify to the cycles of war, famine, and drought. Yet they offer no explanation of the historical context, connected to the slave trade. Recent authors, like N.I.A. de Moraes, A. Delcourt, and Philip Curtin, likewise emphasize natural conditions or warfare as explanations for famines, but they fail to point out the close linkage between famines and the slave trade. Yet that, in the final analysis, was the root cause of the widespread violence that reduced all productive forces to nothing.[12]

Charles Becker's recent work emphasizes interactions between natural and climatic conditions (droughts, floods, locust invasions) and the political climate, typified by inter-state warfare and violence within individual states. He concludes that the slave trade was the decisive context for famines and the population drain. Charles Becker's partial summary of the causes of famine and general penury is a good example of interconnections between natural phenomena and the slave trade. He cites references to periods of famine and food shortages lasting a total of about fifteen years in the seventeenth century. Droughts, poor rains, and locust invasions were certainly among the causes; but their consequences were aggravated by warfare, pillage, and the slave trade. Documentary evidence from the eighteenth century points to a definite deterioration of the climate and a degradation of ecological conditions linked to natural and human factors. Famines and shortages were indicated for at least thirty years – a third of that century. Charles Becker lists twelve explicit references to drought or poor rainfall leading to famines or food shortages, four cases of flood, and four locust invasions. Lastly, there is a score of references to famines linked to wars closely related to pillaging expeditions and the slave trade. There is therefore no doubt that ecological conditions deteriorated. In some cases the consequence was a long series of disastrous years, as happened from 1719 to 1725, 1729 to 1737, and, more severely, from 1747 to 1758 and from 1782 to 1789. In addition, the eighteenth century saw an indisputable deterioration in the socio-political climate, a proliferation of armed conflicts, and an increase in the number of pillaging expeditions. The result was an aggravation of conditions in peasant societies across the board.[13]

Still, evaluation of the population drain caused by natural calamities, wars, and slaving raids remains a difficult exercise. What is certain is that all border zones, being particularly exposed to pillage and to slave raids, ended up deserted. Equally depopulated was the north bank of the Senegal River, constantly raided by the Moorish emirates. The relocation of Waalo's capital, from Jurbel on the north bank to Nder on the south, gives a good indication of the migratory trend from north to south. People migrated within individual states too, especially into Muslim settlements where religious regimes offered their followers protection from the depredations of *ceddo* warrior aristocrats. And the *Toorodo* revolution in Futa Toro drew many Wolofs from Waalo, Kajoor, and Jolof to the new sanctuary.

Decreasing rainfall levels were also responsible, from the seventeenth century, for major changes in the region's vegetation cover as well as in the availability of water. Contemporary European documents mention forests in what is now southern Mauritania. Today there is none. In particular, the destruction of gum-producing groves in the region was closely related to the intensity of the gum trade in the Senegal valley and on the Mauritanian coast between Portendick and Saint-Louis.[14]

To sum up, then, deteriorating ecological conditions were closely linked to the Atlantic trading system, which was centered on the slave trade. Given the disastrous economic, political, and social impact of the slave trade, Europeans were caught in a bind in their attempts to achieve two major commercial objectives. Their first objective was to buy the largest possible number of slaves. Their second was to provide regular food supplies for slave factories and slaving vessels. The first objective they achieved by multiplying wars, pillaging expeditions, and local conflicts. But the second required peaceful security in the source countries.[15] Meanwhile, quite apart from the ecological, demographic, and economic consequences of the slave trade, its greatest impact came in the transformation of social and political relationships in Senegambian societies.

## B.     Slaveholding relationships in Senegambian societies

Slavery is an ancient institution in Africa. There is evidence of the use of slave labor on farms, in households, in armies, in handicraft work, and in the trans-Saharan trade, long before the onset of the seaborne slave trade. But the Atlantic slave trade, which dominated the region from the sixteenth century, intensified slave–master relationships in all areas of Senegambian life. The development of domestic slavery was closely linked to demand from the Atlantic trading system for slave labor. Slaveholding regimes in Senegambia developed along two main lines. First, *ceddo* power, in essence the power of royal slaves, became entrenched in political life. Second, in domestic life, there was a build-up of large concentrations of captive laborers in *runde*, where they were employed in production for household needs.

Slavery is the total domination, by force, of an individual or group by a master or masters. It is an institution of long standing, in which slaves were used both as trade goods and as instruments of production. This dual use indicates how important slavery was to existing social and economic systems. That the geographical scope of slavery in Senegambia expanded, and that the institution developed over time, is a matter of clear record. To understand this, we have to take into account both the twin contexts of the trans-Atlantic and trans-Saharan slave trades and the use, in the Senegambian region itself, of slave labor in agriculture, handicrafts, mining, housework and military service. It was this dual function that brought about the important distinction between slaves born into that status and those recently bought or captured.[16]

Wolof society, first of all, had a category of freshly acquired slaves called *jaam-sayoor*. These were absolutely dependent on their masters. Throughout the day they worked on their masters' farms. In turn, their masters were responsible for meeting all their needs. Such slaves could be sold at any moment, given to a creditor to secure a loan, offered in lieu of dowry, removed from their families, separated from their children.[17] During the slave trade, the condition of such slaves became particularly harsh and insecure. The main reason was the generally dangerous atmosphere. But there was also the risk of slave raids, in which both masters and slaves could be captured. The situation of this category of slaves seems to have been the same throughout Senegambia.

Slaves born in captivity belonged to a second category. They were called *jaam juddu* in Wolof. These house slaves were generally integrated into their masters' families. They were given productive responsibilites similar to those of free-born servants known as *surga*. Slaves with their own families worked mornings on their masters' farms, then spent afternoons on their own farms. Alternatively, in some regions, they were given one or two days a week to till their own farms.[18] It took little time for the considerable increase in the number of domestic slaves to produce a segregated residential pattern, with free persons and slaves inhabiting separate villages. This pattern of concentration and spatial segregation was particularly plain in the Muslim theocracy of Futa Jallon. There, the relative protection the kingdom offered from external invasions, coupled with the intense demand for internal slave labor, led to the growth of a large number of *runde*.

The installation of Muslim theocratic regimes led immediately to the mass subjection of Jalonke and Pulli populations long resident in Futa Jallon but unreceptive to Islam. Meanwhile, the Muslim concept of holy war, which the powerful military theocracy of Futa Jallon used as a cover for pillaging neighboring states, soon became the main method for obtaining slaves to meet both the internal demand for farm and craft labor and the external demands of the Atlantic trading system. Several researchers have supposed that conquered populations in the area were reduced *en masse* to slavery. It is an assumption that reduces the history of Futa Jallon to a simple ethnic conflict between invading Peuls and indigenous Jallonke turned *en masse* into slaves. The assumption rides on the ethnic kinship between long-established Jallonke inhabitants of Futa Jallon and slaves captured during raids in the Futa Jallon plateau region. But data on all wars and raids organized by the powerful Muslim state of Futa Jallon indicate clearly that the kingdom reached far and wide in its search for slaves. It went as far as the Niger to the east, to Niokolo in the north, to the Atlantic in the west, and to Toma and Kissi in the south.[19] The point is that a main reason for the large-scale concentration of slaves in *runde* was the use of slave labor both for the Atlantic trading system and for domestic labor. This concentration was possible because Futa Jallon was such a powerful kingdom in northern Senegambia. Its position was similar to that of its contemporaries, the kingdoms of Asante and Dahomey in the Gulf of Benin.

The numerous wars fought against the Solimana, the Sankaran and the Wasulu in the east, as well as against the Kaabu in the Southern Rivers and the north-west, were the principal means by which Futa Jallon obtained slaves. Thus, straightforward capture (*konu*) in wars of conquest waged under cover of Muslim holy wars brought thousands of slaves into the Futa region after each expedition. The second method used for the acquisition of slaves was the *gubali*, in which provincial chieftains or their sons conducted surprise attacks against pagan villages situated next to them. In the nineteenth century, these main methods were reinforced by barter. The armies of Samori and Shaykh Umar exchanged slaves for the cattle they needed for food.[20] Such large-scale purchases of slaves, even after the Atlantic slave trade was to all intents abolished, show how important a part slavery played in the domestic production system of Futa Jallon. It is hard to estimate the number of slaves inhabiting the *runde*. Hecquart, in 1853, estimated slaves to be as numerous as free persons, if not more so. Clearly, their number varied from period to period, and differences must have depended principally on the relative importance of the Atlantic and domestic markets.

Invariably, slaves living together in the *runde* had the lowest social status. Mamadou Saliou Baldé sheds useful light on the role of slaves in agriculture and mining in Futa Jallon. He points out that ironsmiths lived in the slave villages and had the same low social status. The reason for a social structure discriminating between free persons and slaves was the existence of large numbers of slaves. As a rule, the distinction represented a division of labor. Among free persons, especially if they belonged to the slave-owning military and clerical aristocracy, manual work was synonymous with social degradation. Islam, after all, provided an ideological justification for the enslavement of pagans:

God commanded our father Adam to work. But he also created pagans, people with hard skulls and strong arms, fit for nothing higher than to work, and obviously destined to serve believers.

Slavery, then, gave free men, especially the class of Muslim clerics, the leisure to devote themselves entirely to the study of the Koran. Needless to say, they took care to deny slaves any opportunity to obtain the kind of religious education that might lead them to challenge the ideology legitimizing discrimination between the free, cultured person (*gando*) and the ignorant slave (*Maccudo Ko mo jangaa*). The free person was an *ndimu*; the slave, on the other hand, was the man who belonged to someone else, a *jiyaado*. He had no rights, and wielded power neither over himself nor over anyone else. A social cipher, he was known as a *wawaado*. As a piece of private property, he was not allowed to leave the *runde* unless authorized by his master. Otherwise he could be put in chains (*dumbeede*). As an item of movable property, like furniture (*jawdi dariidi*), he could be sold or bartered. By definition he was someone else's property. He himself did not possess even the hat he wore. Children of male slaves inherited their father's slave status. Children of female slaves belonged automatically to their mothers' owners. Slaves were thus totally dependent on their masters.

Slave-owners, nevertheless, did not have powers of life and death over their slaves. They could not deliberately kill them. Slaves could also change masters by destroying the property of a kinder master and getting themselves given to them in lieu of damages. Generally, indeed, harsh treatment was reserved for first-generation slaves. Second generation slaves (*ndiima*) lived under less stringent conditions. Born and bred in the same area, they were normally less tempted to run away. Their children seldom left their master's family. The master avoided selling them outside the kingdom even when forced to trade them. Third-generation slaves were called *ndiima nduka*. The idea was that the relationship between them and their masters was as intimate as that between the snuff box and the snuff taker. They enjoyed the total trust of their masters, who delegated political and economic responsibilities to them, in a relationship strengthened through marriage ties. Third generation slaves, in short, had practically the same status as freed slaves.[21]

Slave labor, then, was the basis of economic activity in the Futa region. Slaves worked five days a week for their masters. They only had two days, Fridays and Saturdays, to take care of their own needs. Slave labor was widely used in farm work in the form of community work, known as *kile*. It was also used in craft work to meet the needs of the aristocracy. Slaves, concentrated in *runde*, took an active part in subsistence farming. But they also worked to supply cereals for export. Slaving vessels plying the coast, for instance, needed supplies of rice. This dual use of slave labor was the reason for the existence of slave-based production relationships in southern Senegambia. However, the institution here developed in a way different from that of the slave plantations of the American South or the Caribbean. The fact that the export of labor power was given priority led, in substantial measure, to the failure of the dominant production mode then, the tributary mode, to develop into other modes such as the purely slave-based mode, the feudal mode, or the capitalist mode. The subsistence economy, in effect, blocked the possibility of any form of social or economic revolution that might have changed political relationships in fundamental ways.

In southern Senegambia, and especially in Futa Jallon, where master–slave relationships were predominant, slaves were excluded from political participation. The best that second- or third-generation slaves could hope for was to enroll in the army as *suufa*. Some also served in the personal guard of the *Almamy* or of heads of administrative *Diwal*. The head man of a *runde*, chosen from among the most faithful servants, was officially known as the *Manga*. In other words, the perpetuation of master–slave relationships was the main condition for the reproduction of the social system. In Futa Jallon, the appearance of large-scale slavery was correlated to the slave trade and the establishment of Muslim regimes. For this reason, the survival of the theocratic regime was closely dependent on the perpetuation of this social relationship. For slave labor freed the aristocracy to take its hand off productive work, concentrating wholeheartedly on politics and slave raiding along with the study and explanation of holy scripture, while nurturing the social groups needed to shore up its domination and to perpetuate it.[22]

The trans-Atlantic slave trade involved the large-scale export of slaves in exchange for European merchandise, chiefly firearms and gunpowder. Domestic slavery, on the other hand, developed as a way to ensure the society's survival within a framework of relationships between villages of free men (*misiide*) and *runde*. In order to maintain the slave labor reserve for meeting domestic needs while at the same time supplying the massive export demand for slaves, slave owners tended to sell more male slaves to trans-Atlantic slave traders, and to keep slave women and children at home. The prior emphasis placed on the export of male slaves was clearest in such slave-based societies as Kaabu and Futa Jallon. Jean Mettas, on the basis of shipping logs for vessels arriving at Parâ and Maranhâo from the Southern Rivers in 1780–1, gives this as the explanation for the disproportionate number of men as compared to women. The log book, incidentally, listed female arrivals separately from males. Mettas counts 624 women out of a total of 2,242 captives, or 28 percent.[23] Occasionally, though, the percentage of women rose higher than the generally preferred norm of one woman for every two men. This happened in Bissau, for instance, where the percentage of women rose to 37 percent from 1758 to 1764, and to 43 percent from 1766 to 1777. In those cases, the slaves were captives of the Bijago, the Balante, and the Felupe, none of whom practiced domestic slavery. So they sold all their captives from the Bahun, Manjaco, and Papel groups, among whom it was easier to capture women than men.[24]

Women slaves played an indisputably important role. They reproduced slave children and were active in economic life. Children born to a woman slave belonged to her master. Moreover, it cost slave owners less to take women slaves for concubines, and a master could marry as many of the *jaariya* as he pleased. However, children of free men born to women slaves were bound to no one, enjoying the same rights as free men. Many highly placed political leaders, from provincial chieftains all the way through to the central regime of the *Almamis*, were born of slave mothers.[25] As a result, the entire society was intimately involved in the slaveholding system. The procedure for crossing over from slave to free status was carefully codified in such a way as to integrate into the community of free men, known as the *rimbe*, selected slaves accorded privileges in return for services rendered to their masters.

Similarly, all along the Southern Rivers coastline, concentrations of thousands of slaves, some belonging to Euro-African slave dealers, some to local chiefs, sprang up and grew in the course of the eighteenth century. Slave traders and chiefs in Rio Nunez, Rio Pongo, and Rio Cacheu kept large numbers of slaves ready for export on a permanent basis. To guard the slave factories, they formed armies from selected slaves. Above all, they used the labor of these slaves for farm work in the rainy season, while waiting to sell them to slaving vessels in the dry season. The slaves had plenty of farm work to do, since demand for rice and millet to supply slave factories and ships crossing the Atlantic was extremely high. Toward the end of the eighteenth century, wealthy slave-trading families like the Caulkers or the Clevelands came to possess large slave villages on the African mainland, across from the Banana Islands. They used the inhabitants for large-scale rice farming. Such massive use of slave labor in the production system became common among Susu chiefdoms on the coast.[26] In 1750, John Newton bought nearly 8 tonnes of rice to feed 200 slaves. John Mathews estimated that between 700 and 1,000 tonnes of rice were required to feed 3,000 to 3,500 slaves sold to slave dealers on the Sierra Leonean coast. The substantial demand for cereals was met by slave villages maintained by Manding, Susu, and Peul groups, as well as by those Euro-African slave traders who opted to use their slave labor for farm work on the coast.[27] Some slave dealers were known to have as many as 5,000 slaves in their factories. Such massive concentrations of slaves created conditions for full-scale slave rebellions.

Slavery in southern Senegambia, in short, was an integral part of the economic, political, and social system dominated by the slave trade. The system here, characterized by the export not of products but of the producers themselves, differed from the American or West Indian system in two aspects: the latter was marked by racism; in addition, it used slave labor as the locomotive force for the capitalist economy serving metropolitan European needs. In that system, Senegambia remained a bottomless reservoir feeding the New World with slave labor, even while within local society as a whole, slaves were integrated into the subsistence production system. Master–slave relationships were part of a tributary mode of production, at the time still the dominant mode in most Senegambian societies. In any case, while in southern Senegambia, especially in Futa Jallon, slaves played a major role in the economic production system, in northern Senegambia their role was different. For the political instability and the frequency of slaving raids there meant that slaves tended to be used more often in a military role, and sometimes even in political struggles. In the Wolof, Sereer, Soninke, and Denyanke kingdoms, royal slaves played a pivotal part in the affairs of established *ceddo* regimes from the seventeenth to the nineteenth century. In this particular respect, the strengthening of the status of royal slaves ran parallel to the development of the trans-Atlantic slave trade, which increased the frequency of wars and predatory raids in northern Senegambia. After the break-up of the Jolof kingdom, the absence of any major power capable of ensuring a secure existence for the peasant population of the hinterland laid the many states of northen Senegambia open to internal conflicts and to raids organized by Berber emirates to the north. For that reason, warfare became the main business of the region's ruling military aristocracies. Sometimes they fought to defend themselves against invaders; sometimes they mounted raids against neighboring states. And there were times when they simply made war on their own subjects. Pillage became the leading economic occupation. The consequence was the reinforcement of the status of royal slaves, functioning as professional soldiers, in the region's political affairs.

Slaves belonging to the king or to members of royal families, known as *jaami buur*, made up the royal bodyguards as well as the core of the armed forces. In political and administrative affairs, they were entrusted with posts as ministers, provincial governors or tax collectors. They were the most effective supports of the royal power of *ceddo* regimes. On behalf of the aristocracy, they took part in raids on ordinary peasants, the *baadolo*. Paying neither rent nor taxes, they became, to all practical intents, members of the ruling strata. It was all the easier for slaves to become integrated into the ruling aristocracy since slave families with a long record of service to the monarchy married into their masters' families, establishing patron–client bonds with them.[28]

The military role played by royal slaves, now functionally indistinguishable from the *ceddo* regimes themselves, gave rise to the misuse of the term *ceddo*, properly speaking an attribute of the ruling warrior group, to refer to the class of slave-born soldiers totally devoted to their masters' interests. In the atmosphere of ubiquitous violence that became the regional norm, royal slaves became key players in monarchical regimes. The rise in status of this *ceddo* group, which took an active part in warfare and raided peasant communities, was closely linked to the development of the slave trade. *Ceddo* warriors, armed with guns, were direct participants in all the succession conflicts that periodically shattered the stability of northern Senegambian kingdoms. They thus came to enjoy a privileged political status, to the detriment of peasants and notables. In all aspects of life, they became instruments of arbitrary rule, agents aiding in the centralization of monarchical power. This role of slaves within the army emerged in spectacular form in the Bambara kingdoms of Kaarta and Segu, lying east of Senegambia. Segu was an especially clear case. For the royal slaves, called *Jonjon*, imposed a new dynasty under Ngolo Jarra (1776–90) which lasted until 1860. Royal slaves, belonging to the dominant group, thus contributed directly to the intensification of the slave trade through warfare and pillage. In the development of domestic slavery as much as in that of the military use of slaves, the export of slaves remained a basic factor throughout the long duration of the slave trade, which to a large extent determined the evolution of the domestic slave-holding system.

Consideration of the impact of the slave trade as a process that put a premium on the large-scale export of slave labor brings us to an important issue: was there, or was there not, a slave-holding mode of production in Senegambia? Since the publication of the work on slavery in Africa edited by Claude Meillassoux, and other work by Suzanne Miers and Igor Kopytoff exploring historical and anthropological angles of the topic, studies on slavery have proliferated in all fields. These studies have now been supplemented by Lovejoy's recent work on slavery in Africa and the work of Claire Robertson and Martin Klein on women and slavery in Africa.[29] These many studies have contributed greatly to the advancement of knowledge on the evolution of slavery in Africa. However, with the exception of Lovejoy's recent study, which resituates slavery within its real historical and chronological context, the other works are primarily case studies in which there is no closely argued attempt to place specific cases within the general context of the institution's historical evolution. The authors of these studies, in other words, instead of examining the institution of slavery across time, as an integral component within the total context of African societies in their interactions with the rest of the world, relegate history to a secondary status behind sociology or anthropology. There lies the problem: studies offering overviews of slavery in Africa antedated the historical monographs in which they ought, in all scholarly logic, to have been grounded. Generalizations covering the entire continent have been rushed into print on the basis of narrow samples. Worse still, the absence of a time dimension has made the research static, incapable of advancing toward explanations of the evolution of the institution of slavery in African societies.

In the particular instance of Senegambia, there is incontrovertible evidence that slavery as an institution existed in most societies in the region in the fifteenth and sixteenth centuries. Slave-holding was part of the dominant tributary mode of production. But it was the trans-Atlantic trading system which, in the course of the slave trade that lasted from the seventeenth to the nineteenth century, gave the institution of domestic slavery a special spin. And in that process the trans-Saharan trade in slaves played only a subsidiary role. The process as a whole needs to be examined in greater detail before the drawing of generalized conclusions.

Clearly, in northern Senegambia the climate of insecurity and warfare did a great deal to reinforce the role of royal slaves in military and political affairs, as instruments of arbitrary aristocratic power. In southern Senegambia, on the other hand, where slaves were concentrated in *runde* to serve the aristocracy, their role in the production system was more important. In both cases, slavery was a fundamental institution designed to ensure the protection and survival of the aristocracy. In the seventeenth and eighteenth centuries as well as in part of the nineteenth century, however, this dual function of the institution of slavery was intimately hooked to the trans-Atlantic trading system. In specific terms, it was harnessed to the export trade in slave labor, generally speaking the dominant commercial activity of the time. In the context of the Atlantic trading system, producers became the main product brought to market. The result was that the evolution of domestic slavery became dependent on a basic reality: the dominance of a predatory economy. The sale of producers as slaves became the principal activity that blocked the emergence of a genuine slave-holding mode of production independent of large-scale exports of slave labor. In this way the slave trade frustrated all possibility of progress toward other forms of the tributary mode of production, which remained dominant. The key factor, in short, was this stalling impact of the slave trade, which blocked the way toward all qualitative change in the society through the stagnation of its economy and its technological infrastructure.

The stall did not prevent the reinforcement of the slave-holding institution in close connection with the impact of the slave trade on Senegambian societies as a whole. A study of that impact remains to be done, region by region, in a series of case studies carefully articulated within their historical context. Such a historical vision is necessary to the understanding of the importance of slavery in Senegambia's societies. Evidence of that importance is provided partly by the seriousness and extent of slave revolts in the region, partly by the links subsequently established between Senegambia and the black diaspora transplanted to America.

## C.    Slave revolts and the Senegambian diaspora

The high concentration of labor power in *runde*, coupled with the presence of large numbers of captives in slave factories on the coast, led to frequent and violent slave revolts during this long era of the slave traders. By the same token, the forced transfer of thousands of slaves from Senegambia to the New World created indissoluble bonds between the two areas. The fate of thousands of Senegambian slaves in the hell of the plantations was the same as that of survivors from wars, raids, and famines back home.

The systematic intensification of slave trading and the parallel development of domestic slavery on a large scale in segregated villages did a great deal to spark slave revolts. From Futa Jallon to the Southern Rivers, the Senegambian region witnessed a large number of slave revolts of a remarkably intense violence.[30]

As early as 1720, the slave trader John Akins referred to a resistance movement led by one Chief Tamba in the Rio Nunez valley. Tamba successfully organized his people to fight the slave traders on the coast and their collaborators. Captured and sold into slavery, Tamba organized a shipboard revolt with help from a woman slave. He was killed by the slavers, who forced his companions to eat his heart and liver before being killed in their turn, to serve as an example to survivors of the clamp-down. Meanwhile, the concentration of thousands of slaves in *runde*, especially in Futa, caused many more attempted breakouts and slave revolts. Substantial numbers of slaves, having fled captivity, created refugee camps from where they put up stiff resistance against attempts at recapture. Of the full scale slave rebellions caused by the high concentration of captives in slave villages, the earliest on record dates back to around 1756. The rebel slaves, having successfully resisted their masters, collectively migrated toward north-western Futa Jallon. There they built a fortified settlement called Koondeah. There are clear indications that Futa Jallon was the theater of numerous slave revolts toward the end of the eighteenth century. Watt's eyewitness account confirms the information that the Futa Jallon aristocracy was constantly on the lookout for slave revolts. Anxious to reduce the chances of such uprisings, they made it illegal for slaves to bear arms. Despite their precautions, Watt cites two rebellions. The first took place in 1794, a few years before he arrived on the scene. The second occurred before he traveled from the coast to the hinterland. He reports an encounter with the official who oversaw the execution of thirty rebel leaders, part of the effort to put down the movement.[31] This serious rebellion coincided with a period of political upheaval in Futa Jallon following the death of the Grand *Almami* Ibrahima Sori. Civil strife did a great deal to weaken the ranks of the aristocracy. This created an opportunity for a slave rebellion. The rebels seized it to mount a challenge to the theocratic state, this time from within. The political danger alerted the nine provincial chiefs who, temporarily putting aside their differeneces, organized a severe repression of the slave revolt.

The massive and constant trans-Atlantic demand for slaves led to concentrations of increasingly large numbers of slaves caught in the hinterland and kept in the Southern Rivers region and all along the coast. According to Matthews, the percentage of slaves among the Susu, Bullam, Baga, and Temne populations was nearly 70 percent, while among the Manding it was higher.

The concentration of large numbers of slaves along the coast was among the reasons for the emergence there, as in Futa Jallon, of large-scale slave rebellions. In the mid-eighteenth century, according to Newton, the entire countryside from Sierra Leone to Cape Mount was rife with slave rebellions. Apparently, not a single year passed without groups of slaves, in permanent rebellion, attacking some slaving vessel. Furthermore, rebel slaves succeeded in establishing free zones on the coast by attracting runaway slaves from all over the area. These liberated slaves, having gained their freedom in the face of their former masters' attacks, defended it by settling in areas that were often inaccessible. The development of such maroon communities amplified the general trend toward slave rebellions on the coast during the last quarter of the eighteenth century. Given their relatively high degree of organization, rebellious slaves exerted an increasing influence on the regional balance of forces. In one instance, rebel slaves sided with the Susu, fighting against their former Manding masters in a bid to consolidate their independence. In the great 1785 revolt, slaves dealt out severe punishment to their masters by beheading many members of the Manding aristocracy and setting fire to their rice fields.[32]

The success of these revolts put slaves in a position to build fortified settlements at Yangueakori, Kania, and Funkoo in Susu territory. The town of Yangueakori had particularly strong defenses. Perched in mountainous terrain, it was surrounded by a wall twelve feet high with watch towers at the corners to ensure the site's defensive security. Thus strengthened in their fortifications, marroon slaves mounted raids against the villages of their former Manding masters, capturing the inhabitants for sale in their turn. For a decade, the marroons organized guerrilla campaigns, and this finally forced the Manding and Susu slave-owners to forget their differences and join forces against the slave revolt spreading throughout the coastal region. From 1795, combined Susu and Manding forces attacked and destroyed the weakest marroon slave villages. Some of the inhabitants were slaughtered, others sold to slave traders. In January 1796, the long siege of the fortified town of Yangueakori began, two months before Thomas Winterbottom visited the battlefield. Rand, a mercenary hired by the coalition of Manding and Susu slave-owners, estimated that the number of soldiers laying siege to Yangueakori was 2,500. The marroon slaves, led by Dansage, fought courageously. But the siege was long, and the attackers used large-bore cannon. The resistance cracked, and the inhabitants of Yangueakori were either massacred or enslaved. The severity of the clamp-down following the fall of Yangueakori was a good indication of the major scope of the slave rebellion, and the threat it represented to slave-owners and the slave traders on the coast, with their common interest in maintaining the slave trade.[33] All along the coast, moreover, slaves organized numerous revolts. Sometimes their motive was to escape from captivity; at other times, their rebellion was against the prospect of forced of exile to the Americas. In 1791, for example, slaves in Rio Pongo took advantage of the absence of their master John Ormond and rebelled, sacking his warehouse and destroying merchandise valued at £30,000 sterling.[34]

The size and frequency of the many slave revolts point to the intensity of slave exploitation even within the framework of the subsistence economy. Marroon slaves who organized large-scale rebellions capable of posing a serious threat to the political and economic balance of a Senegambian region dominated by the slave trade certainly had a clear awareness of their situation.

Rebellion was a constant reality among slaves. Starting in the hinterland, it continued during the coastal transition, and remained a real possibility throughout the long middle passage, all the way to the hell of the New World plantations. Instances of slave revolts at the loading wharf or aboard the slaving vessels during the middle passage were numerous. Still, millions of Senegambians were shipped by force to the New World. Among them, the memory of the homeland remained sharp. This memory strengthened the unshakeable resolve of certain slaves to escape the hell of slavery and to return home. Examples were Job Ben Salomon of Bundu and Abdurahman of Futa Jallon. Yuba Suleyman Ibrahim Jalo, known in the exotic literature of eighteenth-century Europe as Job Ben Salomon, was born in Bundu around 1700. The son of a marabout, Ben Salomon was on his way to Gambia to sell slaves when he was caught by a gang of bandits who themselves sold him to slave traders in 1730. A few months later, Ben Salomon found himself on the tobacco plantation of one M. Tolsey, in Maryland. He proved quite incapable of adapting to the rigors of slave labor. He therefore tried to escape. Caught and tried, he told Judge Thomas Bluett that he was by birth an aristocrat. Impressed by his religious devotion and his knowledge of the Arabic language, the provincial society of slavers gave him permission to write a letter to his father, to be conveyed through the good offices of the slave trader Vachell Denton. Translated at Oxford, his letter earned him his freedom in 1733 from the Director of the Royal African Company, James Oglethorpe. In quick order, Ben Salomon became a parlor celebrity in London, receiving an invitation from the king and the royal family. Following a formal reception at the Gentlemen's Society of London, Job Ben Salomon set sail for Gambia. He landed at Fort Saint James on 8 August 1734, then traveled to Bundu by road. In April 1735, he finally returned home.[35]

It turned out that the liberation of Yuba and his return to his homeland were designed to further the interests of the Royal African Company, eager to obtain a British monopoly in Senegambia. So, in January 1736, Yuba became an escort to a mission led by Thomas Hull to prospect the gold mines of Bambuk. In December 1736, the Director of the French fort of Saint-Joseph at Galam, opposed to the British, had Yuba arrested. But in a movement of solidarity with Yuba, traders in the area rerouted caravans to Gambia, penalising the French and giving the British an advantage. Thereafter, Yuba maintained close bonds with the British, remaining an active slave trader until his death in 1777.[36] The slave trade was the foundation on which all business affairs rested. Hence the return of Yuba, the freed slave, to his old business, that of slave trader.

The other known case of the return of a slave to Senegambia was that of Abdurahman, son of the *Almami* Ibrahima Sori, born in the Futa Jallon town of Timbo. Taken prisoner in a war between Futa Jallon and Kaabu around 1788, Abdurahman was sold to a Mississippi farmer, Thomas Foster, in Natchez. In the thirty-nine years he spent in the service of his master, Abdurahman never for a single day lost hope of returning to his homeland. In 1826, using his knowledge of Arabic, he wrote a letter to the Sultan of Morocco, who interceded with the President of the United States to have him freed. Freed alone, he undertook a vast campaign in the northern part of the United States to raise money to buy the freedom of his wife, children, and grandchildren, with help from the American Colonization Society. Abdurahman found himself at the center of a North–South controversy about slavery, the heat of which forced him to leave the United States for Liberia in a hurry. At the age of sixty-five, the old slave, after thirty-nine years of servitude in Mississippi, was getting ready to leave Liberia for his native Timbo when, on 6 July 1829, he died.[37] This stubborn desire to return home remained the unfulfilled dream of thousands of Senegambian slaves whose presence in the New World was to mark the destiny of the black diaspora, forever linked with the homeland.

Slave trading was the cornerstone of commerce between Europe, Africa, and America. The slave trade, which dominated Senegambian history throughout the eighteenth century, was in this respect a contributory factor to the accumulation of finance capital that made the Industrial Revolution possible in Europe. Thus strengthened, Europe became capable of bringing the slave trade to a halt in the nineteenth century, turning Africa into its direct periphery. From then on, Senegambia, having first supplied men, was given a new role: to supply raw materials for use by Europe's rapidly expanding industries. The new phase dictated the primacy of legitimate trade over slave trading. Above all, it required colonial conquest.

*Part III*

Senegambia in the first half of the nineteenth century: legitimate trade and sovereignty disputes

The first half of the nineteenth century saw another round of major upheavals that changed all aspects of life in Senegambia. The slave trade had dominated preceding centuries. Colonial conquest would come in the second half of the nineteenth century. This was a time of transition, marked by the triumph of legitimate trade.

The 1814 Congress of Vienna signaled the resurgence of British and French power in Senegambia after a long eclipse due to the Imperial Wars. This resurgence coincided with a gradual transition from commercial mercantilism to industrial capitalism. The shift enabled Europe to impose new forms of domination over the pre-capitalist economies of the African periphery. From the start, Britain, committed to the new doctrine of free trade because it was the leading industrial nation, abolished the slave trade once it lost its usefulness as an instrument for primitive capital accumulation. Senegambia, after three centuries of uninterrupted slave trading, acquired a new function: to devote itself exclusively to the supply of raw materials and agricultural produce to Europe, and to use the proceeds for buying the manufactured products of the European industrial system, then in a state of full-scale expansion. The dependency relationship that the shift required has persisted, in all essentials, to this day. It emerged gradually in accordance with European needs, ultimately achieving dominance. Above everything, its development depended on the real capacity of capital to organize production on the spot.

The assertion of European control over Senegambia, after a long eclipse, occurred initially in the midst of a serious commercial depression caused by the abolition of the slave trade. The crisis was worsened by rivalries between Britain, France, and Portugal. Their wrangling was complicated by claims from such new powers as the United States, Belgium, and Germany. On the whole, Britain, France, and Portugal held on to the positions they had secured in previous centuries. Each power tried, according to its own needs, to cope with the new conditions of legitimate trade. Trade in produce developed first in southern Senegambia, though a substantial contraband trade in slaves, sheltered by the many estuaries of the Southern

Rivers, coexisted with legitimate commerce. Trading companies based in Gorée, Gambia, and Sierra Leone fought to gain control over the Southern Rivers. They also tried to monopolize the new trade in such produce as coffee, palm oil, and, above all, peanuts, in addition to traditional produce from Futa Jallon. The continuation of a considerable contraband trade in slaves brought into the open a long simmering conflict between old slave-trading families in the Southern Rivers and new French and British trading companies, which relied on their respective countries to help them create zones of influence. French–British rivalry centered on Freetown and Bathurst, which the British used as bases in the fight against contraband slave trading.

Contraband slave trading was substantially reduced in northern Senegambia, where the French were trying to cope with new realities by establishing plantations in Waalo and the Cape Verde peninsula. The failure of these schemes worsened the depression in the trading system, then dominated by speculative gum trading in the Senegal valley. The depression, which lasted throughout the first half of the nineteenth century, forced traders based on Gorée Island to try and gain control of the Southern Rivers market, where large-scale peanut farming was then developing. Meanwhile, the trading companies of Marseille and Bordeaux had opted for peanut oil as an industrial lubricant for use in France. British trading companies, on the other hand, preferred palm oil. These options were largely instrumental in shaping occupation patterns in Senegambia. Thus, peanut farming, first in the Southern Rivers area, then in Kajoor, led to the occupation of most of Senegambia by France, and it took little time for the French to run into conflicts over sovereignty with states in the region.

The abolition of the slave trade and the development of legitimate trade, while leading to a multiplicity of sovereignty disputes between local states and the European powers, also caused profound changes in the economic and political evolution of Senegambian states. For instance, Futa Jallon, an inland power eager to combine profits from contraband slave dealing and legitimate commodity trading, began a policy of vigorous territorial expansion toward the coast. But this old Muslim theocracy was internally weakened by secessionist forces. More seriously, it faced massive popular revolts.

Of these the Hubbu movement was typical. Futa Jallon's conquest of the Southern Rivers and Kaabu coincided with France's conquering thrust into the same region from its bases in Saint-Louis and Gorée. In northern Senegambia, the gradual abolition of the slave trade weakened the aristocracy considerably. And the development of legitimate trade finally gave peasants a chance to throw off the *ceddo* yoke. The aristocracy, pressured by European territorial and economic claims, was now forced to confront a vast marabout movement that culminated in a holy war led by Shaykh Umar.

After upsetting the entire Senegambian region with his religious and political campaigns, Shaykh Umar embarked on the conquest of western Sudan. By then the sovereignty of the Senegambian states was already under serious challenge, since the European powers had decided on colonial conquest. In 1854, France began the process by annexing Waalo.

This colonial conquest coincided with the rise of such new leaders as Maba Jaakhu, Cherno Brahim, and Amadu Sekhu. Emerging from the rank and file, these men attempted to unite northern Senegambia under the banner of Islam. They were opposed by a coalition of legitimist rulers and the colonial regime, which took advantage of the marabouts' defeat to establish its control over the whole of Senegambia.

# 9    The crisis of the trans-Atlantic trading system and the triumph of legitimate trade in the first half of the nineteenth century

Britain's decision, at the Vienna Congress of 1814, to force all European powers to abolish the slave trade led to profound changes in the trans-Atlantic trading system on the Senegambian coast.

In southern Senegambia, established Euro-African slave-trading families, led by John Ormond and Benjamin Curtis, dominated economic affairs and kept up a contraband slave-trading business until the mid-nineteenth century. However, the parallel development of legitimate trade soon attracted British and French trading companies, especially into Rio Nunez. Once having arrived, they tried to gain control of the Southern Rivers. The economic prosperity of southern Senegambia contrasted sharply with the depressed state of northern Senegambia. There, the failure of colonial plantation schemes led to speculative gum trading from 1830 until peanuts emerged as a miracle crop capable of saving the colony of Senegal.

In both cases peanut farming created the economic conditions France needed to conquer colonial territory, thus pioneering the territorial partition of Senegambia.

## A.    Contraband slave trading and legitimate trade in the Southern Rivers region

As in the fifteenth and sixteenth centuries, when Portugal had a trading monopoly there, the Southern Rivers region, compared to northern Senegambia, was an economic zone of capital importance during the entire first half of the nineteenth century. For this region was both a hot-bed of contraband slave trading and the busiest market for legitimate trade, which boomed after the abolition of the slave trade.

Even before the Vienna Congress, Britain, leading the abolitionist movement, had consolidated its base in the colony of Sierra Leone. It used Freetown, a settlement founded in 1787 by a group of philanthropists with help from the British government, as its operational base in the anti-slavery campaign. The effectiveness of the abolitionist campaign was considerably muffled by the bad faith of the other powers. Portugal, France, and the

United States, in particular, still had substantial interests in the slave trade. They refused to have their vessels boarded and searched by British cruisers. Moreover, the British patrol system could do nothing to stop clandestine slave trading by Euro-African slave traders, who had established a strong presence in the Southern Rivers region since the eighteenth century. The natural layout of the Southern Rivers region, with its many estuaries, greatly facilitated contraband slave trading, which flourished throughout the first half of the nineteenth century in Rio Nunez, Rio Pongo, and Rio Cacheu. The old slave-trading families had grown even more powerful, thanks to their many matrimonial alliances with various ruling aristocracies in the Southern Rivers. So they had produced a second generation of Euro-Africans such as William Fernandez, son of a woman named Bramaya; John Ormond and John Holman, sons of one Bashia, William Skelton, son of Kissing, and Emmanuel Gomez, son of Bakia. The group, reinforced by several Afro-Americans, formed a sort of local bourgeoisie, closely knit and powerful.[1] Taking advantage of the long eclipse of the European powers during the revolutionary Imperial Wars, these Euro-Africans, trained in elite British schools, managed to turn the new economic order, under which slavery was now forbidden, to profitable use. For quite a while, they kept the Southern Rivers under their domination, against the claims of new trading companies supported by the metropolitan powers France, Britain, and Portugal.

In the first place, all these Euro-Africans carried on a profitable contraband trade in slaves which, despite intensive patrolling by the British from their base in Freetown, flourished in Rio Pongo and Rio Cacheu. Given the contraband nature of the trade, statistical data on the number of slaves involved are extremely scarce. What is certain is that there was a constant demand for slave labor from the New World, where slavery was maintained until 1865 in the southern United States, and later in Cuba and Brazil. This demand kept the slave trade going and developed it, especially since the British, on their own, could not stop clandestine trading. It is certain that, in the decade between 1820 and 1830, the number of slaves traded surpassed totals registered in previous centuries.[2] J. Corry, for instance, suggests that, in 1807, some 2,600 slaves were shipped out of Rio Pongo and Rio Nunez. Though it was a risky business, the trade boomed because of rising prices for slaves, from 40 francs in 1832 to 100 francs and more in 1847.[3] On account of the huge profits brought in by the contraband trade, Rio Pongo, with its numerous patrol-frustrating estuaries, and Rio Geba, where slave trading remained legal for a long time, became the favorite haunts of slaving vessels constantly plying the Southern Rivers.

Along the Rio Pongo, in particular, contraband slave trading continued unchecked into the second half of the nineteenth century, owing to the activities of the powerful families of Benjamin Curtis, John Irving, Sam Perry, Wilkinson, John Holman, Louis Gomez, and, above all, John Ormond, who maintained their dominance over economic life in the region, with occasional forays into politics.

Slave trading remained a fixture of life. But abolitionist agitation pushed it underground, creating a transitional situation in which legitimate trade coexisted with contraband slave trading. Throughout the Southern Rivers, this duplicity led to a period of upheavals and trade wars. In Rio Pongo, there was first of all a struggle for economic and political dominance. On the one hand there was the Curtis family, sponsored by the Kati family, who controlled the right bank. On the other, there were the Ormonds, supported by Styles and Baily Lightburn, Thomas Curtis, son of Kissing, Paul and Mary Faber, and the Wilsons, who controlled Bangalan River. The two parties clashed sporadically for years, until John Ormond died in 1833.[4]

Despite their ruinous rivalry, the Rio Pongo slavers were able, in 1817, to scuttle the intervention in the Southern Rivers region of missionaries, accused of serving as informants for British cruisers based on the Loos Islands. In an effective response to the challenge of the British abolitionists, these slavers coupled slave trading with legitimate commodity trading. For the Euro-Africans, a defining moment came with the capture of a slaving vessel, the *Rosalia*. Shaken by the experience, they decided to invest in coffee plantations. By 1826, they had planted nearly 10,000 coffee bushes along the Rio Pongo. They used their coffee plantations as a perfect front for the pursuit of their slaving activities, still their dominant business interest. Slaves were set to work in the rainy season planting coffee. In the dry season they were sold along with the coffee they had produced. John Ormond, for instance, owned 5,000 to 6,000 slaves, and Lightburn also owned several thousands. The slaves planted coffee while waiting to be loaded onto contraband vessels, which were able at any time to find a full load in the Rio Pongo area. Slave trading was especially profitable around 1830. Helped by his organizational skills, John Ormond put an end to rivalries among slave traders by setting up a quota system for slave sales. At the same time, he promoted the extension of the Futa Jallon regime's control over Rio Pongo, a development that was to his advantage. For by that stroke, Rio Pongo became the most convenient outlet for produce – and, above all, for slaves – coming from Futa Jallon.[5]

John Ormond's death in 1833 marked the end of the era of slave traders completely integrated into local political life thanks to their marriages to daughters of the aristocracy, and able, until then, to develop their economic power with no interference from European powers. The powerful coalition of Euro-Africans dominated Rio Pongo until the 1840s and even later, by cagily mixing legitimate trade with contraband slave trading. Furthermore, the military presence of Futa Jallon from 1838 to 1842 for a while consolidated the role of slave traders in Rio Pongo, where coffee farming, followed by peanut farming, provided a pretext for the gathering of thousands of slaves in factories. The practice provided a cover for continued clandestine slave trading all the way into the second half of the nineteenth century.[6]

Relative prosperity in Rio Pongo attracted John Emerson, a partner in the company of Smith and Emerson, with its headquarters in Freetown, to the trading post on the river. There he married a daughter of Styles and Baily Lightburn, who, with Paul and Mary Faber as well as William Ormond, had inherited control of the upstream market. The marriage gave Emerson strong ties with the Euro-African trading bourgeoisie of Rio Pongo, still the closest outlet for slaves and produce coming from Futa Jallon to the coast.[7]

The situation in Rio Nunez was different. From the start, the difficulty of clandestine operations in the single estuary there made continued slave trading impossible. So the shift to legitimate trading was faster than in Rio Pongo. It was further accelerated by the numerous civil wars that broke out at the time, leading to the large scale immigration of a new class of traders who ousted the old slave-trading families and the local aristocracies. Thus, John Sebastian Pearce, son of John Pearce, who represented the interests of Nalu traders, clashed with John Bateman over control of the Rio Nunez economy. John Bateman was a protégé of Monsieur Fortune, who had formed an alliance with the Landuman in order to move the trading center from Kakandy to the upstream town of Boké.[8]

The background to the dispute was that John Pearce, descendant of a Yani woman and an American slaver, and himself married to a Towl woman, was very closely connected to the aristocracy and the Nalu traders. Indeed, he had become something of a leader in Landuman society. When he died in 1818, the Nalu trade monopoly was breached by his rival John Bateman who, with help from the Landuman, tried to divert the caravan trade from Kakandy toward Boké. The conflict diminished trade along the Rio Nunez considerably. Meanwhile, around 1820, several factors helped to speed up the transition from slave trading to legitimate trade. Charles MacCarthy, newly appointed British governor of Sierra Leone, attempted immediately upon his arrival to close Freetown to American traders. In 1823 he sent troops to occupy the Loos Islands with a view to promoting legitimate trade in the Southern Rivers. In this he was encouraged by the British firm of Macauley and Babington. MacCarthy also tried to open a new, direct trade route from Timbo to Freetown. For this initiative he obtained the agreement of the *almamis*, who wanted to reduce the influence of the middleman population in the Southern Rivers. They also wanted to break the *de facto* control over the caravan trade exercised by the powerful province of Labé to the disadvantage of Timbo, the regime's capital. All these factors, combined with the success of British cruisers patrolling out of Freetown, played a significant part in the decline of slave trading and the development of legitimate trade in such products as leather, ivory, gold, and, above all, coffee and peanuts, from 1840.[9] The rapid development of legitimate trade predictably caused problems in Rio Nunez. A number of local chiefs tried to reinstate the status quo by force. Others preferred to exploit the new trading system by attempting to control the collection of customs duties. In the end, the triumph of legitimate trade in the Southern Rivers, especially along the Rio Nunez, coincided with the large-scale installation of trading companies funded by metropolitan capital and operating from bases in Saint-Louis, Gorée, Bathurst, and Freetown. French trading companies based in Saint-Louis and Gorée led the influx. They moved into the Southern Rivers, ousting British and American traders who until 1835 had dominated the scene.

At the time, the French colony in Senegal was in serious trouble. After a long absence during the Napoleonic wars, the French had resumed business in Saint-Louis, Gorée, and Albreda in 1817. The campaign against contraband slave trading was much easier along the northern Senegambian coastline than on the coast of the Southern Rivers. So the abolition of the slave trade led to a long-lasting economic depression in northern Senegambia. Trying to ride out the crisis, the French experimented with a string of plantation schemes. When these failed, they regressed to wild and speculative gum trading in the Senegal valley.

**B.      Experimental plantation schemes and the crisis of the trans-Atlantic trading system in Northern Senegambia**

At the Vienna Congress of 1814, France retrieved its colony of Senegal from the British. What this meant in practice was the retrieval of French trading posts at Saint-Louis, Gorée, and Albreda. Still, it was not until 1817, after the wreck of the *Méduse*, that what remained of the crew occupied the island of Saint-Louis under the leadership of Governor Schmaltz. From that point on, France committed itself to the business of coping with the new conditions attendant on the abolition of the slave trade. It did this by trying out a series of plantation schemes in an effort to save the colony of Senegal, now reduced to living without its principal business, slave trading. The slave revolt in Santo Domingo (Haiti) had ruined the sugar colonies. France was therefore forced to use African slave labor in Africa, instead of shipping it to the New World as in the past. The crops would be the same: cotton, sugar cane, and tobacco.

The new option also coincided with a new economic situation in which the nascent capitalist industrial and financial system was bent on integrating Africa into the capitalist system as a periphery yoked directly to the

European center.[10] In the beginning, however, France had only limited resources for achieving this integration. It therefore opted to operate within the simple framework of an economic protectorate geared to the production of export crops to feed French industry. So Africa, having spent centuries selling human population to work on New World plantations, was now assigned a fresh function: to sell raw produce, and only to industrial Europe.

Governor Schmaltz selected Waalo, at the mouth of the Senegal River, as a testing ground for this experiment in colonial plantation agriculture. The kingdom was chosen because it was close to Saint-Louis. On 8 May 1819, the Governor signed the Treaty of Ndiaw with the local ruler, the *Brak* Amar Fatim Mborso, who ceded land to France for its agricultural enterprise. The rulers of Waalo had already been frightened by Fleuriau's military expedition in 1818. But they were attracted by the French promise to protect them from the pillaging Moors of Trarza. More than anything else, their mouths watered at the prospect of new customary payments. The French promised to pay an annual fee of 10,358.64 francs. This was triple the income of the ruling aristocracy. They signed the treaty, turning Waalo into a kind of economic protectorate.[11]

Schmaltz chose Dagana as the station for the colonial plantation scheme. He set to work immediately building blockhouse forts along the banks of the Senegal River to protect the plantations. The French Ministry gave the project implementational credits worth 11,223,358 francs between 1818 and 1824. From 1822 to 1827, the governors who took office after Schmaltz, especially one Baron Roger, tried to expand the plantations on a large scale by setting up an agribusiness company with its base at the Richard Toll experimental farm. Yields of cotton, tobacco, and sugar cane, however, were disappointing. So France decided, from 1831, to end this initial experiment in plantation agriculture.

There were several reasons why the plantation scheme failed. The neighboring states of Trarza, Futa Tooro, and Kajoor, scared of the potential consequences of this agricultural enterprise which looked suspiciously like a base for colonial conquest, formed a tripartite alliance that created a climate of insecurity detrimental to agricultural development. The states of Trarza and Futa took turns claiming sovereignty over Waalo, and France was forced to sign treaties with both in the hope of achieving peace in the region. But the signatories did nothing to guarantee the hoped-for peace.

The plantation scheme also ran into land tenure problems resulting from conflicting interpretations of various clauses in the Treaty of Ndiaw. The local aristocrats did not think the payment of annual dues gave France outright ownership of the land ceded. But company staff at Saint-Louis assumed they had paid cash for Waalo land, and it should belong to them outright. The Waalo aristocracy, eager to get their hands on the money, went along with the treaty. But the inhabitants themselves, angered by the huge land concessions, began systematically smashing dikes built by the French.

A further cause of failure was that three centuries of the slave trade had depopulated the land, and labor was scarce. The inhabitants refused to work on French plantations. The French therefore recruited indentured laborers. This was an indirect way of prolonging slaving practices. Later, in the period of outright colonialism, they replaced indentured labor with forced labor.

One last reason why the plantation scheme failed was the resistance of traditional gum and slave traders doing business with Saint-Louis. French retailers and Euro-African traders in Saint-Louis fought tooth and nail against the economic revolution based on the expansion of legitimate trade through agricultural development. They felt threatened by the influx of industrial and commercial capital into this zone where they had formerly enjoyed an unchallenged monopoly.[12]

The French tried another plantation scheme, under private auspices, in the Cape Verde peninsula. It failed for the same reasons as the Waalo project. But there was another factor, a particularly strong one: the ruling *Damel* of Kajoor was determined to prevent the French from operating outside the strictly commercial limits of their trading posts at Saint-Louis and Gorée.[13] Those two centers, incidentally, were from that point on known as the colony of Senegal.

In addition to these attempts at agricultural development, the Saint-Louis trading company was working to develop its business in the Senegal valley. It wanted to establish a strong presence in the upper valley, the better to divert to its own advantage the caravan trade that otherwise went to British companies in the Gambia. It also wanted to control the gold mines at Bambuk. To do that, it had to get its hands on hundreds of slaves, disingenuously referred to as indentured laborers.[14] Indeed, the French, now again in control of the Saint-Louis trading post, were most willing to turn a blind eye to continued slave trading. Under these circumstances, slave shipments went as high, at least, as 1,000 a year between 1814 and 1831. Despite the stiffening of the campaign against contraband slave trading, in the form of a law passed by the French parliament in 1831, the practice of indentured labor in the French possessions did a great deal to facilitate continued slave trading up until – and even beyond – the abolition of slavery in the colony of Senegal in 1848.[15] But by now the French authorities in Saint-Louis were planning to use their expanded market in the upper Senegal valley as a stepping stone toward the conquest of the Niger Bend. For they had heard accounts of its fabulous wealth, and their appetite for conquest was aroused.

Meanwhile, the choice between free trade, as advocated by promoters of the new capitalist order, and the old monopoly system left over from the chartered companies of the mercantile era, had become a thorny problem. The business class in Saint-Louis was immersed in unregulated competition. States along the Senegal River were sliding into deepening political crisis. These were the circumstances that led to the creation of a company with special rights, the Galam Company, along with the construction of Bakel Fort by Baron Roger. But the Galam Company, funded from the colonial budget, soon became a honey pot for metropolitan French companies operating from Bordeaux, leaving the petty traders of Saint-Louis and the local African traders of the Upper Senegal valley with slim pickings. For that reason, even though the Galam Company registered profits as high as 100 percent on its investments, set up entrepôts at Sénedebu and Sansanding on the Falémé as well as at Makhana, Kenu, and Medina on the Senegal, and in 1846 alone sent out cargoes aboard 251 vessels, it was abolished in 1848.[16]

In point of fact, the failure of the various plantation schemes, like the winding up of the Galam Company, points primarily to the failure of economic protectionism as a route to the expansion of trade after the decline of the slave trade. The failures were also symptoms of the transitional problems besetting the trans-Atlantic trading system at the time. In the period of colonial conquest (the latter half of the nineteenth century) France would organize production for its own profit and ensure the triumph of free trade. But until then, the French trading posts at Saint-Louis and Gorée faced an enduring crisis. In an attempt to break out of that depression, the French trading houses ventured into speculative gum trading, while also trying to gain markets in the Southern Rivers area.

For the failure of the plantation schemes had restored gum to its former importance in the produce trade. That meant a return, as well, to unbridled speculation. Around 1830, the population of Saint-Louis was gripped by nothing less than gum fever. "Gum," wrote an eyewitness, "has become the Eldorado of trade and industry in Senegal." The sticky resin was the imperious object of commercial worship. Whoever had any other notion of ways to get rich in Senegal was considered a heretic.[17] In 1825, when Senegal's export trade brought in 1,643,632, francs gum already accounted for 75 percent of the total. The following table shows the value of other produce:

| Wax | 88,425 francs |
| Leather | 255,894 francs |
| Ivory | 32,848 francs |
| Gum | 12,227,029 francs |

According to Courtet, gum collectors brought in a great deal more than 4,000,000 kg in 1838 and 1839, the figure for the first year being 4,475,857 kg. But the speculative fever raised by this trade ruined the traders. The hardest hit were petty traders working at the smaller trading posts as sub-contractors for the companies in Saint-Louis. The free trade system, established between 1818 and 1833, was so devastating that the authorities broke with it and gave special privileges to a new company in a bid to safeguard the interests of the trading system. In 1836, trade was again liberalized; the next year, free trade was once more abolished. The confusion did nothing to ease the commercial crisis. It peaked in 1838 and 1839, due to the shortsightedness of traders who (not for the first time) imported quantities of cotton fabric (then known as *guinea*) far beyond the purchasing capacity of Senegal's colonial markets.[18]

In any case, in Senegambia, the plantation scheme in Waalo was merely a limited experiment. Its failure revealed the depth of the depression into which French commerce had slumped in its search for new ways of adjusting to the abolition of the slave trade. In northern Senegambia, speculative gum trading was simply a stop-gap measure, an attempt to fill the hole in the system left by the abolition of the slave trade. From 1817 to 1848, then, it marked the transitional phase from the era of trading companies to that of colonial imperialism.[19]

Colonial conquest began in the mid-nineteenth century. By then, the commercial crisis, particularly acute in Saint-Louis, and most severe in Gorée, had driven the trading companies of Bordeaux and Marseille into a frenzied search for market control in the Southern Rivers region. French commerce was looking for new directions. Senegambia itself was entering a new historical era. That era would in time be dominated by metropolitan trading companies and the development of peanut farming. For on top of the economic depression ravaging the trading posts at Saint-Louis and Gorée, colonial traders in Senegal were themselves in the throes of a serious crisis. French businessmen, working through their large trading enterprises in Bordeaux and Marseille, dominated the European or Euro-African traders on the spot, forcing them to become mere petty subcontractors. Major companies like Devès and Maurel & Prom did not simply control the gum trade at trading posts along the Senegal River; they also pushed Euro-African, Wolof, and Tukulor petty traders into the risky Southern Rivers markets. There, more often than not, bankruptcy awaited them. When, in 1848, the decree abolishing slavery went into effective implementation, the economic doom of this class of Euro-African middlemen was definitively sealed.

Mamadou Diouf and Abdoulaye Bathily are right when they assert that this was the period when the death warrant of Senegal's comprador bourgeoisie was signed. Samir Amin, who supposes that it was in 1920, with the arrival of Lebano–Syrian merchants, that the fall occurred, is off the mark.[20] At the same time, these trading houses, wielding great clout in metropolitan France, had a direct influence on the policy of colonial expansion in Senegambia, designed to meet French industrial demand for peanuts. Right from the first half of the nineteenth century, France had opted to promote peanut oil as an industrial lubricant, unlike Britain, which preferred palm oil. These oil options were largely instrumental in determining the modalities of colonial partition in Senegambia. Peanut farming was first developed in the Southern Rivers area before spreading to Kajoor, where it really came into its own. The development of peanut farming, then, provided some temporary relief from the depression of the trans-Atlantic trading system. Beyond that, it also set in motion the process of the creation of a colonial system.

## C.    The introduction of peanuts and the creation of a colonial system

Throughout the first half of the nineteenth century, the English, the French, the Portuguese, and the Americans tried, separately, to solve the problem of the trans-Atlantic trade depression. In Senegambia, the double game of mixing legitimate trade with contraband slave trading continued until peanuts rose to dominate the export–import economy. The growth of peanut farming was closely tied to the creation of a colonial system. That system meant the organization by European powers of African production for the benefit of European trading corporations. In this case, the introduction of peanut farming opened the way for colonial conquest and the partition of Senegambian territory. France set the process in motion when it took steps to deal with the trade depression hitting Saint-Louis and Gorée. From 1840 on, peanuts were considered a miracle crop capable of lifting the colony of Senegal out of the economic doldrums. The choice had nothing to do with geographical determinism. It resulted from a calculated decision by France to use peanut oil in this crucial phase of industrial development, unlike the British, who chose palm oil.

Industrial progress in the nineteenth century created an urgent need for various types of oil and grease. In particular, the metropolitan economies needed massive supplies of cheap soap, indispensable for the maintenance of hygiene in the new industrial cities. The British, having opted for palm oil, concentrated on the Niger Delta. That meant abandoning Senegambia to the French, who were totally committed to peanuts.[21] The French decision to break the British palm oil monopoly by promoting peanut oil as a key industrial lubricant was facilitated by several factors. First, in 1840, peanuts were given preferential customs tariffs. So by 1845, peanut oil had eliminated such rival lubricants as sesame, linseed, and poppyseed oil from the French market. Second, Chambers of Commerce in Marseille, Nantes, Rouen, Le Havre, and Bordeaux formed a powerful financial lobby dedicated to the promotion of the peanut trade through their companies in Senegambia. These companies, based particularly in Gorée, where the trading system was facing ruin, launched a campaign to capture the Southern Rivers market. Legitimate trade had got off to an earlier start there. Coffee and peanuts had therefore merged smoothly into the trading system, dominated in preceding centuries by the infernal trade in slaves.

With the support of André Dagorne, the energetic commandant of Gorée from 1835 to 1843, French, Euro-African, and Wolof middlemen were dispatched in large numbers to trading posts in the Southern Rivers region to work for colonial trading corporations based in Bordeaux and Marseille. The Valantin brothers and René D'Erneville settled at Boké on the Rio Nunez in 1836, while at Katukuma, Charles Boucaline, La Porte, and Auguste Santon started a coffee plantation called Bel Air. Along with this new group of French and Euro-African middlemen, there were also many Wolof and Tukulor traders from the colony, such as Ismael Malamin, Maalik Mbaye, and Samba Joop. These traders now represented the interests of the big trading companies, who wanted to dominate trade on the coast. They did a great deal to change the business climate in the Southern Rivers region. For one thing, they ensured the triumph of legitimate trade, especially in Rio Nunez.[22] From this point on, the dominant trading companies in the Southern Rivers were the French firm of Verminck, Gaspard, Devès & Company and the English firm of William Henry Randal, Fisher & Company. Putting increasing pressure on the colonial authorities, they sometimes asked for investment guarantees, sometimes for undisguised military intervention. In a word, they pioneered the infamous system of gunboat diplomacy even before the major military campaigns of colonial conquest during the second half of the nineteenth century.[23]

Peanut farming grew at a dizzy pace in the Southern Rivers from Gambia to Sierra Leone, to the advantage of the French trading establishment, the British having opted for palm oil. In 1842 the Americans closed their market to Senegambian peanuts by imposing a tariff of 32 cents a bushel on them.[24] Peanut exports rose rapidly. In Gambia, they increased from 137 tonnes (sold for £1,558 sterling) in 1836 to 11,095 tonnes (for £133,133) in 1851. The amount bought by French companies rose from a value of £3 in 1836 to £114,366 in 1851.[25] The volume handled by French traders rose from 12 tonnes in 1836 to 24,429 tonnes in 1843, leaving aside exports from Albreda. These were not listed in the official statistical log books of the British authorities in Gambia, but have been estimated at 2,000 tonnes in 1845. Peanuts bought in Gambia at 20 francs per 100 kg were sold in France for 37 or 38 francs. By slapping a 3.50-centime tax on foreign vessels, the French created a monopoly for themselves in both the buying and shipping of peanuts in Gambia, to the disadvantage of the British.[26]

We have no data on peanut trading in Casamance before the French set up a trading post at Seeju in 1838. We do know, however, that around 1860 peanuts became a significant commercial commodity in the Southern Rivers and that the region supplied peanuts directly to exporters operating in Gambia and northern Senegambia. Peanut production was just as well developed in Rio Grande, Rio Geba, and Rio Cacheu by Portuguese and Luso-African traders. Traffic was intense, with some thirty sloops and schooners shuttling between Gorée and Bathurst or Cacheu and Bissau. Production rose from 32,000 bushels in 1853 to 400,000 bushels in 1864. Two-thirds of this went to French traders, who dominated the Portuguese.[27] Rio Nunez, Rio Pongo, and Mellakure remained the leading markets for the expanding peanut trade. Unlike the Gambian, Rio Grande, Geba and Cacheu markets, this region soon attracted a sizable group of French settlers, agents of trading companies at Saint-Louis and, above all, Gorée. French statistical sources put the volume of peanut exports from Rio Nunez and Rio Pongo at 300,000 bushels in 1846 and 500,000 in 1848–9. There was also considerable trade in leather, gold, ivory, and coffee (19.5 tonnes in 1843). According to Bouët Willaumez, in 1840 Rio Nunez and Rio Pongo traders exported 8,000 to 10,000 hides of good quality; 30 kg to 60 kg of gold worth 200,000 to 300,000 francs; and 13 to 15 tonnes of ivory worth 80,000 to 100,000 francs. Coffee exports from the Rio Nunez increased from 100 casks in 1840 to 19.5 tonnes in 1843–5 (the cask was 42 cubic feet, or approximately 13m$^3$).[28] Peanut exports experienced a remarkable if brief boom, actually dominating trade in the Southern Rivers from 1860 to 1870. As early as 1859, one Captain Gande remarked that peanuts were the main trade in Rio Pongo and Rio Nunez. Together with Mellakure, the two valleys produced a total far exceeding 10,000 tonnes per year, and accounted for 88 percent of total export value.[29] Exports of other produce also increased appreciably. Almonds and palm oil, for instance, registered 1,000 tonnes each. In 1865, Mellakure valley alone exported 60,000 hides. Sesame seed, wax and coffee exports also rose, but peanuts remained dominant overall in the Southern Rivers.

Indeed, the Southern Rivers region was the incontestable leader in peanut production. In northern Senegambia the situation was different. Peanut farming developed slowly, and did not achieve dominance until the 1880s. In the Siin–Saloum region, production along the Saloum River rose from 500 kg in 1840 to 3.5 tonnes in 1843, then to 36 tonnes in 1844. Along the Petite Côte, production rose from 2.66 tonnes in 1843 to 3,000 tonnes in 1853, and Rufisque quickly achieved prominence as a peanut trading center. In Kajoor and along the Senegal River, peanut trading got off to a slower start. Production rose from 185,000 kg in 1845 to 3,000,000 kg in 1849. Its subsequent growth was ensured through a series of tax relief measures legislated in 1848, 1852 and 1855. Kajoor in particular benefited greatly from such promotional measures. The most instrumental change was the nomination of Louis Faidherbe as Governor (1854, 1861, and 1863–5). His appointment guaranteed the expansion of peanut production in northern Senegambia, with backing from trading firms in Bordeaux, whose economic interests he promoted with great enthusiasm.

In the Upper Senegal valley, the Galam Company conducted a series of lukewarm experiments in peanut trading. Exports rose from 2.5 tonnes in 1839–40 to 10.75 tonnes in 1852–3. In the 1880s, however, high transportion costs cut into company profits, and annual export volume fell back to 5 or 6 tonnes. Peanut production in this zone was superseded by cotton, which went through a boom in the 1860s on account of the Civil War in the United States of America. Gajaaga, for instance, became a major producer of cotton cloth for Senegambia's coastal populations and of raw cotton for the French. But once the American Civil War ended, and with Egyptian cotton also entering the market, cotton grown in the upper Senegal valley proved too expensive on the world market, and production stopped. Indigo went through the same cycle.[30]

Meanwhile, the French trading presence provided a foretaste of things to come. Companies like Devès & Chaumet, Maurel & Prom, and Buhan & Teisseire settled in. By 1860 their turnover had reached some five million francs.[31] Their arrival ruined the Euro-African middlemen, who retreated toward Medina, Nioro, and Kamama, along with their entourage of Wolof subcontractors. The Soninke, on the other hand, adapted by switching to trading donkeys, salt, and household slaves. In 1844, the French exported nearly 3,000 donkeys to Guadeloupe. Soninke traders in this region engaged in slave trading as a sort of adjustment to the end of the trans-Atlantic slave trade. They reinforced domestic slavery, using slave labor for export farming and most of all for head porterage to the entrepôts of Kita and Keniera on the Bakoy River.[32]

It was at this time of adjustment to the abolition of the trans-Atlantic slave trade, following the growth of legitimate trade, that slave villages similar to Futa Jallon *runde* were developed to meet the demand for labor.[33] Early in the second half of the nineteenth century, however, the mercantile interests of trading companies pushed metropolitan administrations towards a policy of conquest in the Upper Senegal valley. Conquest proceeded through the systematic application of gunboat diplomacy as a way of giving the nascent colony access to the wealth of the Sudan (the name the French gave to the West African hinterland).

The British acted similarly in the Gambia. Resuming control of the valley after the Congress of Vienna, they turned it into a haven for British traders ousted from Gorée and Saint-Louis. A second reason for the British return was that the campaign against slave trading had acquired priority status. In

Senegambia it was waged from two bases. The first was Freetown, Sierra
Leone. The second was Bathurst, Gambia, founded in 1816. It took little
time for British traders to regroup, forming a sizable merchant community
around the likes of Richard Lloyd, Charles Grant, W.H. Goddard, and
William C. Forster, representative of Forster & Smith of London. This merchant community, linked to trading companies in London, soon found
itself in competition with the French trading companies of Gorée and
Saint-Louis. The eighteenth century rivalry between the French in Senegal
and the British in Gambia was rekindled. The two sides shared the same
dream: to monopolize trade in the Senegambian hinterland.

At that time, the British were preoccupied with the campaign against
slave trading. They had no interest in developing a plantation economy in
Senegambia. Their attention was focused on leather, ivory, wax and gold
from the interior. To push their aims, they went up the Gambia in 1823 to
set up the trading post of Georgetown on MacCarthy Island.

British–French competition soon erupted into serious conflict over
attempts to control trade from Bundu, at the intersection of the two main
routes leading to the Senegal and the Gambia rivers. British traders faced
constant harassment from the *Almami* of Bundu, who habitually raided
Wuuli and Naani. The British stepped in to stop this internecine warfare,
and especially to put military pressure on the Bundu regime for giving the
French permission to build a fort at Senedubu on the Falémé in 1843, to be
used for blocking trade caravans en route to the Gambia. On the whole, in
Gambia as in the rest of Senegambia, the first half of the nineteenth century
was only a transitional period leading to the triumph of legitimate trade
dominated by the commercial companies of Bordeaux and Marseille, *de
facto* masters of the peanut trade in the entire region.[34]

The development of peanut exports was the fundamental reality in
Senegambian trade at the start of the second half of the nineteenth century.
The French, who had decided, as from 1851, to promote peanut oil for the
manufacture of soap as well as for domestic cooking, dominated the
economy. The peanut option became the driving force behind all French
trade policy in Senegambia. By 1863, for example, peanut exports to France
required as many as eighty ships each weighing from 250 to 300 tonnes. The
French imposed daunting restrictions on foreign ships transporting
peanuts to France. More pointedly, they forbade the import into France of
peanut oil processed in Senegambia. Such regulations laid the groundwork
for French expansionism in the region. They also helped to set up an
import–export trading system based on single-crop peanut production.
The British, the Germans, the Belgians, and the Americans all had their
eyes on Senegambia's resources. If French imperialism eventually won out
in the region, the key reason was no doubt the peanut trade.

Before moving on to a discussion of the period during which the colonial system was established through military conquest, we need to take a closer look at economic, political, and social changes within the Senegambian states throughout this long transitional phase of the trans-Atlantic trading system. It was a period during which, on the one hand, Futa Jallon expanded into the Southern Rivers region, and, on the other hand, conflicts over sovereignty between France and the states of northern Senegambia flared up again. Meanwhile, every region in Senegambia was experiencing a profound political and social crisis that led to the growth of a militant Muslim reform movement directed against both the ancient *ceddo* regimes and the aging theocracies.

# 10 Popular rebellions and political and social crises in Futa Jallon

The parallel conduct of legitimate trade and contraband slave trading caused profound political, economic, and social transformations throughout southern Senegambia in the first half of the nineteenth century. The greatest change was the eruption of full-scale conflict between the powerful Muslim theocracy of Futa Jallon, internally weakened by a string of political, economic, and social crises, and the coastal states of the Southern Rivers, where legitimate trade, stimulated by peanut production, was developing. The decline of the slave trade shifted the trade balance between the two regions. The value of Futa Jallon's traditional market commodities was dropping. By contrast, the value of produce from the coastal states was now constantly rising, with peanuts proving particularly profitable. Smarting from the change in the balance of power, Futa Jallon, a landlocked power cordoned off behind the coastal states of the Southern Rivers, adopted a vigorous policy of territorial expansion, pushing coastward in an attempt to end the economic crisis brought about by the steady progress of legitimate trade. Futa Jallon's drive toward the conquest of the coast, apart from being designed to achieve control over legitimate trade in such produce as peanuts, was also linked to an internal political and social crisis. For new, centrifugal forces had emerged, forcing the old Futa Jallon aristocracy to react.

Throughout the nineteenth century the two royal clans, the Alfaya and the Soriya, had fought over central power at Timbo. To make matters worse, the Council of Elders was also eager to control the central regime. An even greater complication was the tendency of the provincial chiefs in Timbi and Labé, the main beneficiaries from trade with the Southern Rivers, to push for autonomy. The political crisis was sharpened by the social discontent of the majority of ordinary free persons and slaves. They showed their dissatisfaction with the regime that had ruled them since the early eighteenth century by switching their allegiance to new Muslim leaders.

A key feature of the Muslim reform movement was the establishment of new religious centers. An example was Tuuba, directed by the Jakhanke cleric El Hadj Salim Gassama, popularly known as Karamokho Bâ. The reformers' aim was to speed up the peaceful conversion of the coastal population to Islam. Their policy represented a clean break with the policy of holy war, the *jihad*, whose initial purpose had been forgotten in the scramble for slaves and booty. The movement expanded through the establishment of religious centers at Jekunko and Dingiray by Shaykh Umar Tal, advocate of the Tijaniyya school of Islam. From his base in Futa Jallon, the Shaykh set out to convert Senegambia and the Niger Bend. However, it was the open rebellion organized by the Hubbu, under the marabout Mamadu Juhe, which gave the most forthright expression to the radical challenge to the religious, political, and social status quo under the aging Futa Jallon theocracy, posed by a new set of Muslim leaders. The Hubbu movement destroyed, from within, the power of an aristocracy that had ruled since the early eighteenth century, at a time when Futa Jallon was entering into a contest with European powers for the economic and political control of the Southern Rivers region.

## A.     The political crisis in Futa Jallon

The old Muslim theocracy in Futa Jallon had, since the decline of the kingdom of Kaabu, been the main military power in southern Senegambia. It was also, at the beginning of the nineteenth century, beset by a profound internal political and social crisis.[1] In the central regime, the crisis unfolded in the context of a struggle between the two royal clans, the *Alfaya* and the *Soriya*, which dominated the entire first half of the nineteenth century. For, from 1818 to 1848, the power of the *Almami* was considerably weakened by chronic conflicts between rival claimants, at a time when economic changes taking place in the Southern Rivers area required the Futa Jallon regime to engage upon a more vigorous foreign policy if it hoped to stop the European powers settling permanently on the coast.

The nineteenth century began with the reign of Abdul Kader of the Soriya clan. From 1811 to 1822, he tried to get his country to adapt to the abolition of the slave trade by developing legitimate commercial ties with Freetown. From 1822, however, Abdul Kader was challenged by a rival from the Alfaya clan, Bubakar. Bubakar seized power in August 1822, lost it, regained it in March 1824, then lost it once more in February 1825. This rivalry punched large holes in the credibility of the *Almamis*. It also enhanced the importance of the Council of Elders and individual provincial chiefs. When Abdul Kader died, Bubakar finally asserted the effective supremacy of the *Alfaya* faction, in a situation where several claimants were locked in a struggle for leadership of that clan. The wrangling only made the state more politically unstable. Nor did it help matters when the *Alfaya* were forced to hand over power to the new *Soriya* leader, Yaya, from February 1826 to May 1827. Still, Bubakar managed to hold on to his title of *Almami* from May 1827 to November 1836, apart from a three-month interruption in 1831. He had to agree to a condition: that he follow a peaceful foreign policy geared to legitimate trade. By accepting this compromise, he acquiesced in the right of the Council of Elders and the provincial chiefs to oversee the conduct of government affairs. Even so, the threat of a *coup d'état* still hung over his head. Eventually the *Soriya* faction, after repeated attempts, forced Bubakar to yield power to Yaya. There is no doubt that popular pressure and the influence of the Council of Elders both played a part in this.

At this point the two ruling clans tried alternating two-year terms. But this compromise deal was constantly violated. When, in 1841, Bubakar once more came to power, his policy of promoting legitimate trade ran into stiff opposition from several chiefs. These opponents threw their weight behind Umar, the new strongman of the *Soriya* faction. Umar, son of the *Almami* Abdul Kader, had been a refugee in Bundu since 1820. Because he was young, generous and militarily astute, he won the support of the entire younger generation. In November 1842, and again in January 1843, he tried to overthrow Bubakar. A series of skirmishes ensued in Timbo, creating such insecurity and chaos that the two leaders ended up accepting arbitration from the Council of Elders.

In May 1843, Umar was installed as *Almami* for the first time. Following advice given by Shaykh Umar on a journey through Timbo, he formally put into practice the formula of alternating two-year terms. Accordingly, in 1845 Umar transferred power peacefully to Ibrahima Sori, who took over from Bubakar as leader of the *Alfaya* faction. No sooner had he taken power, however, than Ibrahima Sori violated the two-term agreement by attempting to assassinate Umar on his way to his residence at Sokotoro. Six months later, Umar seized power once more. So harsh were the reprisals he took against the *Alfaya* that Timbo, the capital city, shrank in size thereafter, while the secondary clan towns (Daara for the *Alfaya*, Sokotoro for the *Soriya*) grew.

From then on, the *Almami* Umar refused to hand over power. Instead, at a gathering in Timbo in June 1851, he forced his rival to state publicly his acceptance of the principle of alternating two-year terms. Even after that he held on to power for eight and a half years, handing over voluntarily to Ibrahima Sori only in February 1856. The handover, though unforced, was facilitated by three factors: the Hubbu rebellion had caused a serious crisis for the central regime; Shaykh Umar was present in the kingdom; and the Southern Rivers region was undergoing profound economic changes.[2]

## B.     Shaykh Umar's visit to Futa Jallon

Following the success of the Muslim Revolution there, Futa Jallon became the most prestigious cultural and religious center in Senegambia, second only to the Zawaya Muslim centers of Mauritania, directed by Shaykh Siddiya Al Kabir. Several Islamic educational institutions in the kingdom attracted disciples from all over Western Sudan and Senegambia. In addition, various religious leaders traveled to Futa Jallon, settling there for the purpose of devoting themselves to religious instruction. Around 1804, the Jakhanke religious leader, Karamokho Bâ, settled in Tuuba, where a large religious community had grown up dedicated to the peaceful propagation of Islam among the coastal populations.[3]

Around 1840, Shaykh Umar, a renowned pilgrim, arrived in Futa Jallon. His arrival changed the political and religious landscape of the entire Senegambian region for decades to come.[4]

Shaykh Umar was born into a modest *toorodo* family in the Futa Toro village of Halwar, near Podor, around 1793. He grew to be the most famous latter-day adherent of the Islamic reform movement which had stirred up the political, social, and religious life of Senegambia from the time of Nasir Al Din in the late seventeenth century. He was a direct successor to the class of marabouts who had risen to power in Bundu, Futa Jallon, and Futa Tooro, where the success of the three glorious Muslim revolutions had ensured the triumph of a theocratic regime since the eighteenth century. Bolstered by his pilgrimage to Mecca and other Islamic centers in the Middle East, Shaykh Umar became the principal leader (*Khalife*) of the Tijaniyya movement. Originally using peaceful instruction, but later through holy war, the movement aimed to speed up the conversion to Islam of all West Africa. Shaykh Umar was its embodiment. Advancing it by both pen and sword, he ended up, of necessity, reshaping the political, social, and religious landscape of all Senegambia and a large part of western Sudan. The changes he wrought were commensurate with his religious credentials. These were so solid that they made him the most clear-headed political figure of the second half of the nineteenth century, a man capable of embodying the Islamic reform movement at a time when European plans for colonial conquest were taking clearer shape.

Shaykh Umar began by studying under all the great religious teachers in Senegambia, in particular Abdul Karim Al Naqil of Timbo, and under *Jollobe* from Satina to Labé. He then went on a pilgrimage to Mecca lasting from 1828 to 1831. In Sudan he was appointed *Khalife* of Tijaniyya Islam by Muhammad Al Ghali. The pilgrimage was a way to consolidate his education, which he pursued throughout his long return journey by way of Cairo, Bornu, Sokoto, and Hamdalaye in Macina.

Late in 1840 he arrived in Futa Jallon. Wherever he went, his reputation as a holy man, reinforced by the pilgrim's prestige, preceded him. Legend has it that in Mecca and Cairo he had dazzled great scholars with his erudition. It was said that during his seven-year sojourn in Sokoto he won the respect of Mohammad Bello, heir to Usman Dan Fodio. Some said his erudition surpassed that of the most renowned religious leaders, including the Kunta of Timbuktu, masters of the Qadriyya school, until then the only Muslim school known throughout sub-Saharan West Africa. Armed with his credentials as master of the new Tijaniyya school, directly consecrated by Muhammad Al Ghali, Shaykh Umar made it his mission to combat "paganism", to challenge the political and social status quo under the aging Muslim theocracies, and to impose a new and militant brand of Islam.[5]

When Shaykh Umar settled in Futa Jallon around 1840, a transitional period in his career began. In 1852 he mounted a *jihad* to extend his power from Senegambia to the Niger bend. This was an important period, because it was during this first stay in Futa Jallon that the pilgrim marabout, author of a book entitled *Spears*, gradually transformed his disciples into a military spearhead for the conquest of a new empire.

Shaykh Umar settled first in Jekunko from 1840 to 1845, with the agreement of the *Alfaya Almami* Bubakar, a man known for his piety. His plan was to concentrate on the education of his disciples and to write his masterpiece, the *Rimah* (*Spears*). That work, incidentally was to become the manual of Tijaniyya Muslim worship in West Africa. His disciples came from all over: Bornu, Sokoto, Macina. They included freed Aku and Yoruba slaves from Sierra Leone, who traveled from Freetown up the Niger Bend. There were Kabas from Kankan, and numerous disciples from Bundu, Futa Jallon, and Futa Toro. All drawn by Shaykh Umar's reputation for learning, integrity, and piety, this community of various origins came together around the Master to advance their knowledge of the Tijaniyya Muslim way.

In 1846, Shaykh Umar conducted his first tour of northern Senegambia, focusing on his native Futa, where he received a triumphal welcome after his twenty-six-year absence. His objective was to recruit adherents, to wage a holy war with them, and thus to ensure the triumph of Islam. But he ran into opposition from a Jakhanke marabout, Karamokho Taslima, son of the founder of Tuuba, Karamokho Bâ, who, given his commitment to *Qadriyya* Islam as taught by the famous Al Haj Saalim Suwaare, was against the use of force as a means of converting people to Islam. In other areas of Senegambia, though, Shaykh Umar was more successful. Great personalities like Alfa Molo and Maba Jaaxu Ba embraced the Tijaniyya way, along with thousands of new disciples from the Manding, Wolof, and

Fulani communities, who came to join him. In Futa Toro in particular, even though the ruling aristocracy was hostile, he recruited younger members of various families. On the return trip, a large number of Soninke from Gajaaga, as well as Peul from Bundu and Khasonke from the religious center of Gunjuru, also joined his group. Shaykh Umar met the French twice, first at Podor and then at Bakel. He told them what he planned to do: to create an Islamic peace throughout the land, thus ensuring an atmosphere conducive to trade. In 1847, contemplating the impressive size of Shaykh Umar's following, the *Almami* Umar of the *Soriya* clan grew justifiably apprehensive. He therefore tried, for a time, to block Shaykh Umar's return to Jekunko. Reacting to this unfriendly move, Shaykh Umar left Jekunko for Dingiray, a settlement between the Bafing and the Tinkiso on the border of the Tamba kingdom founded around 1820 by the Sakho lineage.

From 1848 to 1849, so rapidly did Shaykh Umar's religious following grow in strength that Yimba, king of Tamba, decided to destroy the fortified settlement at Dingiray. His decision sparked a *jihad* during which Shaykh Umar, the Holy Warrior, in less than a decade conquered a vast empire stretching from Senegambia to the Niger Bend.[6]

The holy war became Shaykh Umar's main objective. For the first time, he linked the goals of conversion to Islam and the Islamic reform movement with that of territorial conquest, his aim being to set up a vast Muslim entity. This new vision was opposed not only by the region's established theocracies, but also by the European powers, whose territorial ambitions were becoming clearer along the Senegambian coast as well as in the Gambia and Senegal valleys. Shaykh Umar concentrated first on conquering the non-Muslim *ceddo* states. This reassured the *Almamis* of Timbo, who had been alarmed at the size of his movement in Futa Jallon. For large numbers of the population there had been attracted to the Tijaniyya movement. They made up the first battalions of Shaykh Umar's army of holy warriors. But if Shaykh Umar attacked the *ceddo* states first, his policy was dictated by strategic considerations. It enabled him to sell captives taken during his holy war in Futa Jallon. He then used the proceeds to buy arms from Sierra Leone and the Southern Rivers, far from Futa Jallon. For his part, the ruling *Almami*, Umar of the *Soriya* clan, considering the holy man's partiality toward the rival *Alfaya* clan, was relieved to see him set off to conquer the upper Senegal valley. At the same time, the *Soriya* faction, like the *Alfaya*, was confronted with an unprecedented problem: the Hubbu revolt, the most terrible civil war in Futa Jallon history. The revolt was led by a marabout, Mamadu Juhe, based at Laminiya in the province of Fode Hajji.

## C.    The Hubbu rebellion

Quite a few historians tend to reduce Futa Jallon history to a political crisis in the central regime fueled by competition between the *Alfaya* and *Soriya* factions. They overemphasize the hostility of provincial chiefs increasingly asserting their autonomy, not to mention the intrigue-ridden Council of Elders caught up in ceaseless power struggles between factions of the ruling class. According to these historians, the two-clan structure lay at the root of the chronic instability of the political system in Futa Jallon. In time it would provide the ideological justification for colonial conquest. This argument leaves out the role of economic changes on the coast. Even more seriously, it ignores the scope of popular rebellions which, in the nineteenth century, gradually undermined the political and social order established by the Muslim theocracy in Futa Jallon, thus preparing the ground for colonial rule.

The Hubbu rebellion symbolized the disaffection of the main mass of free persons and slaves, under the leadership of new Muslim organizers. The regime established by the Muslim revolution at the beginning of the eighteenth century had become the hereditary property of the families that had led the revolution. Now, in the name of Islam, new leaders rose to challenge the power of the aging military and clerical aristocracy. The Hubbu movement, lasting throughout the second half of the nineteenth century under Mamadu Juhe and his son Abal, continued in the form of movements led by Wali of Gomba and Cherno Ndama. Under the banner of Islam, these movements mounted a vast political and social protest against the old theocratic system. That system had grown sclerotic under an oppressive aristocracy that cared nothing for the ideals of the triumphant eighteenth-century Muslim revolution.

Shaykh Umar's criticism of the establishment in the Muslim theocracies of Senegambia and western Sudan was thus reinforced by protests from new leaders like Mamadu Juhe, even if they did not necessarily belong to the new Tijaniyya version of Islam, steadily gaining ground throughout the region.

Mamadu Juhe began his studies in Futa Toro, taking intensive courses from Shaykh Sidiya Al Kabir, the leading exponent of Qadriyya doctrine after the Kuntas of Timbuktu. He then settled in Timbo, where until 1840 he supervised the religious education of numerous children of the aristocracy. He then moved to Laminiya in Fode Hajji province, where his reputation for piety and learning attracted numerous disciples. The overwhelming majority were free men of modest status. But some were slaves escaping economic and political oppression at the hands of the *Almami* in Timbo province. For the central regime, driven bankrupt by constant infighting between the two royal clans, and denied normal revenues from the now more or less autonomous provinces, put the inhabitants of Timbo province itself under intense fiscal pressure.

That is why religious conflict must be ruled out as a basic cause of the Hubbu rebellion. After all, the Hubbu remained attached to Qadriyya doctrine at a time when Shaykh Umar's Tijaniyya faith was in the ascendant. In point of fact, the *Soriya* clan adopted the Tijaniyya approach rather late. As for the *Almami* Umar, his dislike of the pilgrim Shaykh Umar was well known.[7] Blyden, who visited Timbo in 1872, was unambiguous in his perception of the economic and political roots of the Hubbu rebellion:

The Hoobos are renegade Fulani in rebellion against the King of Timbo. Twenty years ago, on account of the impositions of the Almary Umaru, they revolted and migrated with their families, to settle on pasture land between the Futa and the Solima. They are called Hoobos or Hubus because on leaving their homes they chanted a verse from the Koran in which the word Hubu occurred twice. The verse says: "Nihibu Rusul Allahi Huban Wahidan," meaning: "Those possessed of the love of God's Messenger."[8]

An anonymous document from Boké, dated 1873, gives even more precise information on social and political aspects of the rebellion. It states that the republic, led by Abal, son of Juhe, had liberated itself from all obligations toward the *Almami*, that it had no intention whatsoever of recognizing his authority, that it had abolished slavery, and that it welcomed all who freed themselves from their masters.[9] The Hubbu revolt, then, was an expression of latent discontent among slaves who, for the first time, turned to Islam in order to combat the oppression of their masters, after the desperate revolts of the eighteenth century.

As a rule, traditional Futa chronicles reflect the views of the aristocracy. These were hostile to the Hubbu. Even so, the chronicles recognize the social aspect of the rebellion: "Peul migrated from all corners of Futa and gathered at Boketo. Additional numbers of persons weak in *genuine faith* escaped to join them there in order to be rid of this discipline. Having grown numerous, they strengthened the forces of the Literate Ones."[10] Beneath the regime's sneering refusal to acknowledge the orthodoxy of the Hubbu's Islamic faith, it is clear enough that the movement was primarily a social and political revolution.

The Hubbu mobilized their forces, drawing large numbers of the oppressed to the Futa periphery. They included rural Peul of modest origins and status, subject to all manner of impositions and exactions. Some were descendants of pastoral Pulli, recent Peul converts to Islam. Some were diehard Jallonkes. Thousands came from slave villages, where they had been concentrated. The rural Peul in particular, politically disenfranchised and forced to pay excessive taxes on their livestock, fled in large numbers to join the holy man who wished to construct a haven of peace outside the *Almami's* jurisdiction. There the precepts of the *Sharia*, trodden underfoot by the aristocracy, would become law.

In the Wolof, Sereer, and Soninke kingdoms, still under *ceddo* regimes, Muslim communities, though unable to overthrow the ruling regimes outright, set up autonomous enclaves managed by influential marabouts. In course of time, these marabouts worked out a balanced coexistence with the state. Still, throughout their history, there were frequent rebellions, occurring every time the *ceddo* regime put the Muslim communities under excessive pressure. Sometimes these communities became veritable political and territorial enclaves, exempt from the customary pillaging aggressions of royal slave armies.

In the Muslim theocracies that had risen to power since the eighteenth century, a new generation of marabouts emerged. Barred from wielding political power on account of their birth, but vested with religious authority, they criticized incumbent Muslim regimes for their oppressive behavior, basing their strictures on scripture. Unable to change the status quo, they preferred to migrate from the kingdom, taking disciples and property along. They settled on the outskirts of the territory. There they founded new villages, free from the arbitrary rule of the aristocracy.

The Hubbu movement led by the marabout Mamadu Juhe, like Shaykh Umar's *fergo*, in which huge numbers of disciples migrated from the two Futas, was an oblique challenge to the incumbent theocratic regimes. The fact that Juhe was of the Qadriyya sect, and that Shaykh Umar preached Tijaniyya doctrine, did not affect the unfolding process in any way. This makes the difference in doctrinal viewpoints, which certain historians suppose to have accounted for the more or less revolutionary character of one or the other movement, much less important. The determining factor was, without a doubt, the economic, political, and social crisis. That was what gave both Juhe and Shaykh Umar their rationale for mobilizing disciples in the name of a militant Muslim ethos, for the purpose of establishing a new Islamic order.

In this respect, despite the genuine dynamism of his *Tijaniyya* vision, which steadily spread throughout Senegambia, Shaykh Umar's approach was still compatible with the older Qadriyya vision projected by the prestigious Shaykh Sidia Al Kadir from his Mauritanian base. Both had the same dynamic of political and religious protest against the status quo. The faithful adherence of the Hubbu to the Qadriyya was rooted in the teachings of Sayyidi Abdal Qadir Al Jilani, whose doctrine emerged in twelfth-century Baghdad, with its advocacy of tolerance, charity, piety and moral purity, holding out to the wretched of the earth the hope of social justice in harmony with the ethical principles of Islam.

Right from the start, the *Almamis* saw the Hubbu rebellion as a social and political revolution. They were quick to go on the offensive, attacking Juhe's community in an attempt to nip in the bud this autonomous power set up on the Futa Jallon periphery. After coming under several attacks, the Hubbu went on the offensive in 1859, capturing the capital, Timbo when it was abandoned by the two *Almamis*, Umar of the *Soriya* faction and Ibrahima Sori Daara of the *Alfaya* faction. It was now clear that the two *Almamis* were incapable of mobilizing the Futa kingdom against the rebellion. It was not until the hurried return of Bademba, who was on a military expedition to Kaabu when the crisis peaked, that the Hubbu occupation of Timbo ended.

The problem was this: the Council of Elders, a committee of the Federal Assembly of Fugumba, was the only body empowered to order a general mobilization. But it refused to order Muslim soldiers into battle against opponents who were not just fellow Muslims, but also members of the same national community. Beneath this argument lay a deeper reason for the refusal to issue mobilization orders. The opposition of the Council of Elders primarily reflected its members' desire to protect the Assembly's prerogatives from the centralizing encroachments of the *Almami* Umar, the *Soriya* strongman. Umar had exasperated both the Council of Elders and the provincial chiefs, anxious to safeguard their autonomy. So they remained aloof as the rebellion threatened the central authority in Timbo.

There is no doubt whatsoever that it was this danger, which both *Almamis* saw not as a religious challenge but as a political threat, that now brought the *Alfaya* and *Soriya* clans together. As soon as Bademba, a member of the *Alfaya* clan, had liberated Timbo, the *Almami* Umar relinquished power of his own accord, in favor of Ibrahima Sori Daara. He had reigned without interruption for eight and a half years. Now the two clans began making serious attempts to ensure the success of the alternating two-year system. One incumbent yielded voluntarily to the next, without resorting to the sort of civil strife that had steadily weakened the central regime in previous years. The pact between the two clans was the main feature of this second half of the nineteenth century, because the Hubbu movement continued to threaten Timbo, the capital.[11] But from the start of the nineteenth century, the central regime faced a different challenge. Essentially economic and political, this challenge was a consequence of profound changes caused by the gradual triumph of legitimate trade in the Southern Rivers region. It forced Futa Jallon to embark on a vigorous policy of territorial expansion toward the coast, where the European powers had become increasingly active.

# 11    Futa Jallon expansion into the Southern Rivers region

The development of peanut farming enabled the Southern Rivers region to adjust gradually to the abolition of the slave trade. The growth of legitimate trade turned the coast into a magnet for traders from Futa Jallon, at a time when French, English, and Portuguese trading companies were also moving in, hoping to profit from new opportunities in the trans-Atlantic trading system.

Futa Jallon was already a power on the mainland. Now it mobilized all its forces for conquering the Southern Rivers market between the Gambia and Sierra Leone. It tightened its control over Rio Nunez and Rio Pongo, and undertook a vast military campaign against Kaabu and Forria, culminating in the famous battle of Kansala in 1867.

While Futa Jallon was seeking effective control over the Southern Rivers region, European trading companies in the area, notably the French firms, were struggling for monopoly control over peanut production. For a while, economic prosperity muted sovereignty disputes between European powers and the states of the Southern Rivers region. Meanwhile, attempts by new companies backed by metropolitan capital to gain commercial control had already aroused opposition from old slave-trading families. These made common cause with Futa Jallon, expecting to maintain the economic advantages they drew from contraband slave trading. At the same time, the local aristocracies were trying to use the new boom in legitimate trade as leverage in their efforts to challenge Futa Jallon suzerainty in the Southern Rivers region.

The parallel system of legitimate trade and clandestine slave dealing pulled Futa Jallon irresistibly toward the coast. There, it ran into stiffening opposition from French companies drawn into the Southern Rivers area by the growing peanut trade.

## A.    The *Almamis'* policy for coping with the crisis of the trans-Atlantic trading system

The central regime in Timbo was the first to feel the impact of the slump of the trans-Atlantic trading system. This was because it was far from the major routes used by contraband slave traders. These led into Rio Pongo, Rio Nunez, and Rio Geba, controlled by Labé and Timbi provinces. Reacting to this situation, the *Almamis* initiated a policy of commercial ties with Sierra Leone. The opening of roads between the Southern Rivers and Freetown facilitated the move.

Hampered by numerous succession crises between the *Alfaya* and *Soriya* clans, the *Almamis* in Timbo had failed to react promptly to the abolition of slave trading and the development of legitimate trade on the coast. Timbo therefore fell back on economic links with Freetown. But there, the British had made legitimate trade compulsory since the start of the nineteenth century. Anxious to maximize their income within the framework of the coastal trading system, the *Almamis* readily agreed to develop caravan trading along the Kisi-Kisi road to Freetown. This was the only option left if Timbo was to end the chronic imbalance between the resources of the central authority and those of the provinces of Labé and Timbi, which exercised an effective monopoly over trade in Rio Nunez, Rio Pongo, and Rio Geba.

The desire for trade between Freetown and Timbo was mutual. Sierra Leone gave it practical expression by dispatching several missions in the first half of the nineteenth century in an effort to promote legitimate trade with Futa Jallon. But the British missions, one led by O'Brien in January 1821, another by W. Cooper Thompson in June 1842, did not result in sustained trade contacts between Timbo and Freetown. One reason was that following the death of McCarthy in 1824, British policy vacillated. An even stronger obstacle was the inability of the *Almamis* to subdue Limba, Temne, and Susu marauders, who systematically robbed caravans on the Kisi-Kisi and Port Loko roads in a bid to maintain their status as indispensable middlemen.

The one outcome of the Thompson mission was to create a kind of demarcation line between a pro-British *Alfaya* faction and a *Soriya* faction presumed to be pro-French because its leader, Umar, who owed his victory to arms obtained from the French in Bakel, was more or less blamed for the death of the British representative. Another important reason for Freetown's failure was the commitment of the British colony to the promotion of legitimate trade, and its campaign against slave trading. True, a couple of *Almamis*, the *Soriya* Abdul Qadiri and the *Alfaya* Bubakar, tried their best to promote legitimate trade. But up until the mid-nineteenth century Futa Jallon policy in the Southern Rivers region was substantially determined by the boom in contraband slave trading in Rio Pongo, Rio Geba, Rio Cacheu, and, to a lesser extent, Rio Nunez.[1]

Under these circumstances, the Futa Jallon theocracy turned its ambitions toward the Senegambian coast. Henceforth, its main objective would be to conquer the Southern Rivers market between Freetown in the south and Bathurst in the north. This turnabout was accentuated by the parallel nature of trade in the Southern Rivers area. For traders there combined trade in leather, livestock, gold, and ivory with the sale of captives to slave dealers, undisturbed by patrolling British cruisers. Moreover, most of the Futa Jallon aristocracy was against the abolition of the slave trade and the halting of slave raids. After all, most of their income came from these occupations. Finally, the aristocracy needed constantly to replenish the reserves of slave labor it used for domestic production. Many of these slaves had been wiped out in the 1824 epidemic.

In 1826, a *Soriya* leader who wanted to continue slave raids was appointed *Almami* in preference to his *Alfaya* rival, Bubakar, a peaceful abolitionist. This preference was confirmed by several slave dealers who traveled to Timbo from Rio Pongo, such as Lawrence in 1820, and above all the notorious Canot, who traveled to the area in 1827. The purpose of these visits was to organize mass contraband slave trading from Futa Jallon.

The policy of coastward expansion was significantly slowed down by disputes between the *Alfaya* and *Soriya* clans. A second obstacle was the hostility between the central regime of the *Almamis* based in Timbo, and the provincial governments of Timbi and Labé, traditionally vested with nominal Futa Jallon suzerainty over the entire Southern Rivers area. The policy of coastward expansion also ran into unexpected obstacles. The first had to do with the gradual triumph of legitimate trade. The second was the rejection of the Timbo regime's suzerainty claims by local aristocracies despite the collaboration of slave-trading families. The third and most serious was the strengthening of the French presence in the Southern Rivers region.

## B.     Futa Jallon expansion into the Rio Nunez area

Rio Nunez, nominally under the authority of the *Almami* of Futa Jallon, was in practice under the direct control of the provincial chief of Labé. British anti-slaving cruisers found the area, with its lone estuary, easy to patrol. For that reason, legitimate trade became dominant there quite early, around 1840.

Still, a long series of civil conflicts between the Nalu and the Landuman followed the development of legitimate trade. In addition, the many French, British, and Belgian trading companies operating in the area increasingly interfered in its political affairs to promote their commercial interests.

As an alternative to permanent occupation, the Futa Jallon regime used European powers to ensure the security of caravans and to safeguard its economic and political prerogatives in the valley.

Rio Nunez very soon underwent profound changes. Peanut farming, primarily the business of the downstream Nalu, radically changed the local power balance by depriving the Landuman of their control of the slave trade, a prerogative they had exercised through their supervision of the Boké caravan route.

The preoccupation of the Landuman chiefs with the pursuit of their economic privileges, tied to the continuation of the slave trade, paradoxically led to the emergence of the Nalu as a military and economic power in Rio Nunez.[2]

This economic transformation was the cause of political upheavals following the death of Macaude in 1838. The Landuman chief Sarah took the event as a signal to rebel against Futa Jallon suzerainty and to wage war on legitimate trade. He attacked the Futa Jallon garrison at Boké and imposed a stiff surcharge on duties paid by foreign traders. Meanwhile, the conflict between the Nalu and the Landuman, dominated by the rivalry between Salifu Towl and Sarah, sparked an outbreak of colonial gunboat diplomacy with the spectacular arrival of two ships, the *Corvette* and the *Fine*, in November 1838, to protect the interests of trading companies. But the Treaty of 1842, signed with the French, and that of 1843 with the British, clearly ratified the existence of two trading communities as well as the division of the estuary into two separate sections, one under Lamina Towl as Nalu chief, the other headed by Sarah as Landuman chief.

From the second phase of the war between the Nalu and the Landuman in 1843 and 1844, Europeans intervened directly in the conflict, while Futa Jallon gradually gained recognition as an umpire in the settlement of the political crisis. The rapid growth of legitimate trade, and above all the speedy expansion of peanut farming, thus worked in favor of the occupation of Rio Nunez by the French, at the expense of the British. British traders, established in the region for a long period, were more involved in the interminable conflicts between the Nalu and the Landuman over control of trade along the river.[3]

After the double intervention of France and Britain in March 1844, there were hopeful signs of trade normalization. But upon the death of Sarah, the Landuman chief since 1838, that promise evaporated in the political instability that engulfed Rio Nunez. The crisis involved a peculiar conflict: two of Sarah's sons, Tongo and Mayore, not content with fighting each other for the succession, went so far as to block the Modière royal line, eligible according to the principle of alternate terms, to prevent it acceding to power. At the time that this conflict broke out, the British, who had a base at Kakandy, were against the idea of shifting the capital. The French, on the other hand, were solidly settled at Boké.

The Council of Elders at Bonchevy, which controlled the Simo secret society, favored Tongo at the time, because it wished to protest against the presence of a Futa Jallon garrison commanded by Madiu and stationed at Boké since 1843. Thus, from 1844 to 1846, the downstream portion of Rio Nunez was split between two camps: Tongo was securely installed at Kakandy as well as in the towns of Kisasi and Kanduma; Mayore, for his part, supported by Madiu, the Peul resident, and Lamina Towl, the Nalu chief, occupied the strategic location of Boké. Because of this political crisis, caravan traffic from Futa Jallon was diverted from Rio Nunez during the commercial year 1846–7, in an effort to force the Simo society or the Council of Elders to change their minds.

Around this time, reacting to the general slump in trade, the French financed an expedition of Mayore's forces, backed by those of the Nalu chief Lamina Towl, against Kakandy. Once Tongo was defeated, Madiu, the resident Peul representative, convened a meeting for the purpose of electing a new chief. This was in February 1848, a period when the alliance between Lamina Towl, Mayore, and the French had brought about radical changes in the balance of force, provoking the British into calling in the warship *Grappler*, commanded by Lysaght, to defend their interests. In this way the rift between Nalu and Landuman was worsened by the rivalry between foreign powers, with the British supporting Tongo while the French and the Futa Jallon kingdom threw their weight behind his younger brother and opponent Mayore, in the scramble for power among the Landuman.

Now the British put a great deal of energy into securing their interests. In February 1847, they signed a treaty with Tongo committing him to combat slave trading and to guarantee freedom to British traders, with the same privileges accorded vessels and traders from other European nations. On the French side, from 1846–7 the Board of Gorée, backed by the Bordeaux Chamber of Commerce, demanded permission to build a fort in Rio Nunez. Competition between the powers began to place considerable limits on the effectiveness of the 1845 Franco–British anti-slaving agreement, which also required that all territorial acquisitions be submitted to the approval of the other signatory. Despite Lysaght's exertions, Madiu, the Timbo representative, under the influence of Villeneuve, confirmed Mayore as Landuman chief, with Boké as his capital. Furthermore, the resident Futa Jallon representative henceforth guaranteed the interests of European powers, in return for the right to collect customs duties from foreign traders. However, the reinforcement of Futa Jallon suzerainty in Rio Nunez promptly drove Lamina Towl, the Nalu chief, into signing a treaty with the Belgian lieutenant Van Haverbeke, on the ship *Louise Marie*. The agreement ceded land situated between Victoria and Rapas to Belgium, for an annual rent of $1,000. But at the end of the year 1848, once the French, British, and Belgian gunboats had left, foreign trade in the region was again without protection in the agitated political climate of Rio Nunez.

Lamina Towl had found the terms of the earlier accords unsatisfactory. Now he took advantage of the changed situation to demand extra fees from French traders operating between Rapas and Victoria. At the same time, hostilities flared up again between Mayore and Tongo, disrupting trade. Called in by traders from the respective countries, the British warship *Favourite*, the French *Recherche,* and the Belgian *Louise Marie* moved up the Rio Nunez to provide protection. For his part, the *Almami* Umar dispatched his envoy Madiu with formal instructions to end the Landuman civil war by peaceful means. If that proved impossible, he was instructed to cooperate with the European powers to end the conflict, which had cut off supplies of salt, indispensable for livestock, to the Futa region. With Madiu's agreement, the French and Belgians bombarded Boké and drove out Mayore, replacing him in March 1849 with Tongo, who ceded land near the capital to the two powers.

These accords notwithstanding, peace did not return to Rio Nunez. For Mayore, backed by Lamina Towl, opposed the alliance between Tongo and Futa Jallon backed by the European powers. Since MacDonald, the Governor of Sierra Leone, had chosen to focus his attention on the Sherbro, in the southern part of the colony, it was not until after the arrival of a new resident (the *Almami*'s brother, incidentally) at the head of a large army that it became possible to reinstate Tongo as legitimate chief of Boké. Thus, massive intervention from Futa Jallon in 1850 resulted in a considerable reduction of the freedom of action of the Landuman and Nalu chiefs, now obliged to accept the partition of Rio Nunez into two political divisions directly controlled from Timbo.

After 1850, the situation on the Senegambian coast was to a great extent determined by two factors. The first was competition between European powers, in particular Belgium, France and Britain. The second, and more decisive, was the development of their economic interests, linked with the triumph of legitimate trade. Very soon, however, Belgium gave up its prerogatives in accordance with the Treaty of 1849, while Britain claimed £5,000 sterling in damages for the Franco–Belgian attack on the property of Braithwaite and Martin. With Belgium out of the running, only two contenders, the British and the French, remained. London had instructed British agents in the area to do nothing outside the colony of Freetown. The French had become increasingly committed to an expansionist policy under Napoleon III. Indeed, France's vigorous expansionism in the Southern Rivers region, pursued from the colony of Senegal, was a logical development. French interests were predominant there. In addition, there was the economic option in favor of peanuts. One expression of this expansionist French policy in Senegambia, following the pull of the peanut crop, was the 1 November 1854 Decree establishing the new colony of Gorée and the Dependencies. This also covered the Southern Rivers region.

In 1860, as part of the campaign against contraband slave trading, the British occupied Bulama Island. In 1861, they annexed a large portion of Sherbro region south of Freetown, in a bid to ensure control over the palm oil trade. The French took these moves as a justification for their policy of territorial expansion in Senegambia. Eager to promote the interests of Rio Nunez branches of trading companies based in Bordeaux and Marseille, Faidherbe was particularly active in the Southern Rivers region. He visited it in 1860. From then on he pushed to get a fort constructed at Boké. Its purpose would be to protect traders against violence from the local population, to draw in more trade from Futa Jallon, to combat the British presence in Sierra Leone, and to counter the Portuguese presence in Rio Geba. The plan was immediately set in motion by the dispatch of Lieutenant Lambert to Timbo, with the purpose of requesting the *Almamis* to cede Boké to the French.

This was a time when the two *Almamis*, Umar and Ibrahima Sori, happened to be on good terms. Very reluctantly they agreed to the construction of a French post at Boké. They knew it was all too likely, in time, to prove fatal to Futa Jallon's own expansionist drive toward the coast. But following the arrest of a large number of Peul who had taken slaves to Sierra Leone, the *Almamis* closed the road to Freetown. Lambert, for his part, promised the *Almamis* substantial tribute. And they hoped, in particular, to use the French presence as a means of maintaining order in Rio Nunez. All these factors favored a positive response from Timbo. Besides, the agreement of the *Almamis* was a roundabout way of enabling the central authorities to improve their influence in the face of the challenge from the *Alfas* of Labé, traditionally vested with Futa Jallon suzerainty over the Rio Nunez. As a matter of fact, the provincial chief of Labé, reacting to the agreement the *Almamis* had concluded over his head, refused Lambert permission to visit Labé.

In any case, French interests and those of Timbo were now linked in an effort to end the depredations of Landuman marauders, who endangered the trading system as a whole. In May 1860, Landuman fighters attacked caravans from Futa Jallon and kidnapped nearly two thousand slave porters. They refused to give them up, thus encouraging large numbers of slaves to escape from their *runde* in search of freedom on the coast. From 1861 to 1863, Futa Jallon caravans lost 4,000 porters at Boké. In fact, the slaves, whether runaways or kidnapped porters, ended up doing hard labor planting peanuts for local chiefs or old slaving families. The large-scale use of slave labor for peanut production thus worsened life for slaves on the coast. For these reasons, the *Almami* Umar wished to see the French strengthen their presence in Rio Nunez, for the advancement of their mutual interests.[4]

French control was somewhat delayed on account of Faidherbe's military campaigns in northern Senegambia, especially in the Senegal valley and in Kajoor. Meanwhile, a steady stream of complaints from trading companies in Senegambia led Chambers of Commerce in Bordeaux, Nantes, and Rouen to demand warship patrols and the establishment of military posts to ensure security in Rio Nunez.

Interpreting, rather disingenuously, the British annexation of Sherbro as a threat to take over the Southern Rivers, the French signed a series of new so-called protectorate treaties. The main purpose of these treaties was to strip the coastal states of their sovereignty. For example, the 28 November 1865 treaty with Yura, a Nalu chief, turned his country into a French protectorate. He ceded his right to collect duties from vessels anchoring in local waters to the French, in return for an annual cash payment of 5,000 francs. In January 1866, a 470-man expedition, under the commanding officer at Gorée, launched a surprise attack on the Landuman, forcing Duka to give up Boké plateau for the French to build their fort on. But in 1867, a combined force of Futa Jallon Peul and local Landuman fighters attacked the fort in an attempt to reverse the French coup.

Cauvin took severe reprisals against this anti-French opposition movement. Alfa Kafa, son of the Alfa of Labé, a man opposed to the French presence which benefited the central authorities in Timbo, was killed in action. The Landuman chiefs Duka and Diong were arrested. This French victory marked the failure of the Futa Jallon policy of coastward expansion. From now on the French, while paying lip service to Timbo or Labé control over Rio Nunez, worked resolutely to limit Futa Jallon influence, to their own advantage.[5]

## C.     Futa Jallon expansion into Rio Pongo

The steady advance of legitimate trade created conditions conducive to the French takeover of Rio Nunez, at the expense of the Futa Jallon's expansionist ambitions, as well as of the sovereignty of the Landuman and Nalu inhabitants over their own region. In Rio Pongo, however, the triumph of legitimate trade came much more slowly. One reason was that contraband slave trading persisted there until the 1860s. For, since 1824, with the connivance of old slaving families closely integrated into local politics on account of their many marriages into the area's royal families, Futa Jallon had exercised direct control over Rio Pongo. Rio Pongo was one of three remaining outlets for the contraband trade in slaves, the other two being Rio Geba and Rio Cacheu.

Futa Jallon support for the Ormond family up to 1833, then for those of Mary Faber and Lightburn from 1838 onward, produced two results. First, it entrenched slave trading families in political life in the Rio Pongo valley. Second, it stunted legitimate trade. For instance, in 1842, Futa Jallon engineered the military occupation of Thia, considerably delaying the takeover of Rio Pongo by European powers, especially France.

While Rio Nunez was the theater of permanent civil conflict between the Landuman and their Nalu neighbors, Rio Pongo, on the whole, was more stable. This gave the old, politically integrated slaving families there the breathing space they needed to adjust to the new economic situation without having to cope with European interference. The price they paid was greater subservience to the Futa Jallon regime. In the early part of the century, slave-trading families fought over the monopoly enjoyed first by the Ormonds and then by the Fabers. The conflict was eventually resolved. The resulting peace was briefly interrupted when Yati Yende Kati of Thia died in 1842.

The ensuing succession struggle pitted the Futa Jallon protégé Balu Bangu of the Cumba Bali family, who had been kept out of power by Uli Kati since 1800, against Yati Yende Kati's younger brother Culom (Mathias) Kati, who also happened to be the son-in-law of Thomas Curtis. Culom had the backing of the Simo secret society. As in Rio Nunez, the Council of Elders, in charge of that secret society, opposed the Futa Jallon presence. But the Futa Jallon resident representative, Alfa Siakha, backed by a slave army owned by the Euro-Africans Mary Faber and Bailey Lightburn, rivals to Culom Kati's ally Thomas Curtis, got Bala Bangu installed by force. Alfa Siakha moved the political capital to Bofa and forced Bala Bangu to consult him and the Council of Elders regularly, while letting Culom Kati's opposing group remain at Thias to safeguard Thomas Curtis's property.

This compromise, brokered by Alfa Siakha, restored peace to Rio Pongo for nearly ten years. It also helped the old slave trading families to switch gradually to legitimate trade. In the peaceful interlude, the Curtis, Faber, Lightburn, and Wilkinson families were able to carry on their contraband slave-trading business with no interference from European powers. A reason for the political stability enjoyed by Rio Pongo was that all these Euro-African families had integrated into local royal clans through numerous marriages. A second reason was their alliance with Futa Jallon. But once the crisis in Rio Nunez was resolved, and French commercial interests began to expand into the Southern Rivers region from the mid-nineteenth century, intervention from the European powers became a regular fact of life in Rio Pongo.[6]

For, once the Rio Nunez trading circuits were reopened, Bala Bangu's Futa Jallon allies abandoned him. Under pressure from his rival Culom Kati, he agreed in January 1852 to sign a treaty with the British. Its terms called for him to take an active part in the anti-slavery campaign and to protect British trade. The Faber, Styles, and Lightburn families, together with Richard Wilkinson, chief of Dominguia, frightened by the prospect of an alliance between Bala Bangu, Thomas Curtis, and the abolitionist colony of Sierra Leone, organized a powerful army of their plantation slaves for an invasion of Rio Pongo. This new war of the Euro-African families was complicated by the participation of Susu and Baga chiefs, who, motivated by hostility to the Futa Jallon presence, and responding to the threat from Bangalan slave traders, banded together to protect Kati.

The battles around Dominguia produced heavy casualties, and Alfa Siakha had to intervene to rescue his brother-in-law, Richard Wilkinson. Sporadic skirmishing between the Susu and the Lightburns did not stop until 1855, when the latter capitulated. Alfa Siakha, drawing the necessary conclusions from the outcome, deposed Bala Bangu in 1858, replacing him with Culom Kati. The victory of the coalition of Susu and Baga chiefs over the slave army levied by the Fabers, Lightburns, and Wilkinsons strengthened the Curtis family's position in Rio Pongo. Nevertheless, the river basin in its entirety remained under the command of the Futa Jallon resident representative, Alfa Siakha. Siakha opted to protect the interests of the Bangalan traders, defeated in the recent war.[7]

As in Rio Nunez, the colony of Sierra Leone showed very little interest in a policy of territorial expansion in Rio Pongo after its disastrous failure in the Moria region in 1853. The British colony continued in its lukewarm attitude even though there were many British traders in the Southern Rivers region. In this part of Senegambia, the major concern of the British was the campaign against contraband slave trading, particularly active in Rio Pongo. There, in 1860, the British government ordered the Governor of Sierra Leone, Hill, to destroy slave collection points teeming with captives brought in by numerous slave-trading caravans from Futa Jallon. From 1855, the British presence was reinforced by the settlement of a good number of missionaries of African origin, sent by the West Indian Church. These missionaries admitted members of Euro-African families to their schools. Earlier in the century, members of the Church Missionary Society had been driven out by the slave-trading families for preaching against slave trading. The new set of missionaries received a better welcome. Their arrival coincided with the triumph of legitimate trade. And peanuts ruled the new economic order.

Peanuts, indeed, were the major attraction that drew increasing numbers of French traders from their already secure bases in Rio Nunez and Mellakure to Rio Pongo. Following Faidherbe's trip in 1860, a second war involving Euro-Africans, the Koli-Sokho War, broke out in Rio Pongo in 1863. It pitted Manga Culom, alias Mathias Kati, supported by the

Lightburn and Faber families, against the slave-trading faction of Bala Bangu, allied with the Curtis family and the Futa Jallon regime. Taking advantage of these upheavals, France signed a protectorate treaty with Mathias's successor William Kati on 15 February 1866. Thus, having built a fort at Boké on the Rio Nunez in January 1866, at Benty on the Mellakore in February 1867, and finally at Bofa on the Rio Pongo in June 1867, France, by signing a series of protectorate treaties, became the colonial power in *de facto* control of most of the Southern Rivers region from Gambia to Sierra Leone.[8]

The main reason why France was able to take such early control of so much territory to the detriment of the British, with their bases in Freetown and Bathurst, was that France, being the leading consumer, exercised an economic monopoly over peanut production. By now, French control over Senegambia was practically a reality. For, having blocked all possibility of northward expansion of the colony of Sierra Leone by occupying Mellakure, the French were now considering all manner of compensatory concessions to induce the British to allow them to annex the Gambia. That territory remained a subject of continuous bargaining until the First World War. The French also dreamed of a Senegambian colony stretching from Saint-Louis to Freetown. But their plans ran into opposition from Portugal, which had its own territorial ambitions in the Southern Rivers area between Rio Geba and the Casamance River. Apart from this colonial rivalry between France, Britain, and Portugal for the conquest of the Southern Rivers region – a rivalry lasting until the end of the nineteenth century – Futa Jallon also, being a continental power, was to become the prime victim of this initial colonial push into the Southern Rivers region. Futa Jallon's efforts to control Rio Pongo and Rio Nunez, once the plan to open a trade route from Timbo to Freetown had failed, was in large part motivated by this continental power's need to adjust to economic trans-formations beginning in the early nineteenth century with the triumph of legitimate trade. For most of the first half of the nineteenth century, Futa Jallon, the main slave supplier during the eighteenth-century slave trade, was well positioned to adapt to the new economic order on the Senegambian coast, given its participation in both legitimate trade and the contraband trade in slaves along the southern waterways. However, the triumph of legitimate trade, and in particular the emergence of peanuts as the leading cash crop throughout the Southern Rivers region from Freetown to Bathurst, created an economic imbalance between the coast and Futa Jallon. With time the gap widened steadily. From 1850, peanuts accounted for at least 66 percent of annual exports from the Southern Rivers region, leaving hides, ivory, and gold far behind. And produce from Futa Jallon was a scant one-sixth of total trade value.

The commercial imbalance between the coastal and interior regions worsened as the campaign against contraband slave trading intensified on the coast, depriving Futa Jallon of its market outlet for slaves. At the same time, the attempts of the Futa Jallon regime to occupy the Rio Pongo and Rio Nunez estuaries so as to benefit from legitimate trade were blocked by the construction of French forts at Benty, Boké, and Bofa. The one remaining option for Futa Jallon was northward expansion. The most inviting routes lay through Niokolo and the Upper Gambia valley in the north-east, and toward Kaabu, Rio Geba, and Rio Cacheu in the north-west. To succeed, alas, this new policy required the fighting of a battle at Kansala. The combat exhausted both Kaabu and Futa Jallon, softening the ground for Portuguese penetration. In the event, Portugal divided up the portion of the Southern Rivers region between the rivers Gambia and Nunez with the British and the French.

### D.    Futa Jallon expansion into Kaabu and Foria

Futa Jallon expansion into Niokolo, and especially into upper Gambia, Kaabu, and Foria, came later. It was due to a combination of demographic, political, and economic factors. These coincided to a considerable degree with the development of peanut farming in the region between Rio Nunez and Rio Geba, at the end of the first half of the nineteenth century.

The province of Labé led Futa Jallon expansion to the north-east and north-west. In the north-eastward push, throughout the nineteenth century, the powerful Alfa of Labé organized regular slave raids against isolated communities in the area from Niokolo all the way to upper Gambia. Most often targeted were the Jallonke, Basari, Konyagi, Bajaranke, and Fulakunda minorities. At a very early stage, following the effective occupation of Rio Nunez and Rio Pongo by the French, Labé province and the Futa Jallon regime in general became primarily interested in controlling the coastal region between Rio Nunez and Rio Geba.

Another motive for the drive toward conquest was the continuation in this region of two parallel trading systems – legitimate commodity trading and contraband slave dealing. Territorial expansion followed intensive settlement. Migrants from the Senegambian hinterland, especially from the Futa Jallon plateau, gradually settled in Kaabu and Foria between Rio Grande and Rio Geba. People moved from Futa Jallon to the coast because the plateau was becoming increasingly overpopulated while its natural resource base was shrinking. The problem had long been obscured by the slave trade, but after the abolition the problem became obvious. Poetry from the time contains frequent – and justified – references to the region as a country of sterile rocks, famished beggars, and ragged wretches ("leydi kaaye, kooye-kolde"). It was logical for large numbers of people, many of them Peul, to flee coastward, drawn by the promise of fresh pastures close to salt basins. That migration also meant an escape from oppressive livestock taxes was an added incentive.

Indeed, a notable aspect of the Hubbu movement, which developed in the Futa Jallon hinterland from 1850, was the migration of populations from all social strata. Taking their livestock and other property, they went to settle on the outskirts of Futa, far from the reach of provincial or central regimes. An example was the Juhe movement. Its members settled east of Timbo, in hilly Fitaba. After their migration came a revolt led by Modi Iliyassu in Timbi Madina. The Alfa of Labé crushed the uprising with great severity. Modi Iliyassu's followers dispersed, heading for the coast, which had become a meeting place for large numbers of people from the Senegambian hinterland. They were drawn there by the growth of peanut farming, which, while using a great deal of slave labor, also provided employment for hired seasonal workers. Such were the roots of the peanut-farming labor system now known as the *navetane*.

Groups from Gajaaga, from the remoter reaches of the Falémé and Bafing valleys, and from Bundu, migrating in greater numbers than ever before, headed south down the Gambia basin, all the way to the Rio Grande. Migrant communities of Jakhanke, Bundunke, Khaasonke, and even Futanke traders gradually transformed their seasonal caravans into settlements. Their slaves, no longer saleable, became part of their settlements. In the mid-nineteenth century, the migratory shift from the hinterland was accelerated by the rising demand for labor on peanut plantations and farms. Peanut production grew especially fast on agribusiness units known as *feitorias*. Some of these belonged to Euro-African traders, others to European trading companies. Hundreds of these *feitorias* sprang up, and their production in the Rio Grande valley alone rose above 1,200,000 bushels. They drew in a massive influx of Manjak migrants, who specialized in peanut monoculture along a pattern that would later develop into the *navetane* system. In addition, increasingly large numbers of Peul from Futa Jallon and even more from Kaabu settled in Foria.

In both cases, large numbers of Peul wanted to escape the oppressive regimes of Futa Jallon and even harsher conditions in Kaabu, where power struggles had taken on the characteristics of an ethnic conflict between Manding and Peul. The settlers included free Peul, known as *Fulbe rimbe*, as well as even larger numbers of slaves, known as *Fulbe jiaabe*. The latter belonged either to the political aristocracies of Kaabu or to those of Futa Jallon. As a matter of fact, it was this social and political aspect which considerably muted the importance of the ethnic factor in the war between Futa Jallon and Kaabu. In my opinion, Mamadu Mane, Joye Bowman

Hawkins, and Bakary Sidibé, by sticking too closely to oral tradition, over-emphasize the ethnic factor.[9]

Such an emphasis obscures the reality of a permanent social struggle between *Fulbe rimbe* and *Fulbe jiaabe*. It also overlooks the direct threat to the Beafada of Foria, overwhelmed by the massive flow of migrants from the hinterland. This movement constitutes the keystone of the history of the period, dominated throughout the second half of the nineteenth century by pressure from the states of Bundu and, to an even greater extent, Futa Jallon. These states ran into resistance from the ancient Kaabu kingdom, until then the supreme regional power.

Futa Jallon expansionism coincided with a deep political, economic, and social crisis in the ancient Kaabu kingdom. Kaabu was considerably weak-ened by rebellions in the outlying provinces and by conflicts dividing the military aristocracy. It was impoverished by the loss of income from the slave trade, and by the new commitment of peasant and Muslim commu-nities to export agriculture. An additional problem was the revolt among the Fulakunda minorities. Recent converts to Islam, they were ready to solicit outside aid in their determination to throw off the Soninke yoke. It was this combination of factors which led to the disastrous confrontation at Kansala, where the Futa Jallon and Kaabu regimes fought to a state of mutual exhaustion.

The province of Labé spearheaded Futa Jallon's expansionist drive into Kaabu and Foria. It organized a long series of raids before the battle of Berekelon in Sankolla in 1850. The battle signaled the start of large-scale hostilities between the two states. Claiming that the time was ripe for a holy war, Alfa Ibrahima, provincial chief of Labé, raised an army of nearly 6,000 men for an assault on the *Korin*, Nhalam-Sonko. The *tata* of Berekelon, Kaabu's strongest rampart, was finally conquered after a long siege. Alfa Ibrahim then married the *Nyaanco* princess Kumacha Saane. She later gave birth to the renowned Alfa Yaya who, legend has it, inherited his out-standing courage from his Kaabu ancestors.[10]

The battle of Berekelon was followed by a lull lasting from 1851 to 1858. It ended abruptly when the combined forces of Alfa Ibrahima of Labé and Bubakar Saada of Bundu once again went on the offensive, laying siege to the *tata* of Tabajan. The defeat of its defender, Sisan Farandin, opened the gates of the capital Kansala to the armies of Futa Jallon. In this crucial period, Kaabu was already considerably weakened by the gradual loss of its outlying provinces, internecine conflicts between the remaining provinces, and power struggles between the two royal lineages.

The civil war in Kantora was aggravated by warfare between Sankolla and Tumana, as well as fighting between Wuropana and Jimara. Simultaneously, following the death of Mansa Siibo, civil strife broke out between the two royal families, the Saane and the Maane. The proximate cause was that the Saane of Saama kept the Mansa's death secret for a whole year. When the legitimate heir from Pacana, Janke Wali, heard of it, he was furious. With support from the Peul of Kaabu, the Saane of Saama then called for help from Futa Jallon against the Maane of Pakane.[11] The political crisis was compounded by a religious and social resistance movement among Fulakunda minorities exploited by the *Nyaanco* aristocracy. At the same time, a marabout faction opposed to Soninke violence emerged. For in the wake of the success of Shaykh Umar's holy war throughout Senegambia, there was no way Kaabu could escape the advancing wave of Islam. In this case, Islam served as a rationale for Futa Jallon expansion toward the coast.

There was a general call to arms. The *Almami* Umar himself led the huge army. Such a mobilization indicates the economic and political importance of the Futa Jallon expedition against the ancient kingdom of Kaabu. The Futa army was estimated to number 32,000 men, including 12,000 cavalry. In many respects it resembled the force led by the *Almami* Abdul Kader of Futa Toro at the time of the invasion of Kajoor under Amari Ngoone Sobel. At that time, the *Almami* had mobilized the entire population, from the youngest to the oldest, in the name of Islam, for the purpose of crushing the *ceddo* state. On this campaign the *Almami* Umar was accompanied by the majority of the provincial chiefs. Noteworthy among them was Alfa Ibrahima, chief of the *Diwal* of Labé, supported by the army of the *Almami* of Bundu, Bubakar Saada.

Janke Waali, overwhelmed by the sheer numbers of his enemy, holed up in the *tata* of Kansala, together with all the warriors of Kaabu, determined to resist to the last man. The resulting siege of Kansala was exceedingly bloody. Both armies suffered heavy casualties. The carnage was later remembered as a *turuban*, meaning a hecatomb, inside the *tata* of Kansala. Outnumbered by his assailants from Futa Jallon, Janke Wali preferred to blow himself up by setting fire to his powder kegs and perishing in the flames with his soldiers and wives, determined to honor the *Nyaanco* code by resisting the invaders to his last breath. The battle ended in the mutual annihilation of the antagonists.

To this day, nostalgic Manding griots celebrate the courage of the last Kaabu king in song. They chant his praises to fevered *kora* rhythms recalling the end of a whole era, that of the *ceddo* regime, destroyed, at a horrendous price, in a few moments amid the ruins of Kansala. Listen to the poet recount the story of the battle, *Turuban*:

> This is the place
> where the shaft of black iron
> finished men.

Plate 8 The *Almami* Umar (from *Voyage au Fuuta Jallon de M. Lambert, Tour du Monde*, 1860, p. 396)

Men counting prayer beads,
men swinging gourds of gin – all
married death here in Kansala
the place of extermination.[12]

Thus ended the Kaabu regime, one of the oldest in Senegambia. It was one, also, that symbolized in outstanding style the *ceddo* ethic battered by the Muslim *jihad* just before the triumph of colonial imperialism. Janke Wali, the last great king of Kaabu, earned his place as the quintessential warrior-hero in the tradition of the *Nyaanco* aristocracy. Even traditional chroniclers on the victors' side agree that the conflict was horrific, and that Kaabu resistance was intense. They recall that Kaabu, though going down in defeat, succeeded in destroying any future Futa Jallon might have hoped to have, because the flower of its youth died in the flames of Kansala, along with their enemies. Here was a pyrrhic victory if ever there was one. To the victor fell no spoils. For on the way back from Kansala, the Futa Jallon army, taking with it nearly fifteen thousand prisoners, was decimated by yellow fever. The *Almami* Umar himself did not live to celebrate his victory. He died of the disease on the way home. And shortly thereafter, it was his country's turn to face an invading enemy: France.

Right after the Kansala expedition, conditions grew ripe for the rise of the Fuladu kingdom under Alfa Moolo Egge. The new kingdom grew on the ashes of Kaabu. Peul slaves, freshly converted to Islam, and fighting alongside the armies of Futa Jallon and Bundu, played an important role in the fall of Kaabu, since the rebellion of the kingdom's oppressed lower strata undermined its internal cohesion.

The leader of this internal revolution was Moolo Egge. Born to a Manding slave father and a Peul mother, he took the name Alfa Moolo after converting to Islam and finishing his religious studies in Futa Jallon. Back home, he channeled the discontent of the Fulakunda inhabitants of Firdu province into a movement under the Islamic banner. His forces were active alongside the Futa Jallon army in the war against Kaabu, his motivation having more to do with national interests than with religious or ethnic solidarity. Starting in Firdu, he organized the rebellion of Peul slaves, known as *Fula joon*, in Tumana and Kantora provinces. In the process, he created the nucleus of the Great Fuladu, which expanded steadily all the way to Foria. He obtained help from Futa Jallon, which continued to conduct punitive expeditions into Kaabu until 1878.[13] By the end of his reign, Fuladu had practically engulfed the old provinces of Pata, Firdu, Kamako, Mambua, Naampuya, Patim, Jimara, Kakana, and Pakane.

Just as Fuladu was consolidating its status as a political power under Alfa Moolo, Peul migrations into Foria increased considerably. The migrants came from Kaabu, Badora-Ussera, and Kanadu. Large numbers of free Peul (*Fulbe rimbe*) settled in the Beafada territory south of Rio Corubal, along with their slaves (*Fulbe jiaabe*). From 1868 to 1874 the Beafada fought desperately to keep their land. Then their chief Inchola was forced to flee with his retinue to Rio Nunez. He left the area under the control of Bakar Demba of Kontabani, a protégé of the Alfa of Labé, the real overlord of Foria. From 1878, Beafada resistance in Foria became absolutely impossible. The remainder of Kaabu fell under the authority of Bakar Qidali, himself tightly supervised from Futa Jallon.

So the fall of Kansala led to the emergence of three political power centers. The first, in Firdu, was under the control of Alfa Moolo; the second, in Foria, under Bakar Demba; and the third, in Kaabu, under Bakar Qidali. Still, these new states remained under Futa Jallon suzerainty, with the greatest control going to the Alfa of Labé, in direct administrative control over the conquered territories beyond his borders. Meanwhile, Futa Jallon had to mount numerous expeditions just to maintain its territorial gains, at a time when the appointed local chiefs were also busy jockeying for leadership in the region.

Warfare became endemic between Bakar Demba of Foria and Bakar Qidali of Kaabu. Alfa Moolo, for his part, took advantage of the prevailing turmoil to extend his authority throughout the region, from his Fuladu base. On top of this struggle for hegemony, there was also a profound social crisis which peaked in a rebellion of Peul slaves against free Peul in Foria, where slaveholding had become the social norm.[14] At the same time, a major contradiction arose between Futa Jallon's drive toward territorial expansion and the desire of local Fulakunda chiefs to assert their independence by getting rid of their former ally, now an excessively demanding encumbrance. In particular, Musa Moolo, successor to Alfa Moolo, extended Fuladu authority over the entire region, and then combated the Futa Jallon presence by seeking support from France, Britain, and Portugal. From then on, those European powers battled for possession of this region between the Gambia and Rio Nunez. Its conquest was a matter of time.

The mid-nineteenth century was dominated by the large-scale territorial expansion of Futa Jallon, the continental power, into the Southern Rivers. More than anything else, the process typified attempts by the Senegambian states to adjust to the new conditions governing the trans-Atlantic trading system in the transition from the old slave trade to the triumph of legitimate trade. In many ways, this policy of coastward expansion was quite similar to the tremendous efforts made by the Asantehene, king of the powerful Ashanti kingdom, to achieve control over the coastal populations of what is now Ghana, at the start of the nineteenth century. Like the *Almamis* of Timbo, the Asantehene, feeling the loss of income from slave trading, wanted to secure the advantages of legitimate trade by expanding his kingdom coastward. The same dynamic was at work in Dahomey, where King Glélé improved his profits by using slave labor to develop oil palm plantations on the coast. In the case of Futa Jallon, the attempt by a continental power to adapt to changing circumstances ran into opposition from the coastal communities. It was also opposed by the European powers, determined thenceforth to occupy the coast definitively and to turn its resources to their own profit.

From 1867, with the construction of French forts at Boké, Bofa, and Benty, on account of the sizable peanut trade, opportunities for Futa Jallon to expand toward the coast were considerably reduced. The failure of Futa Jallon opened the way for Britain, Portugal, and France to divide up the Southern Rivers region in the second half of the nineteenth century. For strategic reasons, however, the conquest of southern Senegambia was delayed for a few years, pending the annexation of northern Senegambia and the West African Sudan, the main French objectives from 1854 to 1890. Already, it had become plain that the Futa Jallon regime's capacity for territorial expansion had dwindled considerably as a result of the kingdom's serious internal political crisis. This made it increasingly less capable of coping with the ambitions of the European powers, themselves increasingly committed to a policy of colonial conquest.

## 12     The colony of Senegal and political and social crises in northern Senegambia

The crisis of the trans-Atlantic trading system, the failure of various colonial plantation schemes, and the ruinously speculative gum trade soon led to sovereignty disputes between France and the northern Senegambian states, where profound economic, political, and social changes had been taking place.

In Waalo, the introduction of colonial plantation agriculture plunged the local aristocracy into civil war. Already bickering, they became more sharply divided over the sharing of new customs duties paid by the Saint-Louis traders. The political crisis in turn opened the gates to the revival of the marabout movement. Led by Njaga Issa and his disciple Diile Fatim Cham, the movement declared a holy war in 1830. Civil war, together with the occupation of Waalo by the Trarza Moors and the deep trade depression, gave Faidherbe an opportunity to begin the process of colonial conquest in 1854. The French wanted to stop paying customs duties at their trading posts on the Senegal River. They also wanted to create secure trading conditions. Their practical determination to conquer the Senegal valley as a passageway to the resources of the Niger Bend, however, coincided with Shaykh Umar's *jihad*. That holy war plunged all Senegambia into turmoil.

In Futa Toro, Shaykh Umar crystallized discontent among a population tired of increasing inequalities within the Toorodo regime, whose practices now fell short of the ideals of the triumphant eighteenth-century revolution that had brought it to power. Finding it impractical to change the political regime, which had become a hereditary system monopolized by leading Toroodo families, Shaykh Umar recruited a large number of followers from all social strata. With this army he was able in a few short years to conquer the entire upper Senegal valley, before embarking on his great Sudanese campaigns. But in 1857, the French, alarmed by the huge size of the *jihad*, reacted at the battle of Medina. The result was the elimination of Shaykh Umar from the Senegambian political scene.

Meanwhile, in the Wolof and Sereer kingdoms, the power struggles and civil wars of previous centuries continued within the *ceddo* aristocracy, which enjoyed a monopoly of political power. Inter-clan conflicts were aggravated by the peasants' gradual attempts to emancipate themselves from the *ceddo* yoke by earning an income from peanut farming. Muslim communities mushroomed. Under the leadership of marabouts like Njaga Issa, they initiated programs transcending the scope of the traditional states. They grew steadily in strength. The decline of the slave trade, meanwhile, cut into the income of the *ceddo* aristocracy. In self-defense, they tried to neutralize the marabout movement and to curb the territorial ambitions of the French operating from Saint-Louis and Gorée. Peanut earnings, a major economic and political prize, provoked numerous sovereignty disputes between the *ceddo* aristocracies and the marabout movements on the one hand, and the French on the other. Internal crises had by now become inextricably linked with the process of colonial conquest initiated by the annexation of Waalo in 1855.

## A.     The conquest of Waalo

Internal political wrangles and sovereignty disputes began particularly early in Waalo. It was there that, in 1819, the French obtained the Treaty of Ndiaw, designed to safeguard export crop production. That treaty signaled a fundamental change in French business in Senegambia. It enabled the French to abolish the policy of offshore trading posts established in the seventeenth and eighteenth centuries. Now France had an undisputed foothold on the African continent. From the new base, it set about systematically destroying the sovereignty of the Senegambian states. Thus, though the colonial plantation scheme in Waalo was only a limited experiment that failed, it helped provoke a profound economic, political, and social crisis in most of northern Senegambia. The experiment was especially alarming to the states of the Senegal valley. They put intense pressure on Waalo in an effort to stop the French obtaining a foothold on the continent.

The Trarza emirate and the kingdom of Futa Toro took turns claiming sovereignty over Waalo. They thus forced the French to pay duties to ensure the security needed for farming. Furthermore, the French paid internal duties to assure the collaboration of the Waalo aristocracy in the plantation scheme. This intensified the political crisis from the preceding period which involved the power struggle between the three royal matrilineal clans. Their chronic rivalry was now complicated by another aspect of the political crisis: a major kingmaker, the *Jawdin* Majaw Khor, rebelled against the sovereign *Brak*. Majaw Khor was a member of the *seb ak baor*. Traditionally vested with the land rights of the old *Lamans*, this group had been reduced to the status of mere electors since the emergence of the monarchy. Now it was suddenly pushed to center stage because the plantation scheme entailed large allocations of land. The French at Saint-Louis gave Majaw Khor financial support, strengthening his political position. Using the money to hire *ceddo* mercenaries ready to fight for the highest bidder, he defied the *Brak*, Fara Penda. Taking advantage of the political upheaval, Diile Fatim Cham overran Waalo. Under the banner of Islam, he abolished the regime of the *Braks* and also expelled the French.[1]

The political crisis created favorable conditions for a revival of the marabout movement in the Wolof kingdoms, even though the *jihad* initiated by the Muslim theocracy of Futa Toro at the end of the eighteenth century had failed. The *ceddo* regimes in power in Waalo, Kajoor, and Baol, with support from the slave traders of Saint-Louis and Gorée, had at that time defeated the invading forces of Abdul Kader, allied with powerful factions from the Muslim provinces of Njambur. Even in defeat, the Muslim faith spread among the *baadolo* peasants, perennial victims of *ceddo* pillage. Furthermore, Muslims achieved an extremely important breakthrough when the Cap-Vert peninsula seceded from the *Damel*'s authority. The new Lebu Republic became a permanent rallying point for Muslim partisans from Kajoor, after the clampdown organized by Amari Ngone Ndella. For that reason, his successor Birama Fatma Cuub, as *Damel* of Kajoor (1809–32) and *Tiin* of Baol 1817–32), sought an alliance with the renowned marabout family of the Kuntas, as a ploy to neutralize the agitation of Muslim leaders in Njambur and Tuube.[2] In this way, the *Damel* exploited the prestige of the Kunta family to counter every revolutionary argument based on Islamic pretexts advanced by the local Muslim leadership, who had grown into a significant force in political terms. Measured by the amount of territory they occupied, their power was also substantial.[3] This alliance between the *Damel* Birama Fatma Cuub and Shaykh Bunama Kunta was the second attempt, after that of Lat Sukaabe Faal, to induce Muslims to accept the traditional monarchical framework, as a means of ensuring the survival of the *ceddo* system. For instance, in order to diminish the power gained by the Muslim faction as a result of the territorial concessions given them, for administrative purposes, by Lat Sukaabe Faal, Birama Fatma Cuub laid a special emphasis on the religious function of *Qadi* answerable to the *Damel*'s central authority. Yet this policy did not stop the Muslim clerics of Njambur from rebelling, under the leadership of *Seriñ* Njaga Issa of Koki, in 1827.[4]

Njaga Issa had a towering reputation within the Muslim community, quite apart from his official appointment as *Seriñ Lamb* by the *Damel*. He was the *Damel*'s brother-in-law. And he belonged to the *Damel*'s retinue. So when he proclaimed a holy war against the status quo, he spoke with the backing of multiple sources of authority.

The *Damel*'s reaction was fierce and effective. Blocked, Njaga Issa led his troops to Waalo, where his disciple Diile Fatim Cham had taken advantage of the raging civil war to rise to power and to fight against the French presence.[5] From then on, the marabout's partisans were hemmed in by no frontiers. They were free to go all out in their militant campaign to bring down the *ceddo* regime clinging on to its national prerogatives. Waalo was in a state of open political crisis that started with the rebellion of the *Jawdin* Majaw Khor against the *Brak* Fara Penda. This provided fertile ground for the marabout campaign, which channeled peasant discontent against the *ceddo* power structure.

Diile Fatim came from a family of jewelers. By the norms of the traditional caste system, he belonged to the *ñeeño* caste, excluded from power by definition. In Islam, he found the one ideology capable of destroying the *Garmi* power system. At the head of three thousand warriors massed at the frontier between Waalo and Kajoor since 1827, Diile Fatim Cham, Njaga Issa's disciple, invaded the kingdom. By 7 March 1830 he had overrun it completely. The defeated *Brak* Fara Penda had to flee. He went to Richard Toll to ask for help from the French. Meanwhile, the rebellion of the *Jawdin* Majaw Khor made it impossible for the *ceddo* regime to put together any kind of coalition against the Muslim faction. Diile continued in complete control over Waalo, until he attacked the French forts at Richard Toll and Dagana. The French governor, Brou, reacted brutally. Using canon fire, he completely wiped out Diile's army at Mbilor. Diile Fatim Cham was captured. After being forced to recant his claims of being a prophet, he was sentenced and hanged on the spot. Survivors from the massacre at Mbilor, along with their leader Njaga Issa, took refuge in the Cap-Vert peninsula. There a new Muslim theocracy had been established, and it steadfastly rebuffed the French demand for the extradition of Njaga Issa.[6] This refusal gives a good indication of the power of the marabout faction, as well as of the supra-national nature of the religious movements it led. Having failed to assert his rule over Kajoor, Njaga Issa moved his forces to Waalo. When his main disciple, Diile, was defeated by the French forces, he found inviolable sanctuary in the Muslim theocracy of Cap-Vert.

One significant fact stands out from this episode. Once again, just when the marabout movement had achieved a resounding victory over a divided aristocracy grown incapable of resisting its program, the French stepped in from their base at Saint-Louis to decapitate the movement. Quite clearly, Diile's movement was a direct successor to that of Nasir Al Din in the late seventeenth century. Times had changed, however. A Muslim revolution of the type that occurred in eighteenth-century Futa Toro could no longer succeed. The French had come to stay. They could no longer tolerate the emergence of a politico-religious force capable of resisting their territorial ambitions in Senegambia. However, there was nothing preventing the

Muslim movement from building up its strength prior to going on the offensive throughout Senegambia against the *ceddo* regimes. The marabout offensive was all the more vigorous as the decline of the slave trade had pushed the aristocracy into aggravating their pillaging of the peasantry. Unlike the Southern Rivers region, the coastline of northern Senegambia offered few shelters for contraband traders. Slave trading therefore declined, and the local aristocrats found themselves with only a fraction of their former earnings. To make up for their economic losses, the *ceddo* regimes subjected their own peoples to even worse exploitation. That created conditions for the marabout movement to develop with unprecedented vigor in those Wolof kingdoms where, until then, *ceddo* regimes had resisted the Muslim onslaught. The *ceddo* regimes were caught between pressure from the Moorish emirates on the one hand, and, on the other, the French, who were determined to set up a colony in Senegal. Against old regimes thus embattled by new challenges, the Muslim clerical movement channeled the discontent of peasant populations squeezed by their rulers' greed.

The decline of the trans-Atlantic slave trade saw a revival of the old trans-Saharan slave trade. Trarza and Brakna Moors acted as middlemen, and, in return for their services, their emirates exercised firmer control over the Wolof kingdoms. The emirates of Trarza and Brakna, as a matter of fact, took advantage of the now chronic state of crisis, and of the temporary withdrawal of the Saint-Louis trading company after the failure of the plantation scheme, to interfere constantly in the political conflicts of Kajoor, and especially in those of Waalo. In one instance, Mohamed El Habib, the powerful Emir of Trarza, took advantage of civil strife between Fara Penda's partisans, supported by the famous *Linger* Jombot and practically all the petty traders of Saint-Louis, and those of Kherfi Khari Daaro, supported by the colonial administration, to gain lasting control over Waalo. Feeling cornered, and wishing to avoid pillage by the Moors, Waalo dignitaries gave the country's most beautiful princess, the *Linger* Jombot, to the Emir of Trarza, Mohamed El Habib, at a marriage ceremony on 18 June 1833. This alliance immediately strengthened the position of Mohamed El Habib, making him the strongman of the Senegal valley. The prospect of the Moors becoming a dominant force on both banks of the Senegal River alarmed the French Governor Quernel. Such a development was likely to slow down French colonial expansion in the region for a long time. He therefore mounted a series of military expeditions which completely devastated Waalo. In 1834, Jombot and Fara Penda took refuge at Ngik in Njambur, with help from the *Damel* Meyssa Tend Joor, a relative of the *Linger* from Waalo. The Trarza Moors, having nothing to fear from French reprisals, diverted the gum trade to Portendick, where the British transacted business worth 600 million francs with them. Waalo lay completely ruined. The French colony had gained nothing for its exertions. Adjusting to the situation, Pujol signed the Treaty of 30 August 1835 with Mohamed El Habib. By its terms, El Habib gave up his claims and those of his descendants to the kingdom of Waalo, based on his marriage with Jombot. A second treaty, signed on 4 September 1835, once more recognized Fara Penda as the *Brak*. It also authorized the exiles in Kajoor to return to Waalo. But now that Waalo was under direct threat from the French colony of Senegal, the political crisis deepened, at the same time as the Emir Mohamed El Habib was consolidating his position in the kingdom.

Political affairs in Waalo were at this time dominated by the strong personality of Jombot. Indeed, she remained in charge until her death in 1846, using mercenary *ceddo* soldiers. She was succeeded by her sister Ndate Yalla, wife of Maroso, Prince of Kajoor. A soldier of fortune, the latter tried to set up a faction nationally around Sidia, son of Ndate Yalla. The idea was to support him against Ely, heir to Jombot and Mohamed El Habib, the representative of the Moorish faction. The national faction was against the pillage committed by the Trarza Moors in collusion with certain dignitaries avid for booty. It was also against the territorial ambitions of the French at Saint-Louis, who wanted to encroach on Waalo sovereignty. Residents of Saint-Louis doing business at various trading posts in Waalo were repeatedly pillaged. And even though the French colony suspended payments of customary dues pending receipt of compensation, Ndate Yalla refused to pay damages.

In 1852, the Saint-Louis traders sent a petition asking the Governor to use force to destroy the trading posts and to set up permanent, fortified trading centers at Dagana and Podor. The Governor, Protet, was all in favor of a policy of colonial conquest. By March 1854 he had the resources to back up that policy. He ordered an expedition to Podor under the command of a captain of the Engineering Corps, Faidherbe. After a fierce battle at Jalmat, which ended in the defeat of Futa Toro, Faidherbe built the fort. France thus asserted its determination to assume sovereign powers over the Senegal valley. When later Faidherbe was appointed governor, he wasted no time in tightening French control over the south bank. He did this by organizing military expeditions for the conquest of Waalo, in the lower basin, as a way of protecting his rear. His aim was to keep Mohamed El Habib's son Ely from the Waalo throne, as well as to end Moorish domination of the south bank by establishing French power there. On 25 February 1855, a combined army of Waalo and Trarza Moors was defeated near Jubuldu. With remarkable ease, the territory was conquered after a lightning campaign in which Faidherbe torched more than twenty-five villages. That caused a population exodus from Waalo. The *Linger* Ndate

Yalla took refuge in Kajoor. Ely and the Moors retreated into Trarza territory on the north bank.[7]

Thus the cohesion of Waalo was put at substantial risk by several factors:
the chronic power struggle between the Joos and the Teejek; the *de facto*
occupation of the territory by Trarza Moors in alliance with various factions; and the predatory exploitation of the peasantry by *ceddo* warriors.
All this led to a situation of political and social crisis which made it impossible to organize any form of national resistance on the ground. Once
Waalo had been emptied of its inhabitants, the French turned it into a base
for the conquest of a colonial empire in Senegambia. Faidherbe forced all
parties to recognize the Senegal River as the frontier between Moors,
restricted to the north bank, and Black Africans on the south bank. This
artificial demarcation of boundaries promoted the interests of the Saint-
Louis traders, who were eager to encourage peanut farming by the black
population on the south bank, and cared little about the north bank now
that the gum trade had slumped into insignificance. This French option
provided a strong motivation for the conduct of military campaigns of conquest southward all the way along the Senegal River basin, into the peanut-
producing regions. The conquest of the northern Moorish emirates was to
be postponed until much later. In the early stages, Faidherbe's abiding preoccupation was to gain control over the entire Senegal basin, where the
security of the French trading system was considerably jeopardized by the
activities of Shaykh Umar. For the Shaykh had stirred up the whole region
from Futa Toro to Bakel, gateway to the riches of the Sudan.

B.      **Shaykh Umar's activities in Futa Toro and the upper Senegal
        valley**

Like Waalo, Futa Toro drew its importance from its strategic location
astride the Senegal valley, on both banks of the natural route along which
trade from Saint-Louis was to penetrate into the upper Senegal basin and
beyond, toward the Sudan. The success of the *Toorodo* revolution had put
Futa Toro in a position to ensure its own territorial integrity and to resist
pressure from three sources: from the Moors to the north, from the
Bambara states to the east, and from the Saint-Louis trading company to
the west. However, like all other areas of Senegambia, Futa Toro was itself
undergoing profound economic, political, and social transformations.
These transformations lay at the root of the religious campaign mounted
by Shaykh Umar at the end of the first half of the nineteenth century, at a
time when the French colony of Senegal had begun its expansion into the
Senegal valley. The choice of Waalo as the base for the French plantation
experiment in the early nineteenth century, however, relegated Futa Toro to

a secondary status as far as the interests of the Saint-Louis traders were concerned. At that time, the company in Saint-Louis was satisfied to buy gum and grain from various trading posts along the river. So during the first half of the nineteenth century, in which the trans-Atlantic trading system was undergoing a depression, internal political problems were the dominant feature of Futa Toro history.

Given that the territory was spread over a distance of 300 km, the *Almami*'s central authority was very weak right from the start of the Muslim revolution. Real power under the *Toorodo* regime was in the hands of the Council of Electors, known as the *Jaggorde*. The electors of Boséa and Yirlabé were particularly powerful. From 1807 to 1819 the elector Ali Dundu, representative of the dominant Kane lineage of Dabiya in Boséa province, dominated political affairs in Futa Toro. So chronically volatile was the political system that from 1806 to 1854, no fewer than twenty different candidates held power as *Almami*. The position changed hands forty-five times. Lively as the succession turnover was, it was restricted to just a few families: the Ly, Jaba, and Hebiabe lineages, plus the Wane of Mbumba. The resulting competition did not fundamentally disturb the real autonomy of the provinces from the central authority, weak from the start. The imbalance of provincial power was a key factor in political affairs. Central Futa predominated over western and eastern Futa, which had practically no representatives on the Council of Elders, and presented no candidates for the post of *Almami*. On both the provincial and national levels, it was basically around the Wane family of Mbumba, in the *Law* area along with Biran and his son Mamadu, linked by marriage with the Ly family of Cilon, that a real dynasty emerged, ready to face down the opposition of Eliman Rindaw Falil, the most influential elector, after Ali Dundu, up to the mid-nineteenth century. However, at both provincial and national levels, the political rulers had ceased to have any connection with the Islamic *Sharia* law, imposed by the *Toorodo* movement at the start of the revolution. At the top of the social pyramid, the rulers had turned into a privileged political class with hereditary prerogatives restricted to the dominant Kane, Wane, and Ly families. These kept all other strata in the society from gaining access to power in the *Toorodo* regime. The excluded classes were furthermore subjected to exactions similar to those imposed by the former Denyanke regime. For these reasons, the *Toorodo* regime drew corrosive criticism from a new generation of marabouts trying to direct a reform movement within this aged Muslim theocracy. The movement called for a return to the austere purity of the founders of the *Toorodo* revolution. Its leading incarnation at this time was the renowned Shaykh Umar, who, after a long trip abroad, had returned home to work for the triumph of the Tijaniyya brotherhood.[8]

Shaykh Umar settled down at Jekunko, on Futa Jallon's eastern border, around 1840. From that moment, he presented himself constantly as a reformer throughout the Senegambian region. His reputation as a reformer was particularly strong in his Futa homeland to which, after some twenty years of foreign travel, he had returned. During his initial trip, Shaykh Umar recruited large numbers of disciples with whom he founded his new community at Dingiray. In addition, he reaffirmed his status as a strict critic of the incumbent regime in Futa Toro. He was scathing in his denunciation of the practice of assigning political functions as a hereditary right restricted to a clannish circle of electors and candidates. He lambasted the rich for embezzling religious alms. And he excoriated the supposed religious guides, the Imams, for their ignorance. In the process, he reconnected with the religious, political and social ideal first projected by Sulayman Bal, father of the *Toorodo* revolution. Shaykh Umar went farther. He deplored the exploitation of his fellow Toro citizens by the central authorities of Futa. He denounced the regime's generally weak response to Moorish and French pressures. Lastly, he worked hard at reviving the spirit of religious zeal and the holy war ethos against the *ceddo* and Bambara states, especially those to the east of Senegambia.[9] As happened with Juhe in Futa Jallon, Shaykh Umar, not being of aristocratic stock, was at first excluded from political power by the hereditary ruling class, who plainly detested the Tijaniyya leader. Unable, therefore, to take on the established order head on, Shaykh Umar began by gathering thousands of disciples from all parts of the Futa region, who flocked to him on account of his message and his social and religious ideal.

This political setback happened at a time when the French from the colony of Senegal were beginning to exert military pressure in their drive to conquer the Senegal valley. In 1854, the same year in which Shaykh Umar completed his conquest of the upper Senegal valley above the fort of Bakel, the French were trying to consolidate their position from their base in Saint-Louis. In January that year, Malivoine was assassinated. The incident provided Protet with an excuse for expediting the construction of a fort at Podor in western Futa. The local force sent on the Dialmath expedition was massacred. The new *Almami*, Mamadu Biram, could do nothing to stop that defeat. The massacre signaled the determination of the French at Saint-Louis to obtain a foothold on the continent. Confronted with this new challenge, the *Almami* Mamadu and the majority of chiefs answered Shaykh Umar's call to arms and joined him at Farabana in November 1854. So great was the popularity of Shaykh Umar at this time that he was able to decide when the *Almami* could return: he requested that the latter administer Futa Toro in his absence, while inviting his compatriots to join the war against Kaarta. Thus Shaykh Umar, having failed to achieve political dominance in the two old theocracies of Futa Jallon and Futa Toro, adopted a different objective: for the time being, he would recruit soldiers and disciples for the conquest of the upper Senegal valley, starting from his base at Dingiray.

Following Shaykh Umar's victory over the kingdom of Tamba, the holy warrior immediately turned his attention to the upper Senegal valley, a crossroads region whose various states had been undergoing a profound economic and social crisis since the turn of the century. In less than six months he conquered Bambuk. Having become ruler of Bundu since the death of the *Almami* Saada in 1852, he mounted an attack on Khaaso in Gajaaga territory from May to November 1854. With the help of numerous allies, he won an easy victory. Early in the nineteenth century, Khaaso had been dismembered by an invading force of Massassi Bambara from Kaarta. They captured the capital Konakari and subjugated the entire territory. Khaaso as a political entity was shattered forever. The entire north bank of the Senegal River remained under the domination of the Massassi Bambara. Meanwhile, Hawa Demba (1808–33) was able to exercise his authority on the river bank only through astute military and diplomatic maneuvering. Into this situation stepped Shaykh Umar, God's messenger come to regenerate the world. Taking advantage of the country's weakness, he conquered Khaaso. Following the capture of Jokheba, news of Shaykh Umar's victories so frightened the chiefs of Khaaso that they joined him in his war against the Massassi Bambara of Kaarta.[10] His victory over the Soninke kingdom of Gajaaga was equally swift. Throughout the first half of the nineteenth century, that kingdom had been torn by a long series of civil wars between the enemy clans of Gwey and Kamera. Conflicts dating back to the era of the warlords had continued unchecked in Gajaaga because of the opposition between Samba Yasin of Makhanna and Samba Khumba Jaaman, one of the most prestigious *Tunka Lemmu* of the time. Samba Yasin, who from 1817 to 1821 first saved the country from invading Bundu forces and their Futa Toro allies, tried to rule Gajaaga. But from 1827, he encountered opposition from Samba Khumba Jaamu, a member of the powerful Bacili faction of Gwey, whose economic stature had improved following the construction of French trading posts there. In 1834, Samba Yasin destroyed Ciaabu. That sparked a conflict that lasted some twenty years, and incidentally paved the way for the intervention of neighboring countries in the affairs of Gajaaga. Futa Toro and Bundu sided with Gwey against Kamera and its ally, Kaarta. Gajaaga's cohesion was thus seriously compromised by revolts in the majority of towns in Gidimakha. Trade in the area suffered a profound recession on account of the permanent strife between the Kamera and Gwey factions. Further, the country fell prey to incessant Moorish raids. In short, chaos ruled.

This was the situation when Shaykh Umar arrived in the upper Senegal valley with his forces in November 1854. He began by sacking Farabana in Bambuk. He then destroyed Makhanna and invaded Bundu before finally occupying Khaaso and Kaarta. The holy warrior now had the entire upper Senegal valley under his control. His clear success owed a great deal to support from many political quarters. For instance, the disorder and insecurity that had prevailed in Gajaaga during a half century of civil war and foreign intervention motivated the marabouts of Daramaane to support Shaykh Umar's movement, in the hope that it would restore the peace they needed for profitable trading. Furthermore, the peasants, laboring under heavy taxes levied to support the military establishment, made common cause with Shaykh Umar, forming a vast popular movement directed against the aristocracy and the economic interests of French traders. At this crucial juncture, even the internal cohesion of the ruling class was shattered. For the Bacili clan of Ciaabu, long damaged by the civil war, was delighted at the destruction of Makhanna and the invasion of Kaarta by Shaykh Umar's troops.[11]

It was not long before the French reacted to Shaykh Umar's lightning-swift conquest of the upper Senegal valley. They were well aware of the strategic importance of the region for their trading interests as well as for their plans to expand their power into the Sudan. Faidherbe therefore strengthened the garrisons at Bakel and Sénedebu. He also committed himself, as from 1855, to supporting the claims of Sambala against the followers of Shaykh Umar in Khaaso. For that purpose, he speeded up the construction of a fort at Medina, as well as getting the local authorities to accept a protectorate treaty. In pursuit of his plans, Faidherbe also struck up an alliance with Bokar Saada, the Bundu crown prince, who had turned against Shaykh Umar ever since he embarked with all his forces on the conquest of Kaarta. The local aristocracies, taking advantage of the resistance Shaykh Umar faced at Kaarta, rebelled and allied themselves with the French. In all this, the main objective of the French was to tighten their hold on the upper Senegal valley, thus preventing Shaykh Umar's seemingly unstoppable movement from engulfing western Senegambia. For that would have thwarted their policy of territorial expansion as clearly defined from 1854 onward. For his part, Shaykh Umar was quick to react to this French interference in his recently conquered domain, especially since French intervention threatened his freedom of movement between these new domains and his native Futa as well as his base at Dingiray.

In April 1857, Shaykh Umar ordered the siege of Medina, at that time defended by Paul Holle. The siege lasted until July, when the river's rising level enabled the French to send troops to relieve the fort. Shaykh Umar's army suffered numerous casualties in the battle, and had to abandon the siege. His failure to take Medina in 1857 signaled the emergence of the new French imperialism. It was a fateful defeat. For following it, though the holy warrior continued to replenish his forces from his native Futa, he had to shift his conquering ambitions eastward toward the Sudan. So Segu became the new center of gravity for his empire. Using help from Samba Jaay, an architect and engineer he had seduced away from the French arsenal at Saint-Louis, Shaykh Umar had a few damaged canon captured from the French repaired and installed in stone fortifications at Kundian and Konakori. Thus equipped, he had the technical superiority he needed to continue the conquest of a vast empire on the ashes of the powerful Bambara kingdom of Segu and the Peul kingdom of Masina. In the process, he turned his attention for a while away from Senegambia, which was already partly under the control of the French at Saint-Louis.[12]

Before returning to France in September 1858, Faidherbe had two new trading posts built, at Salde and Matam, meeting little resistance in the process. He also secured the right to keep patrol boats at the smaller trading posts. The boats were needed partly to protect trade, but above all to keep Shaykh Umar away from the French sphere of influence in the upper Senegal valley. From now on, as was his habit, Faidherbe combined diplomacy with violence in pursuit of a policy aimed at dismembering Futa Toro. The *Almami* Mamadu Wane, in a rather timid attempt to block this French policy of interference, built a dam at Garli to stop patrol boats going upstream. Faidherbe, on the defensive now, kept clear of any confrontation that could have brought the holy warrior back to the Futa region of the lower Senegal valley, the heart of the emerging French colony. For his part, Shaykh Umar, during his last trip to Futa Toro, set up his headquarters at Hore Fonde from July 1859, with the aim of exhorting his countrymen to migrate en masse from a territory polluted by the French presence. But he was opposed by most chiefs in central Futa, still resentful of his common birth. In his native Toro, however, his call fell on receptive ears, and the *fergo* pulled in more than 40,000 Futanke followers. All members of the ruling class, notably the *Almami* Biran, avoided any confrontation with Shaykh Umar as he brought into the *fergo* Futanke from all social strata. The migrants included such influential *Toorodo* partisans as Falil Acc, the venerable elector from Rindaw, Mamadu Kane of Dabiya, grandson of Ali Dundu, Saada Kane of the *Alkati*'s family, Hamat Sall, the *Lam Tooro*, and the marabout establishment in Futa. Over 20 percent of the population thus migrated from Futa Toro, leaving the land desolate behind them.

Having left Futa, Shaykh Umar launched a series of lightning campaigns aimed at restoring his authority over Kaarta, conquering Segu and the Masina, and thus creating a vast empire in the Sudan, to the east of Senegambia. All this occurred in the space of just a few years, before his death in 1864. For his part, Faidherbe, as soon as he returned to Saint-Louis in February 1859, took advantage of Shaykh Umar's total absorption in the conquest of the Sudan to set up protectorates in the eastern and western provinces. That done, he continued with the dismemberment of a Futa Toro considerably weakened by Shaykh Umar's *fergo*. Faidherbe was satisfied simply to water the seeds of division in this country where the ruling class in central Futa, led by Abdul Bokar Kane, was trying to cope with the economic, political, and social consequences of Shaykh Umar's campaign. The holy warrior's impact on the fate of his homeland was, in effect, still great. Similarly, the upper Senegal valley, devastated by Shaykh Umar's expansionist wars and by French reprisals against the holy warrior's followers, remained an important strategic prize for Faidherbe, his aim being to control the vast triangle formed by the towns of Bakel, Medina, and Sénedebu, as a step toward the penetration of the resource-rich Sudan.

Medina came to symbolize French military superiority. Henceforth, it was clear that a garrison of a handful of soldiers, operating from a fort equipped with artillery, could, in a colonial war, hold enemy forces a hundred times more numerous at bay. The fact was not lost on Shaykh Umar either. So for the moment he gave up his dream of marching in triumph to the sea, to concentrate on conquering the vast eastern spaces, far from any colonial interference. France's immediate aim was to gain control over the Wolof and Sereer kingdoms of Kajoor, Baol, Siin, and Saalum, territories capable of meeting the rising demand of French industry for peanut oil. Kajoor and Baol, in particular, were becoming increasingly important in the plans worked out by Faidherbe, the real founder of the colony of Senegal.

### C.    Faidherbe's reaction to the political crisis in Kajoor and Baol

Competition between the colony of Senegal and the Trarza Moors for control over Waalo affected relations between Saint-Louis and Kajoor directly. For despite the achievement of peace in 1835, Trarza hegemony over the Lower Senegal Basin was a fact. Kajoor was under direct threat from the powerful Mohamed El Habib now that Waalo was no longer a buffer. In 1842, Mohamed El Habib, upon receiving a call for help from Sakhewar Binta Maasamba in a conflict with the *Damel* Meyssa Tend Joor, invaded central Kajoor. The *Damel* then sought an alliance with the French colony of Senegal. However, it was not long before conflicting interests blew that alliance apart.

The problem was that the *Damel* opposed direct trading relations between the colony and Jolof, which had turned into a major gum producer. In 1848, when slavery was abolished in the colony, the slave-based domestic economy collapsed. That worsened the conflict. As a result, the *Damel* switched over to an alliance with the Trarza emirate. And Trarza now took effective control over Kajoor in a bid to protect its gum monopoly. The main conflict, however, remained the increasingly open opposition between the Colony of Senegal and Kajoor. The reason was that the development of the peanut trade, apart from catalyzing profound social changes, was also turning Kajoor into a key trading partner for Gorée and Saint-Louis. Kajoor had merely been a secondary trading partner for the colony during the slave trade. Suddenly, with the development of the peanut trade, it had grown so important that, from 1852, the *Damel* was demanding a tax of 2 kg on every 30 or 40 kg of produce exported from the trading posts at Ganjol, Rufisque, and Portudal.

Peanuts were grown mainly by peasant farmers. The boom in the peanut trade therefore tended gradually to reduce the central regime's monopoly over trade with the colony, while the *Lamans* and other local chiefs were profiting the most. The economic emancipation of the peasantry intensified centrifugal tendencies in the outlying provinces of Ganjol and Njambur, a trend actively encouraged by the French trading company in Saint-Louis. When Meyssa Tend Joor died in 1854, the sovereignty dispute became, to all intents, an open conflict between the *Damel* and the Governor of Senegal. The *Damel* wanted to impose customs duties on the new peanut trade. The Governor wanted total deregulation in order to deal directly with producers. To complicate matters, the peasants were desperate to liberate themselves from *ceddo* rule. They hated the old rulers for their rapacious violence. Local revolutions, in effect, coincided with French plans for colonial conquest. Here, more than in Waalo and the Southern Rivers region, colonial conquest involved a definite clash between the community of European traders, formerly restricted to the islands of Saint-Louis and Gorée, and the kings of Kajoor and Baol. The break hinged on a sovereignty dispute during a period when the social and political consequences of the developing peanut trade were forcing *ceddo* regimes to explore new ways of resolving the crisis in all its aspects.[13]

Here again, in his contacts with Kajoor and Baol, Faidherbe stands revealed as the master architect responsible for the expansion of colonial power alongside the expanding peanut trade in Njambur, Tuube, and Jander, with Rufisque as the principal export outlet. The emergent colonial system gradually came into conflict with the traditional system, the political and economic domain of the *Damel* and the ruling class. Faidherbe's policy of territorial expansion, in its first phase, required French control of the area between the Senegal and Gambia rivers. To implement it, Faidherbe resorted to diplomacy to keep Kajoor from taking sides in the general conflict initiated by simultaneous expeditions launched from Saint-Louis and Gorée. He worked to engineer the extradition of Moorish and Waalo refugees from Kajoor, alternating promises of friendship with threats of war, constantly using divisive tactics to segment the ruling class. With Machiavellian guile, Faidherbe succeeded in achieving his main aim at a time when the kingdom of Kajoor was also undergoing an unprecedented crisis that weakened the central government at the death of the *Damel* Meyssa Tend Joor.[14] From 1854, as the French threat became more precise, the Geej dynasty, in power since the days of Lat Sukaabe Faal in the late seventeenth century, came to an end. This situation posed a serious threat to the unity of Kajoor. For the revolt of the *Jawdin Mbul* exposed deep cleavages in the kingdom, with several forces fighting for control. The Gej clan, wielding central authority, opposed the royal branch of the Faal Majoor clan, an ally of the unconfirmed heir to the title of *Jawdin Mbul*, as well as of the Muslim religious faction in Njambur, in particular. It was in the midst of this incubating crisis that Faidherbe set off on his notorious punitive expedition to Ñomre. He planned to force the Njambur marabouts to give up the refugees from Waalo, including Sidia, son of the *Linger* Ndate Yalla.

The column set out from Saint-Louis in 1856, burning some fifty villages on the way to Ñomre. There, when the religious leader Ngiit staunchly refused to hand over the refugees, on the grounds that the law of hospitality forbade such betrayal, the French military torched the town. French reprisals against Ñomre were followed immediately by a revolt among the marabouts of Njambur against the *Damel*, Birama Ngone Latir. The marabouts, however, were divided into two factions. The first, under Silimakh Joop, a religious leader, was linked to the Gej clan and hostile to the colony of Senegal. The second, led by Seriñ Lugga, Njuuga Lo, sided with Faidherbe, and aimed to replace the Gej dynasty with the Faal clan. Faidherbe thus became an active participant, indeed a key player, in the habitual use of political violence in Kajoor. Through an infernal strategy of intriguing alliances, he fanned the flames of civil war. By the end of Birama Ngone Latir's term, this policy had yielded three major concessions. First, the colony acquired the right to fix duties and tariffs on agricultural produce traded in Ganjol, Tuube, Cap-Vert, and Rufisque. These towns thus became market enclaves for the peanut crop from Kajoor. The second concession was military and territorial: the Colony could henceforth recruit volunteers from these outlying areas for its empire-building expeditions. The third was political: Faidherbe, behind the scenes, pulled strings to get an ally of his elected to the Council of Electors.[15] The prevailing political crisis, which gradually opened the way for French interference in the political affairs of Kajoor, worsened when Makodu of the

Gelwaar matrilineal clan acceded to power. The Njambur establishment, eager to recover their traditional prerogatives from the monopolistic Gej clan, gave substantial support to the Gelwaar. Still, Makodu tried to reassert the *Damel*'s sovereignty over all Kajoor by denouncing the spurious treaty of 1861. Unfortunately, the situation on the ground favored French domination, despite the marabout partisans' attempt to counter the French, on account of their hostility to the colony following the Ñomre expedition. This opposition was expressed through the development of relationships between Shaykh Umar's envoys and the marabouts. These contacts led to the emergence of Lat Joor Ngone Latir. It was a development that, in all respects, symbolized a compromise between *ceddo* and Muslim regimes, at a time when, to satisfy France's industrial demand for peanuts, Faidherbe was planning the military conquest of Kajoor.

## D.     Political crisis in Siin and Saalum

In the kingdoms of Siin and Saalum, the development of peanut production had a similar impact on the unfolding political and social crisis as in the coastal states of Senegambia during the nineteenth century. There was one difference, though: in previous centuries, different European traders and companies had been intermittently active on the Petite Côte. The French push here therefore came comparatively late, especially since at this time Faidherbe's primary concern was to consolidate his hold on the Senegal valley and on Kajoor. It was not until the arrival of Pinet-Laprade, well after Dakar was founded in 1857, that a concerted policy of expansion into the Sereer kingdoms and the Southern Rivers region in general commenced. Even before then, however, as early as 1849, given the rapid development of peanut production, French traders were active at Fatick and Kaolack, signing treaties with the rulers of Siin and Saalum for the protection of traders, in return for an annual fee and customs duties.[16]

The central authority in the kingdom of Siin had maintained its power intact and reinforced it over the centuries. Even so, it was not immune to the changes that transformed the trans-Atlantic trading system from the start of the nineteenth century. The political crisis peaked in spectacular fashion when, in 1820, the ineligible Sandigi Njoob maneuvered his son Ama Juuf Faye Gelwaar into power as *Buur* in place of the legitimate successor Ama Kumba, forcing the latter into exile. Again in 1833, the rightful successor Sanumoon Faye was pushed aside in favor of Kumba Ndoofen Juuf as *Bumi*. Kumba Ndoofen Juuf ended up during most of the second half of the nineteenth century ruling as a powerful *Buur*, king of Siin. Quite early in his reign, though, he had to cope with the arrival of Catholic missionaries, who settled at Joal and Ngazobil. The king lost no time in banning their activities, which he saw as promoting the interests of the trading company at Gorée.[17]

Saalum was patently a less cohesive kingdom. In the first half of the nine-teenth century, it went through greater political instability than Siin. In 1825, Balle Nduugu Ndaw maneuvered his way into power as *Buur*. During his rule, which lasted until 1853, he protected the peanut market of Kawoon from pillaging *ceddo* warriors. He also curbed barter trading, thus break-ing the vicious circle of peasant debt and conflicts between producers and traders. His death led to a long succession crisis in the kingdom of Saalum between two royal houses: that of the Gelwaar princess Kewe Bigge and that of Diogop Bigge. The latter won out, giving the lineage five *Buurs* without a break. But with the death of Bala Adam Njaay in 1856, this monopoly was shaken. In 1859, the candidate representing Kewe Bigge's lineage, Kumba Ndawa Mbooj, was killed. Another candidate, Kumba Dianke Butong, died at the same time. This created an opening for the can-didate of Jogop Bigge's lineage.

The political crisis brought on by ceaseless infighting between the various royal lineages was here also aggravated by a serious economic and social crisis following the introduction of peanut farming. Income from the new crop gave peasant producers more money. So they bought weapons for self defense against the pillaging *ceddo* ruling class.[18] The entire region was well served by a network of tracks and creeks useful for transporting the peanut crop by camel, donkey, and canoe. Peanut production therefore developed rapidly, focusing increasing attention from the trading companies of Gorée to the mushrooming markets of Saalum.

France, which controlled the peanut trade, now planned to take over Saalum so as to block its British competitors operating from their base in Gambia. So following his victories in the Senegal River valley, Faidherbe decided to renege on the established treaties. He made up an excuse, alleg-ing unsubstantiated pillaging of company traders. Taking advantage of the resulting conflict, he imposed French rule over Siin–Saalum by force. Using a column of 200 local infantry and 160 marines backed by hundreds of Lebu volunteers, he burned Fatick on 18 March 1859, then pushed on to Kaolack. There the newly installed king, Samba Lawbe Faal, surrendered his sovereignty to France without a fight. Kajoor's development was now intimately tied to that of Saalum, in an environment dominated by Faidherbe's expansionist policies. The French governor forced the Petite Côte region into a French protectorate, constructing administrative posts at Rufisque, Joal, Kaolack, and Portudal after this lightning campaign. Sovereignty disputes, between the *Buurs* of Siin and Saalum on the one hand, and the French on the other, grew frequent. For the French now refused to pay customs duties. Pinet-Laprade's 1861 campaign did not end

these sovereignty disputes, whose scope was at the time substantially determined by the French decision to give high priority to developments in
Kajoor and Baol, the main peanut-farming areas.[19]

Kajoor was strategically located in the peanut producing region, midway
between Saint-Louis and the new site, Dakar. The campaign against the
kingdom dragged on over some twenty years. Because of this intense
concentration on Kajoor, France's involvement in Siin–Saalum was somewhat half-hearted in this period. This gave newly emergent Muslim social
groupings the leeway they needed to wage successful struggles against the
*ceddo* establishment, as well as to pose a serious threat to the French presence in all of northern Senegambia. In Saalum, more than anywhere else,
the influence of the holy warrior Shaykh Umar took tangible form in the
activities of Maba Jaakhu, his most prestigious disciple in Senegambia.

# 13 Defeat of the holy warriors in northern Senegambia

Shaykh Umar's defeat at Medina in 1857 forced the holy warrior to turn his attention exclusively to the construction of a new empire to the east of Senegambia. The task absorbed his energies until his death in 1864. Even so, he continued to influence the course of Senegambian history, partly through his *fergo* campaign, partly through the activities of his disciples, at a time when the region was having to face, in increasingly direct terms, the reality of colonial conquest.

The period saw the rise of an unbroken string of leaders in northern Senegambia, all intent on turning Shaykh Umar's vision into reality. These leaders challenged established aristocratic regimes. Their programs spilling over the frontiers of the old states, they set up large political units behind the banner of a militant Islam. From 1861 to 1867, throughout northern Senegambia from the Gambia River to the Senegal, Maba Jaakhu stood out as the greatest disciple of Shaykh Umar. At one point he succeeded in uniting the Muslim community, and in the process directly challenged the French presence in the region. After the failure of Maba Jaakhu came Cherno Brahim, followed by Amadu Seekhu. All, in the name of orthodox Islam, shook up this region, starting with Futa Toro, from 1869 to 1875. In their holy war, Maba Jaakhu the disciple of Shaykh Umar, Amadu Seekhu the Madiyu, and Cherno Brahim the disciple of Shaykh Siddiiya Al Kabir, aroused the resistance of established political authorities. Leaders of reigning regimes, representatives of traditional legitimacy, either collaborated with the new Muslim leadership or fought them, according to their immediate interests. For instance, Lat Joor, at a time when his position in Kajoor was shaky, momentarily joined forces with Maba Jaakhu and Amadu Seekhu as a step toward retrieving lost power. Alburi Njaay in the kingdom of Jolof did exactly the same. Neither hesitated about abandoning Maba Jaakhu or fighting Amadu Seekhu when the Muslims threatened their royal power. Similarly, Kumba Ndoofen Juuf fought Maba Jaakhu tooth and nail to safeguard *ceddo* power in Siin. Abdul Bokar Kane, the strongman of Boséa, also combated the religious and political protest movement organized in the Futa Toro theocracy by Cherno Brahim and Amadu Seekhu.

On balance, French support favored legitimate regimes struggling against emerging Muslim leaders. The final defeat of the marabouts, after they and the traditionalists had exhausted each other, made colonial conquest much easier.

## A.    Maba Jaakhu's *jihad*

Maba Jaakhu was born in Rip, of *toorodo* parents from Futa Toro. The Rip area had a cosmopolitan environment where Wolof and Peul ethnic minorities, having converted to Islam, soon formed tight Muslim communities for self-protection against *ceddo* ruling classes in Saalum and Badibu. Maba obtained his basic education in well-known Muslim schools at Kajoor, as well as from the Zawiya Moors. He returned to Rip to carry on his father's work as a religious teacher. Around 1850, Maba met Shaykh Umar, who initiated him into the Tijaniyya brotherhood, mandating him to proselytize for Islam in this Senegambian region.[1] Around 1860, this area of southern Saalum was already undergoing profound social change due to the development of peanut farming. The new crop gave peasants the means for self-defense against the depredations of the reigning *ceddo* regime. Patterning his work after Shaykh Umar's, Maba Jaakhu galvanized Muslim forces, then issued a call to holy war throughout northern Senegambia. In 1861, Maba Jaakhu defeated Math Jaakher, the *Mansa* of Badibu. That victory gave the Muslims a chance to consolidate their forces in the Ñoomi district, and to gain gradual control over the entire region between the Gambia and the Saalum, a slice of territory 150 km wide, reaching all the way to the Jolof frontier. In short, by 1863 Maba had emerged as the key political player in northern Senegambia, supporting the marabouts Shaykh Usman Joop, Samba Usman Ture, and Manjaay Khoreeja in their struggles against the ruling *ceddo* regimes in Kaymor. He also intervened in the conflict between Makodu and Samba Lawbe Faal for control over Saalum. Benefiting from the political crisis, and taking advantage of the weakening of *ceddo* power in Kajoor and Saalum in the wake of French intervention, he emerged as the new master of the region. The *jihad* enabled him to force *ceddo* chiefs to convert to Islam, and in particular to impose Muslim law on his new domain, using members of important clerical families in each community as mediators. Soon enough, Maba's expansionist program collided with that of the French, now also established in northern Senegambia.

   The situation on the north bank of the Gambia River became clear when the British showed they were not interested in territorial gains in Senegambia. The French Governor D'Arcy was initially quite pleased to see the Muslim forces victorious. After all, their success promised to bring peace to the territory, creating suitable conditions for peanut production and other commercial pursuits. The Soninke and *ceddo* regimes, on the other hand, promised only chaos with their daily routine of pillage and violence. Further, Maba, who bought his arms in Gambia, easily won over the British by acknowledging Ñoomi independence in 1863. He was more interested in the Saalum area to the north, whose rich salt ponds and fast developing peanut production brought in a sizable income. Maba's northward expansion, however, brought him into collision with France. One reason was that political conflicts in Kajoor and Saalum were intermeshed. From 1861, developments in Kajoor, where the French had explicit interests, produced immediate repercussions in Saalum, on account of marriage ties between the ruling classes of the two kingdoms.

Faidherbe had imposed his will throughout the Senegal River valley. Now his major aim was to annex Kajoor. To that end, he organized a military expedition in January 1861, with the purpose of building military posts at Mbijen, Benu Mbot, and Lompul. When Makodu refused to ratify the 1861 treaty guaranteeing French interests in Kajoor, Faidherbe organized fresh military campaigns in March and May 1861. The result was the fall of the *Damel*, who had to flee for refuge to Saalum. There, with the support of Maba Jaakhu, he claimed the throne, even if this meant deposing his own son, Samba Lawbe Faal. Meanwhile, the people of Njambur, caught between the *ceddo* rulers and the increasingly harsh reprisals of the French colonial forces, defected. Faidherbe, taking advantage of the disruption caused by the economic depression, the political crisis, and the defection of Njambur, set up Majojo Degen Kumba as *Damel* of Kajoor and Samba Maram Khaay as *Jawdin Mbul*. Majojo's enthronement did not resolve the crisis in Kajoor. Neither did it guarantee a definitive triumph for French influence. The Faal–Majoor faction, increasingly shunned by the anti-colonial population of Njambur, lost influence. In addition, Makodu and Lat Joor were pressing in on the frontiers of the kingdom.

On 12 January 1862, following a revolt of the inhabitants of Njambur, the defeated Majojo was forced to flee to Lompul for refuge. From then on Njambur supported Lat Joor. And for an instant of time, from May to June of 1862, Lat Joor actually took over as *Damel*.[2] Young though he was, Lat Joor already appeared to be the only major figure with the power to confront the threat of colonial conquest at this time of political and social crisis in Kajoor. Initially, he was handicapped by the fact that his claim to power was patrilineal, through the Joop clan. In principle, that made him ineligible, since succession had so far been restricted to the Faal clan. However, in 1860, his half-brother, the *Damel* Birama Ngone Latir, died, leaving no heir from the powerful Geej lineage. Lat Joor stepped into the vacuum, seizing the opportunity to make his mark in political affairs.

In the event, he did not have the time needed to consolidate his power.

For in 1863, Faidherbe returned from France with a mandate for a second term as governor of the colony of Senegal. He came determined to impose a final solution on the power equation in Kajoor. It took over fifteen French columns, crisscrossing Kajoor on patrol, to push Lat Joor into seeking refuge in Maba Jaakhu's stronghold in Rip. Faidherbe reinstalled Majojo as *Damel*. But Majojo proved inept at ruling a Kajoor economically ruined by colonial military campaigns, and politically shredded by Njambur dissidents and a section of the *ceddo* aristocracy. His policy of indirect rule having failed, Faidherbe decided to take direct charge of Kajoor. He deposed Majojo on 17 February 1865, annexed the kingdom, and divided it into five provinces.

Faidherbe appointed a set of royal slaves, or *jammi buur*, along with selected provincial chiefs of the old regime hostile to Lat Joor, as provincial chiefs. That done, he retired from the colony, persuaded that his final solution for the problem of Kajoor would work. He was far from imagining the threat to French possessions in northern Senegambia posed by the new alliance between Lat Joor and the marabout Maba Jaakhu.[3]

The question is often raised as to whether, in converting to Islam, the *Damel* Lat Joor acted in good faith. The question is irrelevant. For the record, Lat Joor was born a Muslim. He was nonetheless a traditional ruler of *ceddo* lineage. What set him apart was his willingness to depend more heavily on Muslim partisans than his predecessors had, in his effort to shore up the *Damel*'s power, beset as it was by the French threat and internal political strife. This was the context in which Lat Joor, driven from Kajoor by Faidherbe, took refuge in Rip with his retinue of seasoned *ceddo* warriors. His arrival strengthened the hand of Maba Jaakhu, already in control of Saalum after the death of the two heirs Makodu and Samba Lawbe Faal. Now, supported by Lat Joor and Alburi Njaay, the future *Buurba* of Jolof, Maba Jaakhu set out to conquer the *ceddo* states. Fighting all the way, he reached Jolof, which he took on 22 July 1865.

Having conquered most of northern Senegambia, Maba Jaakhu launched an intense diplomatic campaign aimed at getting the Trarza Moors and the rulers of Futa Toro to challenge the French presence. The French colonialists had until now been rather friendly to Muslim forces, since they were effective at stopping the marauding *ceddo* warriors from pillaging the country. But now Maba Jaakhu posed a direct threat to Kajoor and Baol, in the heart of the peanut-producing region. The French attitude changed.

Maba Jaakhu's main aim, like that of Shaykh Umar, was the pursuit of his holy war. He considered himself the head of the Muslim community. That meant his authority now covered the kingdoms of Siin, Saalum, Kajoor, Baol, and Jolof. As sovereign of this entire domain, he reasoned that the internal affairs of these kingdoms were none of France's business, and that therefore the French should restrict themselves exclusively to their trading concerns. This, once again, made sovereignty disputes inevitable. Faidherbe, in a letter to Maba, warned the marabout that he was free to organize the kingdom of Saalum provided he did not touch Baol and Kajoor, which formed an integral part of Saint-Louis.[4] Even though the Treaty of 1864 recognized Maba's authority over Badibu and Saalum, Pinet-Laprade, alarmed at the scope of the marabout's conquests, marched on Saalum on 25 October 1865 at the head of 1,600 regulars, 2,000 cavalry raised to fight for the colony, plus 4,000 volunteers and footsoldiers. The famous battle of Patebajaan, fought on 30 November 1865, ended, strictly speaking, in a military victory for Maba Jaakhu. Pinet-Laprade was himself wounded into the bargain. He could take consolation in the boast that he had torched more than thirty-two villages filled with wealth and the previous year's harvest, and had left the Paos valley littered with the bodies of the marabout leader's soldiers. The battle made it clear, however, that France, its military superiority notwithstanding, could not risk another campaign far from its bases, unless it was prepared to suffer heavy casualties.[5]

After the battle of Patebajaan, Pinet-Laprade had to cope with budget cuts and a reduction in military resources imposed from Paris. He therefore avoided any direct confrontation with Maba Jaakhu's forces. Instead, he contented himself with strengthening the fortifications at Kaolack and organizing raids near the French posts to ensure security in Siin. Meanwhile, Maba, with logistical support from Lat Joor, held on in Rip. To the north, however, his position became more and more difficult. Even so, he was finally able, a few days after his victory at Kaolack, to launch an attack on the powerful Siin kingdom, after six years of waiting. Taking Jakhao, the capital, after a surprise attack, he burned it, before facing the entire Siin army in a pitched battle in July 1867. Later, Kumba Ndoofen Juuf organized Siin resistance with, according to tradition, opportune help from the Sereer spirits (called *pangole*). It is a fact that at the famous battle of Somb, torrential rains doused Maba's ammunition. Their powder wet and useless, his troops were routed. Maba Jaakhu, the holy warrior, died in the débâcle. His chief lieutenant, Lat Joor, after staring defeat in the face, fled to his homeland, Kajoor, dreaming of fighting his way to the throne. This victory of Kumba Ndoofen Juuf, the *ceddo* representative, over the Muslim forces, was spectacular. In the long run, however, it only presaged victory for the French. For, without French help, Kumba Ndoofen Juuf had ended the career of a marabout poised to reunify the old Jolof confederation, the one entity that could, in the name of Islam, have put up a more effective resistance to French imperialism.[6]

**B.    The *jihad* of Cherno Brahim and Amadu Seekhu**

With Maba Jaakhu gone, it fell to Cherno Brahim and, to an even greater extent, to Amadu Seekhu to continue the holy war against the local aristocracies, whom they saw as too inclined to connive with French interference throughout northern Senegambia. Their program of religious and political protest started in Futa Toro. Massive Futanke migration during Shaykh Umar's *fergo* had created a lasting economic and political crisis there. The punitive expeditions of the French colony had only worsened matters. For following the dismemberment of Futa and Faidherbe's establishment of a French protectorate over the eastern and western provinces in 1859, Shaykh Umar's resounding victory in the Masina in 1862 gave ruling-class agitation against the French presence a new lease of life. The entire population waited for his return. Until the last moment, they expected the holy warrior to lead a triumphal march to the sea, avenging his 1857 defeat at Medina and expelling the French from the African continent.

Instead, it was Jauréguiberry who, from Saint-Louis, organized a series of campaigns from July 1862 to February 1863, inflicting severe punishment on the protest movement in Futa. The campaigns were known as *duppal borom*, the governor's fire, because they involved the torching of hundreds of villages. By these campaigns, Faidherbe, on his return to Saint-Louis, forced the *Almami* Mamadu Biram to accept conditions leading to the dismemberment of Futa, sanctioned by the Treaty of August 1863.

In this atmosphere of ruling class capitulation, the young Abdul Bokar Kane, grandson of the powerful kingmaker Ali Dundu, emerged as the real master of central Futa. Faidherbe at the time had eased his military pressure on the Senegal valley, turning his attention to Kajoor. This gave Abdul Bokar Kane the opportunity he wanted. He had no ambition to be a political or religious reformer in the style of the *Almamis*. But he was supremely confident in his identity as a man from Boséa, descended from the most influential lineage represented on the *Jaggorde* Council of Electors. In his time he had fought, with his army of young Peul, *ceddo*, and Moorish warriors, who had no connection whatsoever with the Toorodo tradition of Islam, against Shaykh Umar's *fergo*, blaming it for depopulating the land. He was therefore able to get himself recognized by his compatriots as the only man capable of restoring peace to the Futa kingdom and safeguarding its integrity.

Abdul Bokar Kane was a warlord fashioned precisely after the model of the eighteenth-century *satigi*. His problem was that, as from 1865, he had to face the challenge of a fundamentalist religious movement led first by Cherno Brahim in eastern Futa and then, with greater impact, by Amadu

Seekhu in western Futa.[7] Amadu Seekhu was particularly active beyond
the frontiers of Futa Toro, in the kingdoms of Jolof, Waalo, Kajoor, and
Baol. In a sense, he reversed the itinerary of Maba Jaakhu, whose movement beginning in southern Gambia, had spread toward the Senegal River
valley in an attempt to unite northern Senegambia against French intrusion.

Cherno Brahim studied under the Daymani marabouts, masters of the
Zawiya tradition of Nasir Al Din. For his higher education he went, like
Mamadu Juhe, the Hubbu leader, to the renowned *Qadriyya* teacher
Shaykh Siddiya Al Kabir. Returning in 1864, he settled at Magama. To this
sanctuary he called his compatriots to come in their numbers, away from
the town of Matam, polluted by the French presence. His simple lifestyle
and learning drew many disciples eager to escape from the burden of taxation. In 1865 he attacked the French fort at Matam, threatening Bakel as
well. At the same time, with reinforcements from Maalik Hamat, he soon
brought the authority of Abdul Bokar Kane in eastern Futa under direct
political threat. Abdul Bokar Kane sought help from Bokar Saada of
Bundu, marrying his niece Jiba. He also appealed to Gajaaga and Khaaso
for help, and went so far as to request the French contingent's aid in driving
Cherno Brahim out of Magama in May 1868. Abdul Bokar Kane took
advantage of the situation to strengthen his authority in eastern Futa, but
he was forced to organize a second campaign with nearly 7,000 men to
capture Magama after several days of fierce fighting. His allies from
Gajaaga and Khaaso then decided to hang the holy man, captured in the
1869 siege. On his return from the campaign at Magama, Abdul Bokar
Kane was confronted with another religious movement. This time it was led
by the famous Amadu Seekhu, a man whose program far transcended the
borders of Futa.[8]

In the region of western Futa, the combined effects of Shaykh Umar's
*fergo* and the French presence created an unprecedented economic and
political crisis in the 1860s. This facilitated the emergence of the Madiyu
movement under the leadership of Amadu Seekhu. The construction of a
fort at Podor, coupled with the establishment of a French protectorate in
1859, bolstered the authority of the *Lam Tooro*, whose jurisdiction included
the villages of Hayre, Haylabe, and Walalbe. However, the French presence
also intensified immigration into Nioro. And when, from November 1868
to May 1869, a huge outbreak of cholera killed 25 percent of the population of Podor, 33 percent of that of Bakel, and 50 percent of that of Matam,
in all about 20 percent of Futa's total population, the economic, political
and social crisis hit its lowest point.[9] The epidemic also ravaged the Wolof
kingdoms of Waalo and Kajoor, where the recent imposition of French rule
had brought added suffering to the population. The French routinely con-

fiscated harvests, commandeered livestock, and burned villages. So the epidemic outbreaks of yellow fever in 1866–7 and cholera in 1869, wiping out thousands of lives throughout western Senegambia, were just the last straw.[10] The massive death toll rekindled sparks of dissent, creating an atmosphere receptive to Amadu Seekhu's religious propaganda. For the marabout had proclaimed himself the Mahdi, come to combat the hypocrites collaborating with the French, whose program of expansion from the coast into the continental hinterland was anathema.

Like Shaykh Umar, Amadu Seekhu came from a long-established family of literate Muslims. His father Hamma Bâ, an early Tijaniyya adherent, joined the coalition led by the Wane of Mbumba in 1828. Following its defeat, he focused on a new mission: to purify Islamic practice in Futa. The hostility of the ruling *Toorodo* regime did not stop him building a substantial settlement at Wuro Madiyu near Podor. He strengthened his position by marrying into the powerful marabout families of Kokki in Kajoor as well as the Wane family of Mbumba. Hamma Bâ, a man who had received his education at home, actively opposed the mass departure of the Futanke followers of Shaykh Umar in 1850. When he died, his two sons, Amadu Seekhu, chief of Wuro Madiyu, and Ibra, who had stayed on in Kokki with his maternal relatives, interpreted the cholera epidemic as a sign that the time had come for a purification movement among their Madiyu followers throughout western Senegambia, a land sorely tried by the French occupation. So Amadu Seekhu took up the message of Shaykh Umar, Cherno Brahim, and Maba Jaakhu. Since he had a considerable following of Peul, Tukulor, and Wolof adherents right within the French colony, a confrontation with the colonial occupation forces was inevitable.

Alarmed at the flourishing movement, Samba Umahani joined forces with a French contingent to destroy Wuro Madiyu in the absence of Amadu Seekhu, who had gone with his followers to besiege and capture Kokki after the expulsion of his brother Ibra by his uncle, the *Seriñ Kokki*. At this juncture, Amadu Seekhu and Ibra formed an alliance with Lat Joor, eager to recapture the throne of Kajoor. In July 1869, they inflicted a humiliating defeat on the French contingent in central Kajoor. The victory left Amadu Seekhu free to return to western Futa, keen to avenge the assault on Wuro Madiyu. Around November 1869, his followers put themselves in a position to stop all boats moving beyond Podor. That made French control over Futa totally ineffective. Meanwhile, French reprisals, organized with the collaboration of Samba Umahani, the *Lam Tooro*, speeded up mass migration into Nioro. Soon, it pushed Amadu Seekhu into central Futa, where for a time he reinforced the position of his brother-in-law the *Almami* Sada Wane of Mbumba, under threat from the energetic Abdul Bokar Kane. The latter, however, was maneuvered into yielding political precedence to Amadu Seekhu who, in March 1870, sent out a solemn appeal to his compatriots in central Futa to liberate western Futa from French control. Abdul Bokar Kane, just as he did during the itinerary of Shaykh Umar, carefully avoided direct confrontation with the leader of the Madiyu movement. Amadu Seekhu, having waited in vain for a national uprising, left Futa with all his forces for Jolof, where he set up his headquarters until his death in 1875.[11] Using an army made up for the most part of Wolof disciples who had followed Maba Jaakhu into Futa and Rip, Amadu Seekhu easily dethroned the *Buurba* Bakaram Khadi in August 1870. His victory came all the faster because Jolof, being somewhat remote from the French zone of influence, was not of vital importance to the colony. Still, knowing that Amadu Seekhu's influence in the Wolof kingdoms was tremendous, the French Governor banned all Tijaniyya ceremonial gatherings in the town of Saint-Louis. He also sought new allies for the struggle against the Madiyu. Now Jolof had become Amadu Seekhu's headquarters. There, opposition to his movement came mainly from Sanor Njaay and Alburi Njaay, both claimants to the ancestral throne. Sanor, taking refuge in French territory, asked their ally, the *Lam Tooro* Samba Umahani, to help him attack Amadu Seekhu's army in July 1871. The latter once more marched upon Tooro. But the French governor Valière's cannon forced him back to Jolof. Having tried a second time to conquer Jolof, and having failed again, Sanor submitted publicly to Amadu Seekhu in 1873. The latter in return recognized him as *Buurba*. From then on, the only opposition to Amadu Seekhu came from Alburi Njaay and Lat Joor. The latter had become increasingly hostile to the marabout, who since 1874 had turned his ambitions toward Kajoor.[12]

France, defeated by Germany, had since 1870 been forced to postpone all plans for colonial expansion. Knowing from experience what to expect from an alliance between Maba Jaakhu and Lat Joor, and wishing to avoid a war on two fronts, Governor Valière tried to reach an understanding with Lat Joor. And Lat Joor, after agreeing to an alliance with the dominant Muslim leader of the hour, went back on his word in an attempt to bolster his chances of becoming king of Kajoor. The result was that, on 15 July 1870, Valière once more recognized Lat Joor as *Damel* of Kajoor. The Treaty of 2 January 1871 ratified his compromise with the colony of Senegal. Lat Joor then made several attempts to help Alburi Njaay to recover the Jolof throne, all in vain. By now, Lat Joor had become the principal opponent of Amadu Seekhu, who, apart from wanting to take over Baol, posed a threat to Kajoor with his multitude of followers in Njambur. In 1874, the dispute over Baol brought the latent antagonism between Lat

Joor, who hoped to unite all the Wolof states under his authority, and Amadu Seekhu, who now had the support of Sidia Léon Joop, a paramount chief of Waalo who had turned against the French, to a definitive split. Oddly enough, Amadu Seekhu obtained additional support from the energetic Abdul Bokar Kane, who gave vent to his dislike of Ibra Almami by siding with the marabout. The forces arrayed against Amadu Seekhu were considerable. Yet he won two victories at Kokki in July 1874. In November of that same year, he defeated the combined forces of Lat Joor, Ibra Almami, and Mamadu Sile at the frontier of Kajoor. This double victory gave Valière an excuse to intervene. In February 1875 he organized an expedition of 560 regular troops and 67 *spahis* (cavalrymen serving in the squadron in Senegal colony) bolstered by heavy artillery in support of Lat Joor. The ensuing battle of Samba Saajo was bloody. When it ended, Amadu Seekhu lay dead, along with hundreds of his followers. The Madiyu movement thus came to a sudden end.[13] Prior to this battle, Lat Joor had betrayed Sidia Léon Joop to the French colony, in violation of the law of hospitality. In the last analysis, this victory of Lat Joor's was, like Maba Jaakhu's, really a French victory.

So all Muslim reformers who led movements aimed at the triumph of a militant brand of Islam in Senegambia – Maba Jaakhu, Cherno Brahim, Amadu Seekhu – came to the same tragic end as their model, Shaykh Umar.

Maba Jaakhu benefited from the support of marabout communities established in Rip, Saalum and Jolof. They took an active part in the holy war against the *ceddo* states of the old Jolof confederation. Occasionally, he also obtained logistical support from Lat Joor and Alburi Njaay. The two aristocrats, who had recently switched over to Islam, were attempting to protect their political prerogatives as legitimate rulers of Kajoor and Jolof against rival claimants on the one hand, and French encroachments on their sovereignty on the other. Maba Jaakhu was finally defeated by the resistance organized by the *Buur* of Siin, Kumba Ndoofen Juuf. As a *ceddo* ruler, the *Buur* was opposed to the marabout's attempt to establish a new religious and political order through a holy war in the name of a militant Muslim orthodoxy. With Maba Jaakhu's death ended the most innovative attempt to unify northern Senegambia, from the Gambia to the Senegal River, on the eve of the era of colonial conquest.

Cherno Brahim's rebel movement was restricted to Futa Toro. In many respects it was like the Hubbu movement in Futa Jallon. That movement was an attempt by a reformist marabout to shape his followers into a community outside the jurisdiction of the oppressive theocratic state. The movement was decapitated in a repressive assault organized by the Boséa chief, Abdul Bokar Kane, intent on protecting his political and economic privileges as a *toorodo* ruler. Significantly, he had no qualms about turning to the kings of Gajaaga and Khaaso, who had nothing to do with the religious issue, for help in putting down the movement.

Amadu Seekhu presented a much more complex case. For his movement provoked a chain reaction of alliances and counter-alliances in which religion was not a relevant factor. Furthermore, active French intervention in these conflicts underscored the complexity of the shifting alliances. Above all else, what they indicated was the seriousness of the political and social crisis throughout northern Senegambia as the region faced the prospect of colonial conquest.

In Futa Toro, Amadu Seekhu began by waging war on those collaborating with the French. Later he formed an alliance with the Wane clan of Mbumba in an effort to oppose the authority of Abdul Kane, the powerful chief of Boséa. In the Wolof kingdoms, he ran into hostility from the *Seriñ* of Kokki, while initially getting support from Lat Joor, eager to recover on the Kajoor throne. However, following the conquest of Jolof, and in the light of the threat this posed to the independence of Kajoor, Amadu Seekhu found himself facing opposition from Lat Joor and Alburi Njaay. Neither of them hesitated to collaborate with the French in their determination to protect their power as legitimate rulers.

In all three cases, the physical liquidation of the Muslim leaders brought their supra-national movement, the only contemporary challenge to colonial conquest, to a brutal end. Committed to preaching and organizing a holy war, these warrior clerics often left behind conquered territories far from their home bases. But they left no heirs worthy of the heritage. Saddest of all, they never really had time to organize their kingdoms efficiently. After their passing, a trend emerged among the old legitimate rulers, heirs to the reigning aristocracies in the states born of the territorial breakup of sixteenth-century Senegambia or the conquering Muslim revolutions of the eighteenth century: collaboration with the colonial French. That was their way of protecting their power against ambitious new Muslim leaders with authority over constituencies far larger than the traditional states of Senegambia. The all-out struggle between legitimate sovereigns and new Muslim leaders effectively cut Senegambia's capacity for resistance in half. Such were the debilitating circumstances under which France decided, a few years later, to intensify its drive toward colonial conquest. Initially, however, the defeat of Maba Jaakhu, Cherno Brahim, and Amadu Seekhu caught the French off guard. Their forces were regrouping. For the next few years, all they dared do was to hold on to their conquered territories. In short, they put their program of territorial expansion on hold.

The decisive clash between the Senegambian states and the French colonial authority over sovereignty was thus postponed. That left room for political and social crises to erupt into central prominence in each state. Such legitimate rulers as Lat Joor, Kumba Ndoofen Juuf, Alburi Njaay and Abdul Bokar Kane now tried to restore their authority, considerably undermined by the Muslim uprising as well as by the first salvoes fired by the machinery of colonial conquest.

*Part IV*

Senegambia in the second half of the
nineteenth century: colonial conquest and
resistance movements

Waalo was conquered in 1855. Shaykh Umar was defeated at Medina in 1857. The two events marked the real beginning of the partition of Senegambia by the French, the British, and the Portuguese. The process of partition, lasting until the end of the nineteenth century, involved a long series of military campaigns punctuated by lulls and periods of negotiation. As it unfolded, the states and peoples of the region resisted colonial conquest in a variety of ways. The drive toward colonial conquest was fragmented on account of competition between the European powers. The process was therefore jumbled, with piecemeal advances here, uncoordinated thrusts there; hence the artificiality of today's frontiers in the Senegambian region.

Colonial conquest took place against a historical background in which the major economic issues of the first half of the nineteenth century remained essentially unresolved. The heat of military activity, combined with the clash of rival European powers, tended to blur the motives behind the new European drive toward empire that emerged after the mercantilism of the previous centuries. Indeed, the conquest of Senegambia was an integral part of a general context of colonial imperialism in which the dominant concern was the determination of Europe's industrial states to carve up the world.

As far as Senegambia was concerned, colonial conquest took the form of territorial conquest directly related to the immediate economic interests of France, Britain, and Portugal in this region. For that reason, the resulting partition was to a great extent determined by the commercial status of those three powers in the first half of the nineteenth century.

France, for obvious reasons, got the best deal. At that time, its territorial ambitions were closely tied to the development of peanut farming along the coast from Saint-Louis to Freetown. Secondly, it wanted to get hold of the resources of the Sudanese hinterland. It was therefore motivated to take over the region. The conquering thrust followed three main axes. In the first phase, the emphasis was on violent operations spearheaded by the French navy. Smarting from the 1870 defeat inflicted on France by the Prussian army, the French military turned to colonial conquest with brutal enthusiasm. The conquest of the area from the Senegal River to the Niger began in 1854 with the conquest of Waalo. From there, it proceeded with inexorable force until the victory over Amadu at Segu in 1890. Indeed, even after that it continued until 1898, when Samori was defeated in the remote forests of the Ivory Coast.

The salient feature of the second phase was the conquest of the coastal strip along the Saint-Louis–Freetown axis. This ensured a French monopoly over the peanut trade. In this phase, France occupied Kajoor, Jolof, Siin, Saalum, and most of the Southern Rivers region. The result was an end to the sovereignty disputes which in the past had compromised the economic interests of the trading companies.

The purpose of the third – and last – phase was to link the Sudanese region with that of the Southern Rivers. This would integrate Futa Jallon into the Senegambian environment, thus creating an outlet from the Niger Bend to the sea.

The French thus exercised *de facto* hegemony in the region, enabling them to control both the territory and the economy. Their control, however, came under constant challenge from the British and the Portuguese, who had similar ambitions. When the dust settled, these powers had managed to hold on, fighting to the bitter end, to their enclaves in Gambia and Guinea Bissao. Competition between France, Britain, and Portugal, each jealously pursuing its national interests, thus resulted in an artificial partition pattern that violated the region's natural and historical contours. For years to come this pattern would persist, frustrating the possibility of Senegambian unity.

In northern Senegambia, the process of conquest was exclusively French. France resumed its military campaigns in 1876 with the appointment of Brière de Lisle. By then, all the new leaders of the Muslim holy war had been eliminated by the coalition of legitimist rulers and the French colony of Senegal. Once the marabouts had been dispatched, the French colony turned on the traditional legitimist rulers. The latter organized last-ditch resistance efforts, but their desperate reaction came too late to matter. France now organized a series of military campaigns designed to satisfy its appetite for territorial conquest. One after the other, traditional rulers trying to preserve their heritage – Lat Joor in Kajoor, Alburi Njaay in Jolof, Kumba Ndoofen Juuf in Siin, Abdul Bokar Kane in the Futa Toro, and Saer Maty Ba in Saalum – and all fell on the field of battle.

The conquest of southern Senegambia came much later, except for individual footholds along the Southern Rivers occupied by Britain, France and Portugal since the mid-nineteenth century. The occupation of the hinterland was delayed by competition between the three powers throughout the second half of the nineteenth century. Into the vacuum thus left stepped new leaders like Sunkari, Fodé Silla, Ibrahima Njaay, and especially Fodé Kaba. They revived the movement led by Maba Jaakhu. Leaving the colonial presence aside, the warrior marabouts concentrated on organizing a *jihad* against the Joola, Baïnuk, and Balante groups of the Lower Casamance basin, as well as against Soninke aristocracies on the southern bank of the River Gambia. In the end they were defeated by a combined British–French operation. After that the two powers tightened their control over the region as from the 1880s.

Similarly, in an extension of the holy war that the Futa Jallon regime organized against Kaabu in the mid-nineteenth century, Musa Molo, who succeeded Alfa Molo at the top of the Fuladu power structure, formed an alliance with France in order to free himself from the Alfa of Labé's overlordship and to gain control over the entire region down to the Rio Geba. In the end, his territory was divided up between France, Britain, and Portugal. Musa Molo, for his part, having tried to play the three rival powers off against each other in a bid to consolidate his kingdom, remained a prisoner in Gambia until he died in 1931.

Meanwhile, France conducted a mopping-up campaign, occupying the territory around Rio Pongo, Rio Nunez, and Mellakure in preparation for the creation of the colony of French Guinea. First, France gradually eliminated the political influence of Futa Jallon. Then it abolished the privileges of the Baga, Landuman, Nalu, and Susu aristocracies. French forces defeated Diina Salifu and Sara Tongo in Rio Nunez, John Katty in Rio Pongo, and the *Almami* Bokari in Mellakure, one after the other. In this way France extended its territorial reach beyond the perimeters of the forts of Boke, Bofa, and Benty. The occupation of the Kaalum peninsula (the site of present-day Conakry) and the area around Dubreka consolidated the foundations of French Guinea. The main beneficiaries of this development were the trading companies.

Up until 1896, Futa Jallon had not had to face operations of military conquest. This long period of immunity was due to the country's geographical location, to French–British rivalry, and, above all, to the fact that France gave higher priority to the conquest of northern Senegambia and the Sudan. This enabled the kingdom to face down several internal challenges to its unity from 1870 to 1890, while preserving the old theocracy's autonomy by exploiting French–British competition. But the occupation, one after the other, of Senegal, Sudan, and the Southern Rivers enabled France to surround Futa Jallon. From 1890, France organized the encirclement of the kingdom, intensified its military and diplomatic pressure, and astutely exploited the country's internal political crisis. The defining moment came in 1896 at the battle of Poredaka, which ended in a French

victory. Like the legitimist rulers of northern Senegambia, Bokar Biro, isolated, sought vainly to defend the centuries-old heritage of his ancestors,
and failed.

After the battle of Poredaka, practically all of Senegambia fell under
French, British, or Portuguese control. To all intents, the process of colonial conquest ended as the nineteenth century turned into the twentieth.
Mopping-up operations continued for a few more years because, showing
an unsuspected vigor, the Joola, Basari, and Konyagi people conducted a
long campaign of popular resistance in an effort to preserve their freedom.
The resistance movements lasted into the early years of the twentieth
century.

# 14    Colonial imperialism and European rivalries in Senegambia

The long transitional period from 1814 to 1876 was dominated by the triumph of legitimate trade and the recurring cycle of sovereignty disputes. It ended with the rise of colonial imperialism, which plunged France, Britain, and Portugal into a process of military conquest and the partition of Senegambia.

It was a violent process, conducted by regular armies from metropolitan Europe reinforced by local recruits. The immediate objective was territorial conquest. A useful distinction may be made between the conquest of northern Senegambia and that of the south. The former was entirely dominated by France. In southern Senegambia, however, the process of partition involved considerable competition between France, Britain, and Portugal. That circumstance left a profound imprint on the outcome. In every case, the acquisition of territory unleashed a continent-wide storm of violence in which formerly sovereign states were subjugated. The ferocity of inter-European rivalry eventually found a resolution in the 1885 Berlin Conference. That conference was convened for the purpose of defining rules for the partition process in the hope of averting a generalised conflict in metropolitan Europe.

## A.    French colonial imperialism in northern Senegambia

France was the sole power involved in the conquest of northern Senegambia. Beginning in the early 1850s, France reinforced its position through Faidherbe's conquests in the Senegal valley, starting from Saint-Louis and going along the seaboard from Kajoor to Saalum, with Gorée as the base.

Under Faidherbe, who served two terms as governor, the colony went through a period of expansion. His successor, Pinet-Laprade, consolidated Faidherbe's gains. But under the next governor, Valière (1869–76), there was a long lull. The colony had a hard time coping with a cholera epidemic, and metropolitan France went through a period of depression and withdrawal after its defeat by Prussia in 1870. Valière's 1876 instructions still defined the colony of Senegal simply as a trading post. They explicitly ruled out any attempt at territorial expansion.[1]

Even though Paris imposed limitations that reduced military intervention in Africa to a minimum, successive governors maintained and developed as much as possible the colonial administrative machinery inherited from Faidherbe, and kept the kingdoms of northern Senegambia under constant pressure.

In religious matters, France promoted the influence of Shaykh Siddiyya Al Kabir's grandson in Saint-Louis. His quietest strain of Islam made a convenient counterpoise to the militant brand of those Muslim leaders who had demonstrated their hostility to the French presence. An influential Muslim community friendly to the French thus grew up in Saint-Louis around Saad Bu of the Kunta family and his disciple Shaykh Mamadu of Futa Toro, as well as the famous Arabic interpreter Bu El Mogdad, an intimate of Shaykh Siddiyya's family, and Hamat Njaay. Similarly, there was a large community of subcontractors like Njaay Sar and Gaspard Devès. They formed an indispensable buffer between the colony and local rulers, harmonizing their relationships. Meanwhile, such notables as Alioune Sal, Mademba and Rasine Sy, Mamadu Mbow, and Abdoulaye Kane made themselves useful to the French Governor, doing whatever was required to promote colonial expansion, in the hope of wangling a choice post in the administration at some future date.[2] Furthermore, by passing the Emancipation Act, the colony of Senegal encouraged the flight of slaves toward Saint-Louis, Gorée, Podor, Matam, Rufisque, Funjun, Kaolack, and their outskirts. The colony thus created a series of enclaves capable of surrounding the Senegambian kingdoms. Not only that, they could also serve as vectors of humanitarian ideas likely to enable the colony to take a more direct part in the political and social affairs of the Senegambian states.[3] The tendency toward encirclement intensified at a time when French military superiority over local armies had increased considerably. French forces were no longer restricted to firing salvoes at trading posts from gunboats plying the Senegal River. Now they could organize full-scale campaigns in the hinterland, using artillery as well as machine guns and cannon. The colony created a real professional army by organizing mercenaries throughout Senegambia, the well-known Senegalese Rifle Corps.

In 1876, the drive toward colonial expansion in northern Senegambia led to territorial conquest. Two events gave the revival of expansionist policies a boost: Republicans in France rose steadily to leadership roles in government and the civil service, and Brière de Lisle was appointed Governor of Senegal. Brière, like Faidherbe, was an advocate of colonial conquest. Trading companies in Bordeaux and Marseille jumped at the chance to lobby once more for colonial expansion. The appointment of Jauréguibéry, a former governor of the colony of Senegal, as Navy Minister reinforced the position of the colonialist faction, and it provided Brière de Lisle with the resources he needed to expand the colony by force.

The policy of colonial expansion took practical form in the imposition of a general poll tax, intensified recruitment of slaves into the Senegalese Rifle Corps, and the creation of more trading centers like Rufisque, with Saint-Louis and Gorée serving as models. Above all, colonial policy required the conquest of the Sudan. That in turn presupposed total control over Senegambia, plus the construction of railroads. Plans for a Dakar–Kayes railway line, and to an even greater extent for a Dakar–Saint-Louis line, signaled the start of a new phase of all-out imperialism based on a clear determination to secure military and economic control over con-quered territories in the Senegambian hinterland.[4]

By the mid-nineteenth century, the northern Senegambian economy had become a one-crop system, with peanut production rising steadily year by year. From 8,772 tonnes in 1870, peanut exports rose to 45,061 tonnes in 1885. By 1883, peanut exports to France already accounted for 14,653,000 francs out of a total export value of 20,508,960 francs. The *de facto* peanut monoculture now meant a considerable reduction in subsistence farming. The *Moniteur du Sénégal* reported the fears of a number of district admin-istrators whose areas risked famine.

The huge boost in peanut production motivated trading companies to support the Dakar–Saint-Louis rail project, the construction of wharves in Saint-Louis, and the development of Dakar.[5] Brière de Lisle now set out on a campaign of military conquest needed to carve out the colonial space required for peanut production. A related aim was the construction of a railway line to help break the Moorish caravan monopoly and end the resis-tance of the Wolof and Sereer aristocracies. The railway line was also expected to help boost peanut production and bring the hinterland under firmer colonial control. But for this policy to succeed, the ruling aristocra-cies of northern Senegambia – in particular those of Kajoor, Baol, Siin, and Saalum, the main peanut farming areas – had to be eliminated. Colonial military control remained the only way to ensure the peace and calm required for peanut farming and trading in the new market system involv-ing the French colony and the emergent peasant producers.[6]

For these reasons, colonial imperialism aimed to bring down the ruling aristocracies. The latter, for their part, fought to defend their legitimate eco-nomic and political privileges. The subjugation of northern Senegambia, under exclusive French rule, was part of the French plan to penetrate all the way to the Sudan. Because the French reigned supreme in both of these areas, they ran into stiffer opposition when they moved to conquer south-ern Senegambia. In that region, opposition came from Portugal and, to an

Plate 9 Soldiers of the Senegalese Rifle Corps (from Gallieni, *Deux campagnes au Soudan Français, 1886–1888*. Paris: Librairie Hachette, 1891)

even greater extent, from Britain. For both these powers were also enthralled by the dream of a fabulously wealthy West African Sudan.

## B.    European rivalries in southern Senegambia

The outstanding feature of the conquest of southern Senegambia was doubtless the initial rivalry between France, Britain, and Portugal. Germany also took part in the land grab, though to a minor degree. For a while, the drive toward territorial expansion superseded economic considerations. Nevertheless, economic interests underlay the general process of colonial conquest.

French–British competition was the central feature of European rivalry in this region. It found a resolution in the 10 August 1889 Convention. Earlier, the 1885 Franco–German Convention had ratified the abandonment of German claims, and, on 19 May 1886, a Franco–Portuguese Convention fixed two frontiers, the first between Portuguese Guinea and French Senegal, the second between Portuguese Guinea and French Guinea.

Still, border incidents continued to occur until the beginning of the twentieth century, when the colonial order was definitely established. In any case, rivalries between the various colonial powers soon transcended Senegambia to merge with Europe's immense drive toward global conquest following the Berlin Conference.

The conquest of southern Senegambia coincided with the end of the peanut boom and the beginning of the rubber boom, which dominated trade in the region up until World War I. Peanuts were the main export crop of the Southern Rivers region into the 1880s. But after that, peanut production slumped for various economic, political, and social reasons, most of them related to the division of the region into French, British, and Portuguese zones of influence. France's preference for peanut production in Kajoor, once the Dakar–Saint-Louis railway line was finished, was a prime cause of the crop's slump in the Southern Rivers region. For there, formerly dominant French traders now had to operate under restrictions imposed by British and Portuguese administrators. In addition, of course, there were ecological, economic, political, and social causes peculiar to each area in the Southern Rivers region. So peanut production there was gradually superseded by that of rubber and assorted produce, often gathered wild.

Indeed, from the early 1880s, plummeting exports were followed by a series of poor harvests in Rio Pongo and Rio Nunez. By 1885, peanut production had dropped to an insignificant percentage of exports. Here, though, the depression was the result of a deliberate economic option. For France had decided to drop peanuts in order to promote a new produce –

rubber – from the savanna hinterland of the Southern Rivers region. Rubber was a new strategic material, indispensable for the development of the bicycle, the motorcycle, and, later, the automobile industries in the European economy. Rubber prices continued to rise. The result was a rubber boom, and by 1890, rubber already accounted for 62 percent of exports from Rio Nunez, Rio Pongo, and Mellakure. In 1882, peanut producers in Rio Pongo conducted a boycott against the traders' decision to pay them only half the going rate. The boycott marked the resistance of peanut farmers, whose crop had been supplanted by rubber from the Futa Jallon hinterland of the Southern Rivers region. In this respect, the resumption of the drive toward colonial conquest of the hinterland was closely linked with the rubber boom that signaled the first phase of commercial life in what later became French Guinea.[7]

Similarly, the peanut trade in Rio Grande and Rio Cacheu, under Portuguese control, slumped into a deep depression. The huge production centers known as *feitorias* had numbered one hundred in 1877. Now they folded one after the other, until by 1887 only thirteen were left. Peanut exports from Boloma, from a total of 1,120,820 bushels in 1878, fell to 136,113 bushels in 1888. One reason for the slump was that the Portuguese were unable to stamp out the slave revolt in Foria in which the Peul *jiaabe*, former slaves, were battling it out with their former masters, the *rimbe*. Another reason was the transfer of the former trading giants, the French firms of Maurel–Prom and Gaspard–Devès, to the French colony of Senegal. France had decided to promote peanut farming in the Peanut Basin there, free from the impositions of Portuguese customs officials.[8]

France's decision to create a distinction between northern Senegambia (as a specialized peanut production zone) and southern Senegambia (as a zone supplying such gathered produce as rubber) took very clear form in the Casamance. There, as in other parts of the Southern Rivers region, the period from 1880 to 1900 saw the almost complete abandonment of peanut farming and the rise of rubber tapping in the Lower Casamance forests. From 1885 to 1890, several trading companies rushed into Lower Casamance, eager to exploit these opportunities. Rubber tapping, which brought in 59 tonnes in 1885, rose to 252 tonnes in 1896, pushed upward by constantly rising prices paid to Gambian Aku and Guinea-Bissao Manjak traders, who pioneered the development of the rubber trade before the Joola and the Balante took it up.

Following an attempt by the Société Agricole de Casamance to set up two plantations, the first at Seju, the second at Mangakunda, other companies lured by the high profit margins offered by rubber, obtained government concessions. For instance, on 16 January 1890, Cousin established the Compagnie Commerciale et Agricole de la Casamance (C.C.A.C.). With a capital base of 800,000 francs, the new firm obtained a fifty–year concession to operate on the forested left bank of the River Casamance between Kajinol Creek and Balmaadu, for an annual fee of 1,000 francs. In 1898 a series of problems, including fierce competition from such rival firms as the Compagnie Française d'Afrique occidentale (C.F.A.O.), forced the C.C.A.C. out of business. It was replaced by the Compagnie Coloniale Franco-Africaine (C.C.F.A.), which in turn was replaced by the Compagnie de Caoutchouc de Casamance (C.C.C.), with a capital base of 500,000 francs.[9]

It needs noting that, right from the start, France opted to make northern Senegambia the area that specialized in peanut production, while rubber became the main product in southern Senegambia. As a matter of fact, the creation of these two economic zones merged smoothly into the process of colonial partition, the dominant reality of the final third of the nineteenth century – a period in which France obtained the lion's share of Senegambian territory, leaving Britain and Portugal with the residue.

In 1883, France occupied Bamako. The plan for the conquest of the West African Sudan was on going ahead. The fall of Bamako signaled a speeding up of the occupation of Senegambia. Now the three European powers in contention were racing against time. Each wanted to expand its colonial possessions as fast as was feasible. All operated not just in relation to their initial positions in Senegambia, but also in connection with their interests in other parts of Africa and throughout a world dominated by European powers bent on dividing it up. So hot did the competition become that the Berlin Conference of 1884–5 was convened to draw up ground rules for the colonial partition of Africa. The idea was to obviate any possibility of armed conflict on European soil.

One outcome of the Berlin Conference was the institution of freedom of navigation along the Niger and Congo rivers. Henceforth, each European power was obliged to furnish proof of effective occupation in both coastal and hinterland zones. In addition, each power was required to keep its rivals informed of the content of protectorate treaties signed with African rulers. This provision was meant to prevent diplomatic disputes. The Berlin Conference led immediately to a frenzied scramble for territory. As a rule, effective conquest was preceded by the signing of a plethora of so-called protectorate treaties, each designed to prove that one European power or the other had exclusive rights over some piece of territory, in Senegambia or elsewhere in Africa.

France was securely established in northern Senegambia and the Sudan. But in its attempt to expand into southern Senegambia, it ran into stronger opposition from Britain, Portugal, and, to a lesser degree, Germany. Indeed, the British enclave in Gambia, like the Portuguese territory of Guinea Bissao, compromised France's overall hegemony in Senegambia.

Under these circumstances, Franco–British rivalry was certainly the main concern, underlined by frequent border clashes between the British colony of Sierra Leone and what was to become French Guinea. There were also clashes between British Gambia and French Senegal. France, in fact, had a hard time asserting its sovereignty in Mellakure, Rio Pongo, and Rio Nunez, mainly because of a powerful British trading presence in the area, coupled with the economic weight of the port of Freetown. On 28 June 1882, after a year of tough negotiations, an Anglo–French Agreement was signed. It fixed official boundaries for the possessions of each power. France obtained complete control of the Mellakure river, Britain over the Scarcies rivers. The Agreement implicitly recognized Futa Jallon as a French protectorate under the terms of the 5 August 1881 treaty signed with the two *Almamis*. Even though the French parliament refused to ratify it, it laid the groundwork for the General Agreement of 1889, which assigned fixed boundaries to the possessions of the two countries in the Southern Rivers region, with particular reference to the Gambia River valley.[10]

France used these agreements to organize its protectorates in the Southern Rivers region. To start with, it established a new post, that of Lieutenant-Governor. The move signaled a shift away from the interests of the colony of Senegal, dominated by Bordeaux traders, to those of what would later become French Guinea, dominated by traders based in Marseille. In 1885, Bayol was appointed Lieutenant-Governor of the Southern Rivers region, with his residence at Conakry. It was not until 1890, however, that the new colony responsible for the protectorate of Futa Jallon became administratively autonomous from the colony of Senegal.[11]

Franco–British competition along the Gambia River was a great deal livelier. That river, after all, provided the easiest access to the Sudan. From the beginning of the nineteenth century, the British presence in Gambia was a double headache for the French. First, it reduced trading opportunities for their colony in Senegal. Second, it greatly hampered France's ability to expand into the Southern Rivers and Futa Jallon regions.

From 1866, there were several attempts to work out a deal in which Britain might give up the Gambia in return for French possessions in the Ivory Coast or Gabon. But the negotiations reached a deadlock in 1866, partly because France refused to give up all of the Ivory Coast and, more importantly, because British traders wanted to maintain their stake in the Gambia, as a step toward future conquests in the Niger Bend. To complicate matters further, certain French traders with major interests in the Gambia sabotaged the exchange agreement because they wanted to continue profiting from customs and tax breaks given them by the British colony. In any case, given the global context of a frenzied European scramble for African land after 1885, the idea of a Gambian exchange became increasingly unworkable, even if the possibility kept surfacing sporadically in discussions until the end of World War I.

Meanwhile, imperialist rivalries grew more heated. France, busy at war in the Saalum basin, posed a direct threat to British positions on both sides of the Gambia River. Border conflicts continued to break out until the two powers negotiated the General Agreement of 10 August 1889, laying down ground rules for their expansion throughout West Africa. The agreement placed a 10-km wide corridor along each bank of the Gambia from the coast to Yarbatenda under British rule. France gave up parts of Wuuli, Kantora and Firdu. In addition, it pledged not to undertake any development on territory within 170 km of the Gambia river. The agreement, in effect, cut the colony of Senegal in two.[12]

In the meantime, competition between France and Portugal played a central role in the partition of the Southern Rivers region. The Portuguese had operated in Rio Cacheu and Rio Geba for centuries. For reasons both of national prestige and of economic interest, they were determined to hold on to their possessions and to found the colony of Guinea Bissao in the bloody whirlwind of imperial conquest sweeping over Senegambia in the 1880s. Having obtained Bulama Island from Britain with American mediation, Portugal made a decisive stand against France for the possession of the Casamance, Rio Nunez, and Rio Kasini valleys.

First, Ziguinchor station, under Portuguese control, was claimed by French trading interests based at Karabane and Seju. Ziguinchor was a well-sited port, accessible to steamships. It had the additional advantage of making the trans-shipment of goods – required at the Pointe de Piédras wharves because the river there was too shallow to allow deep draught vessels to go all the way to Seju – unnecessary. The slump in peanut production in the Middle Casamance valley, the spectacular leap in rubber production, plus rising demand for palm and other nuts, all gave the Lower Casamance fresh importance. French trading interests reacted by vigorously asserting their claims over the Joola region. And they specifically wanted control of Ziguinchor.[13]

The Portuguese, for their part, claimed Rio Nunez and Rio Kasini, on the grounds that for centuries these had been their zones of influence. The paradox was that in this area of the Southern Rivers region, French trading interests were paramount. Because French trading companies in Seju and Karabane offered lower prices, they were able to attract traders away from the Portuguese posts at Cacheu and Farim. Similarly, Portuguese firms trading in Rio Kasini were harassed by major French tobacco smugglers operating from Rio Nunez. Portugal's territorial ambitions collided with France's determination to turn the whole of Senegambia into a French zone in close contact with France.[14]

In the face of all these complications, the prevalence of narrow nationalistic interests was ratified by the Franco–Portuguese Agreement of 13 May 1886, which fixed Portuguese Guinea's frontiers with Senegal and

French Guinea. By the terms of the agreement, Portugal ceded Ziguinchor to France in exchange for the Rio Kasini valley. Portugal also recognized Futa Jallon as a French protectorate.[15]

The last dispute was between France and Germany. At stake was control over Koba and Kabitaye, between Rio Pongo and Mellakure, where German interests were represented by a company called Colin & Cl. Following a visit by the Imperial Commissioner Nachtigal, France rapidly signed a series of treaties with Kabitaye chiefs on 30 January 1885. The agreements confirmed French sovereignty over the area. They also updated an older treaty with the Bramaya. By the terms of the 1885 convention, France persuaded Germany to give up all claims to Koba and Kabitaye, in return for recognition of German control over Porto Seguro and Petit Popo on the Slave Coast.[16] Germany's sudden incursion into Senegambia as a colonial power was a fluke, the outcome of a private initiative. Germany had no coherent design for acquiring colonies in Senegambia, already occupied by three powers with long established interests (France, Britain, and Portugal).

In the outcome, these were the powers that divided up southern Senegambia. Partition became a reality in 1889. To start with, there was an agreement in principle, followed by numerous negotiations to fix frontiers, lasting until the beginning of the twentieth century. Now the onus was on each colonial power to exercise effective sovereign control over the region's states and populations. The latter responded by resisting the colonial onslaught in a variety of ways during the final quarter of the nineteenth century.

The rise of colonial imperialism in the latter half of the nineteenth century was a worldwide phenomenon. It was the expression of a determination among European powers to take over foreign territories, bringing them under direct metropolitan control, economic as well as political. The process of conquest worked mainly through the destruction of all traces of local opposition to the establishment of a market nexus tying European trading companies to a subjugated African peasantry toiling to supply raw materials for European industry. It was natural, in such a context, for France, Britain, and Portugal to encounter opposition from the ruling aristocracies of the region. These rulers took up arms to defend their political and economic privileges even if, right from the start of the process of colonial conquest, the odds against them were heavy. The resulting resistance movements were fueled by despair, and the old legitimist rulers of northern Senegambia symbolized this desperate resistance most aptly. They were the first to come under attack from French imperialism, then in unchallenged control of the process of colonial conquest in the region.

# 15 Last-ditch resistance movements of legitimist rulers in northern Senegambia

The defeat of the three main Muslim leaders, coupled with France's retreat after the disastrous defeat of 1870, gave the rulers of northern Senegambia some breathing space. They used it to restore their authority, each within his own state, in the name of a centuries-old tradition of legitimacy.

Lat Joor had again risen to be *Damel*, thanks to a compromise agreement with the French colony. Now he had to deal with a revolt among the *jaami buur*, the royal slave army. Their leader, Demba Waar Sal, was gradually taking on the role of main overseer and operative agent of colonial power as the French hold on Senegambia tightened. From 1883 onward, the conflict between Lat Joor and the French over French plans to build a railway line led to an open break. The issue was resolved in 1886 when the *Damel* was defeated at Dekhele.

Alburi Njaay went through a similar experience. First he regained the Jolof throne using French aid. Then, taking advantage of the remote location of his kingdom, he reinforced his authority, coopting the Muslim revolt that lasted from 1875 to 1890 in the process. After the defeat of Lat Joor, his main ally, Alburi Njaay tried to work out a Tijaniyya alliance with Saer Maty of Rip and Abdul Bokar Kane of central Futa. Still he had to abandon Yang Yang to the French. He then joined forces with Abdul Bokar Kane in Futa, and later with Amadu of Segu, during his exile in the east.

Meanwhile, Kumba Ndoofen Juuf, who had defeated Maba Jaakhu, was shot at point-blank range by the French for insisting that he was the legitimate and sovereign ruler of Joal. After his death came the 1887 campaigns against Maba's successors. The annexation of Siin and Saalum followed.

Lastly, Abdul Bokar Kane, chief of Bosea, taking advantage of a lull in French activity as well as of the political crisis that followed the death of Amadu Seekhu, asserted himself as the real ruler of Futa. In 1879, however, the French resumed their Sudanese campaign against Amadu of Segu and Samori. A quarrel about their plans to lay a telegraph line led to a clash with Abdul Bokar Kane. Once more, the clash ended with the defeat, in 1891, of Abdul Bokar Kane. The annexation of Futa Toro followed.

With the four main legitimist rulers of northern Senegambia fallen in battle, the way was clear for the French conquest of the Southern Rivers region, the Sudan, and Futa Jallon. This conquest created the final conditions for the establishment of what was to become the colony of Senegal. Nevertheless, for a quarter of a century after the resumption of France's policy of colonial expansion around 1876, mopping-up operations continued, until the region was finally pacified.

As a rule, in sum, resistance to French conquest was led by legitimist rulers. The one exception was the marabout Mamadu Lamine Darame. Leading a sudden insurgency in 1887, like the marabouts of the previous generation he challenged the French presence in the Upper Senegal valley. But it took little time for him to succumb to the force of Gallieni's artillery, backed up by the forces of a coalition of traditional rulers from Futa Toro, Bundu, and Fuladu.

## A.    Lat Joor and the conquest of Kajoor

The first kingdom to fall victim to the revived French policy of colonial expansion was Kajoor. Lat Joor, the *Damel*, had been trying ever since the death of Amadu Seekhu in 1875 to reassert his authority. It had been considerably diminished by the chronic political, economic, and social crisis in the state since the start of the nineteenth century. In Kajoor, the *ceddo* regime, using an army of royal slaves, had defeated a series of Muslim insurrections, beginning in the time of Lat Sukaabe Fal. Now it was entering the final phase of its development.

The army of royal slaves had become a pivotal force in the state's political affairs. And now its command structure was under the control of a single family, that of Demba Waar Sal, the *Farba* of Kajoor. As commander of the royal slave army, Demba Waar Sal was in fact the real ruler of the country. Far more lucidly than the aristocrats clinging to their pedigrees and privileges, he understood that the only way the rulers could safeguard their prerogatives was to line up behind the colonial power. Having seen various aristocratic armies go down in defeat one after the other, Demba Waar Sal had opted to serve the colonial power as headman and steward. In this role, one of his aims was to counter the political impact of the increasing wealth of peasant communities, which tended to follow Muslim religious leaders.

Lat Joor had already antagonized the marabout movement by joining the assault on Amadu Seekhu. Now in 1879, hoping to bring the royal slaves back to their traditional job as tools of royal power, he sacked Demba Waar Sal. This move cost him the support of the *jaami buur*. This slave army, the foundation on which *ceddo* power had always rested, retained its fundamental importance in the royal power structure even after the ruler converted to Islam. Now it abandoned Lat Joor. Lat Joor was also abandoned by the majority of the nobility and the Muslim communities. Thus isolated, he had to confront the French colony of Senegal, expanding steadily as peanut production gained ground. The Dakar–Saint-Louis railroad was basically designed to consolidate and expand the French colonial system. It now became the main cause of war between Lat Joor and the colony of Senegal. Unlike Faidherbe and Pinet-Laprade, the French governor Brière de Lisle did not try to get a puppet *Damel* elected. Instead, he tried to manipulate the royal slave army, the only serious force in the state, into doing his bidding.

Lat Joor had turned down the railroad project in June 1879. In September that same year, he went back on his decision and gave permission for construction work. This was a tactical retreat, designed to buy him time to combat centrifugal tendencies and growing insurgent groups in his state of Kajoor. Sensing their opportunity, the aristocratic opposition appointed Samba Lawbe Faal, who accused Lat Joor of treason. In 1881, however, Lat Joor again reversed his decision. In signing the treaty of 1879, after all, his key objective had been to keep his territory intact, even if that meant entering into an alliance with the French. His hostility to the railroad project reopened the rift with French colonial officials. From December 1882 to January 1883, they organized a campaign to drive all opponents of the railroad project from Kajoor. The idea was to create a climate conducive to its completion. When the French appointed a puppet *Damel*, one Samba Yaya Faal, Lat Joor and Samba Lawbe Faal reacted by reinforcing their alliance with the Afro-European traders Devès and Crespin. The latter wished to see a member of the Geej clan return to power, because they wanted to block the construction of the line. For, once built, it would create a direct link between European traders and African producers in the hinterland, cutting out middlemen like themselves.

Still, the 1883 campaign enabled France to start construction work on the railroad in a depopulated Kajoor, most of the population having followed Lat Joor and Samba Lawbe Faal to Baol, Saalum, Jolof, and Waalo. In exile, the two leaders found support from Alburi Njaay, Abdul Bokar Kane and the Moors.

Samba Lawbe Faal tried several times to defeat the French, and failed. Finally, he made a public submission to France, which appointed him *Damel* in August 1883, hoping the move would bring back the peanut-producing peasant population. By now Lat Joor's forces were seriously depleted. Moving from Rip to Jolof country, he spent two years constantly harassing French outposts. In 1885, however, Jolof was hit by a famine which forced Alburi Njaay to sign a separate peace agreement with the

Plate 10 Saint-Louis, headquarters of the French establishments in Senegal

French. The signature coincided with the completion of the rail line. Now the French colony could deal from a position of strength. An incident that took place on 6 October 1886 symbolized the new power equation. Asked to settle an argument between the *Damel* and Alburi Njaay, the French sub-lieutenant Minet had Samba Lawbe Faal shot by a firing squad at Tivawaan. The accusation: disrespect for France.[1]

With Samba Lawbe Faal dead, Lat Joor saw a new opportunity to take back the throne. He expected support from the Afro-European middlemen of Saint-Louis, whose privileges the French had abolished. As for the French colony, it now depended, in effect, on the fidelity of the royal slave army under Demba Waar Sal, Chairman of the Kajoor Confederation of Chiefs, now divided into six provinces. On 26 December 1886, the French army maneuvered Lat Joor into fighting a pitched battle at Dekhele. There the last great *Damel* of Kajoor, knowing he faced certain defeat, accepted battle as his way of underscoring the honor of the *ceddo* regime.

Lat Joor had spent years collaborating with the French colonialists, all in a bid to keep his position as *Damel*. He hoped this last spectacular gesture would erase the record of betrayal from popular memory, retrieve his lost honor, and leave his fame imprinted in Kajoor legend.[2]

In our opinion, he achieved this goal. Today this moment of national pride is remembered in the marvelous poetry of Samb:

> Here in Kajoor and Baol
> I tasted all life's pleasures
> savored all honors due to power
> and also drank my fill
> of all life's bitterness.
> Today, before the sun sets
> I shall be dead;
> But first my blood shall flow
> free over this earth
> this earth of my ancestors.[3]

### B. Kumba Ndoofen Juuf, Saer Maty Ba, and the conquest of Siin and Saalum

To some extent, the campaigns in Kajoor coincided with the conquest of Siin and Saalum. The annexation of the two coastal Senegambian states was closely connected to the spread of peanut farming. The triangular area between Saint-Louis, Dakar, and Kaolack, being particularly suited to peanut cultivation, was destined to be the prime producing basin for the crop, the centerpiece of the emerging colony of Senegal. The ancient aristocracies of Siin and Saalum opposed French expansion southward. So did the successors of the marabout movement led by Maba Jaakhu. Opposition also came from the British, inveterate rivals of the French, who held on tenaciously to their possessions on the Gambia River.

In Siin, Maba Jaakhu's death signaled the triumph of Kumba Ndoofen Juuf. Flushed with victory, he challenged the validity of concessions accorded to the French at Joal. He also reinforced his power beyond the boundaries of his kingdom. However, one day, when Kumba Ndoofen Juuf went to Joal with a large retinue to collect customary fees from French traders, he was shot at point-blank range by an assassin called Beccaria. The ensuing succession struggle between Salmoon Faye and Semu Maak Juuf, in which the latter called for French aid, thoroughly exposed weaknesses in the political system of the kingdom of Siin. In the end, in September 1877, Colonel Reybaud recognized Salmoon Faye, a notorious sadist, as king. As a payoff, the new king confirmed the 1854 and 1861 treaties. In February 1878, though, Salmoon Faye died in the course of a dispute with the king of Saalum, Saajuka Mbooj, an ally of Semu Maak Juuf. The latter thereupon took over the kingship. But in November 1881 he committed suicide. After his death the kingdom went through a series of civil wars between the different claimants to the throne. In five years five different kings came and went. Each in his rise appealed for help from the French or from neighboring kingdoms, then fell, making room for the next.

Invariably, during the internal wrangling, loyalty to individual families and factions took precedence over the defense of the state against the invading French. Furthermore, from 1866 onward, Siin was split between followers of marabout leaders, headed by Nokhobay Juuf, and those of the anti-marabout faction, headed by Mbake Ndek. All this while, the French colonialists were planning their final campaigns for the conquest of Siin and Saalum.[4]

Indeed, it was in Saalum, where Maba Jaakhu's passing had left deeper traces, that the ceaseless warfare between different Muslim factions eager to succeed the late marabout, on the one hand, and chronic conflict between Muslims and royal *ceddo* forces on the other, paved the way for French intervention. For Maba Jaakhu had died in battle in 1867 before he had had the time to organize his conquests. Because his son Saer Maty was too young then, the Council appointed his brother Maamur Ndari as successor. Maamur Ndari fought the British twice, in 1871 and 1872, in an attempt to gain control over Ñoomi, and in pursuit of a plan to invade Kombo. At the time the British preferred diplomatic means to military confrontation. So in 1873 they signed a treaty with Maamur Ndari recognizing his sovereignty over the north bank of the River Gambia from Serekunda to Wuuli, except for the enclave of Niani. On the home front, however, Maamur Ndari had to deal with opposition from a number of marabout families and the king of Saalum, still hoping to reconquer his lost territories. Externally, there remained the threat of conquest by the French colony of Senegal.

From 1877, Maamur Ndari was powerless to prevent the marabout Biram Siise of Kaymor building his own fortified village, then declaring himself independent of Nioro, which abandoned its claims to sovereignty over Niani and Wuuli. At this point the Muslims split into two factions. On the one hand there was Maamur Ndari, allied to Fodé Kaba. On the other hand, there was Biram Siise, allied to Musa Molo and the king of Saalum, Gedel Mbooj. Taking advantage of all this factional warfare, the king of Saalum reconquered part of the territory annexed by Nioro. Gedel Mbooj, in particular, was well placed to regain control of Dagaminian south of Kaolak and partially to reinforce his authority by engineering the defection of the followers of Kewe Bigge from the marabout movement. Still, the Lagem area as well as the entire eastern part of Saalum, mainly inhabited by Wolofs, stayed under Muslim control. And they were having to face increasingly intense pressure from the invading French.[5]

In 1876, negotiations between France and Britain for the exchange of Gambia broke down. That failure came at a time when the new imperialist drive was on. All participants aimed to grab as much territory as possible ahead of their competitors. The appointment, in 1884, of Bayol as Lieutenant-Governor of the Southern Rivers region marked the beginning of a campaign to conquer a slice of territory ensuring control of a north–south axis. That meant that the French had to get hold of Siin and Saalum to forestall any possible British thrust from Gambia. In the face of this threat, several rulers, including Lat Joor, Alburi Njaay, and Abdul Bokar Kane, tried from 1878 to 1887 to reconcile Maamur Ndari and Biram Siise. The movement of Muslim solidarity in aid of the Rip region took on the shape of a Tijaniyya league against the French colony of Senegal. However, infighting among the Muslim partisans intensified when, on 27 March 1885, Saer Maty Ba assassinated Ali Khoja Ba. This provoked the intervention of Birame Siise's armies. Eager to protect their trading interests, the British signed a treaty with both warring parties, Saer Maty Ba and Biram Siise, in February 1887. Now the French took fright at the progress of British diplomacy. They were particularly alarmed by the existence of a Tijaniyya league in the form of the alliance between Alburi Njaay and Saer Maty. As a matter of fact, the alliance spread as far as the upper Senegal valley, to incorporate Mamadu Lamin. To counter it, in April 1887 the French put together a column under Colonel Coronnat.

Prior to these developments, the French had confirmed Gedel Mbooj as ruler of Saalum. Now he repaid them by giving them his *ceddo* warriors as auxiliaries. Thus reinforced, the French column, using artillery, destroyed the fortified village of Goumbof east of Kawoon. Next, Nioro fell to

Colonel Coronnat, who had mounted a fierce campaign in pursuit of Saer Maty. The latter fled for shelter to the British at Bathurst. There he remained until his death in 1897. The three remaining Muslim leaders, Biram Siise, Maamur Ndari, and Omar Khoja Na, surrendered to the French, who then made them joint head chiefs over the territory bequeathed by Maba Jaakhu, now a French protectorate.[6]

The defeat of the marabout movement in Rip opened the way for the conquest of Jolof and Futa Toro. To a degree, the subjugation of this territory was linked with the conquest of the Sudan, with the Senegal valley serving as a route to the Niger valley. These conquests put the finishing touches to French control over all of northern Senegambia. Earlier, though, Gallieni's march into the Sudan had been brought to a sudden halt by the rise of the Soninke marabout, Mamadu Lamin Darame, in the upper Senegal valley. For a while, the holy war led by this marabout compromised the security of the French presence in this strategic region located between Senegal, Niger, and Gambia.

### C.     Mamadu Lamin's holy war and the recapture of the upper Senegal valley

Shaykh Umar had conquered the upper Senegal valley with great ease between 1852 and 1854. In 1857 it was retaken by Faidherbe, after the Holy Warrior's defeat at Medina.

During the entire second half of the nineteenth century, however, the region continued to feel the impact of the struggle between France and the empire of Amadu of Segu, on account of its strategic situation between the French colony of Senegal to the west, the Sudan to the east, and Futa Jallon and Gambia to the south. In the upper Senegal valley, the French had set up a long string of forts at Bakel, Medina and Senedebu. This cordon was the centerpiece of France's offensive war machine, designed for the conquest of western Sudan. Ever since the time of Faidherbe, that region had been considered the major objective of the colony of Senegal. For his part, the Sultan of Segu, who still ruled over part of the upper Senegal valley on the right bank, was anxious to ensure free circulation of persons and goods along the corridor between Nioro and Futa Toro.

This dual pressure from external sources set up conditions for an economic, social, and political crisis conducive to the rise of Mamadu Lamin Darame. He was one of the last Muslim leaders to try to reestablish a state and to challenge the French presence in this region of northern Senegambia.

Amadu, successor to Shaykh Umar, using Segu on the Niger Bend as his base, had worked to stabilize his power on the north bank of the Senegal

River. From 1870, he continued to wield substantial influence over the Senegambian states, the French presence notwithstanding. Still bathed in the afterglow of his father's aura, he dreamed of dominating the Muslim community beyond his frontiers as unchallenged head, and as defender of the territorial integrity of the region's states in the face of France's expansionist drive. In pursuit of these aims, he undertook an intense diplomatic campaign, while waves of migrants, drawn by his charisma, continued to flow toward Nioro and Segu, mainly from Futa Toro and the upper Senegal valley. He also exercised direct influence over the Soninke provinces of Jombokho–Jafunu, along with the main towns of Gidimakha. His domination, however, very soon provoked the hostility of the Juula, who disliked his embargo against the French trading posts. In addition, the local authorities, chafing under the obligation to pay tribute to Segu, also turned against him. As for the population at large, while they had always supported Shaykh Umar's holy war because it helped them free themselves from their traditional *Tunka* rulers' heavy taxation and brutal ways, in 1876 and 1885 they went into open rebellion against the authority of the Sultan of Segu, who had begun to demand too many sacrifices from the inhabitants of the territories his father had conquered, as part of the war effort. Amadu put down the revolts in two bloody campaigns, provoking an exodus of thousands of Soninke from Jafunu, Jombokho, and Gidimakha.

On the one hand, then, the region's population had to cope with pressure from Amadu's empire. Now in addition, they had to deal with the increasingly oppressive presence of the French authorities, making steady inroads into the states of the upper Senegal valley. From 1874 the *Tunka* Sina Hawa decided to block the French advance. To that end he got together with the Bacili in February 1875 to form an armed coalition against the French colony of Senegal. In 1879, France began to use overbearing methods, dragooning people into working on rail and telegraph lines linking Senegal to the Sudan, a region whose conquest had become a major French objective ever since the revival of its policy of colonial expansion. The reaction of the French high command at Kayes on the upper Senegal River was proof of this determination to expand its colonial possessions. Furthermore, it indicated the full extent of the importance of the upper Senegal valley in the rush toward the Niger. At this time, however, France did not have sufficient resources to back up its policy of conquest. It therefore made excessive use of forced labor on its local projects, causing a deterioration of the farming system in the upper Senegal valley. Apart from the local population, the Juula were also upset. The French had set up a group of so-called free villages. Slaves of the Juula were flocking into these places, where they worked as indentured laborers to buy their freedom. So serious did the hostility of the local population to forced labor become that the rulers of Bundu,

Kamera, and Khaaso, convened by the *Tunka* of Gwey, sent a protest against the practice to the colony of Senegal. France therefore considered bringing in Chinese coolies to do the work. In the end, it brought in 1,500 Moroccan laborers to finish it. On the domestic scene, all these upheavals contributed to the rise of the marabout Mamadu Lamin Darame. Focusing the population's discontent, he declared a holy war planned to end in the establishment of a new state in the upper Senegal valley.[7]

In many ways, Mamadu Lamin Darame's career was like that of Shaykh Umar and his Senegambian disciples, Maba Jaakhu and Amadu Seekhu. Mamadu Lamin also called upon his disciples to rise up in a massive holy war to establish a new political and social order based on the *Sharia*. There was nothing surprising about this. For Mamadu Lamin came from a long established family of marabouts, the Darames, who had served the ruling class of Gajaaga for countless generations. On account of the religious and commercial activities of his ancestors, Mamadu Lamin was also related to the main ethnic groups in this part of the upper Senegal valley, the Jakhanke and the Khaasonke. Around 1850, Mamadu Lamin went on a pilgrimage to Mecca. This was the time when Shaykh Umar was introducing Tijaniyya Islam into Senegambia. Mamadu Lamin returned around 1870, at a time when Amadu was struggling to maintain his religious and political authority over the vast empire conquered by his father. The newly arrived pilgrim had great prestige. He did not mince words in his criticism of the programs of Shaykh Umar and his son. In reaction, Amadu the Sultan kept him under a form of house arrest at Segu until 1885. Meanwhile, Mamadu Lamin's reputation for holiness had spread before him throughout the upper Senegal valley. Slipping past Amadu's guards, he finally reached Gunjur early in July 1885. The town lay within the line of French forts. Once there, Mamadu Lamin, whose hostility to Amadu was no secret, openly announced his loyalty to the French, and declared his intention of using his influence to bring his compatriots peace and justice. By September 1885, Mamadu Lamin had practically attained the status of a political leader. He had gained the support of the entire political establishment in Gajaaga. Even Sambala, king of Khaaso, supported him. In addition, he could count on the support of the marabout class throughout the upper Senegal valley. The peasant masses, traumatized after numerous wars, and increasingly dazzled by his miracles and the *baraka* that made his life seem such a charmed one, adored him. For all these reasons, events propelled him into political prominence. Soon, the marabout began buying arms and dispatching envoys here and there in the upper Senegal valley. This worried the French.

Mamadu Lamin set up his first command post in Gwey, where the Falémé river flows into the Senegal. His intention was to carve out for himself a land base from Gamon and Tenda territory. The move seemed well timed, since the Sultan of Segu, Amadu, was tied up with an invasion of Jambokho; the French had committed their troops against Samori in the upper Niger valley; and, most importantly, Bokar Saada, France's faithful ally in Bundu, had just died. His death was followed by a civil war pitting Umar Penda against Usman Gasi. Taking advantage of the confusion, Mamadu Lamin's main army of disciples, made up of 2,000 men armed with rifles, invaded Bundu. In February 1886 the army occupied Balebane, then Senedebu, encountering no resistance whatsoever. The invasion ended the rule of the Sisibe family in Bundu. The place became Mamadu Lamin's new headquarters. Meanwhile, Usman Gasi, disappointed because his ally had failed to deliver on some promise, switched over to the French at Bakel, ready to fight for them against Mamadu Lamin. As for his rival Umar Penda, he sought refuge at Damga with Abdul Bokar Kane, chief of Bosea and an ally of the family of Bokar Saada of Bundu. Now Mamadu Lamin's army numbered some 6,000 to 7,000 men. Large numbers of Soninke joined it from Gwey, Kamera, Gidimakha, and Jafunu. It also drew Jakhanke fighters from Bundu, Manding from Bambuku and Niani, Khaasonke from Logo and Niataga, and even Peul and Tukulor from Futa Toro and Bundu.

Mamadu Lamin thus mobilized the majority of people from all strata in the upper Senegal valley. This sudden build up of a new force at the rear of French forces operating in the Sudan became a major source of worry for the French colony. The upper Senegal valley was strategically located between the colony of Senegal and the Sudan, which France was busy conquering. France therefore decided to go on the offensive. On 13 March 1886, the French authorities arrested members of Mamadu Lamin's family at Gunjur. The marabout immediately besieged Bakel, then fought a bloody battle in the town. Avoiding direct confrontation with French artillery, Mamadu Lamin left Bundu and went to the upper Gambia valley. But the French, in a series of reprisals against his followers, arrested and killed his son Suayibu. This prompted the Sultan Amadu, despite his hostility to Mamadu Lamin, to protest against French brutality.

Having regrouped in the upper Gambia valley, Mamadu Lamin returned to Bundu on 16 July 1886. He killed Umar Penda, thus becoming the sole effective ruler of the entire area between the upper Gambia valley and Bundu. The French, determined to remove the obstacle that had thus appeared behind their lines at a time when they were preparing to fight decisive battles against Samori, quickly dispatched Gallieni to deal with Mamadu Lamin. Using repeater rifles, Gallieni pursued Mamadu Lamin until he finally fell in an ambush set by Musa Molo, king of Firdu, who had recently switched over to the French side. The French took the marabout's head to their camp as a trophy. Thus ended the meteoric reign of Mamadu Lamin, the man who, a half-century before the French effectively occupied the region, galvanized the upper Senegal valley into a short-lived resistance movement.[8]

Hrbeck has advanced the opinion that Mamadu Lamin embodied the nationalist aspirations of the Soninke, frustrated by the occupation of their territory by the French on the one hand and by Amadu's Tukulor empire on the other. This view presents the Soninke marabout's holy war as a Soninke nationalist reaction to Shaykh Umar's program in the upper Senegal valley.[9] However, even if most of his disciples were Soninke compatriots to start with, Mamadu Lamin's movement very quickly grew beyond the Gajaaga homeland, spreading to embrace the whole of the upper Senegal valley all the way to the upper Gambia. So Abdoulaye Bathily is perfectly right when he sets Mamadu Lamin's program within a wider perspective, that of a general protest mounted by the people of the upper Senegal valley against the colonial power established since 1857.[10]

Like Shaykh Umar, Maba Jaakhu, and Amadu Seekhu, this Muslim leader trying to institute a new order also died in battle. For the French colony of Senegal could no longer tolerate the creation of an autonomous state in Senegambia, which was inexorably falling under its influence. The defeat of Mamadu Lamin paved the way for the conquest of Senegambia south of Gambia. The hinterland region here was relatively isolated. That allowed leaders like Musa Molo and Fode Kaba to carve out fiefdoms even while France, Britain, and Portugal were busy with the scramble for territory. For the time being, though, once Mamadu Lamin was defeated, French troops were free to move on to the conquest of Amadu and Samori. And the colony of Senegal could go ahead and finally annex Jolof and Futa Toro, thus completing the conquest of northern Senegambia.

### D.    Alburi Njaay and the conquest of Jolof

As in Kajoor, the defeat of Amadu facilitated the return of Alburi Njaay to the Jolof kingdom. Because the kingdom was rather isolated, it had remained for a long time untouched by French military maneuvers. And Alburi Njaay represented legitimate power there. Alburi Njaay, the lion of Yang Yang, having learned his lesson from the two holy wars of Maba Jaakhu and Amadu Seekhu, set about reinforcing his authority in Jolof from 1875 to 1890. He began efficiently, by securing control of the *Kangam*. This he did by marrying into the Jolof nobility as well as into most royal families in the neighboring kingdoms. Furthermore, he established himself as a Muslim ruler, thus gaining the support of the marabouts, in return for letting them complete the conversion of the population to Islam by peaceful means. Alburi Njaay's political genius, and above all his long career as a fighter with Maba Jaakhu's followers helping Lat Joor, gave him the standing to cope with his rivals Bara Ba and Biram Njem. For that reason, their attempts to dethrone him failed.[11] By 1880, however, Alburi Njaay had to join the struggle waged by rulers of the neighboring kingdoms against the colony of Senegal, which was gradually tightening the noose around Jolof. First, he supported his cousin and comrade in arms, Lat Joor, in his efforts to stop the construction of a railroad across Kajoor. In 1883, he sheltered Lat Joor in Jolof, affording him a base from which their joint armies could harass the French in Kajoor. At the time the colony of Senegal could not afford to intervene directly in Jolof territory. All it could do was to support Samba Lawbe, who was trying unsuccessfully to channel the discontent of some *Kangam*, opposed to Alburi's alliance with Lat Joor and his anti-French policy, into a revolt against the incumbent. Alburi Njaay took advantage of the situation to reinforce his alliances in Futa Toro by arranging marriages with members of the family of Abdul Bokar Kane, the powerful Bosea chief, whose son Mamadu Abdul married Khar, daughter of the *Buurba* of Jolof. Around 1884, seeing his rival Samba Lawbe allied to the French while Lat Joor was in Jolof, Alburi Njaay thought it best to seek a compromise solution. Famine struck Jolof at this time, and the French, whose forces by now encircled the kingdom, imposed a trade embargo on it. Thus Alburi Njaay was forced into signing the Treaty of 18 April 1885.

Aside from the entirely nominal recognition of French protectorate powers over Jolof, the main objective of this treaty was to neutralize Samba Lawbe's program against Alburi and Lat Joor's against the French presence in Kajoor. The clause making this possible was slow in its implementation, but it did give Alburi Njaay some breathing space. Using it to good effect, he crushed the *Damel* Samba Lawbe Fall at Gille in June 1886. The victory entitled him to claim Kajoor as war booty. But the French lieutenant Minet interceded, and he agreed instead to take a tribute of 300 head of livestock. Samba Lawbe Penda took refuge at Saint-Louis until 1890. The death of Samba Lawbe Fall, and especially that of Lat Joor in the famous battle of Dekhele in 1886, propelled Alburi Njaay into the position of leading figure in the resistance movements of the last independent states of northern Senegambia.[12]

While avoiding direct confrontation with the French colony of Senegal, Alburi Njaay nevertheless participated directly in all the fighting between the rulers of northern Senegambia and the French by sending troops to fight for his fellow rulers. After helping Lat Joor to the very end, in contravention of the clauses of the Treaty of 1885, Alburi Njaay reinforced a sort of tripartite alliance with Abdul Bokar Kane of Bosea and Saer Maty of the Rip. The French Governor, already increasingly worried about the existence of a powerful Tijaniyya league made up of Futa Jallon, Futa Toro, Jolof, plus the states under Samori and Amadu of Segu, took considerable fright at this development. By 1887, Alburi Njaay was the only remaining major Senegambian ruler whose land was still not under the direct control of the French colony of Senegal. This meant his power on the domestic front was substantially consolidated. He therefore felt free to intervene in Siin and Saalum to help Nokhobay in his dispute with Mbake Njaay, as well as Saer Maty in his war with Gedel Mbooj. Lastly, during the final campaign in Rip, Jolof cavalry fought alongside Saer Maty's forces in the fortified village of Gumbof until their defeat.

The French conquest of Rip considerably diminished Alburi Njaay's freedom of maneuver. Retreating to Jolof, he waited for the final confrontation with France. From 1887 to 1890, the two sides watched each other while keeping up the appearance of cordial relations. All the while, the colony of Senegal prepared for the coming confrontation with great care. Alburi Njaay, for his part, intensified his contacts with Amadu, Sultan of Segu. As early as 1887, he was contemplating the possibility of going into exile in the Sudan, along with his compatriots. Even so, the two sides signed a second treaty confirming the 1885 treaty, at Yang Yang on 12 July 1889. Then, in April 1890, the French captured Segu, capital of Amadu's empire. That opened the way for the conquest of Jolof and Central Futa, the only territories in northern Senegambia still nominally independent.

The French forces were led by Colonel Alfred Dodds, an Afro-European from Saint-Louis. They were a motley army, including North African mercenaries and *ceddo* warriors from Njambur and Kajoor. When, on 25 May, they marched into Yang Yang, Alburi Njaay abandoned his burning capital and headed for exile in Futa Toro with hundreds of his compatriots. As for his perennial rival Samba Lawbe Penda, Dodds appointed him ruler of Jolof.[13]

This was the beginning of a long exile for Alburi Njaay. First he took refuge in central Futa. But there his ally Abdul Bokar Kane could not long guarantee his safety. He himself, after all, faced the threat of a French assault on his territory. In July 1890, Alburi and Abdul Bokar Kane were forced to cross the Senegal River to seek refuge at Kaedi. The French immediately shelled that town. Alburi therefore decided to head for Nioro with his family and those soldiers who had remained faithful to him, intending to help Amadu in his struggle against the French. He took personal command of the resistance army in Nioro. Even after the fall of the town, the army continued fighting, inflicting heavy casualties on the French in January 1891.

By July 1891, most of Alburi Njaay's compatriots, eager to get back home to Jolof, had left him. He teamed up with Amadu for the trip into an eastern exile. From all sides the French harassed them, driving them out of Jenne in 1893 and from Say in May 1897. Embattled on all sides, they took refuge in Sokoto, the last Muslim state to remain unconquered. There Amadu died in 1898. Alburi continued his exile, which ended when he fell in battle near Doso on the Dahomey–Niger frontier in 1901.[14]

Alburi's exile, like the death of Lat Joor at Dekhele, has become the stuff of legend. To this day the memory of the determined refusal of the lion of Yang Yang to submit to French domination until his death is kept alive in traditional lore. Jolof poetry still sings the long exile of the last *Buurba*, who traveled thousands of kilometers so he could fight and win at Segu, instead of dying at Yang Yang, overwhelmed by the sheer number of his enemies. The griot Samba portrays the feelings of Alburi as he prepares to leave Yang Yang with his army for Segu in these words:

> People: Segu is worth more than the gold of Bure, more than the ingots of Falémé.
> A man thinking no but saying yes, afraid to speak the truth, lives on swill.
> He is brother to the pig.
> Our children's children will read our message
> Under swallows' wings. Their foreheads will not stoop into dust;
> they shall defy the sky.
> Who is deaf to this sound, who calm before advancing doom?
> What can these heavy underground footfalls mean?
> What is the message of these drumbeats
> Rising from the depths of volcanoes?
> Who is blind to the sight of tomorrow falling from the clouds,
> Dressed in fine clothes, radiant as a bride?
> Let Segu rise, seed watered with our blood,
> And birds stroke the shoot smiling in freedom's eyes.[15]

## E.     Abdul Bokar Kane and the conquest of Futa Toro

The conquest of Jolof coincided with that of Futa Toro. This was particularly true of Central Futa, whose independence was safeguarded until quite late by the powerful chief of Bosea, Abdul Bokar Kane. The conquest of Futa Toro proper began in the mid-nineteenth century, with the battle of Dialmath in 1854. From then on, the process continued through a series of ups and downs until the end of the nineteenth century. To a great extent, conquest was particularly slow here because the Middle Senegal valley had become an insignificant region since the decline of the gum trade. From that time, France's main objective had become the conquest of the Sudan beyond the upper Senegal valley, together with that of the peanut-producing Wolof and Sereer kingdoms situated within the Saint-Louis–Dakar–Kaolak triangle.

For the French, then, Futa Toro was a mere corridor. It suffered from the additional disadvantage of being economically uninteresting. Chronic warfare had turned it into a region of penury and famine. In the decade from 1860 to 1870, epidemics struck the area. And all the time, the ceaseless flow of its population, drawn by the religious migration known as the *fergo* toward the empire of Shaykh Umar and his heir Amadu of Segu, left it a desolate land. For a while, Futa Toro continued to experience a sort of autonomy while suffering the political, economic, and social consequences of the vast movements instigated by the Muslim leaders Shaykh Umar, Cherno Brahim, and Amadu Seekhu. Their various attempts at political control failed partly because they were opposed by an alliance of legitimate traditional rulers and the colony of Senegal, bent on combating the marabout movement outside the boundaries of Futa Toro.

Some of the marabout leaders were eliminated by local rulers. Others were liquidated through direct French intervention from the colony of Senegal. Then there was Abdul Bokar Kane of Bosea, who, benefiting from the temporary eclipse of France, beaten into inactivity after the defeat by Prussia in 1870, was able to fill the political vacuum by making himself the real master of Futa Toro until his death in 1891.

Abdul Bokar Kane was an astonishing hybrid, part eighteenth-century warrior in the tradition of Samba Gelaajo Jeegi, part legitimate ruler, heir to the *Toorodo* regime imposed by the Muslim revolution led by Suleyman Baal and Abdul Kader. To consolidate his power, Abdul Bokar Kane had to face down a crop of rising Muslim leaders opposed to the Toorodo regime along with members of the ruling class on the domestic front, and, on the external front, constant pressure from the colony of Senegal. Under the circumstances, he made pragmatic use of every contingency to remain master of an undivided Futa. This was no mean achievement, considering that the country was sapped by civil war, drained of its population by the pull of Shaykh Umar's *fergo* migratory movement, and constantly harassed by French expeditionary forces from Saint-Louis on their way to conquer the Sudan.

In his fortieth year, after the Magama and Madiyankobe crises, Abdul Bokar Kane, chief of Bosea and the most influential leader of the Electoral Council, dealt with increasingly overt hostility from the Wane family of Mbumba. The dispute broke out because Sada and Ibra, supported by the young, energetic Elector from Pete, Mamadu Siley An, wanted to have the *Almami* recognized as superior to the Elector from Bosea. The crisis erupted in the context of the network of traditional alliances in Futa, in the sense that Mamadu Siley An, linked by marriage to the Wanes of Mbumba, depended on other electors, especially the Bas (Mbolo Ali Sidi) and the Lys of Ciloon, to counter Abdul Bokar Kane's influence in the *Jaggorde*

Council. The resulting split within the Council of Electors led to a long series of clashes between followers of the Wanes and those of the Kanes, lasting from 1872 to 1876. The consequence was a high incumbent turnover, with multiple transitional gaps.

Because these clashes took place in Central Futa, the area went through periodic famines. The devastation was worsened by the intensity of migratory shifts from Futa to Nioro.[16]

Meanwhile, France, whose mood of withdrawal following the 1870 defeat by Prussia had halted its expansionist momentum, could not intervene in any significant way. So Abdul Bokar Kane, using an army of *ceddo* and Peul warriors from Bosea and eastern Futa, reinforced by a contingent of battle-seasoned Moors led by Oulad Ely, gradually eliminated his enemies and tightened his hold as sole master of the country. Furthermore, from 1877, he began to implement a policy of reconciliation with his former opponents on the Council of Electors, as well as with Ibra Almami. He also established his reputation as defender of Futa Toro's territorial integrity against the expansionist policy of the colony of Senegal, which had resumed its thrust into the Sudan in 1879.

France had indeed set up a command post at Bafulaabe. This was a clear indication of its intention to expand its holdings into the Niger valley. The laying of a telegraph line, needed for coordinating operations between Senegal and the Sudan, had therefore become the major objective of the French colony. But the attempt to lay a line from Saldé to Bakel, on territory controlled by Abdul Bokar Kane, provoked a series of disputes between Futa and the French colonial authority in Saint-Louis. These disputes slowed down the conquest of the Sudan considerably. In his desire to assert his authority over eastern Futa and to challenge French protectorate powers over the provinces of Pete and Law, Abdul Bokar Kane was proving to be an obstacle. In February 1881, the colony of Senegal decided to break down that obstacle by force. In this scheme they counted on help from the *Lam Tooro*, Mamadu.

In his dispute with France, and especially in his clash with Ibra Almami, Abdul Bokar Kane had solid support from Alburi Njaay, the king of Jolof. In 1884, for instance, when Abdul Bokar Kane was surrounded by enemy forces, the Jolof king sent his cavalry to help him break the siege and keep control of eastern Futa. Ultimately, the conflict ended with the Hore Fonde Treaty of 1885, by whose terms Abdul Bokar Kane was recognized as sole ruler, and the French at Saint-Louis were obliged to agree to pay an annual fee before finishing construction work on the telegraph line from Saldé to Bakel.[17]

By now, Abdul Bokar Kane was at the height of his political power. Adopting the title of Emir of Futa, he was the embodiment of the restoration of Futa's autonomy and prestige, in the tradition of the old warrior-rulers and the founding *Almamis*. The treaty of 1885 meant, in effect, that for the moment France had given up its policy of dismembering the state and had recognized Abdul Bokar Kane's preeminence. In return, Abdul Bokar Kane was to guarantee the security of trading circuits in the area, and to allow construction of the telegraph line. He also, under threat from French pressure, turned a deaf ear to appeals from Nioro calling for the recruitment of Futa troops to reinforce Amadu's forces. For this reason, Eliman Rindaw's recruiting trip to Bosea yielded scant results.

On the other hand, like the ancient *Satigi* warlords, Abdul Bokar Kane, defying the French colonial presence, conducted a series of expeditions outside Futa. In January 1886, he arrived in Rip with a powerful army to intervene in a conflict between Saer Maty and Biram Siise. In the event, he lost a large number of his troops, the best contingents in his army. In any case, with the French occupying Kajoor, Siin, Saalum and Rip one after the other, Abdul Bokar Kane's opportunities for military intervention in western Senegambia were completely blocked. To the east, as soon as he arrived back home, Abdul Bokar Kane had to face the rising Mamadu Lamin in the upper Senegal valley. He did not hesitate to go to the aid of the Sy dynasty in Bundu, with French help this time. He became a partner in the administration of colonial violence by repressing villages supporting Mamadu Lamin in Gajaaga and Gidimakha, pillaging them, and collecting large numbers of slaves and livestock as war booty. In 1888, however, the French regained the initiative. Now they had no more need of embarrassing allies. They were powerful enough to occupy all of western Senegambia as well as to carve out a corridor between the domains of Samori and those of Amadu. The major campaigns conducted from 1888 to 1891 practically dismembered Amadu's empire. Abdul Bokar Kane stood by, a distant observer watching the death agony of Amadu's empire, and did not lift a finger to help him. But once Amadu's empire was gone, the French colonial noose began in turn to tighten around central Futa and Jolof, the only remaining areas of northern Senegambia left with any claim to autonomy.

In May 1890, the French occupied Jolof. The invasion sent Alburi Njaay fleeing to central Futa for refuge with Abdul Bokar Kane. Clement Thomas, the French governor, demanded his extradition. In the name of the right of fugitives to asylum, and in line with the 1885 treaty of Hore Fonde acknowledging his sovereignty over central Futa, Abdul Bokar Kane refused to give up the Jolof king to his enemies. But in the face of opposition from Cherno Molle Bubakar, an ally of the *Almami* Ibra, Abdul Bokar Kane was forced to cross the Senegal River and set up camp in Kaedi. The French and their Futa allies thereupon captured Kaedi, blocking all routes along which the two sovereigns could make their way back to their kingdoms.

This was when Alburi decided to head east into exile to join forces with Amadu. Abdul Bokar Kane, for his part, decided to remain in Chemama. For he hoped to find help from the Oulad Ely and Idawish Moors in a bid to regain his kingdom. In September 1890, Jeandet, the French commanding officer at Podor, was assassinated, along with Shaykh Mamadu, recently appointed chief of eastern Futa by the French. The assassinations provoked the dispatch of an expedition from January to March 1891 for a final assault. The French forces included 1,000 colonial troops, reinforced by 2,000 Wolof and Tukulor volunteers. With auxiliaries from his allies the *Almami* Ibra and Ismaila Siley, Dodds destroyed Dabiya, Boki, Jaawe, and finally Ngijiloon, headquarters of the *ceddo* army. In February 1891, following Amadu's defeat at Nioro, thousands of Futa survivors returned to Futa as refugees or as Archinard's prisoners. The very sight of the terrible condition in which they arrived discouraged all attempts at the organization of a national resistance movement against colonial conquest. In April and May, Abdul Bokar Kane, still holed up on the north bank of the Senegal River, tried to regain control over part of eastern Futa. He failed. The French colonial forces put a price on his head. It was at this crucial juncture that his Moorish allies, terrified at the reprisals organized by the French commandant at Kaedi, left Abdul Bokar Kane, the Bosea chief, in the lurch. On 25 August 1891, he was betrayed and murdered.[18]

Futa Toro, after the battle of Dialmath in 1854 and that of Medina in 1857, was to all intents a conquered territory. Still, it was left to agonize over a long period before being definitively annexed in 1891. In the interval, Abdul Bokar Kane, the new type of warlord, brought up in both the *ceddo* and *toorodo* traditions, refused until the last moment to leave his homeland, Bosea. Throughout, his hope was to safeguard the integrity of his country. But like all the legitimist sovereigns of northern Senegambia, he was defeated by the violent machinery of colonial conquest. His fall signaled the triumph of French imperialism in the region.

There is something similar in the careers of the last kings of northern Senegambia. All failed in their attempts to resist colonial occupation. They failed despite the heroic courage of rulers like Lat Joor, Alburi Njaay, and Abdul Bokar Kane. A substantial part of the reason for their failure lies in the seriousness of the political and social crisis eating away internally at the unity of each of their states. The effort to eliminate opposing Muslim leaders left the legitimist rulers' forces considerably weakened. It also left them without popular support at the crucial moment of the final confrontation with France. The Muslim communities, beaten into submission by both the legitimist sovereigns and French colonial forces, were too tired to aspire to anything more than peace: peace in which they might enjoy the benefits of the peanut trade. In the kingdoms of Kajoor, Baol, Siin, and Saalum, the central peanut-production zone, poor peasants and Muslims traumatized by multiple military expeditions wasted little time before adjusting to the "French peace." This was nothing other than the colonial system; still, under the peculiar circumstances of the time, the new system seemed to offer some security to primary producers. In the case of Kajoor, the alienation of the Muslim community was a considerable factor in Lat Joor's isolation at a time when his authority was being challenged by internal forces roused over a period of centuries by *ceddo* power. Royal slave armies, for instance, had in the past drawn their economic benefits from the habitual pillage of ordinary peasants. Now they switched over to serve the French colony so as to retain their material perquisites. In so doing they left the aristocracy in each kingdom, now more divided than ever along the lines of royal clans, each claiming greater legitimacy than the other, stranded high and dry, to face its doom alone.

Apart from the fact that their internal divisions made them incapable of mobilizing the entire society, the legitimist rulers were also handicapped by their inability to get together to create a united front covering the whole of northern Senegambia and thus capable of resisting colonial conquest. Once the attempts of the marabouts Maba Jaakhu and Amadu Seekhu to unify the region had failed, the legitimist rulers, each clinging to his egotistical privileges within the narrow limits of his own kingdom, could not organize a supra-national force that might have offered effective opposition to colonial conquest. And yet these different rulers were linked by a network of mutual relationships which constituted the beginnings of a nexus covering all of northern Senegambia. Alburi Njaay, for instance, was related to Lat Joor as well as to Abdul Bokar Kane. Such links reinforced a chain of solidarity tying different royal families to each other as far as Bundu, with marriage bonds bringing Abdul Bokar Kane and Bubakar Saada together. But despite these attempts at union, the legitimist rulers were trapped by the policy of encirclement adopted by the French colony of Senegal. Through it, the French eliminated Lat Joor, Alburi Njaay, Abdul Bokar Kane, and Kumba Ndoofen Juuf one after the other. Each at one time or another collaborated with the French, and for that policy paid with his life. Once northern Senegambia was subjugated, the road lay clear for the conquest of southern Senegambia, a region dominated by competition between France, Britain, and Portugal.

# 16 The conquest of the Southern Rivers region

The conquest of the Southern Rivers region in southern Senegambia was a later and much more complex development than that of northern Senegambia. The main reason was the competition between France, Britain, and Portugal for control of the region. A further complicating factor was the interaction between the process of European colonial conquest and the expansion of the Futa Jallon kingdom into the Southern Rivers area, which at the time was undergoing profound political and social upheavals from Gambia all the way to Sierra Leone.

The drive to conquer the Southern Rivers region speeded up after the 1880s partly because France had steadily occupied northern Senegambia and the Sudan, and partly because various European powers were engaged in a race to carve up Africa.

Britain held on doggedly to its possessions along the Gambia River. In so doing, it hoped to keep the strategic advantage offered by this trading corridor along which it might also be possible to thrust into the Sudan on a mission of conquest. Furthermore, Britain wished to secure communications between Gambia and Sierra Leone through Futa Jallon and the Southern Rivers region. For these reasons, Britain countered all French efforts to negotiate an exchange of the Gambia for selected French possessions in Africa or elsewhere.

For obvious economic reasons, as well as from motives of national prestige, Portugal also held on grimly to its possessions in Rio Geba, Rio Cacheu, and Rio Kasini, subsequently using them as a basis for the colony of Guinea Bissao. Here it was the British and the French who lost out.

The Portuguese and British enclaves of Guinea Bissao and Gambia aside, the entire remainder of the Southern Rivers region fell under French control. France's primary objective was to conquer the Casamance, thus expanding the colony of Senegal. This might also provide a means of gradually strangling the British possession of Gambia. Next, there was the need to consolidate French footholds in Rio Nunez, Rio Pongo, and Mellakure. This would lead to the creation of a new colony, French Guinea, a development that would help in any eventual exchange deal for the Gambia, or would help to block British expansion northward from Freetown.

European powers encountered less resistance in the Southern Rivers region than in northern Senegambia. The main reason was that the area was dotted with a multitude of tiny states which for fifty years had been enduring the military onslaughts of Futa Jallon, a continental power. In that sense, the efforts of the region's small states to liberate themselves from the overlordship of the Futa Jallon regime coincided with the conquering drive of France, Britain, and Portugal.

It was the context of external pressure, then, which kept Sunkari, Fodé Silla, Biram Njaay, and Fodé Kaba, disciples of Maba Jaakhu located on the south bank of the Gambia River, from carrying through their program of social and political reorganization. This new generation of warrior marabouts simply ended up waging ceaseless warfare on the Joola, Baïnuk, and Balante populations of the Lower Casamance basin as well as against the Soninke principalities of Gambia, before finally succumbing to the French and the British, who agreed to eliminate the local leaders one after the other, in their respective domains.

A peculiarity of Musa Molo's career is that the Fuladu chief showed a greater interest than his peers in freeing himself from Futa Jallon overlordship by allying himself with France. But the Fuladu policy of expansion into Gambia, Kaabu, and the Foria finally brought about a reaction from the British, the Portuguese, and the French, who eventually divided up Musa Molo's domain.

Lastly, in Rio Nunez, Rio Pongo, and Mellakure, France systematically eliminated Futa Jallon power from the scene. That done, they subjugated the Landuman, Nalu, Baga, and Susu aristocracies, forcing them to give up their economic and political prerogatives to the new colony of French Guinea.

## A.    The war on Maba Jaakhu's disciples on the south bank of the Gambia: Sunkari, Fodé Silla and Fodé Kaba

In the latter half of the nineteenth century the Soninke states on the south bank of the Gambia River went through a period of considerable insecurity on account of the religious activities of Maba Jaakhu's disciples. Taking advantage of the fall of Kaabu following the invasion of Futa Jallon, these disciples went on the offensive against Manding principalities on both sides of the river, defeating them. They also penetrated the forests of the Casamance, to fight against the Joola, the Balante, and the Baïnuk.

Key leaders among the new-style warrior marabouts were Sunkari, Fodé Silla, Ibrahima Njaay, and, most famous of all, Fodé Kaba, whose military campaigns lasted until 1901.

Their religious activities led to numerous wars. Most of the time, the motive was a search for war booty. But they also had a desire to control the new system of legitimate trade, in which peanut production and wild produce gathered from the Casamance forest played a leading role. Their military campaigns, however, ended up merely plunging the trading system into turmoil. The British and the French therefore stepped in to restore order. After eliminating the marabout warlords one after the other, they divided up the region between themselves.

The holy war waged by Maba Jaakhu signaled the start of the disintegration of Soninke regimes on both sides of the Gambia River. After the death of Maba Jaakhu, there was a struggle for political and religious leadership on the south bank under conditions similar to those on the north bank. For instance, the departure of Maba's army from Kiang led to a free-for-all throughout Niamina, Eropina, Jarra, and Fooñi. And again, this succession struggle did not result in the emergence of a leader capable of uniting the old Manding chiefdoms on the south bank of the Gambia and mounting an effective resistance against the advancing wave of colonial conquest.[1]

The principal initiator of a scheme to create a theocratic state south of the Gambia River as an alternative to the traditional Soninke regime or the new colonial state was Fodé Silla. His family, originally from Futa Toro, had moved to the banks of the little River Bintang in the eighteenth century, before settling at Gunjuru. From 1864, Fodé Silla came to symbolize the struggle against the authority of the *Mansa* Siise Bojan of Brikama. Defeated in 1874, the king fled for refuge to the British outpost. Thus ended the Soninke regime.

Fodé Silla had taken power in Kombo. But he still had to face down another marabout warlord, Biram Njaay, who had set up a fortified village at Kafuta around the same time. Biram Njaay was technically a French citizen born in Saint-Louis and working for the Gaspard–Devès company. Deeply impressed by Fodé Kaba's exploits, he mobilized the Manding population of Paka and Yasin for a holy war against the non-Muslim Joola. In June 1884 he torched the villages of Santak and Uonk. Even though the French dispatched a light patrol boat, the *Myrmidon*, against them, Biram Njaay's warriors, extremely rapid in their movements, pillaged several Kalunaye villages and destroyed their farms, sending large numbers of Joola refugees into Baïnuk territory around Adean, Kujundu, and Gudomp. When in December Lieutenant Truche was killed, Colonel Duchemin reacted by burning Selki on 10 February 1887, though he was unable to capture Biram Njaay. But the French victory in the Rip and the capture of Nioro frightened Biram Njaay into agreeing to meet the French commanding officer. He promised then to ensure the safety of traders. But he refused to recognize French sovereignty over Fooñi, reserving the right to wage holy war against the Joola. The population, however, organized themselves to resist him, pushing him steadily back to the banks of the Gambia River. There, when he constructed a fortified village at Kafuta, an angry Fodé Silla reacted. On 2 January 1888, Fodé Silla's warriors destroyed the fortified village. Biram Njaay himself died a few days later in Kunkujang village, much to the delight of the Joola population of Kombo and Fooñi. Biram's cousin Papa Omar Njaay died a similar death. But the many wars waged by various Muslim factions totally ruined the villages of Fooñi near the Gambia river, whose inhabitants all fled. Biram Njaay's defeat reinforced Fodé Silla's position. He took advantage of his new strength to attack the Joola in Kombo. This in turn provoked a reaction from the British and the French, whose overriding concern was to protect their trading systems.[2]

Warfare had become endemic in the region. Eager for booty, Soninke and Toorodo mercenaries from the Senegal River valley trooped south to pillage traders, especially Joolas traveling to Bathurst to sell their forest produce. Fodé Silla's assertion of his authority over Jara and Kombo, with logistical help from Fodé Kaba, Maba Jaakhu's main disciple on the south bank of the Gambia, coincided with the European colonial thrust. When the French took the Rip on the north bank of the Gambia River, the British were motivated to lay definitive claim to sovereignty along the river, as a way of putting an end to the warfare that was destroying trade. In 1894, ignoring various peace agreements and the opposition of the Bathurst Chamber of Commerce, the British colonial authorities trumped up a series of charges against Fodé Silla and dispatched expeditions against Gunjuru, Brikama, Sukuta, and Busumbala.

At their first encounter, Fodé Silla inflicted heavy losses on the British at Brikama. On 26 February 1894 he went on the offensive, laying siege to Bathurst. But Captain Westmoreland, using reinforcements from Sierra Leone and Gibraltar, turned his artillery on him, forcing him to retreat from Kombo into French territory with hundreds of his warriors.

The French Governor Lamothe, for his part, sent sufficient troops into the Casamance from 3 March 1894 to prevent Fodé Kaba from sending reinforcements to Fodé Silla throughout the British military campaign in Kombo. On 10 March, Lieutenant Moreau cut off Fodé Silla's attempted retreat across the river at the frontier post of San Pedro. At that point Fodé Silla offered to surrender. Captain Canard made him lay down his arms. His fighters were marched under guard into the village of Banjikari, where each was ordered to pay a tax of 1 kg of rubber. Fodé Silla was transferred to Kajoor with an escort commanded by Demba Waar Sall, along with some twenty followers who opted to go with him into exile. He died during the night of 19–20 September 1894. His death hastened the integration of the Muslim area of Kombo into the British protectorate.

The French and the British still had Fodé Kaba to deal with. Unlike Fodé Silla, he agreed to negotiate with the French, hoping to retain control of the territory he conquered from the Joola.[3]

There is no doubt whatsoever that Fodé Kaba was Maba Jaakhu's leading disciple on the south bank of the Gambia River. From that area, the marabout carried his military operations into the Casamance forest up until 1901, when the colonial era was already well established. Fodé Kaba was born at Kosse in Wuuli, into a renowned family of Jakhanke marabouts from Tuuba in the Futa Jallon. His father, Fodé Bakari Dumbuya, had crossed the Gambia River with a large following of disciples, settling at Kerewan Dumbutu in the Jimara area. There he clashed with a brutal king, Mamadi Sonko.

As early as 1862, Fodé Kaba, then a young disciple, had enrolled among Maba Jaakhu's forces for the holy war on the north bank of the Gambia. Before leaving, he entrusted his family and property to the care of Alfa Molo, whose authority at that time extended to Jimara. But Mamadi Sonko, with the connivance of Alfa Molo, subjected his family to numerous vicissitudes. Fodé Kaba therefore left Maba Jaakhu's army in a hurry and headed for Jara, the main peanut-producing area. There he founded the village of Dator. From this new base, Fodé Kaba proclaimed a holy war against the Soninke aristocracies on the south bank of the Gambia. He reserved his special fury for the Joola population of Fooñi, terrorizing them with his powerful cavalry. He established himself as a defender of Muslim communities laboring under excessive taxation imposed by Soninke regimes in the Jara area. In his attempt to build a unitary state capable of replacing the multitude of tiny Soninke states along the River Gambia, however, he failed.

Fodé Kaba therefore regressed, for twenty years and more, to simply marauding freely over the territories of Niamina, Jara, Kiang, and Fooñi south of the Casamance River. From his bases at Kiang and Fooñi, he occupied, left, then reoccupied the same territories, depending on his fortunes in battle. The Joola of Basada, Bona, and Nambina were thus the chief victims of Fodé Kaba's wars. Incidentally, he clashed in this same region with the forces of Musa Molo, who wanted to extend the authority of his Fuladu downstream, to the south bank of the Gambia. The two marabout warlords waged ceaseless war on each other. Neither managed to achieve a definitive victory. As happened with Fodé Silla, all this warfare, with marabouts fighting Soninke rulers sometimes, and at other times coming up against each other in factional clashes, did a great deal to damage the economy of the region between the Gambia and Casamance rivers.[4]

The British were the first to view Fodé Kaba's military campaigns with alarm. In 1880, when he settled in Fooñi, they put a price on his head. But Fodé Kaba had just then constructed a splendid fortified village at Medina and another at Dator in Kiang. It was therefore easy enough for him to continue terrorizing the Joola and defying the British and the French. The British were becoming increasingly hostile, however. So Fodé Kaba played the French off against them, taking advantage of their incessant wrangling over borders. For an annual fee of 5,000 francs, he made an agreement ostensibly recognizing French sovereignty. In return, the French recognized his authority over Fooñi and Kiang. Further, they refused flatly to cooperate with the British in arresting the marabout, in retaliation for the protection given earlier by Bathurst to Saer Maty and Biram Njaay.[5] In January 1892, the British attacked Kiang and tried to capture Fodé Kaba. He took refuge at Medina, where the French authorities refused to extradite him despite the Administrator Lewellyn's protests. Lewellyn then stirred up chiefs in western Jara and eastern Kiang to reject the authority of the marabout.

The French, seeing an opportunity in the situation, came to Fodé Kaba's help in his efforts to strengthen his authority in the Joola territories. As a payoff, they made him sign the Convention of 7 May 1893. This new agreement definitively tied Fodé Kaba's fate to France. To start with, the French reduced his jurisdiction to the Casamance area of Kiang plus a scattering of sparsely populated villages. In 1896, the Administrator Adam even considered abolishing the annual payment of 5,000 francs as a way of making it plain that the French authorities had the upper hand.

In June 1900, two British commissioners, Sitwell and Silva, sent to settle a dispute between some Soninke from Jataba and Muslim disciples of Fodé Kaba based at Sankadi in the British section of Kiang, were killed. Their deaths changed the situation, initiating a chain reaction in which both France and Britain turned against the marabout. Fodé Kaba then refused to hand over the men accused of being primarily responsible for the death of the British envoys: Dari Bana Dabo, Lansana Daba, and Bakari Job, who had fled from Sankandi. So the British organized an expedition under Colonel Brake of the Gibraltar regiment, supported by Musa Molo who rode into Jara with several hundred cavalry. The British column destroyed Dumbutu and Sankandi, then reinstated British authority in Badibu.

As for the French, they were determined to get rid of their former ally, now an embarrassment. Without delay they organized a column under Colonel Rouvel and dispatched it to capture Fodé Kaba and destroy his fortified villages at Medina and Dator. When the French artillery opened fire on the fortifications at Medina at dawn on 22 March, the old man opted to die in battle. The following morning, Colonel Rouvel raked through the smoking ruins, among the 150 bodies strewn on the ground, looking for Fodé Kaba's remains. He found nothing. Fodé Kaba had sworn to die an honorable death far from any French prison. And he had kept his word. Musa Molo's warriors captured his son, Ibrahima Dumbuya, placing him under arrest with the chief of Firdu at Hamdalaye. Dari Bana Dabo, Lansana Dabo and Bakari Job were handed over to the British.[6]

With Fodé Kaba's death, all resistance to colonization in the downstream areas along the River Gambia ceased. The colonial authorities, however, still had to eliminate Musa Molo if they wanted to assert their authority over the whole of the Upper Casamance region. The war against Musa Molo, again, involved the three colonial powers, since Musa Molo's territory extended over areas singled out for conquest by France, Britain and Portugal.

### B.     Musa Molo and the partition of Fuladu between France, Britain, and Portugal

The religious campaigns of Fodé Kaba and Fodé Silla were linked with Maba Jaakhu's holy war. The political career of Musa Molo, by contrast, was an extension of the holy war launched by Futa Jallon in the latter half of the nineteenth century against the *Nyaanco* military aristocracy of Kaabu. In this particular instance, Musa Molo, heir to Alfa Molo, liberator of Fuladu, aimed not simply to get rid of Futa Jallon overlordship, but also to expand his territory from the Upper Gambia valley to the Foria in Rio Corubal.

To achieve his objective, Musa Molo supported the French and the British in their campaigns against Mamadu Lamin, Fodé Silla, and Fodé Kaba. In addition, he played off the rival colonial powers against each other, as a way of consolidating his power. In the end, though, France, Britain, and Portugal carved up his territory among themselves. The ruler of Fuladu, at the end of his life, was a prisoner of the British in Gambia, powerless even to set foot in his own country, now divided into two zones, one French, the other Portuguese. He remained a prisoner until he died in 1931, when the colonial system was in its heyday.

In 1867, Firdu broke free of Kaabu under the leadership of Alfa Molo. Alfa Molo had drawn support from Bundu and, most of all, from the Futa Jallon regime, for which the conquest of the Southern Rivers region had become a major policy objective in the latter half of the nineteenth century. But then Alfa Molo himself, and after him, Musa Molo, with even greater intensity, embarked on an expansionist policy which impacted on most of the Southern Rivers region between the Gambia and Corubal rivers. This brought Musa Molo into conflict with the Futa Jallon regime. It also precipitated the intervention of the French, the British, and the Portuguese, then ready to divide up the region.

In any case, after the death of Alfa Molo around 1881, the Muslim holy war lost all its religious meaning. And the attempt to create a theocratic state encountered increasingly stiff hostility from populations conquered in the first place by an army bent primarily on looting. Hard upon Alfa Molo's death, there was a succession crisis pitting his brother Bakari Demba against his son Musa Molo, and lasting practically from 1883 until 1892. Taking advantage of his uncle's anti-marabout policies as well as his hostility to European interests, Musa Molo sided with the French, who gave him strong support against Bakari Demba. Armed with that support, in the form of a regiment of Senegalese Rifles commanded by Lieutenant Bertrandon, he began a decisive campaign early in 1892 against Bakari Demba in his fiefdom at Korop. Bakari Demba retreated to the British-controlled area of Ñaani, where he founded the village of Bakari Dembakunda.

To consolidate his power, Musa Molo had to fight another battle, this time at Pata in Jimara, against his brother Dikori Kumba, whose popularity he considered a threat to his authority. Dikori Kumba obtained support from Fodé Kaba, but that did not prevent him getting killed by Musa Molo's warriors.[7] Right from the start, Musa Molo's career was dependent on French support. For a start, he signed the Treaty of 3 November 1883. That agreement gave France a set of sweeping concessions. These included the right to construct an east–west railway line, the elimination of any possible future claims by Portugal and Britain, the opening up of the Upper Casamance valley to French trade, and, above all, the opportunity for expansion toward Futa Jallon by a north-west route. Musa Molo's reward was to be France's help in consolidating his power. For Musa Molo dreamed, in the long term, of profiting by his collaboration with the French to gain new territories taken from the Futa Jallon regime.[8]

This policy of expansionism based on Fuladu, the main peanut producer until the 1880s, evolved at the same time as export traders were abandoning this zone to cash in on the rubber boom elsewhere. Meanwhile, the central authority at Hamdalaye, controlled by old Peul *jiaabe*, ran into opposition from the outlying provinces ruled by Peul *rimbe*. For instance, Nbuku Niapa, head of Kanadu province, the commercial pivot of Rio Geba, rebelled against the central authority, and was followed by other provinces like Sankolla and Kolla, also controlled by Peul *rimbe*. Musa Molo launched periodic attacks against the rebels, and the incessant fighting ruined the trading *feitorias* along the Rio Geba valley. Nbuku Niapa then struck up an alliance with the Portuguese, who saw Musa Molo as an agent of French expansionism in their colony.

To deal with him, Marques Geraldes mobilized a large army with which he inflicted heavy casualties on Musa Molo, obliging him to sign a peace treaty with the Portuguese. Nevertheless, Musa Molo attacked Panabo early in 1887. He also subjected Kanadu, Kolla, and Sankolla to continuous harassment up until 1890 and even later. As a matter of fact, the struggle between the central authority in Hamdalahi and the outlying provinces was primarily due to the refusal of the Peul *rimbe* to acknowledge the new order established by Alfa Molo, which benefited the Peul *jiaabe*, recent converts to Islam allied with the Futa Jallon regime.[9] This social and political aspect was even more prominent in the clash between Musa Molo and the Foria and Kaabu regimes, both of which, like the Firdu regime, were offshoots of the break-up of the old kingdom of Kaabu after the Futa Jallon victory in 1867. The situation was made even more complex by the fact that apart from the conflict between the Foria and Kaabu, there was interference from both Futa Jallon and Portugal. For these two powers wanted, each for reasons of its own advantage, to assert sovereign rights over the region. Meanwhile, the region itself was thoroughly ravaged by a slave revolt pitting the Peul *jiaabe* against their supposed masters, the *rimbe*.

The conflict here dated back to the victory at Kansala. In its wake, this entire region had been turned, in effect, into slave territory, since the Futa Jallon regime demanded crushing tribute from Bakari Demba, the Foria chief, in the form of slaves and livestock. Unlike Fuladu, these two provinces were dominated by Peul *rimbe*. The impositions led the Foria and Kaabu into a long civil war, with the Peul *jiaabe* building fortified villages as from 1879, to defend themselves against their *rimbe* masters.

In this atmosphere of political and social crisis, the first Governor of the Province of Portuguese Guinea, Agostinho Coelho, actively supported the Peul *jiaabe* in their struggle against their masters, the *rimbe*, supported by Futa Jallon. Large numbers of slaves settled around the Portuguese post at Buba, using it as a base from which to attack their former masters. In return for this protection, the former Peul slaves served the Portuguese as auxiliaries in their colonial campaigns in the Foria region and elsewhere, as they tried to abolish the customary payments demanded of traders by the *rimbe* and the Futa Jallon regime all along Rio Grande.

In 1882 the Portuguese, using 2,000 Manding and Peul *jiaabe* auxiliaries, attacked Bakar Qidali, aiming to force him to sue for peace. But the Portuguese policy, aimed at restoring peace at all costs in order to keep up peanut production levels at the Portuguese trading posts, was shaky in its implementation. For one thing, in the single decade from 1879 to 1889, no fewer than seven different governors came and went as chief administrators of the colony. Sometimes the Portuguese supported the former slaves. At other times they adopted the self-deceiving tactic of proclaiming their neutrality, while the conflict, utterly ruinous to the economy supporting their trading posts, dragged on. In 1886, however, the Portuguese perceived a clear threat: the Futa Jallon regime looked set to intervene in the Foria and Kaabu areas, to affirm its sovereignty. That brought the Portuguese round, in gradual stages, to supporting the local *rimbe* aristocracy against their Futa Jallon overlord, namely the Alfa of Labé. The oppressive policies of Bakar Qidali had led to a reaction from the local Foria chiefs, who appealed to the Alfa of Labé for help. Eager to reestablish his sovereignty, the latter attacked Bakar Qidali, forcing him to seek refuge in the Portuguese fort at Buba. There, unwilling to contemplate the prospect of exile, he committed suicide.

After him, Mamadu Paate Bolola ruled from 1887 to 1890, yielding to Cherno Kaali. Cherno Kaali in turn yielded to Mamadu Paate Koyada, who ruled over both the Foria and Kaabu. He was a worse ruler than Qidali, habitually demanding exorbitant tribute from Foria, abducting women, and rustling livestock. So Cherno Kaali, overcoming the reticence of the Peul and Beafada chiefs, brought them together to end Koyada's oppressive rule. The ensuing war between Mamadu Paate Koyada and the combined forces of the Alfa of Labé and Cherno Kaali completely ruined the economy of the Foria region. In particular, peanut production in Rio Grande was wiped out throughout the 1890s.[10] While this situation of social and political crisis lasted, Musa Molo, who made no bones about using French support to free himself of Futa Jallon overlordship, started a war with Foria and Kaabu, intending to prepare the ground for Fuladu expansion into that region.

Given the depth of hostility between the Peul *jiaabe* and their former masters, the *rimbe* aristocracy, plus the aggravating circumstance that the Firdu chief was determined to control Kaabu, the conflict between Musa Molo and the Embalo family became a permanent fact of life. Sellu Koyada insulted Musa Molo, calling him a slave. Rubbing salt into the wound, he named his horse after Musa Molo's mother, Kumba Wude. That brought the two kingdoms to war. When Sellu Koyada was taken hostage, Mamadu Paate Koyada appealed to the Portuguese to join the war against Musa Molo. The Portuguese, who considered Musa Molo an agent of French expansionism in their colony of Guinea Bissao, readily agreed. Indeed, the Portuguese blamed Musa Molo for every disaster in the area, especially the trade depression in the Gerba and Farim regions. Musa Molo's repeated attacks around the year 1890 also helped reinforce the alliance between the Peul *rimbe* aristocracy and the Portuguese. The latter organized several campaigns against the Papel and the Balante populations in their determination to carve out the colony of Guinea Bissao. Soon, however, Musa Molo, frustrated by the lack of any clear military gains, abandoned his designs on the Foria and Kaabu regions, to concentrate on asserting his independence from the Futa Jallon regime.[11]

In pursuit of his desire for independence, Musa Molo now stopped paying any tribute to the Futa Jallon regime. Distracted by internal chaos, the *Almami* could not mount a serious military campaign to bring him to heel. And for the time being, Musa Molo could count on help from the French, since they planned to use him in their plan to push into the West African hinterland. Meanwhile, the Alfa of Labé had had some caravans from the Sudan passing through Niokolo and Tenda country attacked. Under the guise of reprisal, the French Governor Lamothe suggested it would be a fine idea for Malik Turé of Bundu and Musa Molo to raid the Alfa's vassal territories of Pakesi, Ndama, Bajar, and Damantang. So, in 1894, Musa Molo helped the French to attack Ndama, and to mount an especially fierce assault on Pakesi, whose chief Bamba Dalla had for years irritated the French captain Baurès. On 9 July 1894, Bamba Dalla defeated the French troops at Parumba. The French then sent in a reinforcement of sixty riflemen under Lieutenant Moreau to help Musa Molo annex Pakesi to Fuladu. On 21 January 1895, the combined forces set fire to Kandelifa. Defeated, Bamba Dalla fled to Kadé, seeking refuge with the Alfa of Labé.

Prior to all this, Musa Molo had signed an agreement on 11 January agreeing to pay half of all tax receipts collected in Fuladu to the French. He also gave the go-ahead for the construction of a military post at Hamdalaye. Despite the integration of Pakesi and Bajar into Fuladu, Musa Molo had become a prisoner of the French. On 25 January 1896 they forced him to ratify the earlier treaty. They also ensured that thenceforth they could control all his activities. As a result, France gradually strengthened its hold on Fuladu. The kingdom's dependencies, Bajar, Ndama, and the Konyagi area, were placed under the jurisdiction of French Guinea in May 1897. Pakesi was divided between French and Portuguese Guinea. In 1902, Musa Molo suffered an even keener disappointment: all tax collection was brought under the direct control of the French Administrator Lebretoigne du Maze.[12] Smarting under the numerous impositions of the French, Musa Molo drifted gradually into the embrace of the British. But like the Portuguese, the British also considered him as no more than an agent of French colonial expansionism in their domain.

In any case, on account of the expansion of Fuladu into the British zone, Musa Molo signed an agreement with the governor of Bathurst in 1901 by which he gave up the right to collect taxes in those parts of Fuladu under British control. In return, the British would pay him a annual flat fee of £500 sterling. This agreement came at a time when the French had decided to exercise greater control over the domestic and foreign policies of Musa Molo. Now, early in 1903, the French summoned Musa Molo to Seju. Suspecting the worst, he left Fuladu, taking refuge in the part of his kingdom under British control. Justifiably frightened of going into exile, Musa Molo took advantage of the absence of the French commanding officer De la Roncière to organize an exodus of the population. On 14 March 1903, having first burned Hamdalaye, Ndorna, and several other villages, he set out on the road to Gambia.

Musa Molo's departure was good news for the authorities in the French colony of Senegal. They had for years reinforced Musa Molo's power. Now, when it was too late, they turned to criticizing his governance. Meanwhile, upset at the destruction of villages and property, along with what they saw as the compulsory exodus of the population, they tried to stem the outflow of people. Musa Molo, from his exile in Gambia, kept pointing out that the people were leaving of their own free will. The French tried to make the British extradite Musa Molo, but failed. The British allowed him to settle at Keserekunda, on the understanding that he would give up all political activities throughout his former kingdom. The kingdom itself was divided up between France, Britain, and Portugal.

The British refused to extradite Musa Molo mainly because they hoped his presence on British-controlled territory would attract people there from French-controlled Fuladu who might help develop peanut farming more actively. As for Musa Molo himself, he remained in Gambia until his death, except for a short exile in Sierra Leone during World War I.[13]

Musa Molo's career presents a number of aspects unique in Senegambian history. First, his activities constantly overlapped and interacted with those of the three colonial powers, Britain, France and Portugal. Second, he was able for a while to play these powers off against one another. He used the French to eliminate his domestic competitors, to expand the Fuladu frontiers, and to free himself of Futa Jallon tutelage. But in the end he abandoned his first allies to take refuge with the British. The British kept him as nothing more than a prisoner. Meanwhile his kingdom fell definitively under French and Portuguese control, and the European powers simply kept him out.

The point is that the moment he signed the 1883 treaty with France, intending to consolidate his personal power in Fuladu, Musa Molo condemned himself to the role of colonial collaborator. By supporting European forces in their wars against Mamadu Lamin, Fodé Silla, and Fodé Kaba, he did a great deal to facilitate colonial penetration into the area, leading to the partition of the Southern Rivers region between the three powers, Britain, France, and Portugal.

## C.     The conquest of Rio Nunez, Rio Pongo, and Mellakure

The conquest of Rio Nunez, Rio Pongo, and Mellakure was primarily a French achievement, and it gave France the lion's share of the Southern Rivers region. The preponderance of French peanut trading interests in the mid-nineteenth century, coupled with the construction of forts at Boké, Boffa, and Benty in the three river valleys as early as 1867, gave France a head start in the scramble for territory, restricting its rival Britain to Gambia and the area south of the Mellakure River, while doing a great deal to limit the Portuguese presence to Rio Cacheu, Rio Geba, and Rio Kasini. The French conquest of Rio Nunez, Rio Pongo, and Mellakure laid the foundations for the new colony of French Guinea. The main loser here was the continental power of Futa Jallon, which gradually lost all political and commercial control in the Southern Rivers region. However, from 1869 to 1879, with the slump in the peanut trade, the French came to see their possession of the three river valleys merely as a bargaining counter in nego-tiations with the British for possession of the Gambia. Then rubber started making spectacular leaps and bounds as a trading commodity, and sud-denly the region assumed its former importance as a strategic base for penetration into the African hinterland. The French therefore strengthened their hold on the three river basins, then secured the connection between the supposedly rich markets of the Sudan and the sea by conquering the Futa Jallon. Concurrently, they developed the new zones of Conakry and Dubreka, to reduce the pull formerly exercised by Freetown as a trading center serving the entire Southern Rivers region between Gambia and Sierra Leone.

The aim behind the creation of this new economic and political center was to free the colonial powers from the many harassments imposed on them at the trading centers of Boké, Boffa, and Benty in their dealings with the old aristocrats, avid for economic handouts and political privileges, and their slave-trading allies. The three river valleys had a long trading history. The old aristocrats and slave-trading families had only slowly begun to tolerate the French presence as a means of freeing themselves from the Futa Jallon yoke. After that, they tried to adjust to the decline of the old trading system by setting themselves up as middlemen between the coast and the hinterland. For the interior regions now produced rubber, the main trading produce since the 1880s. In time, though, on the instigation of the major trading companies, the colonial authorities tried to consolidate French control along the coast, suppressing the middlemen's trading posts in the process. This meant the disappearance of the privileges of the Baga, Landuman, Nalu, and Susu aristocrats, and they fought stoutly against the new system. One by one, the French destroyed them: Diina Salifu and Sara Tongo in Rio Nunez, John Katty in Rio Pongo, and the *Almami* Bokari in Mellakure all paid dearly for daring to oppose the conquering French as they advanced into the Southern Rivers region. After that, the region became a base for the conquest of the Futa Jallon.

In 1867, the French constructed a series of forts at Boké, Bofa, and Benty in Rio Nunez, Rio Pongo, and Mellakure. The forts marked the beginning of a new era in relationships between France and the Southern Rivers region on the one hand, and between France and the Futa Jallon on the other. Initially, the authorities at Timbo did not react to the French move into the area. After all, they hoped the French would help them create a secure trading atmosphere in the remote Southern Rivers region. And safer trading conditions would increase revenue from trade with the Futa Jallon. But conflicts between the Nalu and the Landuman continued to create considerable havoc, making the peace needed for trade in Rio Nunez elusive. Most foreign trading posts were established on Nalu territory, but the Landuman were bent on maintaining a monopoly on trade by stopping caravans heading for Nalu areas. In the midst of the upheavals, France tried to impose a 4 percent tax on all produce exported from Rio Nunez and Rio Pongo. The idea was to use this tax income to pay for peacekeeping in the region.

Peacekeeping was further complicated by the constant demands of the Alfa of Labé. As nominal overlord of Rio Nunez, he sometimes made demands contrary to the interests of the central regime in Timbo. In 1867, the Alfa of Labé sent his lieutenant Alfa Kafa to pacify the area and collect the annual tribute from the Landuman. He ordered Duka, the Landuman chief, not only to pay double the customary tribute, but also to join his army for the purpose of expelling the French from the valley. The resident French officer Cauvin, in a panic, opened fire, killing a nephew of the Alfa of Labé. Alfa Kafa's army was scattered. Duka and Diout, the leading Landuman chiefs, were arrested and transferred to Saint-Louis. Flize, the commanding officer at Gorée, was quickly dispatched to Boké to calm the Landuman and Futa Jallon authorities, as well as to get Cauvin recalled, so as to avoid reprisals against French traders. Flize requested that Alfa Kafa be replaced. He also guaranteed that the Landuman tribute would be paid to the Alfa of Labé, and that pillaging raids, especially those involving the kidnapping of slave porters from the Futa Jallon, would be stopped. In 1868, however, the commanding officer at Boke, even though he acknowledged Futa Jallon sovereignty as a practical reality, tried to limit its scope in order to prevent the Futa Jallon from intervening militarily in the area under any circumstances whatsoever.[14]

The French occupying forces also encountered opposition from the British. In 1867, for instance, they protested against customs duties imposed by the French in the Mellakure estuary in particular. After securing equal treatment for British traders, Britain was willing to leave the Rio Pongo and Rio Nunez markets to the French, provided it could keep the Mellakure, a zone near Freetown where for centuries it had had strong influence. In February 1870 the French were ready to accept a demarcation along those lines if Britain would give them Gambia in return. But the Bathurst Chamber of Commerce was against the scheme, and it was abandoned in September 1871. Implicitly, the British had agreed to French settlement in the three river basins.

But here too, the French policy of withdrawal after the 1870 defeat kept them from asserting their authority. The Landuman people, whose main desire was to take advantage of the French presence to liberate themselves from their Futa Jallon overlords, were still terrified of the French post at Boké, because of its cannon.[15] France became steadily more and more involved in internal conflicts, signing numerous treaties with local chiefs to supplement its inadequate territorial coverage in the Southern Rivers region.

In 1877, France signed two new treaties in Rio Nunez. The first gave the Landuman chief, Duka, an annual fee of 2,000 francs, besides the customary commercial duties. The second was aimed at ending the civil war ravaging the Nalu homeland ever since Yura announced his abdication to make room for Diina Salifu. France obliged Yura to stay in power, awarding him a 5,000-franc annual payment, with the understanding that Bokari would become his successor. This, however, did not mean the end of the succession crisis.

In Rio Pongo, Yangi Will's death in 1874 forced France to dispatch Captain BolièvE to ensure that the new king would not prove rebellious. Still, not until 1876 did John Katty acknowledge French suzerainty, in return for an annual payment of 5,000 francs. Even so, his court was opposed to the move. The 5,000-franc annual fee was double the amount agreed on in the 1866 treaty. Nevertheless, it seemed a paltry sum indeed, considering that trade in the valley was estimated to total 8,600,000 francs in 1878, and annual customs receipts averaged 85,000 to 90,000 francs. Hence the frequency of subsequent complaints from John Katty. Furthermore, he tried to keep up a relationship with the British colony of Sierra Leone, which continued to pay an annual fee to the king of Rio Pongo, as required by the 1852 treaty.

The Mellakure valley continued to experience upheavals even after the French paid Bokari, the *Almami* of Morea, a fee of 3,000 francs. France indirectly encouraged the different *Alkalis* to assert their independence by signing eight similar treaties with them. But Freetown, intent on keeping the Mellakure valley within its zone of influence, continued to offer the French even stiffer competition than before.[16]

It must be remembered that Anglo–French competition in the three river valleys was part of a larger picture in which the two powers sought to outdo each other in West Africa as a whole. Thus, from Pinet-Laprade's death in 1869 to Brière de Lisle's arrival in 1879, the French regarded the Southern

Rivers region, and the Mellakure valley in particular, as bargaining counters to be used for loosening the Gambia from Britain's grasp.

The failure to reach an agreement on the exchange of the Gambia came at a time when peanut production had slumped, yielding place to rubber in the Southern Rivers economy. The French option, in fact, was to make southern Senegambia a key zone for securing supplies of rubber produced in the Futa Jallon and the Sudanese savanna regions of the Upper Niger valley. The new economic policy gave the Southern Rivers region a fresh lease of life as a strategic base for access to the hinterland, needed to secure rubber supplies. For that reason, France reinforced its position in the three river valleys, which eventually became the basis for the colony of French Guinea.[17]

France still faced an old problem: it had an ambitious policy of conquest, but not the resources to implement it. From 1875, peace in the three river valleys was constantly jeopardized by the rise to power of new chiefs less inclined to tolerate the French presence. A succession crisis following the incumbency of the old Nalu chief Yura was aggravated by the interference of Futa Jallon envoys, who deliberately prolonged their visit to the coast, partly because they wanted to meddle in local politics, partly because they had lucrative personal business deals to negotiate. The Futa Jallon regime took to sending its army more often to deal with local conflicts, as well as to recapture runaway slaves who came to the area to reinforce the ranks of the Mikifore. The Mikifore were a band of former slaves. Having run away, they organized themselves not just to pillage trade caravans traveling from the Futa Jallon, but also to attack the local Landuman and Susu communities. To start with, the French bribed the Futa Jallon's military forces to restore order in the river valleys. But in 1875 they switched to direct military intervention, firing on the warriors of Modi Moktar, who had marched upon Yura and Duka to force them to return 600 slaves who had escaped to join the Mikifore and the Baga.[18]

The failure of the Gambia exchange scheme irritated the French. The attempts of the British Governor Rowe to take over the Mellakure valley for use as a base for British penetration toward the Futa Jallon and the Niger River made them even angrier, and they took immediate retaliatory action. In 1877, Brière de Lisle proclaimed the indivisible sovereignty of France over the coastal region between Rio Pongo and the south bank of the Mellakure River. From June 1877 to February 1878, he dispatched Bolième, Political Affairs Director for the French colony of Senegal, to confirm various treaties signed with chiefs in Rio Nunez, Rio Pongo, and Mellakure. In October 1879 the commanding officer at the French post of Boké began negotiations to persuade the Nalu and Landuman chiefs to bury their old antagonisms so as to form a common front to resist future intervention from the Futa Jallon regime. In January 1880, the Mikifore runaway slave forces defeated a Futa Jallon army under Alfa Gassimu. The losers blamed their defeat on French interference, and the angry *Almamis* began turning away trading caravans from the Rio Nunez trading posts.

In October 1882, France appointed a resident Lieutenant Governor of the Southern Rivers region. The move signaled the French authorities' determination to do more to consolidate their authority. The appointment also marked a separation between the interests of the colony of Senegal, dominated by Bordeaux, and those of the Southern Rivers, dominated by Marseille.[19]

Locally, France took advantage of succession disputes after Yura's incumbency to impose a new treaty. This denied power to Bokari on account of his pro-British inclinations, giving it instead to his rival Diina Salifu Kamara. When hostilities flared up again in March 1885, the commanding officer, still supporting Salifu, destroyed several upstream villages, in particular Katinu, where Bokari himself was killed. The Commandant had made up his mind: he wanted to deal with only one Nalu chief, Diina Salifu. One reason was that the man liked the French. Another was that he had demonstrated a capacity to maintain peace in the valley. Diina Salifu had other assets. He was allied with the chiefs of Rio Pongo, and his contacts with the Futa Jallon *Almamis* were good, since he had gone to Koranic school in Timbo. In 1889, Diina Salifu went to France to see the Universal Exhibition, and was awarded the Legion of Honor decoration. In 1890, however, while traveling to Saint-Louis to ask for help against the Yola and the Fulakunda, he was arbitrarily arrested. Hostile traders, taking advantage of the situation, signed a petition requesting his definitive proscription from Rio Nunez. Diina Salifu wrote letter after letter protesting against the injustice and pleading his devotion to France. In vain. He was kept in detention until he died in 1897. Once Diina Salifu was out of the way, the French Administrator was free to impose direct rule. Now it was the French authorities who dealt with all disputes between chiefs in Rio Nunez. France, however, kept the Landuman chief Sara Tongo in power, finding him useful as a go-between for the Commandant in his dealings with the Futa Jallon authorities.[20]

In Rio Pongo, however, things were different. The Commandant at Boffa had only limited powers. The old slave-trading families there were still powerful and as yet France did not have enough fire power to impose respect for its authority beyond a 2-km radius from the post. There was constant warfare on account of disputes between the Katty family and the chiefdoms of Koba, Lakhata, and Bambaya. Frequent disturbances from 1879 to 1883 moved traders to request troops to combat the Kroba, a band of henchmen serving Ben Katty, the brother of the king, John Katty. On 23 November

1884, France forced John Katty to sign a treaty enabling the Commandant to expand the perimeters of the post. Ben Katty opposed the treaty, so France, in a bid to reinforce its position, had to sign separate protectorate agreements with Lakhata and Kolisokho, to the north of Boffa. In 1891, John Katty died. The French saw their opportunity to try and abolish the position of chief. In its stead, they proposed the services of an Afro-European, Thomas Curtis, whom they themselves had appointed Minister. However, the traders still needed a homegrown chief capable of handling misdemeanors committed by local chiefs under his jurisdiction.[21]

Meanwhile, the situation in the Mellakure valley remained confused. The trouble was that even though the French had set Bokari up as sole paramount chief, they were also going around signing separate treaties with other chiefs. This was creating potential enemies for Bokari. In 1880, the French accused Bokari of being too friendly with the British and dismissed him. In his place they supported the *Alkali* of Forekaria, Dauda. Bokari, protesting against his dismissal, appealed to the Temne for help. They obliged, subjecting the Mellakure valley to a series of bloody attacks that ravaged the area until Bokari's death in 1885. The *Alkali* Dauda was, by default, recognized as *Almami* in 1886. But this ruling was immediately disputed by Condetto, the *Alkali* of Laya. At the same time, the presence in the Tamiso area of warriors from Samori's army remained a source of disturbance.[22]

Because of these developments French authority in the three river valleys remained insecure. First, the local aristocracies hated the French colonial administration. Second, and more importantly, the Futa Jallon regime wanted to maintain its privileges on the coast. The Bayol Treaty of 1881 notwithstanding, the Futa Jallon authorities continued to exercise sovereign rights over the region. For instance, they ordered chiefs and traders in Rio Pongo and Rio Nunez to pay an annual tribute. And as from 1881, Futa Jallon armies intervened often in Rio Pongo to stop John Katty robbing caravans passing through. At times the colonial authorities and traders had to cooperate with the Futa Jallon troops to put down disturbances. Such was the case in Rio Nunez in 1885. But the Labé chiefs had a habit of mounting raids every year. This made the situation even riskier. To deal with it, the French had to find new ways of maintaining their authority in the Southern Rivers region.[23]

In point of fact, ever since the establishment in 1882 of the post of Lieutenant-Governor of the Southern Rivers region, France had tried to obtain a foothold in the Dubreka zone. The idea was to escape the problems encountered in Rio Nunez, Rio Pongo, and Mellakure, while establishing unbroken control over the entire coastline north of Sierra Leone. The Dubreka station, far from the traditional trading zones, would give the

French an opportunity to build up a more secure base from which to assert their power throughout the coastal zone, while making sure that their customs tariffs were efficiently observed.

So the creation of an administrative district around Dubreka in July 1885 came at the same time as the reform siting the residence of the Lieutenant-Governor of the Southern Rivers region on Tumbo island. When Balla Demba died in 1886, France took advantage of the temporary vacuum to put down more solid bases in the villages of Tumbo, Conakry, and Bulbine, after burning hostile villages and arresting the principal chiefs. In 1887 the chiefs of Labeya, Kanea, and Sumbuya were brought under control to enlarge the territorial range around Dubreka. The aim was then to make the new post a major caravan station. In 1890, annual payments to chiefs were transferred from the Futa Jallon and Boké to Dubreka and Conakry. The shift marked the definitive rise of this region to a preeminent status.[24] The choice of Conakry as capital of French Guinea put the seal to the new colony's autonomy from Senegal and the Sudan. Thenceforth, the primary function assigned to the colony of French Guinea would be to serve as a base for the conquest of the Sudan. A second function would be to break the commercial hegemony of the British port of Freetown over the entire Southern Rivers region.

The conquest of the Southern Rivers region lasted until around 1896. It was not the result of a series of military campaigns mounted against a unitary state. Rather, it was a long, piecemeal campaign of economic penetration. In the first phase, it involved the gradual elimination of slave-trading families. The second phase saw the installation of a colonial authority which used local chiefs to break the influence of the Futa Jallon regime, then gradually shored up its power by steadily working to eliminate incumbent aristocracies. That the colonial authority worked to defend the interests of European trading companies is a truism. That commitment underlay the way the colonial administration operated in this region. Economic motives were dominant in a process which required the manipulation of local aristocracies in the Rivers area to clear the coast of the influence of Futa Jallon power.

Beginning in 1887, the coastal populations found themselves obliged to give up farming, with peanut production having grown particularly unprofitable. Rubber was the new principal product, and Futa Jallon was the main producer. So the coastal populations turned to working as intermediaries between the productive Futa Jallon and the trading outlets at Boké, Boffa, and Benty. Susu traders, wishing to profit from the new system, set up numerous secondary markets at such points as Damakulima, Kebale, and Sarasene. As for the chiefs of Tene, Bakunji, and Barigu, they specialized in a protection racket, demanding exorbitant payments for ensuring safe access to the coast, failing which they simply pillaged the caravans from the Futa Jallon.

From this time on, the Futa Jallon *Almamis* could no longer control the Susu chiefs, who took advantage of the French presence to avenge humiliations inflicted on them in past times. For the French, once the Futa Jallon was conquered in 1896, the main task was to get rid of the middlemen's markets, giving the French trading companies unimpeded access from the coast to the hinterland.[25] To accomplish this, the French avoided becoming entangled in long military operations likely to create useless disturbances in the steady flow of commercial transactions vital to the prosperity of the Southern Rivers region. So they let the old centers of Boké, Boffa, and Benty vegetate quietly, in order to concentrate on conquering the area around Conakry and Dubreka. From that new base, they would extend their power over the entire coast. Now France was in a position to take care of the linkage of the Sudan with the coast. That linkage required, of necessity, the conquest of the Futa Jallon.

# 17 The balancing act of the *Almamis* of Timbo in their attempts to cope with centrifugal forces

Geographically, the Futa Jallon kingdom was situated in the West African hinterland, away from the main axis of French penetration in the Sudan and the Southern Rivers regions. For that reason, up until the 1890s it enjoyed a degree of autonomy which enabled it to play off one colonial power against the other. The game helped it to preserve its independence for quite a while.

Internally, the central regime, dominated alternately by Ibrahima Sori Dongolfella of the *Soriya* faction and Ibrahima Sori Daara and Amadu of the *Alfaya* faction, went through a period of real calm because both sides were scrupulous in the observance of the principle of alternating terms. The kingdom therefore functioned normally from 1872 to 1890. The resulting stability put the *Almamis* in a position to cope with a revival of centrifugal forces, namely the continuing agitation of the Hubbu movement and the determination of the provincial chiefs in Labé and Timbi to assert their autonomy. In 1883, the *Almamis* asked Samori to help them crush the Hubbu movement by attacking the fortified village of Boketto. Survivors of the movement fled to Ndama and Gomba, where they reinforced new centers of resistance. For nearly forty years the *Almamis* had humored the powerful *Alfa* of Labé, Ibrahima, in his desire for independence. But after he died in 1881, his prospective heirs plunged into a fratricidal succession war. The *Almamis* seized the opportunity to bring the province under their central authority. And they split the province of Timbi between Madina and Tunni, as a way of checking centrifugal tendencies there.

In external affairs, the success of the central regime's balancing act in its confrontation with centrifugal forces enabled the *Almamis* to come to terms with Samori, now the dominant ruler east of Futa. They were, in particular, able to play off the colonial rivals France, Portugal and Britain, one against the other. In this way they preserved the autonomy of their kingdom until the 1890s. This went a little way toward compensating Futa Jallon for its loss of clout in the Southern Rivers region.

## A.    Success of the policy of alternating terms in Timbo

In 1867, Futa Jallon had won a victory at Kansala. But the war against Kaabu had exhausted it. It had cost the regime the life of its *Almami* Umar, the *Soriya* champion. Many of its best warriors also died. The pyrrhic victory left the *Almamis* with a backlog of urgent internal problems. Of these the most serious were the continuing Hubbu revolt and the determination of the provincial chiefs of Labé and Timbi to assert their independence. The *Almamis'* response was to adopt a policy of balance, beginning with the observance of alternating terms for the two ruling factions in Timbo.

The central authorities managed to observe the policy of alternate terms inaugurated by Umar. After his death, this policy was followed by his successor, Ibrahima Sori Dongolfella of the *Soriya* faction, and then by Ibrahima Sori Daara, leader of the *Alfaya* faction. For the first time, relations between the two clans became so cordial that Ibrahima Sori Daara, then awaiting his turn at the head of the regime, spent three months in 1872 at Timbo with the incumbent *Almami*, Ibrahima Sori Dongolfella. The two *Almamis* celebrated the Muslim feast of Ramadan together. They also played host at Timbo to Blyden, the emissary from Freetown, who signed the 1873 treaty with them. Compared to the first half of the nineteenth century, when interminable succession squabbles had marred the kingdom's affairs, the new development was unique. In the past, alternate *Almamis*, for security reasons, did not venture into the capital until their turn came to rule.[1]

But in 1873, Ibrahima Sori Daara died in battle against the Hubbu. His death weakened the *Alfaya* faction considerably, with the result that from 1873 to 1875 Ibrahima Sori Dongolfella remained in power, in contravention of the policy of alternating terms, but with the approval of the Council of Elders. Ibrahima Sori Dongolfella proved to be an authoritarian ruler. This annoyed the President of the Council of Elders, so, taking advantage of Ibrahima Sori Dongolfella's absence, he installed the new *Alfaya* leader, Amadu, as *Almami* for two years, from 1875 to 1877.[2] Still, the alternating rule continued in force, and from 1877 to 1879 Ibrahima Sori Dongolfella resumed power, served his two-year term, and handed over to Amadu once again. Amadu, however, had ruled for barely nine months when Ibrahima Sori Dongolfella overthrew him early in November 1879, thus for the first time violating the agreement, in force since 1856, to alternate two-year terms. One pretext for the coup was that Samori was pressing in on the eastern frontiers of the Futa Jallon kingdom. Indeed, Ibrahima Sori Dongolfella moved swiftly to appease Amadu and the *Alfaya* faction. In the end, bowing to the will of the Council of Elders, he gave up power in June 1881, five months before the two-year term was due to end.[3]

Cooperation between the two royal families was strengthened in foreign policy matters, because the two *Almamis* habitually signed treaties and correspondence with the European powers together. Despite the dominance of the *Soriya* party under Ibrahima Sori Dongolfella, the visiting European envoys Bayol, Noirot, Plat and Briquelot noted that relations between the two royal families were peaceful and cordial. At that time, the system of alternating incumbencies was considered a positive achievement of Futa Jallon's political system. The balancing act lasted until Ibrahima Sori Dongolfella died in July 1890. One thing that made it possible was that the representatives of the two families at the time remained active over a long period, calming political ambitions among potential aspirants in both families from 1873 to 1890. The success of the policy of rotation was also due to the influence of the Council of Elders. Its leader, Modi Ibrahima Diogo, was able to dominate both *Almamis*.[4] To a considerable extent, however, this cohesion within the central regime was a response to the domestic challenge the *Almamis* faced in the form of the Hubbu rebellion and the determination of the provincial chiefs to assert their independence.

## B.    The defeat of the Hubbu movement

The Hubbus had been driven out of Timbo by a coalition of the two *Almamis*. Taking refuge in the impenetrable mountains of Fitaba, they gradually reinforced their position under the leadership of Abal, son of the marabout Mamadu Juhe. Initially, the movement had been reinforced by Fodé Dramé, who left Timbo to join Abal in Fitaba. In 1865, however, Fodé Dramé began to get on Abal's nerves. So he left Fitaba to settle in Sangaran. From there, in 1875 he organized a holy war which made him ruler of the entire territory.[5] Seeing several dissident states emerging and growing stronger on the borders of Futa Jallon, the worried *Almamis* decided to smash the Hubbu rebellion.

It seemed necessary to crush the movement because the Hubbu had turned into pillaging gangs. They raided the territories of the Solimana, and attacked Jallonke and Peul communities in the province of Fodé Hadji. While his father had been known as a great cleric, Karamoko Abal was remembered historically primarily as a redoubtable warrior. Fighting numerous battles, he occupied the entire zone to the south of Fitaba forest, expanding the land under Hubbu control toward the territory of the Firiya and the Solimana.[6] Hunted down by all the region's rulers, the Hubbu ended up simply operating as robbers pillaging caravans traveling from the Upper Niger valley through Futa Jallon to Sierra Leone. The situation became so serious that, in 1872 and 1873, the governors of Freetown decided to dispatch Blyden to Falaba and Timbo to get the two regimes to cooperate more closely so as to stop the Hubbu raids, then causing considerable havoc with the colony's trade.[7]

It was easy enough for Blyden to persuade the *Almamis* of Timbo and the king of Falaba, former enemies, to join forces in an attack on the Hubbu. Still, only in 1873, well after Blyden's departure, did the *Alfaya* leader Ibrahima Sori Daara decide to organize a full-scale military campaign to destroy Boketto, the Hubbu capital. This would be a way to retrieve some prestige for the *Almamis*, whose credibility the rebellion had seriously dented. The incumbent *Almami*, Ibrahima Sori Dongolfella, however, still revered the memory of his Koranic schoolteacher Mamadu Juhe. Furthermore, the Hubbu leader Abal had been a childhood friend of his. So the help he provided for the campaign organized by Ibrahima Sori Daara was half-hearted. Oddly enough, the campaign was timed to coincide with the rainy season – an atrocious time for military maneuvers.

Ibrahima Sori Daara's army was short on provisions. Further handicapped by the rains, it was severely mauled by the forces of Abal, a courageous warrior, in the mountains of Fitaba. This was an all-out disaster for Ibrahima Sori Daara. Caught in an ambush before Boketto, he died in battle along with several of his sons and a large part of his army. Some of his followers fled in the heat of battle, leaving him defenseless. Ibrahima Sori Daara himself refused to run, considering it beneath his dignity to flee before a former subject, a rural Peul who, in his own words, owed him obeisance.[8]

This preference for death before flight in the confrontation with a former subject gives a good indication of the political and social nature of the Hubbu rebellion. Incidentally, after this defeat, the *Alfaya* party lost a great deal of prestige, and for nearly ten years the *Almamis* of Timbo were forced to give tacit recognition to the existence of the Hubbu rebels.[9] It was not until 1883 that they were able to persuade Samori, then at the peak of his power, to destroy the Hubbu fortress of Boketto. Samori was anxious at the time to ensure the safety of trade routes leading to Sierra Leone. That, after all, was where his arms supplies came from. So he organized two long campaigns, one under Kemoko Bilali, the other under Lankan Nfali.

The siege of Boketto was a difficult undertaking. The Hubbu capital was strategically located. All round it there were hills intercut with steep ravines amid thick forest vegetation. Moving through the underbrush was particularly hard because of the abundance of a thorny liana called *koyon*. The Hubbu were masters of the hilly forest terrain. They had set up a system of pillars, planks and cords for controlling passageways leading to the capital. Using it, they could shut down each entryway.

After nine months of siege, the first contingent of Samori's army, under Kemoko Bilali, pretended defeat. This was a ruse to get the Hubbu warriors to drop their guard. In fact, Kemoko Bilali was waiting for reinforcements under Lankan Nfali. When they arrived, they overwhelmed the natural fortress of Boketto with their sheer numbers. Karamoko Abal was executed, along with his generals, brothers and adult children.[10] Samori had to put parts of Karamoko Abal's corpse on public display all the way down to Sierra Leone, as a way of convincing caravan drivers that the route now really was free of Hubbu robbers. A Sierra Leonean weekly newspaper, reporting on Samori's victory, editorialized that in putting an end to the depredations of the Hubbu, Samori had guaranteed "the advancement of trade and civilization."[11]

For thirty years the Hubbu rebellion had defied the authority of the *Almamis* in Timbo. The destruction of the fortified Hubbu village in the supposedly impregnable mountains of Fitaba ended that rebellion. Because Samori left a detachment of his soldiers there, under the command of Kemoko Bilali, to maintain order until the French arrived in 1892, the Hubbu left Fitaba, scattering in several directions. Some went to Sierra Leone and other areas where they revived the movement in different forms under other leaders, all of whom had risen, like Juhe, from lowly origins.

In 1887 the *Almamis* of Timbo had to deal with more trouble. A community of disciples had grown up around the *Wali* of Gomba, Cherno Aliu. Now that community was growing stronger. Its leader, Cherno Aliu, had been born in Kollade around 1820. Like Juhe, he went to Mauritania for his Koranic education. There he became an ardent disciple of the *Shadhilia* fraternity, whose specialty was a reclusive mysticism coupled with religious incantations known as *Diarore*. Many disciples of the sect of Ali Sufi-Al Fasi, based in Fez, Morocco, were closely linked with the Hubbu movement, even if it could not be clearly ascertained that they had personal ties with Juhe.[12]

Cherno Aliu's rebellion against the *Almamis'* authority in Gomba ran along the same lines as the Hubbu rebellion in Fitaba. The *Wali* initially settled along the Futa frontier, where the Susu chiefs made him welcome. He had, after all, brought in a large number of disciples and a huge herd of cattle. Then the community started getting stronger, and the local chiefs became alarmed. All this while, the *Almamis* had been wondering how best to stop the population drain caused by Cherno Aliu's following. They wanted him back in Kebu, so they could have him, his followers and their property under their direct control.[13]

There was an insurrection, under similar circumstances, against the authority of the *Diwal* of Labé, led by Cherno Ibrahima Ndama, a disciple, like the *Wali* of Gomba, of the *Shadhilia* fraternity. From 1875, when his father, Cherno Jaw, died, Cherno Ibrahima Ndama began to show unusual religious fervor and a zealous desire to teach the young. Thanks to his reputation for holiness, he attracted numerous disciples. This turned the *Alfas* of Labé against him. They could hardly tolerate the emergence of a dissident center of political and religious authority on the borders of their province.[14]

Futa Jallon was a hotbed of deep-seated movements of political and social protest. Under the guise of religious movements, these had drawn adherents around influential marabouts. The religious leaders made a habit of moving away from the center of authority to settle in outlying areas of the kingdom, setting up autonomous communities there. Great numbers of faithful disciples from the lower social strata kept leaving Futa, aspiring to live in a community enjoying greater justice, free of exploitation by the reigning aristocracy. That aristocracy was in turn feeling the damage caused by the economic vacuum left by the exodus of the masses, free-born as well as slaves, together with their property. The impact of the Hubbu movement, incidentally, was magnified by the flight of huge numbers of slaves from Futa to the coast. Arriving there, they reinforced the Mikifore, bands of runaway slaves who had formed independent communities, and were pillaging caravans from Futa Jallon traveling in the Southern Rivers region.

The Hubbu movement hurt the central regime of the *Almamis* all the more because it was beset by two dissident movements, one in Fitaba, the other in Gomba on the border of Timbo province, the regime's capital. The rebellion weakened the central regime all the more because the Federal Assembly of Fugumba, along with various provincial chiefs eager to assert their independence from Timbo, refused to support the regime in this fight, leaving the *Almamis* to fight alone.

## C.     The provinces of Labé and Timbi assert their autonomy

One key explanation for the solidarity of the *Alfaya* and *Soriya* factions in the latter half of the nineteenth century was that the *Almamis* were concerned to counter the obvious desire of the provincial chiefs, especially the *Alfa* of Labé, to assert their independence from the central authority.

Provincial chiefs under the Futa Jallon regime had enjoyed a great deal of autonomy ever since the foundation of the kingdom. In the nineteenth century, following considerable conquests made by the provinces of Timbi and Labé in the Southern Rivers region, old autonomist tendencies intensified. The power of Labé province, for instance, was boosted by the fact that within the kingdom, the administration of each newly conquered territory was the direct prerogative of its closest province. On this head the central province of Timbo was handicapped from the start, because one of its neighbors was the powerful Manding kingdom of Solimana. Worse still, in the latter half of the nineteenth century, two new empires, that of Amadu of Segu and that of Samori, rose on its eastern flank.

Given the interplay between the ground rules and the evolving situation, the considerable expansion of Labé province, which took control of the entire Southern Rivers region plus Kaabu, led to a worsening imbalance between the capital and the province. The former remained relatively static; the latter grew in size. In their traditional rivalry, the *Soriya* and *Alfaya* factions in Timbo had lost touch with changes in the system. The *Almamis*, for instance, were no longer sure of being able to impose their protégés on provincial power structures. The *Soriya* faction dominated Labé and Timbi, while the *Alfaya* faction dominated Fugumba and Kollade.[15]

The *Almamis* found the secessionist proclivities of the *Alfa* Ibrahima, provincial chief of Labé, particularly irksome. He had remained in power almost continuously since 1840, thanks to his military skill and his territorial conquests in Niokolo and the Southern Rivers region, achieved with help from Bubakar Saada of Bundu. His province, in popular parlance, was said to make up half of Futa Jallon. Knowing how important this made him, the *Alfa* Ibrahima refused to go to Fugumba for the ceremony of investiture. Instead, it was the *Almami* himself who had to travel to Labé, Ibrahima's provincial seat, to conduct the investiture. Worse, Ibrahima constantly refused to hand over power to the *Alfaya* candidate Gassimu. He got away with his refusal, since the *Almamis* were not strong enough to get most of the provinces to respect the rule of alternating incumbencies. From 1878, the *Alfa* Ibrahima began to make it utterly plain that he was chafing to break free of the central authority in Timbo. On one point all foreign observers of the time agreed: the *Alfa* of Labé was as powerful as the *Almamis*, if not more so.[16]

In 1880, however, Ibrahima, now a very old man and wishing to keep power within his family, handed over to his eldest son Aguibu. He had twelve sons, and was anxious to avoid a succession struggle among them. He was especially concerned to prevent friction between Aguibu and his younger brother Mody Yaya, an ambitious man renowned for his military genius. In any case, Aguibu's accession in no way affected the power equation between Labé and Timbo. In fact, the rulers in Labé were even more inclined to assert their independence from the central regime.

In 1881, the powerful *Alfa* Ibrahima died. His death left a vacuum in the *Soriya* faction, which had held power in Labé for almost half a century. Now the *Almamis* saw their opportunity to get Labé to switch over gradually to the system of alternating terms of office. They took it. In 1881, for instance, *Almami* Amadu wanted the return to power of *Alfa* Gassimu, a member of the *Alfaya* faction, in place of the *Soriya* incumbent, Aguibu. Aguibu tried to hang on to power, but failed. Subsequently, *Almami* Amadu imposed two more *Alfas*, Amadu and Mamadu Aliu, one after the other, in Labé. This interference by the central authority in Labé's internal affairs was facilitated by the intensity of the internal rivalries within the *Soriya* faction ever since the death of the energetic Ibrahima. So fierce did the succession struggle become that in 1883, Aguibu, once more in power, was assassinated by his brother Mody Yaya, the powerful chief of Kade. Ibrahima Sori Dongolfella, the ruling *Almami*, refused to install Mody Yaya. For he was already alarmed by the ambitions of this brilliant warlord who had, with disconcerting ease, carved out a domain for himself on Futa Jallon's northwest frontier.[17]

Now the *Almamis* of the central regime were in a better position to bring the unruly province of Labé to heel. In 1889, for instance, *Alfa* Gassimu used force to keep Ibrahima Bassaya, installed by the *Almami* Amadu, from assuming power. The two *Almamis* immediately raised an army to support their candidate. Gassimu, driven out of Labé, was forced into exile in Khaaso. To underscore the triumph of the central authorities, all his property was confiscated, most of his supporters assassinated.[18]

The *Almamis* of Timbo faced a similar problem in the province of Timbi, which shared control over conquered lands in the Southern Rivers region with Labé. Timbi also had secessionist tendencies, and this worried the central regime's *Almamis*. But here they adopted a different strategy. At an early stage, they maneuvered to get the potentially rebellious province split into two new provinces: Timbi Tunni and Timbi Madina. When the two new provinces began squabbling over control of Kebu, the *Almamis* got an opportunity to move in to settle the dispute, following the death in 1885 of Cherno Madiu. *Almami* Amadu decreed that Kebu would belong to Timbi Madina. By that stroke he boosted the prestige of the central regime.[19]

Futa Jallon really needed to maintain maximum internal cohesion and integrity. After all, on every frontier it faced the threat of foreign invasion. To deal with that multiple threat, it had to organize itself.

### D.    Relations between Timbo and Samori

Externally, it had become indispensable for the central regime to maintain cohesion. One reason was that on its eastern frontier, two powerful rulers, Amadu and Samori, had emerged. More menacingly, in the Southern Rivers region, the British and the French were advancing in a double offensive aimed at the occupation of the region and the imposition of protectorate status on the Futa Jallon kingdom.

To the east, then, the threat came from Samori. Like Shaykh Umar, Samori had decided to construct a vast empire starting in 1860 from Wasulu on the right bank of the Niger. His aim was to recreate the grand political system of old Mali, broken down in the course of the ages. It would be a great enterprise, harbinger of peace and unification. It would establish a reign of security along all the roads leading to the ocean. Since 1876, Samori's plans had become a source of worry for the *Almamis*. This was the time when Samori started out to conquer the left-bank territories of the Niger. In 1878, Samori annexed Baleya, a territory where Futa Jallon habitually conducted slave raids. He also brought the tributary territory of Ulada under his rule. To the authorities in Timbo, these moves were profoundly disturbing. *Almami* Ibrahima Sori Dongolfella protested: in vain. For in January 1879, Samori, then at the height of his powers, invaded the province of Fodé Hadji. Timbo was forced to send envoys to Baleya to negotiate peace terms.[20]

Samori assured the envoys that his intentions toward Futa Jallon were peaceful. At that stage in the construction of his empire, he had no need to conquer the kingdom. In short, both sides could do with a compromise. Samori wanted to buy cattle from Futa Jallon to trade for arms on the coast. For their part, the *Almamis* of Timbo wanted to use this new military power to destroy the Hubbu fortress in Fitaba. So Samori's agents were free to criss-cross Futa Jallon, selling prisoners of war for cattle. The cattle were then traded for arms on the coast, where the triumph of legitimate trade now made the direct sale of slaves extremely difficult.

The fact that Hubbu robbers created a climate of insecurity on roads leading through Farana and Falaba to Sierra Leone reinforced Samori's cooperation with Futa Jallon. Initially, the *Almamis* had been justifiably upset by Samori's annexation of Ulada. But then, under the influence of a marabout from Futa Jallon called Alfa Usman, Samori's new empire had begun increasingly to take on the color of a theocracy. That made the *Almamis* feel friendlier. In 1883, Samori destroyed the Hubbu fortress in Fitaba. The *Almamis*, who had had to live with this threatening rebellion for thirty years, were delighted. Their friendship with Samori deepened.

In May and June 1885, however, two of Samori's lieutenants, Lankan Nfali and Kemoko Bilali, occupied Tambaka and Tamiso. They claimed that they had acted to ensure the safety of routes between the Upper Niger valley and Sierra Leone; and the emperor of Wasulu, Samori, kept sending messages of friendship to Timbo. But the Futa Jallon authorities were not reassured. The invasion had created a siege mentality among them. Soon, though, Samori's troops pulled out, to the relief of the Futa authorities. Not only did Samori want to maintain good relations with Timbo; he also needed those troops to reinforce his army. He was planning battles against Sikasso and the French forces on the Upper Niger river.

In 1886, the specter of an invasion rose again to worry the Futa Jallon regime in Timbo when Samori signed a pact with the French. The two *Almamis*, suing for peace, assured Samori that they would cooperate with him to keep all routes leading from the Upper Niger valley through Limba and Port Loko open and safe. Samori at this point stationed two of his generals between his territory and the eastern frontier of Futa Jallon, with instructions to protect caravans. Furthermore, that same year, when the *Almami* Amadu asked Samori to force Sahan Fodé of Tamiso to accept the authority of Timbo, Samori complied. He now considered safety along the trade routes a priority, as he prepared to march against Tieba and Sikasso.[21] Various factors, in short, helped to strengthen the objective alliance between the *Almamis* of Timbo and Samori. It lasted until 1893, when the two states ceased to have a common frontier, because French colonial power had thrust itself between them. For a while, the *Almamis* had attempted to strengthen their ties with the British colony of Sierra Leone, hoping thereby to safeguard the autonomy of their kingdom.

### E.     Relations between Timbo and the British

European penetration, especially that of the British and the French, was a major concern of the *Almamis* of Timbo. At this juncture in the latter half of the nineteenth century, colonial conquest had become a fact of life for most states in Senegambia and the Sudan. The *Almamis* kept in close touch with the march of the conquering European armies around Futa Jallon. As long as feasible, they maintained their autonomy by playing off the French against the British. For that reason Futa Jallon went through a long respite, lasting until the 1890s, during which the British had more pressing business elsewhere, and the French were preoccupied with plans to conquer the Niger basin from source to mouth. It was around this major objective that the French and the British clashed a number of times from 1870 to 1890 in Futa Jallon. All this while, the *Almamis* tightened their cohesion in foreign policy matters. In this their aim was to postpone their defeat as long as possible, since it was clear that conquest had become inevitable.

In 1866, Kennedy, who had already served as Governor of the British colony of Sierra Leone, returned for another term. He immediately initiated a policy aimed at consolidating British influence on the coast while developing cordial relationships with populations in the hinterland, as a way of promoting trade in the colony. This policy required that routes leading to Futa Jallon and the Upper Niger valley be kept secure, so as to draw trade away from the Rio Nunez and Rio Pongo valleys, now under French control. Twice in 1869, Kennedy had helped to underwrite trips by Winwood Read to Falaba, aimed at locating the sources of the Niger River and prospecting rich gold and copper deposits at Sangaran and Bure. One result of Read's trips was a firmer determination on the part of Governor Kennedy to use customary bribes paid to rulers of various neighboring kingdoms as trade incentives, instead of using brute force, as the French were then doing in their colony of Senegal.

The policy was set in motion in 1871 through the appointment of an agent in charge of security services for foreign traders in Freetown. This was followed in 1872 by the appointment of Mohamed Sanussi, an Aku creole educated in Futa Jallon, as the government's official Arabic translator. Next came the appointment of Blyden as the colonial agent for hinterland affairs. The purpose of all these measures was to neutralize the opposition of the Temne population in Port Loko. They had acted in the past as intermediaries with proprietary rights over trade between Freetown and the populations in the Upper Niger valley, and they wanted to keep their privileges. In a similar vein, Blyden was sent to Falaba in 1872 to persuade the king of Solimana to make peace with his traditional enemy, the *Almami* of Timbo, so that together they could stop the pillaging Hubbu rebels from hijacking caravans heading for the colony.[22]

In 1872, Kennedy was replaced as governor by John Pope Hennessy. Hennessy continued the policy of good neighborliness by sending a mission to Kankan. More importantly, he sent Blyden to Timbo in February 1873 to discuss means for dealing with the Hubbu threat. Hennessy increased customary payments to the Susu, Temne and Limba chiefs with domains straddling the trade routes, to incite them to ensure the safety of traders to and from Futa Jallon. In Timbo, the two *Almamis* gave Blyden's mission a cordial reception, signing the kingdom's first written trade and friendship agreement with a European power. Given the importance of Futa Jallon as a passageway to the Sudan, Blyden agreed to the payment to the *Almamis* of Timbo of an annual sum of £100 sterling. In the absence of a British Resident Representative at Timbo, however, the Blyden mission achieved very little, because Britain was not prepared to assume territorial responsibilities in this region. So once Hennessy and Blyden were gone from the scene, contacts between Timbo and Freetown became increasingly infrequent. For nearly eight years the governors of Sierra Leone failed to pay the agreed emoluments to the *Almamis*. And the *Almami* Ibrahima Sori Dongolfella showed his displeasure by freezing official contacts with Freetown for four years, starting in 1877.

In any case, in 1873 the Freetown market began a steep decline. One reason was a drop in palm oil prices; a second was the weak policy of paying customary fees to chiefs in the hinterland; a third was that the tax policy introduced by Pope Hennessy in 1872 proved disastrous. Hennessy had abolished taxes on all imported products except alcohol, tobacco, and firearms. On the other hand, he had imposed stiff surcharges on export produce from the hinterland. From 1872 to 1877, Futa Jallon traders reacted by diverting export produce such as hides to French trading posts in the Southern Rivers region, while continuing to sell between 3,000 and 4,000 head of cattle for local consumption in Freetown.[23] So for the first time in a quarter of a century, Freetown registered a sizable deficit. The economic recession was aggravated by the instability of the local colonial establishment. From 1873 to 1875, Sierra Leone had no fewer than six governors. Under such circumstances, the policy of penetration into the hinterland, initiated by Kennedy and continued by Hennessy, was suspended.

In July 1875 Rowe, the new governor, reactivated this policy. Moving carefully, he enticed key Muslim dignitaries to Freetown, and sent presents to Ahmadu, the Sultan of Segu. He even thought of constructing a rail link with Timbo. Until 1879, however, no official contacts were established with Timbo. For since 1860 the authorities in Freetown had come to consider the road through Falabaa a better route for penetrating into the Malian hinterland than the one through Timbo.[24] Meanwhile, the Hubbus had been attacking trading caravans; Samori and Fodé Dramé had been conducting wars of conquest; the Futa Jallon regime was at loggerheads with Dingiray; and turmoil in Temne territory had led to the closing of the road to Rokel. The result of all this was an unprecedented 80 percent decrease in Freetown's volume of trade. The situation forced Governor Rowe to send two Manding officials representing the government of Sierra Leone to the *Almami* Amadu of Futa Jallon, Fodé Dramé, Samori, Agibu, and even Abal, the Hubbu leader. Their mission was to coax these rulers into restoring a climate of peace conducive to the development of trade in the colony.

The Alfaya were rather fond of the British. So the *Almami* Amadu gave the envoys from Freetown a warm welcome. In an unprecedented move, he even gave them leave to continue their embassy beyond the Futa Jallon frontiers. In September 1880 the envoys returned to Freetown, having failed, on account of warfare in their region, to meet Abal and Fodé Dramé. Even so, trade began to pick up again. Rubber exports, for instance, rose from 39,220 tonnes in 1879 to 829,636 tonnes in 1880.[25]

Apart from sparking a trade recovery in Freetown, Rowe worked with remarkable determination to revitalize the energetic Kennedy's policy of penetration into the hinterland as a response to French efforts to divert trade from the Niger to the colony of Senegal. On his advice, the British Colonial Office sent the Gouldsbury mission to the region. Its assignment was to explore the Gambia River from the estuary at Bathurst to its source, and then to work its way through Futa Jallon and Solimana to Freetown, from where it would return to Gambia. After numerous discussions, Gouldsbury signed a treaty with the *Almami* Ibrahima Dongolfella on 30 March 1881. The new treaty confirmed the previous one signed by Blyden, in the sense that it was designed to promote trade between Freetown and the countries beyond Futa Jallon. Gouldsbury, however, found Rowe's initiative somewhat irritating. He argued against the idea of the Gambia becoming a prime trade route to Futa Jallon and Mali. And he dismissed the idea that the West African interior was fabulously wealthy.

One outcome of the mission was to call the attention of the Freetown authorities to the need to honor the 1873 treaty. Specifically, this meant paying the agreed customary fees to the *Almamis* in Timbo. An even more important result was that it sharpened French desire to take control of the region. The French feared, in effect, that renewed British diplomatic activity meant that the British were ready to occupy Futa Jallon. So they sent a mission under Bayol in the same year, intensifying their rivalry with the British. It was this rivalry that enabled the *Almamis* to play one power off against the other, thus, for a time at least, preserving their autonomy.[26]

The *Almamis*, incidentally, preferred trading with the British in Freetown, partly, no doubt, because British plans for territorial conquest in the region were clearly limited. But the 1883 agreement reduced British opportunities for expansion toward Futa Jallon. Opportunities for the French, on the other hand, increased. And when they occupied Bamako that same year, the British had to focus their attention on the Niger, neglecting Timbo as a consequence. Top priority was given to the route from Falaba to the Sudan, especially since Samori, having made the eastern trade routes safe again following the defeat of the Hubbu rebels, was now looking toward Freetown in an effort to develop trading links and break through the French cordon surrounding him.[27]

Rowe did not show renewed interest in Futa Jallon until 1887. Even then, he simply asked the *Almami* to help ensure safe travel along the Port Loko–Falaba routes, the main British focus at the time. Rowe paid Amadu the customary fees. He also ordered his representatives to use this eastern route from then on, in order to induce caravans from Futa Jallon to follow suit. But at this juncture the British Colonial Office in London revised its Futa Jallon policy, tacitly acknowledging the validity of Bayol's treaty. In short, the British now saw Futa Jallon as a French protectorate.

The policy change in London upset the colonial authorities in Freetown. Considering the Futa region economically promising, they continued to try to strengthen British influence at Timbo. The *Almamis*, for their part, were keen to maintain contact with Freetown. They found the British focus on trade reassuring, and were pleased to note that they showed no urgent desire to annex Futa Jallon territory. In fact, in order to maintain the British presence as a counterpoise to the more warlike French, the *Almamis* continued for a long time to argue that the treaty of Bayol did not imply a surrender of their country to France. The argument was perfectly correct.

Still, Rowe's hands were tied. The trade treaties signed by Blyden and Gouldsbury in 1873 and 1881 were too vaguely worded to enable him to make a case for British rights in Futa Jallon. More to the point, the British government was completely against any territorial expansion in the region.

Rowe did propose that the Colonial Office send Major Festing on a mission to Samori. The mission would travel through Timbo, and ask the *Almamis* not to cede their country to any European power without British approval. The Colonial Office turned down the proposition.

The main concern of the British government was to respect the status quo at a time when preparations were afoot for comprehensive negotiations aimed at fixing boundaries between British and French possessions in West Africa, Futa Jallon included. Hence the British rejection of Rowe's suggestion. What Britain officially demanded from France was that it protect British trading interests in Futa Jallon, on account of the two British treaties antedating Bayol's treaty.[28]

Meanwhile, Samori, increasingly busy putting down internal revolts, failed to deliver the expected gains in trade with Sierra Leone. This promptly led to a downgrading of the Upper Niger in Freetown's plans. Now Governor Hay and the colonial merchants in Sierra Leone became seriously worried about possible French restrictions on British trade in Futa Jallon. So Hay reopened the Great Scarcies route to Futa. He then sent the head of the Muslim community in Freetown, *Almami* Benaka, to Tambaka and Tamiso in December 1888, to negotiate treaties with chiefs there. But the signature of the comprehensive accord of 10 August 1889, including the recognition of Futa Jallon as a French protectorate, meant that all this work was wasted.[29]

For various reasons related to the balance of diplomatic power in Europe and the interests at stake in West Africa, the British had to give up their territorial claims in Futa Jallon. Another reason for the British withdrawal was that France had established firm footholds in the Southern Rivers region, Senegal, and the Sudan. From these bases it had surrounded Futa Jallon quite early, blocking future possibilities of British involvement. In short, France had pursued a systematic policy of colonial conquest in Senegambia and the Sudan right from the beginning of the nineteenth century. From the *Almamis'* point of view, that made them the principal threat to the territorial integrity of their kingdom, Futa Jallon.

### F.    Relations between Timbo and the French

In 1867 the French built forts at Boké, Boffa, and Benty in Rio Nunez, Rio Pongo, and Mellakure. These moves signaled their determination to establish a foothold in the Southern Rivers region. The forts constituted a solid base from which they could move on to conquer Futa Jallon. That gave the French a head start on their British rivals. Pending the link-up of the Sudan and the Southern Rivers region through Futa Jallon, however, the main French concern was to conquer the Upper Senegal and Niger valleys. So up until 1890, all they did was to keep the *Almamis* of Timbo under intense diplomatic pressure. The aim of this pressure was to secure protectorate rights over Futa Jallon for France, thus forestalling British claims.

In the period from 1867 to 1876, France went into a withdrawal phase. Furthermore, the French authorities wished to focus on maintaining footholds already secured in the colony of Senegal. Relations between France and Futa Jallon were therefore substantially limited to contacts between French officials in the Southern Rivers region and representatives of the *Almamis* or the provincial chiefs of Labé and Timbi resident at Boké, Boffa, and Benty. At this point, Governor Valière saw no urgent need to invade Futa Jallon. He reasoned that the key to the control of the Senegambian region lay not in the Futa Jallon plateau, at the source of the Gambia and Senegal Rivers, but in coastal Saint-Louis and Bathurst, at the mouths of the two rivers.[30] So France concentrated on the Saint-Louis–Bathurst axis, defining the area that later became the Peanut Basin. Then came the boom in rubber production, with Futa Jallon as leading supplier. Private sector interest, in particular among the six French trading companies established in Freetown, grew. An example was the Marseille-based firm of C.A. Verminck, which was on good terms with the *Almamis*. Without informing the government of Sierra Leone, it financed a trip by Zweifel and Moustier in July 1879 to explore the source of the Niger and return through Futa Jallon.

Because the Hubbu rebellion was at its height at the time, the Zweifel–Moustier expedition failed. It was followed by another expedition, under Aimé Olivier, a controversial figure notorious for his nationalistic and personal ambitions. Olivier was both a trader and an engineer. A son-in-law of J.B. Pastré, he also became the director of a Marseille company with subsidiary posts in Casamance, Rio Kasini, Rio Grande, and Mellakure.

Aimé Olivier considered private enterprise the only way to promote French national interests. And he thought the best route to the Niger River lay through Futa Jallon. Having established cordial ties with Alfa Ibrahima, provincial chief of Labé, he dreamed of laying a railway line from the coast through Futa Jallon to the Niger. He considered Futa Jallon well suited to serve as a base for the advancement of western civilization in West Africa, because its upland location gave it a fine climate, while the kingdom itself had a solid political and social organization.[31]

In April 1880, however, the *Almami* Ibrahima Sori Dongolfella, irritated with the French Commandant at Boké, detained the protégé of Alfa Ibrahima of Labé. Then on 2 June 1880, eager to get rid of his unwanted guest, the *Almami* agreed to the construction of a railroad, but only on condition that it stop short of Timbo. And he still prevented Olivier from traveling beyond Futa Jallon. On 10 July 1881, Olivier sent Goboriaud and Ansaldi to get Amadu to confirm the railroad construction permit. At the same time, he sought support for his project from the French government. But France in the 1880s showed little interest in expanding toward Futa Jallon. The conquest of the Sudan had become its top priority, and it preferred to focus on the Upper Senegal valley as the best access route.

Aimé Olivier spent his time tirelessly repeating his conviction that the key to control of the Sudan lay in Futa Jallon. It was a waste of effort; the French authorities had decided he was not trustworthy. To make matters worse, Portugal accorded Olivier the title of Count, fueling French suspicions that he was a Portuguese agent. The *Almami* Ibrahima Dongolfella also challenged the validity of the treaty giving Olivier permission to construct his railroad across Futa Jallon.[32]

But following the signature of the 1881 treaty by Gouldsbury and the *Almamis*, France was quickly shaken out of its indifference toward Futa Jallon. Gouldsbury's mission, it turned out, bore ironic fruit: it whetted France's appetite for territorial conquest. Jauréguiberry, in a dramatic address to the Senate, urged the French not to forget that the British were their implacable rivals, that they were constantly seeking ways to diminish French influence in Senegal, and that they were determined at all costs to push on to the Niger before the French. In March 1881, a mission was hastily organized under Bayol and Noirot. Its mandate: to conclude protectorate treaties with Futa Jallon's rulers, and to explore Bambuk and the source of the River Niger.

In other words, this mission was intended partly to head off British attempts to connect their territories in the Gambia and Sierra Leone, and partly to give trade in Senegal and the Southern Rivers region, formerly so active, a new lease of life.[33] Bayol had difficulty convincing the *Almamis* in Timbo that his mission was not the thin end of the wedge of a military invasion. But he finally persuaded them to sign two documents. The first recognized French suzerainty over the Southern Rivers from Rio Kasini to Mellakure. The second, at least according to the French version of the treaty, placed Futa Jallon under exclusive French protection, in return for an annual payment to be shared out between its various chiefs.

The *Almamis* refused Bayol permission to proceed to the source of the Niger. So he returned to Senegal through Bambuk. Along the way he signed seven treaties with regional chiefs guaranteeing the opening of the north road linking Futa Jallon with French posts in Senegal. Now Bayol was convinced that British influence had been definitively erased, making Futa Jallon exclusively French. But there was a problem. The new treaty, quite apart from violating the older one concluded by Gouldsbury, was based on a profound misunderstanding: the two sides interpreted the concept of a

Plate 11 The Mission welcomed at Fugumba, Futa Jallon (from Gallieni, *Deux campagnes au Soudan Français, 1886 1888*. Paris: Librairie Hachette, 1891, p. 507)

protectorate quite differently. In the *Almamis'* version, written in Arabic, the treaty was about nothing more than an alliance between two countries. It said nothing whatsoever about exclusive trading rights for France.

That the *Almamis* were determined to remain independent was made perfectly clear in a phrase the *Almami* Amadu kept repeating throughout the negotiations: Futa belonged to the Peul, as France belonged to the French, and that was the way things ought to remain. In any case, a Futa Jallon delegation led by Mamadou Saïdu received the red carpet treatment in Paris. But the treaty itself was not published until 1885, because France wanted to avoid violating existing agreements with Britain concerning the acquisition of territory in this region.[34]

On 28 June 1882, after a year of difficult negotiations, Britain and France signed an agreement setting down a line between the Mellakure and the Great Scarcies rivers as their common boundary. This put the French in a better position to expand toward Futa Jallon. Still, they continued to think of that possibility not as a goal in its own right, but as a precaution against British expansion from Sierra Leone into the Upper Niger valley.

Ever since the British declared the Lower Niger basin their protectorate,

Plate 12 The *Almami* Ibrahima's warriors on parade (from Gallieni, *Deux campagnes au Soudan Français, 1886–1888.* Paris: Librairie Hachette, 1891, p. 568)

French colonial officials had known that the British could outpace them in the race to the Sudanese heartland. They had therefore made the creation of an Upper Senegal–Niger axis their top priority.[35] Still, they did not completely overlook Futa Jallon. The Franco–Portuguese agreement of 12 May 1886, for instance, recognized French protectorate rights over Futa Jallon. France, in short, had already begun surrounding the British possessions in Gambia and Sierra Leone, positioning itself advantageously for future boundary demarcation exercises. In the period from 1886 to 1890, when the Southern Rivers colony was established, the responsibility for initiating relations with the Futa Jallon regime shifted more toward the French military authorities in the Sudan, since they were more securely established than the minor posts on the coast.[36]

As a matter of fact, Gallieni had contacted the Futa Jallon authorities as early as the 1886–7 campaign against Mamadu Lamin. At that time, he wanted to block any attempt by the latter to recruit fighters there. And he had obtained support from the Alfa of Labé, who had pledged to block every escape route left open to the marabout. At this point Gallieni advocated a suspension of the French expansionist drive to the east beyond Bamako. Instead, he suggested concentrating on the southern axis, in the direction of the Southern Rivers and Futa Jallon. He thought this would lead to the creation of a unified colonial possession embracing the Southern Rivers region as well as the Upper Senegal and Upper Niger valleys, with Timbo as capital.[37] In pursuit of this dream, Gallieni recommended that a fort be built at Siguiri, and that direct communications be established between the Sudan and the Southern Rivers region through Futa Jallon. He accordingly tried to persuade the *Almamis* that France desired only peace, and that it could protect their kingdom against Samori, should he decide to invade it.

The Plat mission of December 1887 set out to find the best route from the Sudan to the coast. A second assignment was to select a site for a French post in Futa Jallon. This time, Plat forced the *Almamis* to sign a treaty (30 March 1888) making Futa Jallon an exclusive French protectorate while exempting French traders from all duties and abolishing customary fees established in the Bayol treaty of 1881. *Almami* Ibrahima Sori signed the treaty under duress. France was then putting the Senegambian and Sudanese states under unprecedented military pressure, and he feared the alternative to an agreement would be an invasion. Incidentally, Plat faced enormous difficulties during this trip, because the Timbo authorities were against any surrender of their sovereignty. On his return, in any case, Plat recommended a military invasion as a means to break down the *Almamis*' resistance.

In 1888 the French sent another mission, under Levasseur. Assigned to explore the northern reaches of Futa Jallon, it also received a cold reception from the *Alfa* of Labé, who was hostile to the French presence in the Firdu area and in the tributary states of the Upper Casamance valley. And when Captain Audéoud, at the head of 150 soldiers, tried to open a road from Siguiri to Benty as part of a linkage between the Upper Niger valley and the Southern Rivers region through Futa Jallon, the reigning *Almami* was enraged. Ibrahima Sori Dongolfella, while avoiding a head-on clash, did what he could to hasten the departure of the French column. Its passage was seen as preparatory to a major French invasion of Futa Jallon.[38]

Meanwhile, in France, the government had, in February 1888, appointed La Porte as Under-Secretary of State for the Colonies, in place of Etienne. The new appointment meant a considerable change in the official attitude to Gallieni's proposal for a military occupation of Futa Jallon. In September 1888, Bayol took the initiative, asking the commanding officer at Boké to pay the suspended customary fees to the *Almamis*, while asking Paris not to ratify Plat's treaty. Bayol found Gallieni's interference in his jurisdiction insulting. He also feared it might provoke a fruitless war that would merely disturb trade in the Southern Rivers region. In addition, he was sensitive to the *Almamis*' dislike of the abolition of customary payments, and their hostility to the occupation of their country in any form. Confirmation for this new policy came in October 1888, in the form of the terms of reference given to the new Commandant of French forces in the Sudan, Archinard. He was ordered to demonstrate France's peaceful intentions to the *Almamis*. The French therefore dispatched a mission under Briquelot to Timbo. Its assignment was to negotiate the opening of a direct route from the Southern Rivers region through Futa Jallon to the Upper Niger valley. Such a route would enable France to consolidate its conquests in the Sudan while developing agricultural production there. Briquelot, escorted by a light detachment, left Dubreka in December 1888 for Siguiri. But his repeated protestations of France's peaceful and friendly intentions notwithstanding, his reception at Timbo was chilly.

The *Almamis* were decidedly unfriendly. Amadu, whose partiality to the British was no secret, was particularly hostile. The Plat treaty had angered them; Audéoud's military expedition had enraged them; and they were seriously worried by French military activities along the northern and eastern borders of their kingdom, in areas traditionally subordinate to Futa Jallon. Above all, they resented French troops passing through their country. They insisted that, in future, French troops should use a route far to the south if they wished to move from Siguiri and Benty. Their suspicions were strengthened when, in January 1889, a detachment of riflemen under Lieutenant Buat arrived from Siguiri to give Briquelot fresh orders.

On all points, the *Almamis* preferred dealing with the French commanding officer at Boké instead of the one in the Sudan. For news of the extraordinary violence of the French invasion there had reached them in Timbo. Furthermore, the *Almamis* took pains to point out, quite rightly, that their agreement with Bayol was a pact between allies, not that Futa Jallon should become a French protectorate.

Needless to say, Archinard and Briquelot blamed the failure of their mission on the British, who supposedly persuaded the *Almamis* that the French were out to conquer their country. Archinard reacted by planning a policy to encircle Futa Jallon, in such a way as to reduce problems likely to arise in the conquest of this highland plateau, where resistance would be easier to organize than in the Sudanese savanna, where cannon fire was tellingly effective.

French occupation of the territory around the Futa Jallon plateau eliminated all traces of British influence at Timbo. It also put France in an excellent position to impose a military solution, if necessary. The 1889 treaty, in which Samori ceded all land on the left bank south of Tinkiso to France, was part of this scheme. It also underscored Archinard's primary focus on the conquest of the Senegal and Niger basins, and on the drive toward Segu and Timbuktu. In the same vein, the construction in April

1889 of a French post at Kurusa intensified French pressure on Futa Jallon. Now the frightened *Almamis* tried different diplomatic approaches, hoping to reduce the potential for a serious clash with France. One such ploy involved getting the French to put down the revived Hubbu rebellion at various locations in the kingdom, on condition that French troops stayed outside Futa Jallon.[39]

Meanwhile, in May 1889, Etienne returned to the Colonial Office. His reappointment meant a revival of Gallicni's scheme, centered on the need to occupy Futa Jallon to prevent all possibility of British interference as well as to guarantee continued French advances in the Southern Rivers region and the Sudan. The scheme called for the immediate occupation of Futa Jallon. France would then appoint a Resident Representative at Timbo, and establish a military post to guarantee security on the region's roads. The French Minister of Foreign Affairs, however, blocked ratification of the Plat treaty. He also opposed any immediate military action in Futa Jallon that might complicate ongoing negotiations with the British aimed at an amicable delimitation of frontiers between French and British conquests in West Africa. Such French scruples turned out to be pointless. For by the end of 1888, the British government was practically resigned to Futa Jallon becoming a French protectorate. Its sole interest, therefore, was in obtaining guarantees of security and freedom for British trading concerns in the region.

In the event, the 10 August 1889 treaty satisfied most French claims. It confirmed the boundaries established in the 28 June 1882 treaty, fixing a frontier between the Mellakure and the Great Scarcies rivers, extended into the hinterland in such a way that the Bena, the Tamiso, Futa Jallon, and the Hubbu territory fell under French control. An appendix stipulated a frontier so drawn as to give France a useable road linking the Mellakure and Upper Niger valleys through southern Futa Jallon. This clause, which Archinard immediately recommended, testified to the robust refusal of the *Almamis* to let French troops pass through Futa Jallon, where the French did not exercise effective authority.

Britain kept Tambaka, Limba, and Solimana. On balance, France had good cause for satisfaction, even if the agreement did not quite eliminate all possible causes of friction between the two powers over Futa Jallon. Admittedly, in addition, it also left Britain room to expand north of Liberia and toward the source of the Niger River through Falaba.[40] Now France had to assert its authority over Futa Jallon. The *Almamis*, opposed to the occupation of their country in any form, were bound to resist. To break down their resistance, France would have to intensify its diplomatic and military pressure on them.

# 18    Bokar Biro and the conquest of Futa Jallon

In August 1889 France, having shaken off the diplomatic challenge from its rival the British, set out resolutely to implement a policy of peaceful expansion in Futa Jallon. It pursued this policy into the early months of 1896. At the same time, however, France worked to take control of all territories bordering on the kingdom, encircling it and applying constant pressure designed to bring the *Almamis*, by gradual stages, to submit to French authority.

This policy meant a relaxation of military pressure. The two *Almamis*, Amadu of the *Alfaya* faction and Bokar Biro of the *Soriya*, took advantage of the lull to resist French demands. They were thus able, through a vigorous diplomatic counter-offensive, to maintain their independence as long as was feasible. As from 1896, however, France decided to use armed force to push through its program. This decision coincided with a serious political and social crisis in Futa Jallon. This crisis prevented the kingdom from mounting a durable resistance to colonial conquest.

Bokar Biro, strongman of the *Soriya* faction, came to power in 1890. From the moment of his accession, he set about establishing a centralized, unified, and authoritarian regime. His efforts aroused opposition from *Alfaya* and *Soriya* candidates for the office of *Almami*, as well as the hostility of the principal provincial chiefs, namely those of Labé, Timbi, and Fugumba, keen to safeguard their autonomy. And all of Bokar Biro's opponents anxious to preserve their privileges turned pointedly to France, which was just then putting the finishing touches to its encirclement of Futa Jallon, having taken control of the Sudan, Senegal, and French Guinea. When the *Almami* Amadu died in April 1896, France took advantage of the ensuing succession crisis to widen divisions in the ruling class. The policy culminated in a military victory at Poredaka on 14 November 1896. Left alone with his followers to face French forces supported by all those opposed to the rise of a single powerful central regime at Timbo, Bokar Biro was defeated. The fall of Timbo accelerated the occupation of Futa Jallon. French control over most of Senegambia was now complete.

284

## A.       French Diplomatic pressure in Futa Jallon

The Anglo–French agreement of 10 August 1889 designated Futa Jallon as a French protectorate. After it had been signed, France decided to drop Gallieni's aggressive policy. Simultaneously, it made efforts to calm the fears of the *Almamis* at Timbo, which had been aroused by the Plat mission in 1888. De Beckman, the new administrator at Dubreka, was given special orders to assure the *Almamis* that France's intentions were solely peaceful, and that the French were primarily interested in maintaining friendly diplomatic and profitable trading relations with Futa Jallon. France pursued this so-called peace policy until 1896. For once Britain had recognized French rights over Futa Jallon, there was no need for an immediate military occupation. Besides, any use of force at the time might have created too many military fronts, quite apart from disturbing trade in the Southern Rivers region, where commercial interests predominated, all to no useful purpose. Furthermore, the conquest of the Sudan had been a costly enterprise, calling forth sharp criticism from the French parliament. Still, the so-called peace policy ran parallel to a continuous campaign of encirclement in which the French cut off outlying areas of the kingdom. The *Almamis* were meanwhile subjected to systematic, diplomatic pressure, designed to induce them, step by step, to surrender their prerogatives to France. The *Almamis* Amadu and Bokar Biro, far from remaining passive under this French onslaught, mounted a vigorous counter-offensive in which they spared no pains to point out that the Bayol treaty was nothing more than a friendly pact between two sovereign nations. To give substance to their assertions, the *Almamis* continued to develop their commercial and political relations with the British in Freetown, as a counterweight to the French presence. Better still, they provided logistical support for Samori's resistance movement, used the alternating-terms arrangement under which the Timbo regime operated as an excuse to slide out of inconvenient commitments, and played the French authorities in the Sudan, Senegal, and Guinea off one against the other, thus preserving their country's independence as long as possible.

From 1889, the French placed the protectorate of Futa Jallon under the jurisdiction of the new Lieutenant-Governor of the Southern Rivers region. This transfer to a civilian administration was calculated to calm the fears of the *Almamis*, who had naturally found the aggressive policies of the military administrations operating along their frontiers from the Sudan and Senegal alarming. From the beginning, however, relationships between France and Futa Jallon were based on a serious misunderstanding caused by totally divergent interpretations of the Bayol treaty of 1881. The

*Almamis* saw the treaty primarily as a trade and friendship pact between two sovereign nations. The French interpreted it as giving them the right to treat Futa Jallon as their protectorate, including a takeover of the country whenever they decided to do so. Under these circumstances, whenever the French shifted from the seductive tactics of the so-called peace policy to adopt a more threatening posture, the *Almamis* of Timbo reacted promptly to safeguard the integrity of their country.

A constant refrain of the *Almami* Ibrahima Sori Dongolfella was that Futa belonged to the Peul just as France belonged to the French. Moreover, in December 1889, the *Almami* Amadu decreed a boycott of French traders because for two years the French authorities in Conakry had failed to pay the agreed fees, and above all because French troops from the Upper Niger command had cut communication lines between Futa Jallon and Samori's territories. At this point the French sent a mission to Timbo at the prompting of the powerful Marseille-based trading firm, the Compagnie Fançaise d'Afrique occidentale. But it failed to calm the *Almamis'* suspicions. In fact, the *Almamis* turned more and more toward other Senegambian and Sudanese rulers, trying to rally support for a struggle against French imperialism. For instance, they gave serious thought to the possibility of occupying Kurusa, and of harassing French rear bases in the Sudan. In March and April 1890, they requested arms and ammunition from the British in Freetown. But the British had officially recognized Futa Jallon as a French protectorate. They therefore refused to provide logistical support for the *Almamis*. Despite this refusal, the *Almamis* continued trying to play off the British against the French. Thus they maintained trading and political contacts with Freetown, in an attempt to counterbalance French pressure on their country.

France found the intensity of trading relations between Freetown and Futa Jallon a source of constant worry. In February and June 1890, it sent a protest on the issue to London. The British gave a robust response, pointing out that their contacts with Futa Jallon were purely commercial, and that the treaties they had signed in 1873 and 1881, antedating the 1889 agreement, entitled them to such relations. The French then evaded any discussion of the fundamental issue of British trading rights in Futa Jallon until 1893. Then, once they knew for certain that trade from Futa Jallon had effectively been rechanneled toward the Southern Rivers, they argued strongly that since Futa Jallon was now a French protectorate, the British treaties of 1873 and 1881 were null and void. Further, on 21 January 1895, France arranged to have a 7 percent tax imposed on produce exported from Futa Jallon to the British colony of Sierra Leone. The new tax narrowed opportunities for continued relations between Timbo and Freetown still further. In September 1895, Amadu Wakka was sent to Timbo to tell the

*Almamis* that no more customary payments would be forthcoming, and that they were forbidden to buy arms in Freetown. But despite the existence of a pact between the colonial powers, the *Almamis*, especially Bokar Biro, continued to hope that contacts with Freetown might help them break out of French encirclement, an increasingly palpable reality.[1] During this period, France was more concerned with the support the *Almamis* were still giving to Samori's resistance effort in the Upper Niger valley.

The *Almamis* had originally taken fright at the dizzying speed with which Samori expanded his empire. But as his campaigns became focused on resistance against the French for the preservation of Futa Jallon independence, they warmed to him. They thus allowed Soriba, one of Samori's lieutenants, to quarter his troops in the province of Fodé Hajji, from where he harassed French rear bases in the Sudan. Furthermore, when Soriba's troops invaded Dingiray in June 1891, Amadu went along with them. Unfortunately for him, the French lieutenant Maritz defeated Soriba. The latter was therefore forced to flee with his troops to the right bank of the Niger. This made direct communications between Samori and Futa Jallon considerably more difficult. But it did not stop Bokar Biro from working hard from 1891 to 1893 to resupply Samori with modern weapons. In 1893, however, the French built military posts at Hermakono and Farana, putting an end to all communications between the two kingdoms.[2] To deal with the issue of continued relations between Futa Jallon and the British in Freetown, as well as to stop the *Almamis* supporting Samori's resistance, the French sent several missions to Timbo. Their purpose was to apply sufficient diplomatic pressure on the *Almamis* to make them agree that France had exclusive rights to the kingdom. Failing that, the French could always fall back on the use of force.

The De Beckman mission was sent in December 1891. Its arrival marked the beginning of the policy aimed at pressuring the *Almamis* to make increasingly greater concessions. De Beckman bullied Bokar Biro into recognizing the Lieutenant-Governor of the Southern Rivers region as the only official entitled to maintain official contacts with Futa Jallon. Bokar Biro was also forced to pay customary dues to the French at Dubreka. De Beckman obtained further concessions: the abolition of subcontractors' markets between Futa Jallon and the Southern Rivers region, and the halting of all support for Samori's resistance movement.

Immediately after the mission left, however, Bokar Biro wrote to the governor of Senegal and the French Commandant in the Sudan complaining about the way De Beckman had gone about obtaining the new treaty, and thus calling into question its validity. From this point on, the *Almamis* adopted a new policy based on the deliberate exploitation of differences of opinion between the French authorities in Senegal, Guinea, and the Sudan, in the hope of preserving the independence of Futa Jallon. For instance, Bokar Biro and Amadu often cited the peaceful nature of their relations with the French authorities in Guinea when rejecting demands made by the commanding officers in the Sudan. And they used their quarrels with officers in the Sudan as excuses when refusing to meet unacceptable demands from the authorities in Guinea or Senegal. The *Almamis* were able to put this balancing act to good use until 1895, when the French set up the West African Federation, an umbrella unit under which all French posses- sions in the region were administered according to one coherent policy.[3] Furthermore, the *Almamis* used the principle of alternating terms between *Soriya* and *Alfaya* incumbents to wiggle out of commitments imposed on past incumbents by force or threats. Thus, from 1891 to 1896, Amadu and Bokar Biro kept passing the buck between them, using all possible ploys to keep France from imposing a Resident Representative in Timbo.[4]

But as from 1892, De Beckman began to play a weightier role, sustained over a long period, in the shaping of France's Futa Jallon policy. He sug- gested downgrading contacts with the central authorities in Timbo, and concentrating instead on building up alliances with the powerful provincial chiefs of Labé, Timbi Tunni, and Masi, real masters of trade routes leading to the Southern Rivers region. He also recommended the gradual dis- memberment of Futa Jallon through the slow alienation of the subject Susu states: Sukuli, Barigu, and Tene. Meanwhile, the French had occupied the Upper Niger valley, cutting off communications between Futa Jallon and Samori's territories. The French policy of encirclement notwithstanding, the *Almamis* reacted sharply to this new encroachment. They refused to supply the new French posts with cattle, and blocked the return of Manding refugees into the Ulada and Baleya districts, now fallen under French control. At this point, Archinard argued strongly for the resolution of the matter by force. But Delcassé wanted to try the dispatch of one more mission from Conakry, under a civilian, to reassure the *Almamis* that France's intentions were peaceful. The Alby mission achieved nothing, in the sense that the treaty of 23 May 1893, on balance, gave up gains already achieved in Futa Jallon. Bokar Biro and Amadu refused to give up Futa Jallon suzerainty over Kinsan; they refused to allow the settlement of a French Resident Representative in Timbo; they would not permit traders to move freely through their country. Amadu also refused to ratify previ- ous treaties signed by Bokar Biro. Further, he made profound changes in the terms of the 1881 treaty, reasserting that it was nothing more than a friendship pact. He condemned the idea of a protectorate, depriving France at a stroke of the single legal justification for its presence in Futa Jallon. Amadu was so clearly anti-French that Ballay began to appeal more often to Bokar Biro, who seemed more conciliatory. But as from July 1893, Ballay also suggested a shift from peaceful persuasion.[5] De Beckman agreed with this appraisal. He reported that during his February 1894 mission to Timbo, he had found the authorities there generally anti-French, and that the policy of conciliation was bound to prove fruitless. In May 1895, Bokar Biro decreed a boycott of French goods in retaliation against the refusal of the French Commandant in the Upper Niger valley to allow slave trading, or to return runaways who had fled in large numbers from Futa Jallon to areas recently conquered by the French. Futa Jallon authorities showed such constant hostility to the French that the Governor-General of French West Africa organized a coordinated expedition from the Sudan, Senegal, and Guinea, for the purpose of smashing their resistance. In so doing, he wished to take advantage of a deep political and social crisis in Futa Jallon, so as to make the most sparing use of France's military resources.[6]

## B.    The crunch

The profound political and social crisis at the heart of Futa Jallon was a result of several internal and external factors. Ever since the early decades of the nineteenth century, the crisis had steadily gnawed away at the country's unity. In 1896 it peaked, making it impossible for the *Almamis* to continue resisting colonial conquest much longer. Internally, the crisis was rooted in the traditional division between the *Alfaya* and the *Soriya* factions. What made it worse was that within each faction, there was an ongoing power struggle between several claimants, at the very time that Bokar Biro was trying to set up a unified power structure in Timbo. To complicate matters, the provincial chiefs of Labé, Timbi, and Fugumba, eager for greater autonomy from the central authorities, were completely against Bokar Biro's centralizing ambitions. Lastly, the crisis of the central regime rode on a deeper social crisis caused by an smoldering revolt among ordinary people and slaves. Free persons continued to move into dissident centers established by the *Wali* of Gomba and Cherno Ndama, while slaves fled in huge numbers into zones under French control. The crisis wrecking the foundations of the theocratic state of Futa Jallon was clearly nourished by French pressure on all the country's frontiers. The colonial authority also did its best to sharpen divisions within the ruling class. This combination of internal and external pressures was calculated to stampede the *Almamis* into succumbing to French colonial authority.

Internally, since 1872 the *Almamis* had been able to hold their regime together in the face of centrifugal tendencies, thanks to a balancing act. But in 1890, internal divisions surfaced between the two ruling factions, the *Alfaya* and the *Soriya*, following the death, after a long reign, of the *Almami* Ibrahima Sori Dongolfella. The sons of a former *Almami*, Umar, had been waiting for a long time to get a taste of power. Now they saw their opportunity; the competition was on. On one side of the power struggle there was Bokar Biro, the great military chief. On the other side, there was Mamadu Pate, backed by the entire aristocracy, who found his rival's characteristic drive unequivocally alarming. In the event, the Council of Elders crowned Bokar Biro's elder brother king, but then Bokar Biro assassinated him, taking power in a military coup. He then set about consolidating his personal power by appointing to high office individuals of modest social rank, including slaves, all loyal to himself. But he ran into opposition from Mody Abdoulaye, bent on avenging his maternal elder brother, the murdered Mamadu Pate. Even more determined opposition came from Amadu of the *Alfaya* faction, who favored the tradition of alternating incumbencies. So, under pressure from the Council of Elders and Alfa Ibrahima, head of the religious capital of Fugumba, Bokar yielded power to Amadu in July 1892. As a matter of fact, Bokar Biro agreed to respect the principle of alternating incumbencies only because France was putting military pressure on the Futa Jallon frontiers to force the *Almami* to stop supporting Samori's resistance movement. Bokar Biro took power once more in June 1894, at a time when France was beginning to exploit the numerous fault lines within the provincial and central power structures of the Futa Jallon ruling class. He had to cope with the hostility of most *Soriya* partisans, determined to avenge the death of Mamadu Pate. He was accused of surrounding himself with slaves and inconsequential youths. In January 1895, Cherno Cire and Modi Illiasu went to Bakel to seek French help to overthrow Bokar Biro, but without result. Meanwhile, the *Alfaya* faction had also turned against Bokar Biro for his attempt to remain in power in contravention of the principle of alternating incumbencies.

The most visible aspect of the political crisis was the open revolt of provincial chiefs increasingly alienated by the high-handed behavior of the central regime in Timbo. The opposition was led by Alfa Ibrahima of Fugumba. Normally entitled to officiate at the coronation of *Almamis*, he stood to lose his prerogatives under a unified, centralized, and authoritarian regime. But behind the scenes, the motive force of the revolt came from Yaya, the powerful *Alfa* of Labé, who dreamed of making his province independent of Timbo. He was already exploring opportunities for using French aid to counter the central regime, to eliminate his local rivals, and to maintain Labé control over the populations of Rio Nunez and Casamance, all under French rule. Bokar Biro reacted violently to all these centrifugal challenges. Sacking the chiefs of Koyin, Kebali and Fugumba, he appointed his own hangers-on in their stead. Next, he began planning to inflict severe punishment on Alfa Yaya. But the principal chiefs he had sacked united under Mody Abdoulaye, his brother, to ambush and defeat the *Almami* at the now famous battle of Bantignel, on 13 December 1895.[7]

The background was as follows: Alfa Ibrahima Fugumba, feeling his interests seriously threatened, had organized a coalition under Mody Abdoulaye with active help from Alfa Yaya, whose desire for independence was now plain. The coalition sprang into action at Bantignel on 13 December 1895, jumping Bokar Biro in a surprise attack as he was preparing to lead a military expedition north. Narrowly escaping death, he had to hide in the bush for ten days before reaching Kebu. There, with help from the alternate *Almami* Amadu, then at his resthouse, he regrouped his forces. Amadu disliked Bokar Biro's authoritarian policies, but felt even more repelled by the rebellion of provincial chiefs against the central regime. Bokar Biro hastily put together an army of 1,500 Susu soldiers from Kinsan and Sukuli. News of his comeback spread panic among his enemies, and at the battle of Petel Jiga, on 2 February 1896, he defeated them.[8] Alfa Ibrahima Fugumba, the *Soriya* leader Sori Yilili, and *Alfa* Yaya went into hiding in Labé province. Mody Abdoulaye was taken prisoner and brought to Timbo, where, on 13 February 1896, Bokar Biro made a triumphal return. Forthwith, he replaced all the chiefs opposed to his policies, and appointed Mody Saliou in place of *Alfa* Yaya. On 14 March 1896, suppressing his own sorrow, he had his second half-brother Mody Abdoulaye executed. Mody Abdoulaye had attempted to link up with the conspirators, who were now trying, from their base in Labé, to solicit French help to achieve their political aims.[9]

De Beckman had monitored events in Futa with close interest. Now he set out for Timbo, with the firm intention of installing a French military post in the Futa Jallon capital. He arrived on 18 March 1896, with a military detachment under Captain Aumar. Despite this show of French force, Bokar Biro refused steadfastly to bow to French demands. Specifically, he refused to accept a French Resident Representative at Timbo; to let the French build roads throughout the country; to give exclusive trading rights to the French; and to seek French approval before appointing provincial chiefs. But the arrival of French troops was beginning to arouse hostility among the population. To get rid of them, Bokar Biro made a show of signing a new treaty on 13 November 1896, hoping to free his hands for dealing with his internal opponents, already reaching out for foreign aid. This last De Beckman mission marked a watershed. For when, in May 1896, it became clear that Bokar Biro had not really signed the treaty, that he had no intention of traveling to Conakry, and that he was not about to deliver on any other commitment in the treaty, France fixed the end of the rainy season as the date for a final solution of the Futa Jallon problem. The decision was clear: force would be used if needed.[10] The move away from the policy of peaceful persuasion came at a time of internal upheavals which accelerated a clash between France and Futa Jallon.

In April 1896, Captain Aumar's troops withdrew to Sangoya. They moved there to spend the rainy season away from the hostile population, but their withdrawal was interpreted as a victory for Bokar Biro. And he took advantage of the circumstance to bolster his authority. He swore on the Koran to keep the French from returning to Futa Jallon as long as he lived. Matching words with deeds, he destroyed all French installations in Timbo. He deposed *Alfa* Yaya, appointing in his stead as provincial chief of Labé one Mamadu Saliu, a man known for his anti-French attitude. He split Bomboli district from the province of Timbi Tunni, attaching it to Fugumba. He encouraged the systematic spoliation of pro-French individuals. Chief among these was his cousin Sori Yilili who, in June 1896, was sent by *Alfa* Yaya and Ibrahima Fugumba to Sigiri to solicit French aid against Bokar Biro. Bokar Biro's term ended in April 1896. But that was also the time of the *Almami* Amadu's death, an event which created a political crisis. Bokar Biro now declared his wish to stay in power indefinitely. For now he no longer had as counterpart the old Amadu, who shared his hostility to the idea of colonial occupation.

Amadu's death provoked a power struggle within the *Alfaya* faction between the pro-French Umaru Bademba and his opponents, Mody Umaru and Yusuf. To achieve his goals, Bokar Biro first tried to assassinate Umaru Bademba late that April. Then he threw his support behind the opponents of Mody Umaru and Yusuf within the *Alfaya* faction. At that point the succession struggle turned into an arms race. It involved not simply the *Alfaya* and *Soriya* factions, but also internal subdivisions within each faction, since the number of would-be kings was now considerable. On 9 September 1896, Mody Umaru and Yusuf waylaid Umaru Bademba on the road to Fugumba. The incident pushed Futa Jallon to the verge of civil war. The attack by Yusuf and Mody Umaru was repelled, but then they called upon Bokar Biro for help. He stepped in, forcing Umaru Bademba to flee to Sangoya, where he asked the French for military help. Now Bokar Biro refused to hand over power to Umaru Bademba. Furthermore, he decided to tame the Council of Elders, whose members had opposed his plans to install a central regime, strong and unified, in Timbo. Meanwhile he subjected all pro-French elements to systematic reprisals. Frightened by the scale of repression, *Alfa* Yaya made repeated appeals to the French authorities at Seju, Dubreka, Conakry, and Satadugu in September and October 1896, pleading for urgent military assistance to secure the independence of Labé province from the central regime in Timbo.

The French authorities had been following the political crisis with keen interest. They were now determined to impose De Beckman as Resident Representative in Futa Jallon, arrest Bokar Biro, neutralize Bapate Yusuf and Mody Umaru, appoint Umaru Bademba as *Almami*, and proclaim Labé and Timbi independent of Timbo. To this end, French troops from the Sudan, Senegal, and Guinea were mobilized to surround Futa Jallon, ready to crush any resistance. On 3 November 1896, a column under Lieutenant Speiss, accompanied by Sori Yilili from Sigiri, as well as other troops from Sangoya and Wossu under Captains Aumar and Muller, together with Umaru Bademba, captured the town of Timbo after Bokar Biro's partisans had abandoned it. Bokar Biro tried, without success, to persuade the provincial chiefs to help him mount a resistance to the French invaders. He even appealed to the powerful *Alfa* Yaya, his sworn enemy, asking him to forget past quarrels and join him in driving out the French. On 6 November 1896, *Alfa* Ibrahima Fugumba submitted to France. Called to a council of war in Fugumba, Cherno Abdul from Massi, Cherno Ibrahima from Timbi Tunni, Alfa Usman from Kebali, Ibrahima from Koin, and Mamadu from Buria, all said farewell, one after the other, to Bokar Biro. In principle, they were supposed to go to their respective provinces to recruit soldiers for the resistance effort. In fact, none of them planned to return. Forsaken by the aristocracy, still obsessed with their own privileges, Bokar Biro, alone with his closest followers and a few soldiers from Samori's army, went to face the French forces, backed up by the coalition of *Alfaya* and *Soriya* aristocrats. On 13 November 1896, Bokar Biro, courageous to the last, rushed into certain defeat, accepting a pitched battle in which the French were able to use their artillery to wipe out the forces opposed to colonial conquest.[11]

The sight of the plain of Porédaka littered with the corpses of the most valiant Futa warriors was unforgettable. Contemplating the spectacular carnage, a poet uttered these words in remembrance of Bokar Biro, the last great *Almami*.

> Among the great of Futa, some say to you: Farewell.
> Modi says farewell, Modi Sori, son of *Almami* Bokar,
> Son of *Almami* Oumar, son of *Almami* Abdoul Gâdiri,
> Son of *Almami* Sori the Great. He said come Saturday
> on the battlefield at Porédaka, he would not flee.
>
> He kept his word.
> It was a blast of gunshot that took him away.
> And *Alfa*, son of Mother Sonna and Modi Sori,
> Son of Fici and Cherno of Kalâ. He too said come Saturday
> on the battlefield at Porédaka he would not run away.
> He too kept his word.
> It was the boom of cannon fire that finished him.
> The *Almami* Bokar Biro says farewell. Bokar Biro
> Son of *Almami* Abdoul Gâdiri, son of *Almami* Sori the Great,
> warrior who led the well filled life, Peul hero who never fled,
> and feared nothing ever. At the dawn of Porédaka
> he refused to flee. It was a blast of gunshot that ended his days.[12]

# 19    Mass resistance movements among the Joola and the Konyagi

The Joola and Konyagi peoples lived far from the main axes of colonial conquest. They were therefore practically the last groups in Senegambia to face the French. On account of their egalitarian social structures, they were able to mobilize unsuspected energies in the defense of their independence right up until the early twentieth century. The first attempts at colonial penetration into Joola territory go back to around 1850, when Bocandé built a post at Karabane to keep the British and the Portuguese out of the Lower Casamance basin. But the French first consolidated their footholds in the Middle and Upper Casamance basins, where peanut farming was a major activity. Only in the 1880s, when rubber began to attract trading companies, did they begin clamoring for the conquest of the Lower Casamance basin. The colonial regime then ran into a popular, village-based resistance movement that effectively helped the area's inhabitants retain their independence until the outbreak of World War I.

The Lower Casamance Joola, relying on the inaccessibility of their villages, refused to submit to the French authorities. The latter organized expeditions to try and subdue the Karone or Bayot communities. But the people organized their resistance village by village, refusing to cooperate with the Wolof chiefs imposed by the colonial regime, while doing their best to avoid paying taxes on rice, their staple food.

Similarly, the Konyagi, members of the Tenda group, organized a long-lasting resistance movement against the French. Until 1898, their land had been safe from invasion. But that year, the colonial regime decided to bring the Konyagi under French Guinea. The Konyagi, under Alcune, then organized a resistance movement that showed their determination not to submit to the *Alfa* of Labé, their inveterate enemy. Their overriding desire was to stay free. Only after several campaigns, notably that of 1903, did the French succeed in constructing their post at Yukunkun, a symbolic marker of their presence.

## A.    Joola resistance movements

The nomination of Emmanuel Bertrand Bocandé as Resident Representative at Karabane marked the beginning of a policy aimed at extending French influence throughout the Lower Casamance basin, as a way of keeping out the British and the Portuguese. In 1857, however, Joola inhabiting the north bank, who belonged to the Karone group and Chonk-Esil village, challenged the French presence. They attacked Karabane in 1858. And, taking advantage of the inaccessibility of their villages hidden among labyrinthine networks of narrow, shallow creeks, they defied the colonial authorities. To subdue them, in March 1860 Pinet-Laprade organized a strong military expedition which burned the villages of Hilor and Chonk-Esil. It also destroyed rice stocks. As a result, Gibenor, the chief of Karone, was forced to submit to the French at Hilor on 17 June 1860. But in 1865, after the villagers of Jembering had looted a French boat, the *Valentine*, stranded in the local creek, Pinet-Laprade was obliged to organize another expedition against the Joola.[1]

Even under pressure, the Joola refused to pay tax on rice, their cultural staple. They also continued to loot stranded ships. In any case, effective French authority reached no farther than Karabane, since it was hard to organize reprisals against villages isolated from each other by numerous creeks. In fact, following the assassination of Lieutenant Truche in 1886, the Joola of Seleki invented a new form of resistance: at the approach of patrolboats on punitive expeditions, they would quickly evacuate their villages. At the slightest sign of danger, the entire population would take refuge in the forest, bringing food and livestock, and taking care to remove their thatched roofs so as to lower the risk of fire damage. The French had to land troops on 10 February to get the Joola at Seléki to submit. In March 1888, France appointed Gitabarene as chief. But the Joola, whose democratic social structure the French found an intractable problem, continued to resist the colonial system.[2]

Beginning in 1885, in the face of the practically permanent state of rebellion among the Joola, the French decided to take possession of the Lower Casamance valley in order to benefit from rubber production. In 1891, in line with this desire, the administrator Martin set out a policy based on the assumption that Joola society lacked any form of structured authority. Martin supposed he could solve the problem by selecting Wolof soldiers and sailors who had shown particular devotion to France, and making them chiefs over the Joola. The assumption, which overlooked the fact that responsibility among the Joola was individualized, was hasty and false. The policy it subtended proved disastrous. A Wolof named Demba Juuf was appointed chief of the village of Gudomp in 1891–2. Another, Mangone Seye, was imposed on Joola in the Kombo and Karone areas in 1892–3. Unfortunately, these new chiefs and their retinues organized the systematic looting of the Joola people, stripping the territory bare. In 1894, a Joola resistance movement crystallized around the high priest of Karone, called Etea, a man opposed to any dealings with the French. In the Fooñi district also, police operations led by the French commandant from Bignona failed to establish French authority. The people were never totally subdued, because villages resumed their rebellion the moment French troops left. The troops thus had to deal with an increasingly active resistance movement. In October 1897, chief Ayemari of Sutu laid siege to Bignona while Joola resistance fighters took reprisals against Kulaye and Guna Sudugu. So serious did the situation become that the senior French administrator Adam suggested, as a means of imposing French authority, the destruction of several villages along with the exile of hundreds of Joola to Gabon.

In other words, seven years after the signature of the treaty with Fodé Kaba ceding the Fooñi area to France, the situation remained practically unchanged. The Joola were still fiercely determined to remain free. They were helped in this by their natural environment. In particular, the local forests provided secure refuge, since soldiers of the French Rifle Corps feared to enter them. But when French reprisals came, they were often murderous. In April 1879, for instance, the administrator Séguin attacked Niamone, forcing the villagers to evacuate their homes, and confiscating 200 guns. From the south bank the resistance, organized by Bayot Joola inhabiting the frontier between French and Portuguese possessions, was equally determined.

Because Joola fighters were attacking rubber tappers, the commanding officer at Seju felt obliged to organize a large-scale campaign against Etame, Niasia, and Kaïlu. In 1900, the administrator still had a hard time getting the Joola to pay taxes. In fact, Joola resistance was only beginning. It was to last beyond the period of conquest.[3]

In a bid to bring the Joola communities under control, the French installed a Resident Representative at Usuye in the Felupe heartland. Bayot and Seliki communities were also brought under the jurisdiction of Ziguinchor, which was itself placed under a military administrator. At this point, Felupe resistance crystallized around the *Boekin* cult, which strengthened their solidarity with the Joola in Karuheye, on the other side of the French–Portuguese border. In 1901, a *Boekin* cult leader called Jamuyon tried to organize armed resistance with help from his counterpart among the Karuheye Joola, a Jamat, who went around saying he was really Fodé Kaba. This was a period when the Felupe had at least 6,300 flintlock guns loaded with stone projectiles from the villages of Kasalol, Katu, and Yalle in Portuguese Guinea. In 1903, Lieutenant Raymond, the new administrator at Usuye, facing opposition from the Felupe population, had King Silhalebe arrested. Jamuyon, the second leader of the resistance movement, fled to Portuguese Guinea. Silhalebe was imprisoned together with several of his subjects. Since he was forbidden by custom to eat or drink in their presence, he remained on a hunger strike in Seju prison until he died, to the amazement of his jailers. Jamuyon, for his part, traveled from village to village exhorting people not to pay taxes but to fight the European invaders. His agitation helped to consolidate the resistance organized by the notorious "Fodé Kaba" across the border.

In March 1908, Portuguese troops attacked a number of villages: Jamat, Susana, Kassalol, and Keruheye, harboring followers of the self-styled Fodé Kaba. Once more, the resistance leader himself hid in the forest. After a Portuguese column from the military base at Bulam had destroyed several Joola and Balante villages, the villages of Efok and Yutu made a show of submission to the Resident Representative at Usuye. However, as soon as the column left, Joola resistance flared up again under Jamuyon's leadership, inflicting casualties on Portuguese detachments. Again in January 1909, Lieutenant Duval was attacked by large numbers of Jamat fighters supported by militants from Guinea Bissao led by the pseudonymous Fodé Kaba and Jamuyon. Under pressure from the Portuguese army south of the frontier, the Felupe were only grudgingly beginning to acknowledge French authority on the eve of World War I.[4]

In the region of Ziguinchor, the colonial authorities also faced opposition from the Joola communities of Seleki and Bayot, who were particularly hostile to the imposition of a rice tax. The *Ahan Boekin* or cult leader Silaye Sondo of Esil crystallized the struggle, even though he was frequently jailed in Ziguinchor and threatened with exile to Podor or Gabon. The colonial administration conducted numerous police operations, but still failed to subdue the movement. In May 1906, the Fourth Rifle Corps garrisoned at Bignona crisscrossed Kamobeul and Enampore, then camped at Seleki to demand total payment of taxes. Jinabo, the spiritual leader of the resistance movement, was killed leading a night attack on the French camp. Nevertheless, every year, after the departure of the French column, the resistance flared up anew. This went on practically until 1912. In that year, the Bayot community traveled to Ziguinchor to declare their submission. The Seleki, however, remained hostile to colonial occupation. They continued their resistance even after 1914.[5]

On the north bank, the Fooñi and Kombo communities also continued resisting the colonial authorities, despite the many military forays conducted in 1906 by Captain Lauqué at Balingore, Surebe, and Kartiak. Incidentally, at Kartiak the resistance was led by women, determined to keep the French from occupying any part of their territory. In June 1907, Lauqué's camp was besieged in a surprise attack. The column had to drive back more than three hundred Joola fighters. Lieutenant Duval, sent to reinforce Lauqué's column, destroyed the centers of Joola resistance organized by militant women inspired by cult leaders known as *Dilimbaj*. The rebel neighborhoods of Jongol, Jatumbul, and Butengalul submitted, giving up 174 guns to Duval. But, as in most Joola villages in Lower Casamance, their submission was only temporary.[6]

The Joola resisted French and Portuguese authority right up to the eve of World War I. As part of their war effort, the colonial authorities imposed extra demands. This provoked multiple forms of resistance in the region, forcing the colonial powers to carry on military campaigns well beyond the strict period of colonial conquest. In this respect, Joola resistance was much like that of the Konyagi, who also mounted long-lasting resistance movements against French occupation in the region between the Upper Casamance valley and Futa Jallon high plateau.

## B.     Konyagi resistance

The Basari and the Konyagi, members of the Tenda group, have survived thanks to a strongly organized defensive system that for centuries kept out all invaders. In the latter half of the nineteenth century, Tenda territory became a useful hunting ground of slave raiders from Futa Jallon, Bundu, and the Firdu region. After founding the autonomous religious community of Ndama, Cherno Ibrahima tried to conquer the Konyagi area. Like other would-be invaders before him, he failed. The French, as soon as they entered Upper Casamance, threw their support behind Musa Molo, who in turn tried to extend his rule southward over the Pakesi, Ndama, and Bajar territories, thus encroaching on the domain of the *Alfa* of Labé. Still, he was forced to acknowledge the autonomy of the Konyagi and the Basari, fiercely attached to their freedom.[7] Indeed, given its geographical location away from the main corridors of French commercial penetration, the Tenda territory remained free of colonial encroachments for a relatively long time. But in 1898, France laid down the borders of the colonies of Senegal, Guinea, and the Sudan. The move was calculated to reinforce colonial power in the frontier regions which, until then, had remained remote from the major axes of colonial conquest. The Konyagi area, Bajar, and Ndama were defined as part of French Guinea, and, in 1900, a military post was established at Busara to integrate these territories into the new colony.

At this time the colonial authorities knew absolutely nothing about the Tenda territories. They therefore avoided going into the Konyagi districts to take a census of the population for purposes of taxation. The Konyagi were organized as village-level communities, with the entire group forming two autonomous sub-groups known as Nioke and Sukoli. Of these the leaders were Alcune of Iciu and Tugane of Ifane. Under the Konyagi community were the Basari. For centuries the Tenda had resisted domination by any of the neighboring states, especially Futa Jallon. Right up to the start of the twentieth century, the Konyagi continued to resist the many attempts made by Cherno Ndama, under the guise of a holy war, to conquer their country. In 1901 the new French commanding officer Mongorcet decided to reverse the hands-off policy of his predecessor Lucas by taking rapid action to bring the Konyagi under French authority. He feared, failing this, that an independent Konyagi would serve as a model for other communities in the region. After a walkover in his confrontation with Cherno Ndama, a confident Mongorcet decided, on 15 April 1902, to attack Iciu. The Konyagi simply withdrew from the front-line villages, letting the enemy penetrate deeper into the heartland. Meanwhile, reinforcements from all the other villages arrived to help the people of Iciu. Together they overran the French column. Led by Alcune, the resistance forces destroyed the invading column, killing ninety-three of the enemy, including Lieutenant Mongorcet.

Underneath the usual solidarity of the Ifane and Iciu sub-groups, however, there was an undercurrent of rivalry. For that reason, Tugane, coached by Musa Molo, agreed to submit to the French authorities. His followers imposed one condition: that Konyagi territory be integrated into the colony of Senegal. This would prevent the territory falling under the authority of the *Alfa* of Labé, the Konyagis' worst enemy. Moderate as this demand was, the French governor Liotard rejected it. He was determined to make the Konyagi area part of French Guinea. The Tugane and Misigi initiatives, aimed at Konyagi integration into Senegal, led to the Rimbaud mission of 19 December 1902, designed to bring about negotiations with the principal Konyagi chiefs.

Ever since his victory of 16 April, Alcune had come to symbolize Konyagi resistance. He did not attend the meeting with the Rimbaud mission, during which Misigi and Tugane agreed to send delegates to Conakry. The delegates went to Conakry, where they accepted French authority. They then returned home through Senegal accompanied by Hinault, the administrator of French Guinea. The latter's presence was designed to make it clear that the Konyagi henceforth belonged to French Guinea. The Hinault mission left Hamdalaye with a strong military escort on 12 March 1903. Because the French were at the same time preparing for war against the Felupe, and an expedition under Colonel Rougier had set out for the Upper Casamance valley through Netebulu, the mission aroused considerable anxiety among the population.[8]

Faced with the threat of invasion, the Konyagi drew together under Alcune. He formed an alliance with the Kurotti, and strengthened his pact with the Basari. As soon as Hinault arrived, he decided to build a French post on the Bantenkili plateau east of Yukunkun. He also forced various chiefs to fly the French flag. But Alcune, rejecting colonial authority, refused to fly the flag.[9] Matters took a sudden downward turn when Musa

Molo fled to the Gambia in May 1903. His flight dented the credibility of French power in the area. From being a faithful ally of the French, Musa Molo had turned against them. Now he called on the Basari of Ubadji to join him in the Kantora forest, on British territory. Musa Molo's envoys traveled all the way to the Konyagi areas proclaiming his message: the French were not to be trusted; and Musa Molo was determined to make them pay.[10] On 30 June 1903 the war drums boomed at Iciu. All Konyagi fighters assembled there under their chiefs, except Tugane and Pata Tugane. Now two events happened that made Hinault decide to subdue the Konyagi as fast as feasible: Demba Jian, a messenger from Musa Molo, arrived at Iciu. And Momo Bangura, a militiaman, was assassinated in Alcune's camp. Hinault, having obtained adequate reinforcements, was sure he had the upper hand. So he took increasingly bold initiatives, designed to terrorize the Konyagi. On 3 November 1903, Hinault summoned the Konyagi to a meeting. He planned to introduce his assistant, one Mbaye, trained at the colonial school for sons of chiefs, to them. After that, he would move to the principal business of the day: tax collection, the tangible proof that the Konyagi had really submitted to French authority. Tugane promised to pay the tax on the spot, but the chief of Ifane argued that the Konyagi had never signed any agreement to pay any such tax.[11] Judging by the amount of tax collected, out of eighty-one villages, seventy-eight did not recognize France's authority. Hinault therefore concluded that a military attack was needed to clarify matters. On 21 November 1903, an outline plan for the Konyagi campaign was drawn up in Saint-Louis. Five hundred and twenty men were mobilized from Seju in Senegal and Boké in Guinea. They were to be used to smash the Konyagi resistance, while preventing survivors escaping to Guinea Bissao. The French captains in charge of the operation, Bouchez and Lambru, were immediately struck by the alacrity with which most chiefs came to prostrate themselves before the French. So when the French troops surrounded Iciu during the night of 8–9 April 1904, they thought Alcune's surrender was a foregone conclusion.

Now when the French troops arrived in Konyagi territory, one column from the south under Dessort, the other from the north-west under Lambru and Bouchez, the Sande population simply withdrew from their villages, regrouping in the main forest at Iciu. The French forces easily destroyed several villages evacuated in this manner. As they pressed forward, they met only a few isolated marksmen. These in fact were scouts posted to signal the positions of the advancing French troops. Using guerrilla tactics, the Konyagi frustrated the French column for a long time, inflicting several casualties on it. After the bombardment of Iciu, the core resistance group was reduced to fifty men around Alcune, in the ritual forest near the village. Finally exhausted, the Konyagi withdrew, leaving nineteen dead, including Alcune, fallen in battle while defending his country. The leadership of the resistance movement shifted to Kirani. With hundreds of Konyagi, he continued fighting from the bush. The French sent numerous patrols after them, but they remained elusive.[12]

Next, France declared a unilateral ceasefire, lasting over a long period. Sonkoli, Nioke and Biaye fighters, reassured by the cessation of hostilities, finally laid down their arms, a total of 1,950 guns. The number of weapons surrendered gives a good indication of the scope of the resistance movement. Kirani and Bambutan continued their resistance, even though Dessort took hundreds of women and children from Sande hostage, and pillaged livestock herds, all in an effort to force the Konyagi to surrender. On 24 April 1904, Dessort withdrew the garrison, leaving the 9th Company to occupy the territory after the creation of Konyagi district, with Yukunkun as district capital. The arrangement was a truce in disguise. For in 1916, Angoulvant was forced to acknowledge that French authority in the Konyagi area was quite fragile. In truth, France resigned itself to leaving the population entirely to its own devices, making no attempt at administration.[13] But by then, the colonial order was well established throughout Senegambia. From then on the region was open to economic exploitation by Britain, Portugal, and, above all, France, which received the lion's share from the partition of Senegambia.

# Conclusion

Prior to the fourteenth and fifteenth centuries, Senegambia, situated at the intersection of two historic West African zones, the Sahara and the Sudan, functioned mainly as a final destination for migratory populations. For that reason, it was not a theater for particularly important developments. Still, it did serve, even then, as a meeting place and a point of departure for all populations and influences flowing in and out of the savanna, the desert, and the forest zones. The Senegal and Gambia rivers, along with the numerous rivers furrowing the territory all the way to the Kolente, played a key role in the integration of this westernmost part of West Africa into existing economic networks, all oriented, at that time, either northward through the Sahara, eastward through the Niger Bend, or southward through the forest zone.

Because Senegambia was a spillover zone for people migrating from the Sahara desert, the Niger basin, and the forest zone, the region's population was typically diverse. Here were Wolof, Peul, and Tukulor groups, Manding, Serer, and Derber, Susu, Joola and Nalu, Baga, Beafada, Tenda, and so on. This demographic diversity was underscored by a tendency toward geographical variety. The most obvious difference is between northern Senegambia, comprising the Senegal river valley and the western plains between that river and the Gambia river, and southern Senegambia, comprising the Southern Rivers region and the Futa Jallon plateau. All this demographic diversity and geographical variety, however, was framed within unifying orientations expressed in the similarity of political and social institutions, as well as in the complementary meshing of the region's economies. These economies, focused on subsistence needs, centered on the Gambia basin. The Gambia River was a convenient demarcation line between northern and southern Senegambia. It was also a kind of funnel for all the region's remarkably diverse population, drawing them into cultural patterns no less remarkable for their complementarity. By the fifteenth century, most Senegambian societies were already evolving from kinship-based forms of political organization (known here under such names as *Lamanal* or *Kafu*) toward organized, monarchical states. Tekrur and Silla were the first. Then came Jolof, which rose to dominate northern Senegambia, while Kaabu, still dependent on Mali, dominated southern Senegambia. Under both the *Lamanal* and *Kafu* systems, just as under monarchical forms, Senegambian societies tended as a rule to be highly hierarchical. The basic social structure was a caste system. Upon this a set of social orders was superimposed. Monarchical rule here was commonly oligarchical. Based on bilinear succession, it recognized the land tenure rights of the *Laman*, within a tributary production mode in which self-sufficient subsistence production was the norm. Senegambia's local economy, nevertheless, was an integral part of a long-distance inter-regional trading system ensuring complementary relations between the forest, savanna, and desert zones. In the late fifteenth century, the arrival of the Portuguese changed this situation profoundly. The change forced a new role on the region's Atlantic coastline: it became a channel along which European economic, political and cultural influences rose to dominate all West Africa. That role persists to this day.

Starting in the fifteenth and sixteenth centuries, the Portuguese gradually diverted trade from the hinterland to the coast, taking control of Senegambia's inter-regional trading system. This shift was closely linked with the exploitation of the Cape Verde islands. The new trade in gold, ivory, and, soon enough, slaves, brought about profound political and social transformations throughout Senegambia, a region now open on the Atlantic flank. In southern Senegambia, Kaabu broke loose from Malian tutelage, becoming the area's major political power. It rose to dominate the Futa Jallon high plateau and the Southern Rivers region, whose coastal population, made up of Baïnuk, Baga, Nalu, Kasanga, and Beafada communities, had been ruined by the Portuguese trading system. Political and military pressure exerted by Kaabu at this time reached beyond the Gambia all the way into Siin and Saalum, where the Gelowar dynasty was the dominant – and privileged – force. In an earlier period, all of Senegambia had been overrun by the great migration led by Koli Tengela. Koli Tengela's followers migrated first from the Sahel to settle temporarily in Futa Jallon. They then headed north, going past the Gambia to the Senegal River basin, where they founded the Denyanke kingdom in Futa Toro. As this kingdom consolidated its power in the mid-sixteenth century, it hastened the break-up of the Jolof confederation. The seat of power in the disintegrated confederation shifted toward the coast, a move that benefited the littoral provinces of Kajoor, Baol, and Waalo. When these former provinces became independent, they set the seal on the political fragmentation of Senegambia, a development profitable to the new and booming Atlantic trading system boosted by the arrival of new European participants.

The Portuguese had started out enjoying a monopoly. But that was soon challenged by the arrival of the Dutch, the British, and the French. Each of these European powers carved out zones of influence on the coast, bases from which they could better meet the demand of the new trans-Atlantic trading system for slave labor. From the latter half of the seventeenth century, the slave trade became the keystone of the colonial mercantile system, which bound Africa, America, and Europe into a system built on domination. The way the system worked, to paraphrase Samir Amin's concept, was that Europe became the center, America became a periphery working to nourish Europe, and Africa became a sub-periphery working to feed the American periphery working to nourish the European center. And Senegambia was part of the African sub-periphery. The European trading posts at Saint-Louis, Gorée, Fort Saint James, Cacheu, and Bissau turned the Senegambian coast into a vast warren for slaves brought in from as far inland as the Niger Bend.

The estuaries of the Senegal and Gambia rivers, as well as those in the Southern Rivers region, were controlled by the French, the British, and the Portuguese. The deviation of trade from the old caravan routes to the coast completely destroyed the north–south trans-Saharan trade circuits. In their place, the new east–west circuit flourished. The takeover of trade in the Senegal River basin by the French trading post at Saint-Louis, and in particular, the economic, political and social crisis created by the violent nature of the slave trade and the massive exportation of slave labor, provoked a vast Muslim religious movement beginning in the late seventeenth century. Its organizer, Nasir Al Din, declared a holy war in the name of a puritan strain of Islam. His stated purpose was to save Berber society, ruined by the power of the Hassani warriors coupled with the weight of the trans-Atlantic trading system, which was diverting trade from the entire Senegal River valley toward Saint-Louis, to the detriment of the traditional northern circuit. In 1673, this Muslim religious movement triumphed throughout the Senegal River valley. But, in 1677, it was defeated by a coalition of dethroned traditional rulers from Waalo, Futa Toro, and Kajoor, in tandem with the forces of the Hassani warriors supported by the French trading company in Saint-Louis. Its defeat ensured the triumph of the trans-Atlantic trading system and the continuation of the slave trade. That trade in turn deepened the antagonism between the region's military aristocracies and the peasant masses. Faced with the arbitrary impositions of the traditional aristocracies, fully integrated into the trans-Atlantic system, with its dependence on the slave trade, Islam emerged as the main vehicle of popular opposition.

The slave trade, which remained central to the trading system throughout the eighteenth century and part of the nineteenth, determined to a great extent the way the states and societies of Senegambia developed. Accurate statistics on slaves are hard to come by, but it is clear that Senegambia, though only a secondary slave export region, steadily exported an annual average of nearly 8,000 slaves, year in, year out. Slave trading ruined both the coastal and hinterland societies. In the north, along the Senegal River valley, it went hand in hand with the gum trade, which helped Berber communities to become integrated into the trans-Atlantic trading system, while facilitating the domination of northern Senegambia by the emirates of Trarza and Brakna. Similarly, the scope of the slave trade made it possible for slave trading families to establish bases in the Southern Rivers region. The trade also led to the massive use of slave labor for the production of foodstuffs needed to supply slaving vessels. In the era of the slave trade, the monopoly of the trans-Atlantic trade enjoyed by chartered companies was considerably reduced.

Generally, the violence spawned by the slave trade entrenched arbitrary rule and the centralization of monarchical power within the tiny states left over after the territorial break-up of the old Senegambian states in the latter half of the sixteenth century. Soninke and *ceddo* regimes, whose power depended predominantly on royal slaves, placed substantial curbs on the prerogatives and powers of electoral colleges or chiefs vested with autonomous powers. The power thus curtailed went to strengthen the central regime. A new breed of warlords like Lat Sukaabe Faal or Samba Gelaajo Jeegi owed all their power to their monopoly over slave trading and arms purchases. Each kingdom was bedeviled by numerous succession struggles. Above all, the ordinary masses were subjected to constant pillage by the rulers and their armies. All this helped to strengthen the Muslim religious movement. Muslim leaders and their followers created many self-contained communities to protect themselves from the arbitrary exactions of the reigning military aristocracies. Furthermore, Islam became an ideology for the internal revolutions which, in the eighteenth century, gave birth to the three Muslim theocracies of Bundu, Futa Jallon and Futa Toro. The success of these three glorious revolutions ensured the security of Muslim citizens within each of these states. Finally, though, the new aristocracy of Muslim militants and clerics degenerated into a self-indulgent imitation of the old *ceddo* regimes.

That was how the Muslim theocracies became involved, just like *ceddo* regimes, in slave trading. And the impact of the slave trade worsened the economic stagnation and aggravated social conflicts in all aspects of Senegambian life. Wars, slave raids, internal conflicts, all closely linked to the slave trade, prevented the region's peasant societies settling down in all security to carry on their productive farm work. The slump in agricultural production was worsened by a chain of natural disasters punctuating Senegambian history with successive food shortages and famines. This interaction between wars and natural calamities intensified the demographic drain, to the advantage of the export trade in productive labor, the trans-Atlantic slave trade. Here, in a system feeding on chronic violence, producers themselves became the principal merchandise. Needless to say, such a situation held Senegambia back from the achievement of its own agricultural revolution, while helping Europe to finance its industrial revolution. Senegambia regressed in all areas including the handicraft sector, where competition from European ironware and cotton-cloth manufacturers ruined the local production system. Internally, the slave trade deepened social antagonisms and made domestic slavery more exploitative, channeling it into the satisfaction of the foreign demand for slave labor. In northern Senegambia, where *ceddo* regimes ruled through systematic violence, royal slaves came to play a preponderant role in political and military affairs. On the other hand, in agricultural production, the role of slave labor, concentrated in slave villages, was more important in southern Senegambia. In both cases, however, the slaveholding system was adapted to the demands of the trans-Atlantic slave trade. Because that system emphasized the export of slave labor, it blocked technological progress, condemning the economy to stagnation. For a long time, this situation stalled the evolution of the subsistence economy toward a capitalist system capable of liberating society's productive forces and changing the dominant form of production, the tributary mode.

One result was the internal weakening of Senegambia by the slave trade, a system that perpetuated violence in relations between and within states. Moreover, Senegambia came under increasing pressure from the Berber emirates of Trarza and Brakna. These emirates incessantly raided most of northern Senegambia for slaves. From the east, too, the region came under attack from the Bambara kingdoms of Kaarta and Segu toward the end of the eighteenth and in the early nineteenth century. In southern Senegambia, Futa Jallon superseded Kaabu as the major power. This dominance came at a price: continuous warfare against neighboring states, along with the reduction of thousands of captives into slavery. These captives were herded into slave villages called *runde*. In the eighteenth century, throughout southern Senegambia there were numerous slave revolts; and in northern Senegambia, communities under Muslim clerical leadership frequently rebelled against the *ceddo* regimes. These revolts and rebellions presaged a long series of political and social conflicts that ravaged Senegambia in the nineteenth century following the abolition of the slave trade and the gradual triumph of legitimate trade.

In the nineteenth century, the slave trade lost its instrumental role in the accumulation of financial capital in Europe, and was abolished. The abolition disrupted existing relationships between Europe and Africa. Thanks to the triumph of legitimate trade, Africa then became a direct periphery of Europe. The dominant need of the European economy was for raw produce to feed European industry. The changed economic situation entailed radical transformations in the political and social structures of Senegambia during the period before colonial conquest.

In the first half of the nineteenth century, the European powers made a strong comeback on the Senegambian scene. In the mid-nineteenth century, numerous sovereignty disputes broke out, with the Senegambian states struggling against European – mainly French – encroachments. Changes at this time mainly reflected economic, political, and social transformations in Senegambian society following the gradual ascendancy of legitimate trade.

For centuries, slave trading was a monopoly enjoyed by reigning aristocracies. Some were of the traditional *ceddo* type, some headed Muslim theocratic regimes. Slave trading was a royal monopoly because only the aristocracy could mobilize sufficient military force to raid neighboring communities for captives, or to turn their own subjects into slaves. The aristocracy was also the only group capable of conveying slave coffles safely from hinterland to coast, for sale to slave traders. The abolition of the slave trade led to the gradual loss of this economic monopoly. It deprived the aristocrats of their main source of income and power. This period saw Senegambian societies experimenting with different coping strategies in the monumental transition from slave trading to legitimate trade.

In southern Senegambia, traders in the Southern Rivers region maintained a degree of economic prosperity in the transitional period by operating a dual economy, part slave trade, part legitimate trade in primary produce. For a time, the dual economy also consolidated the status of old slaving families established in the Southern Rivers region. The massive use of slave labor on coffee plantations and, even more intensively, in peanut farming, entrenched slave-holding norms. And the region's relative economic prosperity attracted European trading companies, directly linked with the economic interests of French and British finance capital. It also drew in the Futa Jallon kingdom, a continental African power eager to benefit from the coastal trade in primary produce. The construction of forts at Boké, Bofa, and Benty gave French trading companies a monopoly in most of the peanut-producing Southern Rivers region. By the same token, it sowed the seeds of sovereignty disputes between France and the small coastal states, as well as between France and the Futa Jallon kingdom. The Futa Jallon regime's policy of coastward expansion was a response to the double challenge facing the old aristocracy: externally, Futa Jallon had to end the imbalance between the trade in such traditional hinterland produce as leather, wax, and livestock, and the new type of export produce emerging on the coast, like coffee, palm oil, and peanuts. Under the circumstances, the aristocracy was obliged to find ways of making up for losses due to their mounting difficulties as they sought markets for their contraband slave offerings within the newly abolitionist trans-Atlantic trading system. The losses – and the trade imbalance to which they led – probably explained the heightened exploitation of the masses and the slave population in the aging theocracy. They certainly were a major part of the reason for the emergence of large-scale insurgent movements seeking to change the status quo.

One such political and religious revolt, the Hubbu movement, attained vast dimensions, considerably weakening the power of the *Almamis* in Timbo. In any case, they exhausted their forces in the struggle against the Hubbu, at a time when the coastal provinces of Timbi and Labé were asserting their autonomy more strongly by taking control of the economic region of the Southern Rivers between the Gambia and Rio Pongo rivers. The seriousness of the social crisis, coupled with the chronic imbalance between real resources available to the central authorities and to provincial authorities, eventually dealt a fatal blow to the Futa Jallon policy of expansion into the Southern Rivers region. In the end, the region was partitioned between France, Portugal, and Britain. Thus, colonial conquest aborted the embryonic process of unification which Futa Jallon, as a continental power, had seemed about to impose on southern Senegambia.

This imminent process of unification through military conquest, the internal conflicts it provoked between the Futa Jallon kingdom and the coastal states notwithstanding, was the most original response that emerged in southern Senegambia in the transitional phase of the trans-Atlantic trading system. Beyond the rationalization of a holy war, used to justify the conquest of Kaabu in 1867, Futa Jallon expansion into the coastal region was precisely similar to the process of the Asante kingdom's expansionist southward drive in the Gold Coast at the start of the nineteenth century.

In sum, the history of southern Senegambia is dominated by the territorial expansion of the Futa Jallon kingdom. That push itself was part of the strategy of the old Muslim theocratic regime in its effort to resolve its internal crisis and to adapt to the changed circumstances of the trans-Atlantic trading system. By contrast, in northern Senegambia, on account of the impact on the multitude of small states of the crisis in the trans-Atlantic trading system, social and political change was dominated by Muslim revolutions against *ceddo* regimes within various states, or by the organization of holy wars by a new crop of Muslim leaders risen from lowly origins, and bent on creating political structures on a grander scale, all in the name of the *Sharia*.

The serious depression in the trans-Atlantic trading system lasting throughout the first half of the nineteenth century sharpened conflicts between the *ceddo* aristocracy and the Muslim leadership. The abolition of the slave trade, their main source of income, steadily impoverished the *ceddo* aristocracy in each state. To make ends meet, they subjected the peasants to intensified exploitation. In reaction, the latter turned to the emergent Muslim leaders who, with income increasingly drawn from peanut farming, led them in their struggle against the *ceddo* aristocracy.

The previous era had seen the political fragmentation of the Wolof and Sereer kingdoms. The many states that resulted were individually too tiny for their ruling aristocracies to contain the Muslim religious movement, which was active over areas considerably larger than any of these small states. Various royal families in the kingdoms of Waalo, Kajoor, Baol, Siin, and Saalum had grown powerful in previous centuries thanks to the slave trade. Now they exhausted themselves in endless civil wars in which different royal clans fought, usually over issues of succession. In the process, they strengthened the hand of the royal slaves. For, thanks to their cohesion and professional military skills, they became *de facto* masters of the changing situation.

Taking advantage of their position, the uncontrolled royal slave armies of the *ceddo* aristocracy pillaged the peasant population. The peasantry reacted increasingly by taking up arms, setting up Muslim theocracies. The type of holy war mounted by Niaga Issa and Diile Faatim Cham was a far cry from traditional conflicts between self-contained Muslim communities and central *ceddo* authorities within each state. This was, instead, a vast Muslim religious movement transcending the frontiers of each state, expressing a unifying vision on the scale of the ancient Jolof confederation, which had disintegrated in the sixteenth century.

The *ceddo* aristocracy was caught between the demands of the Muslim religious movement and the pressures of the French colony of Senegal, which wanted to organize a colonial environment, the better to resolve the crisis in the trans-Atlantic trading system. This attempt to bring the Wolof and Sereer kingdoms of the coast under control, either in order to try out an agricultural development scheme, as in the Waalo, or to take advantage of profits from peanut production in Kajoor, Baol, Siin, and Saalum, came at the same time as the vast movement led by Shaykh Umar. That movement created tremendous turmoil throughout the Senegambian hinterland, from Futa Jallon all the way to the Futa Toro in the Senegal River valley.

Shaykh Umar's movement, initially consolidated along the eastern borders of Futa Jallon when thousands of disciples from all over Senegambia and western Sudan poured into Dingiray, embarked on the conquest of the Upper Senegal valley in 1854. Because local communities of the Muslim faithful, organized around marabouts, and eager to be rid of the arbitrary rule of reigning aristocracies, supported the Holy Warrior, Shaykh Umar achieved a series of lightning-swift victories over the tiny *ceddo* kingdoms of Gajaaga, Khaaso, and Kaarta, and even added the Muslim theocracy of Bundu.

Shaykh Umar's holy war pushed on into Futa Toro, his homeland. Given his popular support, he achieved *de facto* control of the country. Unable with immediate effect to change the political regime in Futa Toro, Shaykh Umar was happy to recruit the best soldiers of the kingdom into his army of holy warriors, while using indirect means to get the political aristocracy to do his bidding. Meanwhile, he dreamed of returning one day in triumph from his eastern conquests to rule directly over his native land, after incorporating it into a vast Muslim empire.

Shaykh Umar's field of action far exceeded the boundaries of Senegambia. And his activities certainly marked the high point of the militant Muslim ascendancy of the mid-nineteenth century. Shaykh Umar the religious leader was indissociable from Shaykh Umar the political organizer. His activities were intimately connected with the general context of Senegambian and western Sudanese societies, all facing both serious internal political and social crises, and the threat of colonial conquest. In making the Tijaniyya strain of Islam dominant, Shaykh Umar was simply putting the finishing touches to the work of political and social reform begun by the founders of the *Toorodo* revolution, following the Muslim religious movement led by Nasir Al Din in the late seventeenth century. His politico-religious program was given a hostile reception from reigning aristocracies in the theocratic kingdoms of Futa Jallon, Bundu, Futa Toro, and Masina, as well as from the *ceddo* kingdoms of the Upper Senegal valley and Segu. The final obstacle to Shaykh Umar's program, however, was French colonial imperialism. It was French opposition which forced the Holy Warrior, as from 1857, to build his empire away from Senegambia, to the east, in western Sudan. While preparing for a showdown with Amadu of Segu, Shaykh Umar's successor in the Niger Bend, the French were free to complete their conquest of Senegambia.

Before that, northern Senegambia in particular had remained open to new attempts at internal structural reform. These followed in the wake of Shaykh Umar's reform campaign, and were led by disciples like Maba Jakhu or initiators like Cerno Brahim or Amadu Seekhu. The new leaders were individuals of lowly origins. They tried to unify most of northern Senegambia by declaring holy war on the region's *ceddo* states as well as its theocracies. One after the other, they were defeated by a coalition of legitimist rulers bent on preserving their privileges, on the one hand, and the French colonial administration, determined to extend its political and economic domination over this region, on the other.

The defeats of Diile Fatim Cham and Niaga Issa in 1830 in Waalo, of

Shaykh Umar at the gates of Medina in 1857, of Maba Jaakhu at Somb in 1867, of Cherno Brahim at Magawa in 1869, of Amadu Seekhu at Samba Saajo in 1875, of Karamokho Abal at Boketto in 1887, and, last of all, of Mamadu Lamin at Tabakuta in 1887, were stages in a process leading first to the victory of the traditional rulers and then to that of the colonial regime over the Muslim movement in Senegambia. All the new religious leaders were men of common birth. All were inspired to wage holy war as the only way to bring the society under a strain of orthodox Islam capable of transforming Senegambian society. For that reason, they were able to mobilize the peasant masses, who became a significant economic force once legitimate commerce replaced slave trading, and whose contribution to peanut farming was crucial. The new religious leaders fought against both the outdated structures of the status quo and the violent abuses of the *ceddo* regimes. They also combated social inequalities and denounced the exploitation of the ordinary people by the Muslim aristocracies that had been in power since the eighteenth century. It was quite natural, then, that they aroused the hostility of such legitimist rulers as Lat Joor, Alburi Njaay, Abdul Bokar Kane, Kumba Ndoofen Juuf and Ibrahima Sori Dongolfella. These rulers waged war on the Muslim movement as soon as it threatened their political prerogatives in their various states.

As for the French, British, and Portuguese colonial powers, they initially welcomed the peaceful spirit of the Muslim communities, focused as they were on production. But later they turned against them on account of their inclination to start holy wars, which tended to expand territorial spaces beyond the limits of traditional Senegambian states. Shaykh Umar was the first to try to unify most of western Sudan under cover of holy war. Next, Maba Jaakhu and Amadu Seekhu tried to unite all of northern Senegambia. But these attempts provoked the direct intervention of the colonial powers against the Muslim movement. This movement was opposed both to the pillaging practices of the reigning aristocracies and to the extension of European sovereignty on the African continent. This was why the traditional rulers and the colonial authorities joined forces to crush it. Once the movement was defeated, the way to colonial conquest lay open. In effect, the holy wars against the old aristocracies softened up Senegambian society in general on the eve of colonial conquest. The Muslim marabouts had mobilized most of the peasant population behind themselves. Once they were defeated, the traditional rulers were left to confront the colonial powers alone. The clash had become inevitable.

From that point on, even though the traditional rulers organized various resistance efforts to try and safeguard their political and economic privileges against the rapacious colonial powers, the outcome was no longer in doubt. Colonial conquest became necessary because France, Britain, and

Portugal needed to organize production on the spot for their own benefit, making sure that local production went to meet the demands of European industry. France, whose economic interests were tied to the expansion of peanut production, obtained the lion's share of the spoils. Its gains stretched from the Senegal River to the Niger, from Saint-Louis to Freetown along the coast, and from the Southern Rivers through Futa Jallon to the Sudan. Britain held on to its Gambian enclave to the bitter end, while Portugal was limited to Guinea Bissao. The process of colonial conquest took place in an atmosphere of rivalry between the three European powers, each using military violence to crush the resistance of Senegambia's last legitimist rulers.

France mounted a series of bloody military campaigns in the Sudan and northern Senegambia, where Lat Joor, Alburi Njaay, Kumba Ndoofen Juuf, Abdul Bokar Kane, and Saer Maty Ba fell one by one before the French mercenaries. The conquest of southern Senegambia, by contrast, occurred in gradual stages. One reason for this was the play of colonial rivalries between France, Britain, and Portugal. Another was the option of diplomacy as a means of annexing this region, which was of lesser importance than northern Senegambia or the Niger Bend. Still, the division of Fuladu and Gambia, in which Musa Molo, Sunkari, Fodé Silla, and Fodé Kaba were the losers, and the occupation of Rio Nunez, Rio Pongo, and Mellakure, laid the groundwork for the encirclement of Futa Jallon. There, with the defeat of Bokar Biro in 1896, the conquest of Senegambia as a whole was complete. By then the Joola, Bassari, and Konyagi were the only groups left to organize popular resistance movements. For quite some time their remnant resistance movements held out against the colonialists, providing a counterpoint to the overwhelming defeat of traditional rulers.

The region's patchwork of reigning aristocracies succumbed to colonial conquest as if to fate. They put up a desperate fight, but, more to the point, they revealed an obvious inability to inspire deep and determined popular resistance to the foreign invader. Some did consider, in a half-hearted way, the possibility of uniting in a common front. But all ended up simply clinging to their national privileges until they died, intent on preserving their ancestral heritage. This narrowness of vision, mirroring with peculiar sharpness the political fragmentation of Senegambia after the failure of the unifying efforts of nineteenth-century Muslim leaders, was the main reason why last-ditch resistance efforts against colonial occupation failed. The peasant population felt alienated from the political regime. In each state, traditional rulers were internally divided. Little wonder, then, that compared to the campaign waged by Amadu of Segu, or indeed by Samori, who mobilized his solidly organized state in a durable resistance movement, the resistance put up by the Senegambian sovereigns was weak.

Beyond the defeat of the legitimist rulers, colonial conquest put a definitive seal on the political fragmentation of Senegambia. The partition of the region between France, Britain, and Portugal would for a long time shatter its unity. The partition, with the consequent loss of all autonomy, is the most intractable legacy with which those independent states that fall either entirely or partially within the Senegambian region (Senegal, Gambia, Guinea Bissao, Mauritania, Mali, Guinea Conakry) now have to cope. Before facing this major challenge of regional integration, however, Senegambia underwent nearly a century of direct colonization. Throughout that period, Europe imposed its political, economic and cultural domination on the region, laying cast-iron foundations for Senegambia's current state of underdevelopment and dependence.

# Notes

## I SENEGAMBIA FROM THE FIFTEENTH TO THE SEVENTEENTH CENTURY

1 J. Suret-Canale and B. Barry, *"The Western Atlantic Coast 1600–1800,"* in *The History of West Africa,* 2nd edn, Vol. I, Longman, 1976, p. 456.

## 1 SENEGAMBIA IN THE FIFTEENTH AND SIXTEENTH CENTURIES

1 P. Michel, *Les Bassins des Fleuves Sénégal et Gambie: Etude Géomorphologique,* ORSTOM Memoire Series No. 63, 1973, pp. 37–8.

2 Y. Person, *Senegambia.* Proceedings of a Colloquium at the University of Aberdeen, April 1974, pp. 7–8.

3 J. Boulègue, "La Sénégambie du milieu du XVIe au début du XVIIe siècle," Doctoral dissertation, Paris, 1968, p. 117.

4 A. Teixeira Da Mota, "Un document nouveau pour l'histoire des Peuls du Sénégal pendant les XVe et XVIe siècles," *Boletim Cultural da Guiné Portuguesa,* No. 96, 1969, p. 184.

5 This process of territorial amputation, which happened in the sixteenth century under the impact of the Atlantic trade, is examined later in this volume. The process did not fundamentally change the parameters of economic, political, and social institutions in Senegambia before the European intrusion, the subject of this chapter.

6 P. Pelissier, *Les paysans du Sénégal, Les civilisations agraires du Cayor à la Casamance,* Saint-Yrieux, Fabregue, 1966, p. 105.

7 A.B. Diop, *La société Wolof – Tradition et changement. Les systèmes d'inégalité et de domination,* Karthala, 1981, p. 182.

8 B. Barry, *Le royaume du Waalo,* Maspero, 1972, pp. 94–100. The *Jogomay* was the ruler of the waters; the *Jawdin* ruled the land; the *Maalo* was the royal treasurer.

9 *Ibid.,* pp. 100–3.

10 J. Boutillier *et al., La Moyenne Vallée du Sénégal, Etude socioéconomique,* P.U.F., 1962, p. 112.

11 J. Johnson, "The Almamate of Futa Toro, 1770–1836, A Political History," Doctoral Dissertation, Wisconsin, 1974, pp. 24–32.

12 O. Kane, "Les unités territoriales du Fuuta Toro," IFAN Bulletin, Series B, No. 3, 1973, pp. 615–23.

13  *Ibid.*, pp. 626–9. The Denyanke regime, which ruled over Futa Toro from the late fifteenth century to the end of the eighteenth, deserves a study in its own right, a retrospective inquiry related to the triumphant *Toorodo* regime that rose to power after the Muslim revolution of 1776. At the time there was an unduly strong attempt to present a revisionist version of the history of the Denyanke calculated to provide ideological justification for the new *Toorodo* regime while glossing over the claims of conflict between Peul and Tukulor, likely to complicate unduly the appreciation of the history of Futa Toro.

14  P.D. Curtin, *Economic Change in Precolonial Africa. Senegambia in the Era of the Slave Trade,* University of Wisconsin Press, 1975, p. 74.

15  A. Bathily, "Imperialism and Colonial Expansion in Senegal in the Nineteenth Century, With Particular Reference to the Economic, Social and Political Development of the Kingdom of Gaajaga," Doctoral dissertation, West African Studies Centre, University of Birmingham, 1975, pp. 25–6.

16  *Ibid.*, pp. 31–2.

17  *Ibid.*, pp. 262 and 284.

18  Pelissier, *Les paysans du Sénégal*, pp. 41 and 89.

19  We are better informed about the political and social institutions of the Wolof kingdoms thanks to the remarkable pioneering work done by Pathé Diagne coupled with the excellent update produced by Abdoulaye Bara Diop. In addition, there are now numerous historical works facilitating the understanding of these institutions.

20  Diop, *La société Wolof*, pp. 125, 181, and 185.

21  M. Diouf, "Le Kajoor au XIXe siècle et la conquête coloniale," Doctoral dissertation, Paris I, 1980, pp. 47–84.

22  Pelissier, *Les paysans du Sénégal*, pp. 196–9.

23  *Ibid.*, p. 235.

24  *Ibid.*, pp. 401, 411, and 416.

25  G. Brooks, *Kola Trade and State Building in the Upper Guinea Coast and Senegambia, 15th–17th Century,* African Studies Center Working Papers, No. 38, 1980, p. 15.

26  *Ibid.*, pp. 1–2.

27  The name "Southern Rivers" was coined by the French from their Senegalese settlement. The English, from their station in Sierra Leone, called the same area the Northern Rivers region or the Upper Guinea Coast.

28  Pelissier, *Les paysans du Sénégal*, p. 107.

29  *Ibid.*, pp. 710 and 720.

30  The remarkable works of Walter Rodney and George Brooks have given us valuable information on trading networks in this Southern Rivers region, as related to state construction before the arrival of the Portuguese.

31  Brooks, *Kola Trade,* p. 29.

32  *Ibid.*, p. 15.

33  Pelissier, *Les paysans du Sénégal*, p. 674.

34  G. Brooks, *Kola Trade*, pp. 18–19.

35  *Ibid.*

36  M. Mane, "Contribution à l'histoire du Kaabu, des origines au XIXe siècle," IFAN Bulletin, Vol. 40, Series B, No. 1, January 1979, pp. 95–9.

37 *Ibid.*, p. 103.
38 *Ibid.*, pp. 106–7.
39 *Ibid.*, pp. 108–13.
40 *Ibid.*, pp. 114–15.
41 The word "Soninke" was used to designate non-Muslims, allowed to drink *dolo*. It was different from the ethnic name of the Sarakole from Gadiaga. See "Contribution à l'histoire du Kaabu," Mane, 1979, p. 119.
42 J. Suret-Canale, *La République de Guinée,* Editions Sociales, Paris, 1970, p. 47.
43 *Ibid.*, pp. 62–4.
44 *Ibid.*, pp. 65–8.
45 Mane, "Contribution à l'histoire du Kaabu," p. 118.
46 W. Rodney, *A History of the Upper Guinea Coast, 1545 to 1800*, Clarendon Press, Oxford, 1970, pp. 5 and 17.
47 Suret-Canale, *La République de Guinée*, pp. 14–29.
48 *Ibid.*, pp. 30–2.

## 2  SOCIAL DYNAMICS IN SENEGAMBIA

1 Research on populations in the Southern Rivers area remains an unfulfilled task. So far, available studies have focused on their situation in the nineteenth century. But by then they had suffered from a long history of external pressures and extermination on account of the slave trade, during which they were decimated.
2 Pelissier, *Les paysans du Sénégal*, pp. 689–94.
3 Diop, *La société Wolof*, p. 126. Abdoulaye Diop's fine analysis of this process in the Wolof kingdoms may justifiably be applied to the generality of Senegambian kingdoms, with just a few exceptions. Pending the conduct of more detailed case studies, his analysis fills an important gap.
4 *Ibid.*, p. 125 .
5 A.B. Diop, "La tenure foncière en milieu wolof," *Notes Africaines,* No. 118, April 1968, p. 50.
6 Diop, *La société Wolof*, p. 168.
7 *Ibid.*, p. 27.
8 *Ibid.*, p. 46.
9 *Ibid.*, pp. 113 and 116.
10 C. Meillassoux, *Femmes, greniers et capitaux,* Maspero, Paris, 1975, p. 59.
11 *Ibid.*, p. 61.
12 Diop, *La société Wolof*, p. 185.
13 *Ibid.*, pp. 184 and 189.
14 *Ibid.*, p. 202.
15 Curtin, *Economic Change in Precolonial Africa*, p. 68.
16 P. Diagne, *Pouvoir politique traditionnel en Afrique occidentale*, Présence Africaine, Paris, 1967, p. 19.
17 M. Diouf has objected to this concept of a close link between the political and social systems. In my opinion, his objections are unfounded.
18 L. Sanneh, *The Jakhanke,* International Africa Institute, London, 1979. pp. 13–31.

## 3  THE ATLANTIC TRADING SYSTEM AND THE REFORMATION OF SENEGAMBIAN STATES FROM THE FIFTEENTH TO THE SEVENTEENTH CENTURY

1 Curtin, *Economic Change in Precolonial Africa*, p. 202. It is hard to obtain comprehensive statistical data for these remote periods of the Atlantic trade. The difficulty is compounded by the fact that freebooters systematically evaded checks.
2 V.M. Godinho, *L'économie de l'Empire portugais aux XVe–XVIe siècles,* S.E.V.P.E.N., Paris, 1969, p. 185.
3 *Ibid.*, pp. 199–200 and 203.
4 *Ibid.*, 1969, pp. 202–3.
5 Rodney, *History of the Upper Guinea Coast*, p. 153.
6 Godinho, *L'économie de l'Empire portugais*, p. 217.
7 Curtin, *Economic Change in Precolonial Africa*, p. 202.
8 I.D. Moraes, "La Petite Côte d'après Francisco De lemos Coelho (XVIIémé siècle)," *Bulletin IFAN*, Vol. 35, Series B, No. 2, 1973, p. 249.
9 Rodney, *History of the Upper Guinea Coast*, p. 155.
10 *Ibid.*, pp. 158–61.
11 Curtin, *Economic Change in Precolonial Africa*, p. 177.
12 Godinho, *L'économie de l'Empire portugais*, p. 185.
13 Curtin, *Economic Change in Precolonial Africa*, p. 13.
14 Rodney, *History of the Upper Guinea Coast*, pp. 95, 97, and 98.
15 Curtin, *Economic Change in Precolonial Africa*, p. 13.
16 J. Boulegue, "Relation du Fleuve Sénégal de Joâo Barbosa faite par Joâo Baptiste Lavanha vers 1600," *Bulletin IFAN,* Vol. 24, Series B, Nos. 3–4, 1968, p. 509.
17 Rodney, *History of the Upper Guinea Coast*, pp. 171 and 181.
18 G. Thilmans and N.I. de Moraes, "La description de la côte de Guinée du Père Baltasar Barreira 1606," *Bulletin IFAN*, Vol. 34, Series B, 1972, p. 30.
19 Rodney, *History of the Upper Guinea Coast*, p. 72.
20 Curtin, *Economic Change in Precolonial Africa*, p. 228.
21 Brooks, *Kola Trade*, p. 19.
22 *Ibid.*, p. 14.
23 Rodney, *History of the Upper Guinea Coast*, p. 181.
24 *Ibid.*, p. 222.
25 *Ibid.*, p. 199.
26 Brooks, *Kola Trade*, p. 19.
27 Rodney, *History of the Upper Guinea Coast*, p. 110.
28 Boulegue, "Relation du Fleuve Sénégal," p. 212.
29 *Ibid.*, p. 244.

## 4  THE PARTITION OF THE SENEGAMBIAN COAST IN THE SEVENTEENTH CENTURY

1 Barry, *Le royaume du Walo*, pp. 111–26.
2 Curtin, *Economic Change in Precolonial Africa*, pp. 105–9.
3 *Ibid.*, p. 102.

4 *Ibid.*
5 Lemaire, *Les voyages du Sieur Lemaire aux Iles Canaries, Cap-Vert, Sénégal et Gambie...*, Paris, 1965, p. 68.
6 Barry, *Le royaume du Walo*, pp. 135–59. This previous book by the author presents a detailed study of this movement. Readers interested in the discussion of it and the supporting documentation are advised to consult the book.
7 Chambonneau, principal eyewitness to these developments, has left a clear description of the causes of Nasir Al Din's movement. The leader, in his capacity as Chief Servant of God, had a mandate "to warn all Kings to mend their ways by saying their prayers better and more frequently, restricting themselves to three or four women, and dismissing from their entourage all idle griots and libertines; and finally, to warn them that God did not want them to pillage their subjects, much less to kill or enslave them." Moreover, "God does not permit Kings to pillage, kill or enslave their subjects. On the contrary, God enjoins them to support their subjects and protect them from their enemies. For the peoples are not made for Kings, but Kings for the peoples." Until recently, information about Nasir Al Din's movement in its Mauritanian phase was available thanks to a set of *Tarikhs*, historical chronicles of Berber origin, published by Ismaël Hamet. It was the text by Chambonneau, a contemporary of the movement, recently published by Carson I.A. Ritchie, which shed clearer light on the real scope of this Muslim revolution reaching all the way into the states of the Senegal River valley. See Carson I.A. Ritchie, "Deux textes sur le Sénégal, 1673, 1677," *IFAN Bulletin*, Vol. 30, Series B, No. 1, 1968, pp. 338–9.
8 All travelers who visited the region after Chambonneau agreed that the *Toubenan* religious movement owed its success to the ravages of the slave trade. In 1682, Le Maire spoke of a local ruler, the *Brak*, who enslaved people in his country at the slightest offense. He showed clearly that the success of the marabout movement was due to the promise made to the inhabitants of Waalo that "it would avenge them against their kings." Lacourbe in 1685, and Gaby in 1689, reported in similar vein: "The kings have no right to impose any tribute on their people. All their revenues are in the form of captives and livestock. They often go to pillage their subjects on the pretext that they have defamed them, committed theft or been found guilty of murder. As a result, no one is secure in his possessions or his freedom, because their kings take them off as captives. This was the cause of a revolution in their kingdom." All these testimonies have not stopped Philip Curtin from closing his eyes to our interpretation of the economic, political, and social context of this marabout movement. See Philip D. Curtin, *Economic Change in Precolonial Africa*, p. 50.
9 Barry, *Le royaume du Walo*, pp. 137–42. I apologize for a faulty interpretation of the movement in my earlier book due to an unfortunate confusion with developments in Kajoor. See also Lucie Colvin, "Islam and the State of Kajor: A case of successful resistance to *jihad*," *Journal of African History*, Vol. 15, No. 4, 1974, pp. 587–607, p. 197; and Diouf, "Le Kajoor," pp. 122–9.
10 Colvin, "Islam"; Diouf, "Le Kajoor," pp. 122–3.
11 Chambonneau, an eyewitness to these developments, is here again quite explicit about the part played by the Saint-Louis trading post in the annihilation of the Muslim religious movement. In an opening campaign between May and 20 June 1674, De Muchin obtained the support of the Waalo chiefs. He then returned

upstream for a distance of 60 leagues early in July 1674 with "the same vessels and other small boats. The fleet thus reinforced being stronger than during the first voyage, was capable of scaring all the fleets of the Negroes put together...This Naval Army came back down the river after a month and a half. On their arrival in August, all was rejoicing, fireworks and entertainment. A straw effigy of a Burguly bogeyman was burned." Ritchie, "Deux textes," pp. 345–6.

12 This is the principal shortcoming of Curtin's book, and there is plenty of documentation to that effect. It has never been my intention to deny that African societies have had their own internal dynamics. What I have been at pains to point out is that, from the fifteenth century onwards, the evolution of these societies has been increasingly determined by the European presence. This presence incorporated Africa into the developing capitalist system in such a way that, right from the start, the process of African dependence was set in motion. That process continues to this day. As in the past, it is maintained by an alliance between foreign capital and the African ruling classes. There is no way anyone can deny this obvious reality under the guise of "decolonizing African history," unless indeed one's objective is to perpetuate Africa's dependence. In this connection, see the review of my book by Philip D. Curtin in *The International Journal of African Historical Studies,* Vol. 6, No. 4, 1973, pp. 679–81.

## II SENEGAMBIA IN THE EIGHTEENTH CENTURY

1 Ly, *La compagnie du Sénégal de 1637 à 1696,* Présence Africaine, Paris, 1958, p. 35.

## 5 THE SLAVE TRADE IN THE EIGHTEENTH CENTURY

1 J. Copans, "Ethnies et régions dans une formation sociale dominée: Hypothèse à propos du cas sénégalais," *Anthropologie et Société. Minorités ethniques, Nationalismes,* Vol. 2, no 1, 1978, p. 100.
2 Ly, *La compagnie du Sénégal,* p. 35.
3 It must be borne in mind that Senegambia as defined in this book is larger than that defined by these other authors.
4 Curtin, *Economic Change in Precolonial Africa,* p. 162.
5 *Ibid.,* p. 164.
6 *Ibid.* These export figures were based on general estimates of British and French slave trading culled from naval data, with regional attributions made on the basis of varied samples.
7 J. Suret-Canale, "La Sénégambie à l'ère de la traite," *Revue canadienne des Etudes Africaines,* Vol. 11, No. 1, 1977, pp. 125–34.
8 Charles Becker, "La Sénégambie à l'époque de la traite des esclaves," *Société Française d'histoire d'Outre-Mer,* No. 325, 1977, p. 220.
9 Charles Becker and V. Martin, "Journal Historique et suite du Journal Historique 1729, 1731," *IFAN Bulletin,* Vol. 39, Series B, No. 2, April 1977, p. 224.
10 C. Becker and V. Martin, "Mémoire inédit de Doumet 1769," *IFAN Bulletin,* Vol. 41, Series B, No. 1, January 1974, pp. 71 and 73.

11  Rodney, *History of the Upper Guinea Coast*, p. 248.

12  *Ibid.*, p. 250.

13  J. Mettas, "La traite portugaise en Haute-Guinée 1758–1797," *Journal of African History,* Vol. 16, 1975, p. 347.

14  *Ibid.,* pp. 348 and 351.

15  *Ibid.*, p. 359.

16  Becker and Martin, "Mémoire," p. 74.

17  J. Mettas, *Répertoire des expéditions négrières françaises au XVIIIe siècle, édité par Serge Daget,* Société Française d'Histoire d'Outre-Mer, Nantes, Paris, 1978, p. 795. In the course of his lifetime, Jean Mettas began a colossal enterprise. This book, the first volume of a planned series, provides an account of 1,427 expeditions that set out from the port of Nantes alone between 1707 and 1793.

18  Curtin, *Economic Change in Precolonial Africa*, p. 256.

19  *Ibid.*, pp. 126–7 and 156.

20  *Ibid.*

21  C.O. 268/4 Fort Lewis, Senegal, 18 August 1775.

22  C.O. 267/1: "A Petition Presented by the Inhabitants of Senegal for the Redress of Injustices Done to Them by His Excellency the Governor O'Hara at Different Times," Senegal, 22 August 1775.

23  C.O. 267/17, La jurie 1776.

24  Colonies C6 17 Gorée, April 1777.

25  Lamiral, *L'Afrique et le peuple affriquain,* Paris, 1789, p. 171.

26  Colonies C6 17. Presumed date: 1783.

27  C.O. 267/19. Answer to the Questions Proposed to Lieutenant Colonel Maxwell... Saint-Louis, 1 January 1811.

28  Mettas, "La traite portugaise," pp. 358–9.

29  A. Delcourt, *La France et les Etablissements français au Sénégal entre 1713 et 1763,* IFAN, Dakar, 1952, p. 180.

30  S.M.X. Golberry, *Fragments d'un voyage en Afrique pendant les années 1785, 86, 87,* Paris, 1802, p. 196.

31  Delcourt, *La France,* p. 179.

32  *Ibid.*, pp. 179–229.

33  Curtin, *Economic Change in Precolonial Africa*, p. 217.

34  ANF, Col. C67, 23 April 1723.

35  Becker and Martin, "Mémoire de Doumet."

36  Curtin, *Economic Change in Precolonial Africa*, pp. 83–5.

37  Delcourt, *La France,* pp. 341–6.

38  E.C. Martin, *The British West African Settlements 1750–1821*, London, 1927, p. 74.

39  "In the period from 1727 to 1728, the Company was absolutely determined to get rid of the Senegalese concession. To prove that it was bearing the cost of its maintenance, the Company argued that the concession cost it 18 millions. In fact this sum included as much in made-up expenses as in pure losses. But what the company left out of its accounting was that a sum of 35 million was due from Santo Domingo for nine (9) years' worth of sales of slaves and assorted goods exported from Senegal. Then in the years following, that is to say, in 1729 and 1730, there was talk of gold mines; whereupon the Company changed its tune

and no longer wanted to abandon the concession." Unsigned memoir, dated 1762, on Senegal ANF. Sent to the author in Kaolack by Charles Becker, 14 July 1982.

40 Curtin, *Economic Change in Precolonial Africa*, p. 105.

41 *Ibid.*, pp. 113–21.

42 Sane, "La vie économique," pp. 58–9.

43 G. Brooks, "Luso-African Commerce and Settlement in the Gambia and Guinea Bissau Region," African Studies Center Working Papers, Boston University, 1980, p. 5.

44 *Ibid.*, pp. 9–16.

45 B.L. Mouser, "Trade Coasters and Conflict in the Rio Pongo from 1790 to 1808," *Journal of African History*, 1973, pp. 50–4.

46 *Ibid.*, pp. 55–64.

47 G. Brooks, *Yankee Traders, Old Coasters and African Middlemen,* Boston University Press, 1970, pp. 24–49.


# 6 THE STRENGTHENING OF *CEDDO* REGIMES IN THE EIGHTEENTH CENTURY

1 Reforms of outstanding interest initiated by Lat Sukaabe Faal have been highlighted by Lucie Colvin. Mamadou Diouf and Abdoulaye Bara Diop have also expatiated on them. See Colvin, "Islam," pp. 587–97; Diouf, "Le Kajoor," pp. 124–30; and Diop, *La société Wolof*, p. 167.

2 Diop, *La société Wolof*, p. 226.

3 Diouf, "Le Kajoor," pp. 119 and 130.

4 Colvin, "Islam," p. 598.

5 J. Boulègue, "Lat Sukabe Fal ou l'opiniâtreté d'un roi contre les échanges inégaux au Sénégal," *Collection les Africains*, Vol. 9, 1977, pp. 171–93.

6 J. Boulègue, quoting the account rendered by B.N. Godôt, French Manuscript Ms. Fr. No. 13380, "Lat Sukabe Fal," p. 176.

7 C. Becker and V. Martin, "Kajoor et Baol. Royaumes sénégalais et traite des esclaves du XVIIIe siècle," *Revue Française d'Histoire d'Outre-Mer,* No. 226/227, 1975, pp. 286–99.

8 In 1753, Brüe reported that the *Damel-Teeñ* Mawa had, in the course of the year, "sold nearly 400 captives. To our knowledge, none of his predecessors ever sold so many. Since the King takes practically nothing but guns and ammunition in exchange for his captives, we have almost no trade guns left." (C6–14 – Letter from the *Journal du Sénégal* to the Company, 20 June 1753, quoted in Becker and Martin, "Kajoor", p. 289.

9 Delcourt, *La France*, p. 240.

10 Barry, *Le royaume du Walo*, pp. 186–9.

11 *Ibid.*, pp. 208–10.

12 M. Klein, *Islam and Imperialism in Sine Saloum 1847–1914*, Stanford, 1968, p. 26.

13 *Ibid.*

14 *Ibid.*, pp. 27–9.

15 M. Klein, "Serer Tradition and Serer Development of Salum," unpublished manuscript, n.d.

16 O. Kane, "Les Maures et le Futa Toro au XVIII siècle," *Cahier d'Etudes Africaines,* Vol. 14, No. 54, 1974, p. 245.

17 *Ibid.*, p. 246.

18 O. Kane, "Samba Gelajo," *IFAN Bulletin,* vol. 32, Series B, No.4, 1970, pp. 912–24.

19 A. Ly, "L'épopée de Samba Guela Diegui," A doctoral study of an unpublished rendering, Dakar, 1977–8, 560 pages. A.A. Sy, "La Geste Tiedo," Doctoral thesis, Faculty of Arts, Dakar, 1978–80, 676 pages.

20 Sy, "La Geste Tiedo," pp. 365–7.

21 *Ibid.*, pp. 438–9.

22 Kane, "Les Maures et le Futa," pp. 246–7.

23 *Ibid.*, p. 248.

24 *Ibid.*, p. 924.

25 "The Fula country invariably presents the same aspect, that is to say, that it is the perennial prey of the Moors. There is no longer any point in noting the revolutions taking place here, because they bring no changes in the situation of the country. We just pay the customary dues to the king who happens to be in power. Today that much goes without a hitch." Col. C6 13, Lettre du Conseil supérieur du Sénégal, 25 July 1752.

"Once more, the Fula country has a new king. That is about all we have to say about it. It is a matter of no consequence on whose head this crown lands, since all real power is in the hands of the Moors." Col. C6 14, Lettre du Conseil supérieur du Sénégal, 20 June 1753.

26 Bathily, "Imperialism."

27 Mane, "Contribution," p. 128.

## 7 MUSLIM REVOLUTIONS IN THE EIGHTEENTH CENTURY

1 Bathily, "Imperialism," pp. 97–9.

2 P.D. Curtin, "Jihad in West Africa. Early Phases and Interrelations in Mauritania and Senegal," *Journal of African History,* Vol. 12, 1971, pp. 20–2.

3 Bathily, "Imperialism," p. 58.

4 Curtin, "Jihad," p. 22.

5 S. Diagne, "Le Bundu des origines au protectorat français de 1858," Master's Thesis, Faculty of Arts, Dakar, 1975–6, p. 1.

6 W. Rodney, "Jihad and Social Revolution in Futa Jallon in the Eighteenth Century," *Journal of the Historical Society of Nigeria,* Vol. 4, No. 2, 1968, pp. 274–6.

7 Curtin, "Jihad," pp. 21–2.

8 T. Diallo, "Les institutions politiques du Fouta Djalon au XIXe siècle," *Initiations et Etudes Africaines,* No. 28, Dakar, 1972, p. 208.

9 N. Levtzion, "The Early Jihad Movements," *Cambridge History of Africa,* Vol. IV (edited by Richard Gay), Cambridge University Press, 1975, p. 208.

10 Rodney, *"Jihad,"* pp. 280–2.

11 T. Winterbottom, *An Account of the Native African, in the Neighbourhood of Sierra Leone*, n.p., 1803, p. 8.

12 A.I. Sow (ed.), *Le filon du bonheur éternel, par Thierno Mouhammadou Samba Mombeya*, Classiques Africains, A. Colin, 1971, p. 4.

13  O. Kane, "Les unités territoriales du Fuuta Toro," *IFAN Bulletin*, Vol. 35, Series B, No. 3, 1973, p. 622.
14  D. Robinson, "The Islamic Revolution of Futa Toro," *The International Journal of African Historical Studies*, Vol. 8, No. 2, 1975, pp. 201–8.
15  L. Colvin, "Islam," 1974. p. 601. Also, Baron Roger Kélédor, *Histoire Africaine*, Paris, 1829, p. 129.
16  Robinson, "Islamic Revolution," p. 202.
17  *Ibid.*, pp. 209–14.
18  Diouf, "Le Kajoor," pp. 134–9.

## 8  THE IMPACT OF THE SLAVE TRADE: ECONOMIC REGRESSION AND SOCIAL STRIFE

1  Charles Becker, *La Sénégambie à l'époque de la traite des esclaves*, Société Française d'Histoire d'Outre-Mer, 1977, p. 219.
2  Curtin, *Economic Change in Precolonial Africa*, pp.16 and 110.
3  C. Becker, "Les conditions écologiques et la traite des esclaves en Sénégambie. Climat, sécheresse, famines et épidémies aux XVIIe et XVIIIe siècles," CNRS LA 94, Kaolack, 1982 (unpublished). Following the partial efforts of Delcourt, Curtin, and Moraes, Charles Becker not only fills in the gaps in available documentation, but also presents an interesting update on correlations between natural calamities and the slave trade. His analysis and the numerous fresh sources he opens up to scrutiny have provided the basis for the argument here.
4  Carson, Materials, p. 352; quoted by Becker, "Les conditions," pp. 5–6.
5  C6.6, 24 June 1721.
6  C6.8, 28 March 1724.
7  C6.14, Letter from the High Council, Senegal, 20 June 1753.
8  C6.14. Letter from the High Council, Senegal, 3 June 1754.
9  A.N. C6.15. Memoir on Senegal, 1758.
10  Barry, *Le royaume du Walo*, pp. 208–11.
11  F3.61. Folio 239, Letter from Littleton, 1786.
12  Becker, "Les conditions," pp 25–9.
13  *Ibid.*, pp. 34–8 and 40–3.
14  *Ibid.*, pp. 43–51.
15  *Ibid.*, p. 37.
16  M. Klein and P.E. Lovejoy, "Slavery in West Africa," in H.A. Gemery and J.S. Hogendorn, eds., *The Uncommon Market: Essays in the Economic history of the Atlantic Slave Trade*, New York, 1979, p. 85.
17  Diop, *La société Wolof*, pp. 201–2.
18  *Ibid.*, p. 200.
19  M.S. Balde, in *L'esclavage en Afrique précoloniale, L'esclavage et la guerre sainte au Fuuta Jallon*, ed. Claude Meillassoux, Maspero, Paris, 1975, pp. 188–90.
20  *Ibid.*, pp. 191–3.
21  *Ibid.*, pp. 195–201.
22  *Ibid.*, pp. 201–4.
23  J. Mettas, "La traite portugaise."
24  *Ibid.*, pp. 352 and 356.
25  Balde, *L'esclavage*, pp. 205–6.
26  W. Rodney, "African Slavery and Other Forms of Social Oppression on the

Upper Guinea Coast in the Context of the Atlantic Slave Trade," *Journal of African History*, Vol. 3, 1966, p. 439.

27  W. Rodney, "Jihad," pp. 282–3.

28  Diop, *La société Wolof*, pp. 196–99.

29  C. Meillassoux, ed., *L'esclavage en Afrique précoloniale*, Maspero, Paris, 1975, 582 pages; S. Miers and I. Kopytoff, *Slavery in Africa: Historical and Anthropological Perspectives*, University of Wisconsin Press, Madison, 1977, 474 pages; P.E. Lovejoy, *Transformations in Slavery: A History of Slavery in Africa*, African Studies Series 36, Cambridge University Press, 1983, 349 pages; C.C. Robertson and M. Klein, *Women and slavery in Africa*, University of Wisconsin Press, 1983, 380 pages.

30  I. Mendez, "Resistance to Slavery in West Africa During the Eighteenth and Nineteenth Centuries With Special Emphasis on the Upper Guinea Coast," Unpublished document, African History Seminars, School of Oriental and African Studies, 1975, p. 1. It was Walter Rodney who first published evidence of slave revolts in the Southern Rivers area. In his wake, Ivan Mendez undertook a systematic study of this little-known subject. Apart from the seminar here cited, however, we have had no general surveys of slave revolts. There is a clear need for such studies now.

31  J. Watt, "Journal of James Watt," Manuscript, Rhodes House, Oxford, p. 73. Quoted by Mendez, "Resistance."

32  I. Mendez, "Resistance." pp. 8–9.

33  *Ibid.*, pp. 10–12.

34  B.L. Mouser, "Trade Coasters and Conflicts in the Rio Pongo from 1790 to 1808," *Journal of African History*, Vol. 1, 1973, p. 52.

35  A. Bathily, "Job Ben Salomon, Marabout négrier 1700–1773," *Jeune Afrique, Collection les Africains*, Vol. 6, 1977, pp. 195–8. Yuba's biography was published by Grant Douglas in *The Fortunate Slave*, Oxford University Press, 1968.

36  Bathily, "Job Ben Salomon," pp. 198–204.

37  B. Barry, "Afro-Americans and Futa Jallon," in Joseph Harris, ed., *The Global Dimension of the African Diaspora*, Howard University Press, 1982, pp. 285–6. Abdurahman's life story is marvellously recounted in Terry Alford's *Prince Among Slaves*, Harcourt, New York, 1977.

## 9 THE CRISIS OF THE TRANS-ATLANTIC TRADING SYSTEM AND THE TRIUMPH OF LEGITIMATE TRADE IN THE FIRST HALF OF THE NINETEENTH CENTURY

1  B. Mouser, "Trade and Politics in the Nunez and Pongo Rivers 1790–1865," Doctoral dissertation, Indiana University, 1971, p. 39.

2  G. Brooks, *Yankee Traders*, p.112.

3  O. Goerg, "Echanges, réseaux, marchés. L'impact colonial en Guinée, mi-XIXe – 1913," Doctoral dissertation, Paris VII, 1981, p. 35.

4  B. Mouser, "Trade and Politics," p. 130.

5  *Ibid.*, pp. 148–66.

6  *Ibid.*, pp. 216–21.

7  *Ibid.*, p. 183.

8  *Ibid.*, p. 130.

9  *Ibid.*, pp. 137–47.

10  S. Amin, Preface to Boubacar Barry, *Le royaume du Walo, 1659–1859: le Sénégal avant la conquête,* Maspero, Paris, 1972, p. 22

11  For a more detailed treatment of this colonial plantation scheme, see Georges Hardy, *La mise en valeur du Sénégal de 1817 à 1854,* Emile Larose, 1921.

12  Barry, *Le royaume du Walo*, pp. 256–8.

13  M. Diouf, "Le Kajoor," p. 117.

14  Bathily, "Imperialism," p. 181.

15  Curtin, *Economic Change in Precolonial Africa*, pp. 181–90.

16  Bathily, "Imperialism," pp. 181–90.

17  Hardy, *La mise en valeur*, p. 255.

18  M. Courtet, *Etude sur le Sénégal,* Challamel, Paris, 1903. p. 15.

19  O. Sane, "La vie économique et sociale des Goréens entre 1817 et 1846," Doctoral dissertation, Dakar, 1978.

20  Diouf, "Le Kajoor," p. 184.

21  G. Brooks, "Peanuts and Colonialism: Consequences of the Commercialization of Peanuts in West Africa, 1830–1870," *Journal of African History*, Vol. 16, 1975, pp. 29–54. Brooks sheds valuable light on linkages between peanuts and the French conquest of Senegambia.

22  Mouser, "Trade and Politics," pp. 186–7.

23  Goerg, "Echanges," pp. 106–15.

24  Brooks, "Peanuts," p. 37.

25  *Ibid.*, p. 34. and Table I: Gambian Peanuts Exports, 1834–1851.

26  *Ibid.*, pp. 41–2.

27  *Ibid.*, pp. 46–7.

28  Goerg, "Echanges," p. 39.

29  *Ibid.*, pp. 83 and 87.

30  Bathily, "Imperialism," pp. 126–8.

31  *Ibid.*, p. 193.

32  *Ibid.*, p. 218.

33  *Ibid.,* p. 218.

34  Curtin, *Economic Change in Precolonial Africa*, pp. 136–52.


## 10  POPULAR REBELLIONS AND POLITICAL AND SOCIAL CRISES IN FUTA JALLON

1  Thanks to the theses of Mouser on the Rio Pongo and the Rio Nunez, that of Joye Bowman Hawkins on the Foria, and above all, thanks to the outstanding work of Winston Franklin McGowan, "The Development of European Relations with Fuuta Jallon and French Colonial Rule 1794–1897" (Doctoral dissertation, School of Oriental and African Studies, London, July 1975), an overview of the history of southern Senegambia in the nineteenth century is now possible. The author is grateful to McGowan, whose collaboration from 1969 enabled him to build up his own documentation on Futa Jallon history. In his thesis, based on his initial two-volume text, McGowan traces events and data with painstaking exactitude. His accuracy gives us a basis for concentrating on the analysis required for a regional history.

2  McGowan, "The Development of European Relations," pp. 418–22.

3  L. Sanneh, "Fuuta Jallon and the Jakhanke Clerical Tradition," *Journal of Religion in Africa*, Vol. 12, 1981, p. 47.

4 A great deal is now known about the life and work of Shaykh Umar, thanks to several works. But Robinson's forthcoming book is the first study that presents a comprehensive historical overview. We are grateful to him for allowing us to use his manuscript. It fills in numerous gaps in the available data, enabling us to highlight the impact of Shaykh Umar on the political and religious development of Senegambia in the period when the design for colonial conquest was taking precise form.

5 D. Robinson, "The Early Career of Umar Tal," unpublished manuscript, 1982, pp. 3–34.

6 Robinson, "The Early Career of Umar Tal," pp. 120–37.

7 B. Barry, "Crise politique et importance des révoltes populaires au Fuuta Jallon au XIXe siècle," *Afrika Zamani, Revue d'Histoire Africaine*, Nos. 8 & 9, Yaoundé, December 1978, pp. 51–4.

8 E.W. Blyden, *Report on the Timbo Expedition,* n.p., 1873, pp. 267–320.

9 Anonymous Document 1G8, Boké, 15 April 1873.

10 A.I. Sow, *Chronique et recits du Fuuta Jallon,* Librairie Klienksieck, Paris, 1968. p. 137.

11 Barry, "Crise politique," pp. 55–61.


## 11 FUTA JALLON EXPANSION INTO THE SOUTHERN RIVERS REGION

1 McGowan, "The Development of European Relations," pp. 285–96.

2 Goerg, "Echanges," p. 60.

3 Mouser, "Trade and Politics," p. 39.

4 McGowan, "The Development of European Relations," pp. 490–500.

5 Goerg, "Echanges," pp. 65–79.

6 Mouser, "Trade and Politics," pp. 216–22.

7 *Ibid.*, pp. 265–72.

8 Goerg, "Echanges," p. 75.

9 Mane, "Contribution à l'histoire du Kaabu." J.B. Hawkins, "Conflict-interaction and Change in Guinea-Bissau: Fulbe Expansion and Its Impact, 1850–1900," Doctoral dissertation, UCLA, 1980. B. Sidibe, "The Story of Kaabu," The Fall of Kaabu: Conference on Mandingo Studies, SOAS, London, 1972.

10 Mane, "Contribution à l'histoire du Kaabu," pp. 140–1. Hawkins, "Conflict-interaction," pp. 90–1.

11 Mane, "Contribution à l'histoire du Kaabu," pp. 134–5.

12 Poem by Amadou Lamine Drame, presented at the Colloquium on Kaabu Oral Traditions, Dakar, 1980.

13 Mane, "Contribution à l'histoire du Kaabu," pp. 146–7.

14 Hawkins, "Conflict-interaction," pp. 107–14.


## 12 THE COLONY OF SENEGAL AND POLITICAL AND SOCIAL CRISES IN NORTHERN SENEGAMBIA

1 Barry, *Le royaume du Waalo*, pp. 259–67.

2 Diouf, "Le Kajoor," p. 188.

3 Colvin, "Islam," p. 182

4 Diouf, "Le Kajoor," p. 188.

5 *Ibid.*, p. 195.
6 Barry, *Le royaume du Waalo*, 1972. pp. 267–74. The following is the account given by Monsérat of the refusal to heed the extradition request: "The Governor of Senegal presented a request to this chief through the Special Commandant at Gorée. The head of the Republic of Dakar refused explicitly to deliver him to the French. For political and commercial reasons, Governor Brou had to drop this affair. In any case, there was no way he could get the marabout Yagayssa arrested: the man had too great an influence over these communities of Mahometans. Even if we had mounted an expedition against the chief of Dakar, his fellow Muslims would still have rescued him, and he would have found a refuge in the Yolof kingdom." Monsérat, Previously unpublished Memoire on the History of Northern Senegal, 1819. Published with a commentary by Boubacar Barry in the *Bulletin de l'IFAN,* Series B, No. 11, 1970, p. 11.
7 *Ibid.*, pp. 289–306.
8 Robinson, "Islamic Revolution," pp. 18–27.
9 *Ibid.*, p. 37.
10 S.M. Cissoko, *L'impact de la guerre sainte umarienne dans les royaumes du Xaso 1850–1860*, an anthology published in honor of Raymond Mauny, Société Française d'Histoire d'Outre-mer, 1981, pp. 709–11.
11 Bathily, "Imperialism," pp. 371–417.
12 Robinson, "Islamic Revolution," pp. 40–3.
13 Diouf, "Le Kajoor," pp. 200–27.
14 *Ibid.*, pp. 242–50.
15 *Ibid.*, pp. 266–89.
16 M. Klein, *Islam and Imperialism in Senegal–Sine Saalum, 1847–1914,* Stanford University Press, 1968, pp. 41–4.
17 *Ibid.*, pp. 46–53.
18 *Ibid.*, pp. 44–6.
19 *Ibid.*, pp. 54–62.

## 13  DEFEAT OF THE HOLY WARRIORS IN NORTHERN SENEGAMBIA

1 Diouf, "Le Kajoor," pp. 66–7.
2 *Ibid.*, pp. 306–11.
3 *Ibid.*, pp. 311–17. L.G. Colvin, *Historical Dictionary of Senegal*, African Historical Dictionaries No. 23, The Scarecrow Press, 1981, pp. 197–200.
4 Klein, *Islam*, pp. 81–3.
5 Diouf, "Le Kajoor," p. 320.
6 Klein, *Islam*, p. 92.
7 D. Robinson, "Islamic Revolution," pp. 52–7.
8 *Ibid.*, pp. 70–8.
9 *Ibid.*, pp. 79–83.
10 "As a consequence, three thousand volunteers from Waalo, Jolof and Saint-Louis were unleashed against Kajoor in the wake of our columns. Like swarms of locusts which in a matter of hours strip the lushest fields to desert, these pillaging gangs, wherever they roamed, brought ruin, desolation, death. One could say that from this period, these regions, formerly so rich and populous, were

ruined for countless years ahead, thus drying up for a long time one of the most abundant springs of our trade." F.O.M. SII, Dossier 4, quoted in Diouf, "Le Kajoor," p. 325.
11  Robinson, "Islamic Revolution," pp. 83–8.
12  A.C. Eunice, *Precolonial Sénégal: The Wolof Kingdom, 1800 to 1890*, African Studies Center, Boston University, 1977, pp. 67–77.
13  Diouf, "Le Kajoor," pp. 334–44. Charles, "Shaikh Amadu Ba," pp. 72–9.

## 14  COLONIAL IMPERIALISM AND EUROPEAN RIVALRIES IN SENEGAMBIA

1  "The Colony is primarily a trading post, or rather a bunch of trading posts. Their mission is to supply our industries and businessmen with natural produce for processing in the metropolis, as well as to serve as a market for the sale of some of our manufactured commodities. Our policy is tailored to these conditions. It must be peaceful in essence, with no ambition for territorial expansion. For any action to that end would create disturbances in the area from which our markets draw their supplies, forcing us to sacrifice men and money." Orders from Admiral Fournichon to Colonel Brière de Lisle, dated 1876. Quoted in Diouf, "Le Kajoor," p. 348.
2  Robinson, "Islamic Revolution," pp. 104–9.
3  Diouf, "Le Kajoor."
4  *Ibid.*, pp. 348–60.
5  A. Villard, *Histoire du Sénégal*, Maurice Viale, Dakar, 1943, pp. 160–2.
6  Diouf, "Le Kajoor," pp. 348–60.
7  Goerg, "Echanges," pp. 118–19.
8  Hawkins, "Conflict-interaction," pp. 146–7.
9  C. Roche, *Conquête et Résistance des Peuples de Casamance, 1850–1920*, N.E.A., Dakar, 1976, pp. 191–8.
10  Goerg, "Echanges," pp. 144–5.
11  *Ibid.*, p. 147.
12  Roche, *Conquête*, pp. 221–3.
13  *Ibid.*, p. 204.
14  Hawkins, "Conflict-interaction," pp. 167–8.
15  Roche, *Conquête*, pp. 205–6.
16  Goerg, "Echanges," pp. 140–43.

## 15  LAST-DITCH RESISTANCE MOVEMENTS OF LEGITIMIST RULERS IN NORTHERN SENEGAMBIA

1  Colvin, *Sénégal*, pp. 197–200.
2  Diouf, "Le Kajoor," pp. 350–79 and 390–5.
3  Samb, quoted in Diouf, "Le Kajoor," p. 198.
4  Klein, *Islam*, pp. 104–13.
5  *Ibid.*, pp. 96–104.
6  *Ibid.*, pp. 130–42.
7  Bathily, "Imperialism," pp. 428–43.
8  *Ibid.*, pp. 452–76.

9 Hrbeck, "A Fighting Marabout: The Beginning of Mamadu Lamin's Struggle in Senegal," *Praha, Archiv Oriental,* Vol. 44, 1976, pp. 1–2.
10 Bathily, "Imperialism," p. 480.
11 Eunice, "Precolonial Senegal: The Jolof Kingdom 1800–1890," *African Research Studies,* No. 42, Boston University, 1977, pp. 82–92.
12 *Ibid.*, pp. 104–17.
13 *Ibid.*, pp. 123–7.
14 *Ibid.*, pp. 127–31.
15 Cheikh A. Ndao, *L'exil d'Alburi,* J. Oswald, Paris, 1967, p. 88.
16 Robinson, "Islamic Revolution," pp. 89–91.
17 *Ibid.*, pp. 124–38.
18 *Ibid.*, pp. 139–59.

## 16  THE CONQUEST OF THE SOUTHERN RIVERS REGION

1 C.A. Quinn, *Mandingo Kingdoms of the Senegambia: Traditionalism, Islam and European Expansion,* Northwestern University Press, 1972, p. 170.
2 Roche, *Conquête,* pp. 214–7.
3 Quinn, *Mandingo Kingdoms,* p. 184.
4 *Ibid.,* pp. 170–7. Roche, *Conquête,* pp. 132–8.
5 *Ibid.,* pp. 138–45.
6 *Ibid.,* pp. 145–53.
7 *Ibid.,* p. 243. Hawkins, "Conflict-interaction," pp. 211–15.
8 Roche, *Conquête,* p. 239.
9 Hawkins, "Conflict-interaction," pp. 218–37.
10 *Ibid.*, pp. 118–24 and 169.
11 *Ibid.*, pp. 248–51, 260–4.
12 Roche, *Conquête,* pp. 248–59.
13 *Ibid.*, pp. 259–63. Also Hawkins, "Conflict-interaction," pp. 266–75.
14 McGowan, "The Development of European Relations," pp. 524–30.
15 *Ibid.*, pp. 530–4 and 569–70.
16 Goerg, "Echanges," pp. 79–83.
17 *Ibid.*, p. 117.
18 McGowan, "The Development of European Relations," pp. 579–81.
19 *Ibid.*, pp. 585–6, 625 and 640.
20 Goerg, "Echanges," pp. 148–51.
21 *Ibid.*, pp. 151–2.
22 *Ibid.*, pp. 152–5.
23 McGowan, "The Development of European Relations," pp. 646 and 659.
24 Goerg, "Echanges," pp. 153–61.
25 McGowan, "The Development of European Relations," pp. 742–5.

## 17  THE BALANCING ACT OF THE *ALMAMIS* OF TIMBO IN THEIR ATTEMPTS TO COPE WITH CENTRIFUGAL FORCES

1 McGowan, "The Development of European Relations," pp. 544–5; Co 267/320, "Blyden Report on the Timbo Expedition, January–March 1873."
2 *Ibid.*, pp. 550 and 556.

3 *Ibid.*, p. 600.
4 *Ibid.*, pp. 728 and 736.
5 *Ibid.*, p. 592.
6 Ismael Barry, "Contribution à l'étude de l'Histoire de la Guinée. Les Hubbu du Fitaba et les Almami du Fuuta." Graduate Diploma thesis, Institut Polytechnique Julius Nyere, Kankan, 1970–1, pp. 117–22. This excellent thesis has the particular merit of finally presenting the Hubbu point of view, in an account recorded by Ismael Barry as part of his fieldwork.
7 "Considering the amount of trade these Hubbu divert from Sierra Leone every year, and taking the impact of their movement into consideration, it is clearly imperative that the Government take steps to halt the atrocities committed by these vagabonds, otherwise they will end up completely destroying trade with the hinterland." E. Blyden, "Report on the Expedition to Falaba, January to March 1872," *Proceedings of the Royal Geographical Society*, Vol. 17, 1873, p. 124.
8 Alfa Ibrahima Sow, *Chroniques et récits du Fouta Jallon*, C. Klincksieck, Paris, 1968, p. 137.
9 Barry, "Crise politique," p. 57. McGowan, "The Development of European Relations," pp. 549–50.
10 Barry, "Les Hubbu du Fitaba," pp. 140–53.
11 "Samori did a great job for trade and civilization last year when he crushed the Hubbu regime and freed the roads of its cruel exactions. For thirty years the Hubbu, in rebellion against the Futa Jallon government, had defied the two armies of Solimana and Futa." *The Sierra Leone Weekly News*, Saturday July 4th, 1884.
12 Paul Marty, *Islam en Guinée, Le Futa Jalon*, Editions Ernest Leroux, Paris, 1921, pp. 68–93.
13 Alby, on a mission to Timbo in 1893, has left testimony that sheds significant light on the political and social aspects of this conflict "The *Wali* is capable of mobilizing more than 2000 armed young men. Six years ago he migrated from the Kebu region of Futa to escape the war ravaging the area, as well as the taxes imposed on his livestock herds by the *Almamis*. He stresses that his intentions are peaceful, taking pains to point out that his ancestors never belonged to families of chiefs or kings. The cause of the current crisis is the stubborn determination of the *Almamis* to pursue a group of Peul who have left the Futa in search of peace and security in a state independent of their power, chasing them all the way into the neighboring states." A.F.O.M. Guinée II, "Notes de M. Alby en mission à Timbo, du 25 avril au 12 juin 1893."
14 Mamdou Sow Samba, "La région de Labé – Fouta Djallon au XIXe siècle," Graduate diploma thesis, Sorbonne, Paris, pp. 100–5.
15 McGowan, "The Development of European Relations," p. 557.
16 *Ibid.*, pp. 557–63. So palpable was the power of the *Alfa* Ibrahima from this time on, that in those areas of the Southern Rivers region conquered by the Futa Jallon, there was a tendency to suppose that the *Alfa* of Labé was indeed the *Almami* of Timbo. As a matter of fact, until the time of *Alfa* Yaya, the *Alfas* of Labé answered to the usurped title of *Almami*.
17 McGowan, "The Development of European Relations," p. 651.
18 *Ibid.*, p. 737.

19 *Ibid.*, p. 658.
20 Yves Person, *Samori, Une Révolution Dyula*, I.F.A.N., Dakar.
21 *Ibid.*
22 McGowan, "The Development of European Relations," pp. 535–41.
23 *Ibid.*, pp. 595–9.
24 *Ibid.*, p. 569.
25 *Ibid.*, pp. 595–9.
26 *Ibid.*, pp. 613–22 and 635.
27 *Ibid.*, pp. 652–4 and 664.
28 *Ibid.*, pp. 698–705.
29 *Ibid.*, pp. 719–24.
30 *Ibid.*, p. 725.
31 *Ibid.*, pp. 599–606.
32 *Ibid.*, pp. 604–11.
33 *Ibid.*, pp. 622–3.
34 *Ibid.*, pp. 623–32.
35 *Ibid.*, pp. 642–3.
36 *Ibid.*, pp. 668–71.
37 *Ibid.*, pp. 671–5.
38 *Ibid.*, pp. 675–87.
39 *Ibid.*, pp. 706–19.
40 *Ibid.*, pp. 720–6.

## 18  BOKAR BIRO AND THE CONQUEST OF FUTA JALLON

1 W.F. McGowan, "Fula Resistance to French Expansion into Futa Jallon, 1889–1896," *Journal of African History,* 1981, pp. 248–9.
2 *Ibid.*, pp. 247–8.
3 *Ibid.*, pp. 249–50.
4 *Ibid.*, p. 250.
5 McGowan, "The Development of European Relations," pp. 811–15. "Fula Resistance," pp. 246–7.
6 McGowan, "Fula Resistance," p. 253.
7 B. Barry, *Bokar Biro – Le Dernier Grand Almami du Futa Jallon*, Editions ABC, Paris, 1978.
8 The name Petel Jiga means "Vulture Rock." It was given to the site on account of the scavengers attracted there by the large number of casualties.
9 B. Barry, "Bokar Biro," in *Les Africains*, Vol. 12, edited by Charles-André Julien, Editions J.A., Paris, 1978, p. 76.
10 Bokar Biro's ruse was discovered when the French arrived in Saint-Louis. In place of a signature, the *Almami* had simply appended a verse from the Koran to the document, plus a memo saying he would like to meet the Governor of Guinea at a later date, to discuss relations with his country, after consulting his dignitaries and provincial chiefs.
11 Barry, *Bokar Biro,* pp. 76–83.
12 A.I. Sow, *Chroniques et récits du Fouta Djalon,* Librairie C. Klinschsieck, Paris, 1968, pp. 219–21.

## 19  MASS RESISTANCE MOVEMENTS AMONG THE JOOLA AND THE KONYAGI

1  Roche, *Conquête*, pp. 111–15.
2  *Ibid.*, pp. 181–7.
3  *Ibid.*, pp. 267–80.
4  *Ibid.*, pp. 281–4.
5  *Ibid.*, pp. 284–9.
6  *Ibid.*, pp. 289–94.
7  A. Camara, "Les Koniagui 1900–1904," Masters Thesis, Department of History, University of Dakar, 1974–5, pp. 28–35.
8  *Ibid.*, pp. 99–125.
9  According to Hinault, Alcune declared that he would never take a single step toward a European, neither would he ever report at the post; and that the Konyagi were determined that as long as a single one of them remained alive, the French could not occupy their country. Camara, "Les Koniagui," pp. 129–30.
10  *Ibid.*, p. 152.
11  The argument put forward by the chief of Ifane was as follows: The delegates sent to Conakry were not qualified to speak for the country. If they indeed made the declarations attributed to them, it must have been because, having traveled such a long distance over land and sea, they ended up so disoriented that they could no longer tell whence the sun rose, nor where it set. How could the declarations of men who had lost their sense of direction be taken seriously? Camara, "Les Koniagui," p. 173.
12  *Ibid.*, pp. 173–85.
13  *Ibid.*, pp. 186–97.

# Bibliography

Brasseur, P. 1964. *Bibliographie générale du Mali*. Dakar.

Carson, P. 1968. *Materials for West African History in French Archives*. London: University of London, Atheon Press.

Diallo, T., Mbacke, M.-B., Trikdovic, M., and Barry, B. 1966. *Catalogue des manuscrits de l'I.F.A.N., Fonds Vieillard, Gaden, Brévié, Figaret, Shaykh Moussa Kamara et Cremer en langue arabe, peule et voltaique*. Dakar: I.F.A.N.

Johnson, G.W. 1964. "Bibliographic essays. Senegal." *Africana Newsletter* 2, I (entire issue).

Joucla, E.A. 1937. *Bibliographie de l'Afrique occidentale française*. Paris.

Markowitz, I.L. 1970. "A bibliographic essay on the study of ideology, political thought, development and politics in Senegal." Parts I and II, *Current Bibliography on African Affairs*, III, 3 (March 1970), 5–29 and III, 4 (April 1970), 5–35. Westport.

Pollet, G. 1964. "Bibliographie des Sarakolé." *Journal de la Société des Africanistes*, 34: 283–92.

Porges, L. 1977. *Bibliographie des régions du Sénégal*. Dakar: Ministère du Plan et du Développement. Supplement for the period from the beginning to 1965, plus an update for 1966–1973. Paris: Mouton–Lattage-A.C.C.T. 637 pages.

## THESES AND UNPUBLISHED ARTICLES

Barrows, L.C. 1974. "General Faidherbe, Maurel and Prom Company and French Expansion in Senegal." Ph.D. dissertation, U.C.L.A.

Barry, I. 1970–1. "Contribution à l'étude de l'histoire de la Guinée: Les Hubbu du Fitaba et les Almami du Fuuta." Diploma thesis, Institut Polytechnique Julius Nyéréré.

Bathily, A. 1975. "Imperialism and colonial expansion in Senegal in the nineteenth century with particular reference to economic, social and political developments in the kingdom of Gajaaga." Ph.D. thesis, Centre of West African Studies, University of Birmingham.

Boulègue, J. 1969. La Sénégambie du milieu du XVe siècle au début du XVIIe siècle. Doctoral thesis, University of Paris.

1972. Les Luso-Africains de la Sénégambie aux XVIe-XIXe siècles. Mimeographed document. 114 pages. Travaux et Documents, Department of History, Faculty of Arts, University of Dakar.

Cissoko, S.M. 1972. Introduction à l'histoire des Mandingues de l'Ouest: l'Empire du Kabou (XVIe–XIXe siècle). Paper delivered at the Conference on Manding Studies, School of Oriental and African Studies, University of London.

1979. Contribution à l'histoire politique des royaumes du Khasso dans le Haut-Sénégal, des origines à la conquête française, XVIIe siècle à 1890. 2 vols. Doctoral thesis, Paris I, Sorbonne. 1206 pages.

Coifman, V.B. 1969. History of the Wolof state of Jolof until 1860 including comparative data from the Wolof state of Walo. Xeroxed document. Ph.D. dissertation, Ann Arbor (University Microfilms) 458 pages.

Colvin, L.A.G. 1972. Kajor and its diplomatic relations with Saint-Louis du Sénégal 1763–1861, Ph.D. dissertation, Ann Arbor (Xerox), Columbia University. 458 pages.

Diagne, S. 1975–6. Le Bundu des origines au protectorat français de 1858. Masters thesis, Faculty of Arts, University of Dakar.

Diouf, M. 1980. Le Kajoor au XIXe siècle et la conquête coloniale. Doctoral thesis, Paris I.

Gamble, D.P. 1957. The Wolof of Senegambia. London: International African Institute. 110 pp.

Goerg, O. 1981. Echanges, réseaux, marchés. L'impact colonial en Guinée mi-XIXe, 1913. Doctoral thesis, Paris VII. 563 pp.

Harris, J.E. 1965. The Kingdom of Fouta Diallon. Ph.D. dissertation, Northwestern University.

Hawkins, J.B. 1980. Conflict-interaction and Change in Guinea-Bissau, Fulbe Expansion and its Impact, 1850–1900. Los Angeles: University of California.

Howard, A.M. 1972. Big men, traders and chiefs: Power, commerce and spacial change in the Sierra Leone, Guinea plain. Ph.D. dissertation, University of Wisconsin.

Johnson, J.P. 1974. The almamate of Futa Toto 1779–1836: A political history. Ph.D. dissertation, University of Wisconsin

Klein, M. n.d. Serer tradition and Serer development of Salum. Unpublished manuscript.

Ly, A. 1977–8. L'épopée de Samba Guela Diegui – Etude d'une version inédite. Doctoral thesis, Dakar.

McGowan, W.F. 1972. The development of European relations with Fuuta Jallon and French colonial rule 1794–1896. Ph.D., London: S.O.A.S.

Macson, M. 1975. A social history of Saint-Louis du Sénégal 1758–1854. Ph.D. dissertation, Princeton University.

Person, Y. 1974. "Proceedings of a Colloquium at the University of Aberdeen." (April 1974), pp. 7–8.

Robinson, D. n.d. The Holy war of Umar Tal in the Senegal and Niger river valleys (provisional title). Unpublished manuscript, 500 pp.

Sane, O. 1978. La vie économique et sociale des Goréens entre 1817 et 1848. Doctoral thesis, Dakar.

Sidibe, B.K. 1972. "The story of Kaabu: Its extent." Paper presented at the Conference on Manding Studies, School of Oriental and African Studies, University of London.

Sow, M.S. (n.d.). La région de Labé-Fouta Djallon au XIXe siècle. D.E.S. Paris: The Sorbonne.

Sy, A.A. 1979–80. La geste Tiedo. Doctoral thesis. Faculty of Arts, University of Dakar. 676 pp.

## EYE-WITNESS ACCOUNTS AND TRAVELERS' REPORTS

Adanson, M. 1751. *Voyage to Senegal. A natural history of Senegal.* Paris.

Alexis, S.L. de 1637. *Relation du voyage au Cap-Vert.* Paris and Rouen.

Alfonce, J. 1559. *Les voyages aventureux du Capitaine Ian Alfonce Sainctongeois.* Poitiers: Jean de Marnes.

Alvares d'Almada, A. 1946. *Tratado breve dos rios de Guine de Capo Verde.* First published 1594. New edition published by Luis Silveira, Lisbon.

Ancelle, J. 1886. *Les explorations au Sénégal et dans les contrées voisines depuis l'antiquité jusqu'à nos jours.* Paris: Maisonneuve et Leclerc.

Astley, T. 1745. *A New General Collection of Voyages and Travels.* 4 vols. London.

Azan, H. 1863–4. "Notice sur le Walo." *Revue maritime et coloniale*, Vols. 9 and 10.

Barbot, J. 1732. *A Description of the Coasts of North and South Guinea.* London: A. Churchill. 716 pp.

Baron, R.K. 1829. *Histoire Africaine.* Paris.

Barreira, B. 1972. "La description de la côte de Guinée du père Baltasar Barreira." Published by Guy Thilmans and Nize Isabel de Moraes in *Bulletin de l'I.F.A.N.*, 31: 1–50.

Barry, B. 1970. "Mémoire inédit de Monsérat sur l'histoire du nord Sénégal de 1818 à 1839. Published with commentary by Boubacar Barry in *I.F.A.N. Bulletin*, Series B. 32, No. 1 (January).

Bathily, I.D. 1969. "Notices socio-historiques sur l'ancien royaume soninké du Gadiaga." *Bulletin de l'I.F.A.N.*, 31: 31–105. With an introduction and notes by Abdoulaye Bathily.

Bayol, J. 1888. "Voyage en Sénégambie, Haut-Niger, Bambouck, Fouta Djallon et Grand Bélédougou, 1880–1885." Revue maritime et coloniale, 94: 441–73; 95: 72–104, 265–81, 438–66; 96: 155–81, 492–559 (1887–8). Paris: L. Baudoin et Cie. 230 pp. 1 Map.

Becker, C. and V. Martin. 1974. "Mémoire inédit de Doumet 1769." *Bulletin de l'I.F.A.N.*, Vol. 41, Series B, No. 1, January 1974, pp. 25–92.

1977. "Journal Historique et suite du Journal Historique 1729–1731." *Bulletin de l'I.F.A.N.*, Vol. 39, Series B, April 1977, pp. 223–89.

Berenger Feraud, J.L. 1879. *Les peuplades de la Sénégambie : Histoire, ethnographie, moeurs et coutumes, légendes, etc.* Paris: E. Leroux.

Bertrand, B. 1849. "Notes sur la Guinée portugaise ou Sénégambie méridionale," *Bulletin de la Société de Géographie de Paris,* 11, (Series 3): 265–350 and 12: 57–93.

Blyden, E.W. 1873. "Report on the Expedition to Timbo." In Hollis R. Lynch (ed.) *Selected Letters of Edward Wilmot Blyden.* Kto Press, Millward, New York, 1978, pp. 117–39.

Boilat, P.D. 1853. *Esquisses sénégalaises.* Paris: Bertrand. 534 pp.

Bouet, W.E. 1848. *Commerce et traites des Noirs aux côtes occidentales d'Afrique.* Paris: Imprimerie Nationale. 230 pp. With maps.

Bouflers, S.J. (Le Chevalier de) 1875. *Correspondance inédite de la comtesse de Sabran et du Chevalier de Bouflers (1778–1788).* Collected and published by E. Magnien and Henri Prat. Paris. Vol. XVI. 527 pp.

1905. *Journal inédit du second séjour du Chevalier de Bouflers au Sénégal (3 décembre 1786–25 décembre 1787)*. Paris: Editions de la Revue bleue (Issue of 12 August and subsequent issues). 196 pp.

Boulegue, J. 1967. "Relation de Francisco d'Andrade sur les Iles du Cap-Vert et la côte occidentale d'Afrique (1582)." *Bulletin de l'I.F.A.N.* Vol. 29, Series B, Nos. 1–2, pp. 67–87.

1967. "Relation du port du Fleuve Sénégal de Joâo Barbosa, faite par Joâo Baptista Lavanha (vers 1600)." *Bulletin de l'I.F.A.N.*, Vol. 29, Series B, Nos. 3–4, pp. 496–511.

Brosselard, C. 1886. *Rapport sur la situation dans la vallée du Sénégal en 1886, Insurrection de Mamadou Lamine*. Lille.

Ca da Mosto, A.D. 1937. *The voyages of Cadamosto and other documents on Western Africa in the Second Half of the Fifteenth Century*. Edited by G.R. Crone, London.

Caillé, R. 1830. *Journal d'un voyage à Tombouctou et à Jenné dans l'Afrique centrale*. 3 vols., with maps. Paris: Imp. Royale. 475, 426, and 404 pp.

Carrère, F. and P.H. 1855. *De la Sénégambie française*. Paris: Fournier, Didot. 396 pp.

Castro e Almeira, V de. 1934. *Les grands navigateurs et colons portugais du Xve siècle; anthologie des écrits de l'époque*. Vols. I and II. Paris: Duchartre.

Cenival, P. de and M.T. 1938. *Description de la côte d'Afrique de Ceuta au Sénégal (1506–1507)*. Valentim Fernandes. Paris: Larose. 216 pp.

Chambonneau. 1898. "Relation de Sr Chambonneau." *Bulletin de géographie historique et descriptive* 2, 308–21.

1968. "Deux textes sur le Sénégal (1673–1677)." Edited by Carson I.A. Ritchie. *Bulletin de l'I.F.A.N.* 30, 289–353.

Chevalier, A. A. Cigny, and P. Rambaud. 1900. *Une mission au Sénégal*. Paris.

Dapper, O. 1686. *Description de l'Afrique*. Translated from the Flemish. Amsterdam: Wolfgang Waesberge Boom Van Someren. 556 pp.

D'Avity, P. 1640. *Description générale de l'Afrique . . .* Paris.

Doucouré, L. and S. Diaowé. 1967. *Légende de la dispersion des Kusa (épopée Soninké)*. Claude Meillassoux, Lassana Doucouré, and Diaowé Simgha. Dakar: I.F.A.N. 134 pp.

Duguay-Clédor, A. 1931. *Essais sur l'histoire du Sénégal. La bataille de Guilé, suivie de Faidherbe à Cappolani ou les Gandiols-Gandiols au service de la France*. Saint-Louis: Imprimerie du Gouvernement du Sénégal. 143 pp.

Durand, J.B.L. 1807. *Voyage au Sénégal 1785–1786*. 2nd edition, 2 vols. Paris: H. Agasse (1802: 2 vols. 360 and 384 pp.).

1807. *Atlas pour servir au voyage du Sénégal*. Paris: Agasse, VII, 67 pp. With 43 plates.

Estancelin, L. 1833. *Recherches sur les voyages et découvertes des navigateurs normands en Afrique*. Paris: Pinaud.

Faidherbe, L.L.C. 1856. "Populations noires du Sénégal et du Haut-Niger." *Bulletin de la socété de géographie de Paris*, 2 (4th series), 281–300.

1858. "Notice sur la colonie du Sénégal." *Annuaire du Sénégal et Dépendances*. pp. 71–144.

1863. "L'avenir du Sahara et du Soudan." *Revue maritime et coloniale*, 221–48.

1882. *Grammaire et Vocabulaire de la langue Poul à l'usage des voyageurs dans le Soudan*. Paris: Maisonneuve et Cie. 165 pp.

1889. *Le Sénégal : La France dans l'Afrique occidentale.* Paris: Hachette. 501 pp.

Faure, C. 1914–16. "Documents inédits sur l'histoire du Sénégal (1816–1822)." *Bulletin de la section de géographie,* Comité des travaux historiques et scientifiques, 29, 80–127.

Fernandes, V. 1951. *Description de la côte occidentale d'Afrique (Sénégal au cap Monte, Archipels, 1506–1507).* Translated by T. Monod, A. Teixeira Da Mota, and R. Mauny. Bissau. 227 pp., 9 fig.

Flize, L. 1856. "Le Boundou." *Le moniteur du Sénégal et Dépendances,* No. 37, p. 2 (9 Dec.).

1857. "Le Bambouk." *Le moniteur du Sénégal et Dépendances,* No. 51, pp. 3–4 and No. 52, p. 3 (17 and 23 March).

1857. "Le Ndiambour et le Gadiaga (provinces du Sénégal)." *Revue coloniale,* 17,2nd series: 390–8.

1857. "Le Gadiaga." *Le moniteur du Sénégal et Dépendances,* No. 42 (January), pp. 3–4.

1857. "Le Boundou (Sénégal)." *Revue coloniale,* 17, 2nd series (January), pp. 175–8.

1857. "Exploration dans le Bambouk (Sénégal)." *Revue coloniale,* 17, 2nd series (January), pp. 384–9.

1857. "Le Sénégal, le Niger, et le lac Tchad." *Revue coloniale,* 17, 2nd series (January), pp. 276–83.

Froideveaux, H. 1898. "La découverte de la chute de Félou, 1687." *Bulletin de gégraphie historique et descriptive,* 13, pp. 300–21.

1899. "Les mémoires inédits d'Adanson sur l'île de Gorée et la Guyane française." *Bulletin de géographie historique et descriptive,* 14, pp. 70–100.

1905. "Une exploration oubliée de la Falémé (Voyage du Durillon en 1740)." *Revue Africaine,* No. 257 (2nd quarter), pp. 192–204.

1917. "Une lettre d'Adanson pendant son voyage au Sénégal." *Revue de l'Histoire des Colonies Françaises, (R.H.C.F.)* 5, pp. 79–90.

Gaden, H. 1912. "Légendes et coutumes sénégalaises : cahiers de Yoro Dyao." *Revue d'ethnographie et de sociologie,* 3, pp. 119–37, 191–202.

Gaby, F.Y.B. 1689. *Relation de la négritie contenant une exacte description de ses royaumes et leurs gouvernements avec la découverte de la Rivière du Sénégal.* Paris: Edme Conterot. 90 pp.

Gallieni, Lt. Col. 1891. *Deux campagnes au Soudan Français, 1886–1888.* VIII. Paris: Librairie Hachette. 658 pp, 1 plate, 2 maps.

Geoffrey, V.R. de 1814. *L'Afrique ou histoire, moeurs, usages et coutumes des Africains.* 4 vols. Paris.

Goldberry, S.M.X. 1802. *Fragments d'un voyage en Afrique pendant les années 1785, 1786, 1787.* Paris: Trentel et Wurtz, An X. 2 vols.

1802. *Fragments d'un voyage en Afrique pendant les années 1785, 1786, 1787, dans les contrées occidentales de ce continent, comprises entre le Cap-Blanc de Barbarie… et le Cap des Palmes….* 2 vols. Paris: An X.

Gray, W. 1825. *Travels in Western Africa in the Years 1818, 1819, 1820 and 1821.* London. (Paris: Avril de Cartel, 1826.) 391 pp, illustrated.

Guebhard, P. 1909. "Les Peulh du Fouta Djallon," *Revue des études ethnographiques et sociologiques,* 2, pp. 85–108.

1910. *Au Fouta Djallon : Elevage, agriculture, commerce, régime foncier, religion.* Paris.

Ingram. 1847. "Abridged Account of an Expedition of about two hundred Miles up the Gambia," *Journal of the Royal Geographical Society,* 17, pp. 150–5.

Jamburia, O. 1919. "The Story of the Gihad or Holy War of the Foulahs," *Sierra Leone Studies,* 3, pp. 30–4.

Jannequin, R.C. de 1643. *Voyage de Lybie au royaume de Sénégal, le long du Niger, avec la description des habitants qui vont le long de ce fleuve, leurs coutumes et façon de vivre, les particularités les plus remarquables de ces pays.* Paris: C. Rouillard. 328 pp.

Jobson, R. 1932. *The Golden Trade, or A Discovery of the River Gambia.* London. First published 1623.

Kamara, C.M. 1970. "La vie d'El-Hadji Omar." Translated and edited by Amar Samb. *Bulletin de l'I.F.A.N.,* Vol. 32, Series B, pp. 44–135, 370–411, 770–818.

Kati, M.B.El H. 1964. *Tarikh El-Fettach.* Translated by O. Houdas and M. Delafosse. Paris: Maisonneuve. 362 pp.

Labarthe, P. 1802. *Voyage au Sénégal pendant les années 1784 et 1785, d'après les mémoires de Lajaille.* Paris: Denter, An X. 262 pp.

Labat, J.B. 1728. *Nouvelle relation de l'Afrique occidentale.* Paris: Cavelier. 5 vols.

La Courbe, S. de. 1913. *Premier voyage du Sieur de la Courbe fait à la coste d'Afrique en 1685.* Edited by Pierre Cultru. Paris: Champion et Larose.

Lamartiny, J.J. 1884. *Études Africaines : Le Boundou et le Bambouc.* Paris.

Lambert, A. 1861. "Voyage dans le Fouta Djallon, côtes occidentales d'Afrique (février–juin 1860)." *Revue maritime et coloniale,* Vol. 2, 2nd quarter, pp. 1–51.

Lamiral, D.H. 1789. *L'Afrique et le peuple africain considérés sous tous les rapports avec notre commerce et nos colonies.* Paris: Dessene. 400 pp.

Lasnet, Dr. 1900. "Les races du Sénégal. Sénégambie et Casamance," in Lasnet et al., *Une mission au Sénégal.* Paris: Challamel. Exposition Universelle de 1900, pp. 1–193.

Le Blanc. 1822. "Voyage à Galam en 1820," *Annales maritimes et coloniales,* Part 2, Vol. 1, pp. 133–59.

Le Brasseur. 1778. *Détails historiques et politiques sur la religion, les moeurs et le commerce des peuples qui habitent la côte occidentale d'Afrique dépuis l'Empire du Maroc jusqu'aux Rivières de Casamance et Gambie.* Bibliothèque nationale, fonds français 12080. Edited and published by V. Martin and C. Becker, Kaolack, 1975. 24 pp. cyclostyled.

Le Maire. 1695. *Voyage to the Canaries, Cape Verd, and the Coast of Africa under the command of M. Dancourt (1682).* Translated by Edmund Goldsmid. Edinburgh, 1887. Paris: Jacques Collambat. 235 pp, 5 engravings.

Lindsay, R.J. 1759. *A Voyage to the Coast of Africa in 1758.* London.

Lintingre, P. 1966. "Voyage du Sieur du Glicourt à la Côte occidentale d'Afrique pendant les années 1778 et 1779," *Dossiers africains,* No. 3. Reproduced *Afrique Documents,* No. 84. 171 pp. 8 plates, bibliography.

Machat, J. 1906. *Documents sur les établissements français et l'Afrique occidentale au XVIIIe siècle.* Paris: Challamel. 140 pp.

Marche, A. 1879. *Trois voyages en Afrique occidentale.* 2nd edition, Paris, 1882. Paris: Hachette.

Marmol Carvajal, L.D. 1573–99. *La description general Africa, con todos Los*

*Successos de guerras que a avido … hasta el ano del señor 1751.* 3 vols. Granada and Malaga.

Mollien, G. 1820. *Voyage dans l'intérieur de l'Afrique.* 2 vols. Paris: Courcier. 337 and 319 pp.

1967 *L'Afrique occidentale en 1818 vue par un explorateur français.* Edited by Hubert Deschamps. Paris: Calmann-Levy. 300 pp. (1st edition: 1820).

Monod, T., R. Mauny, and G. Doval. 1959. *De la première découverte de la Guinée, écrit par Diego Gomès (fin du Xve siècle).* Memoire No. 21. Bissau: Centro dos Estudos da Guiné Portugesa.

Moore, F. 1738. *Travels into the Inland Part of Africa…* London: Edward Cave.

Monsérat. 1970. "Mémoire inédit de Monsérat sur l'histoire du Nord du Sénégal de 1819 à 1839." Edited and annotated by Boubacar Barry. *Bulletin de l'I.F.A.N., Vol. 32,* Series B, pp. i+43 pp.

Monteil, C. 1905. *Contes Soudanais.* Paris.

1953. "La légende du Ouagadou et l'Origine des Soninké." *Mélanges ethnologiques.* Dakar, pp. 359–408.

Monteil, V. 1966. *Esquisses Sénégalaises.* Initiations et Etudes Africaines. I.F.A.N., No. XXI. Dakar.

Monteilhet, J. 1916. *Documents relatifs à l'histoire du Sénégal.* C.E.H.-S.A.O.F., 62–119.

Morenas, J. 1820. *Pétition contre la traite des noirs qui se fait au Sénégal.* Paris.

Noirot, E. 1883. *A travers le Fouta-Djallon et le Bambouck.* Paris: Dreyfous. 360 pp.

Pacheco Preira, D. 1956. *Esmeraldo de Situ Orbis (Côte Occidentale – Afrique du Sud Marocain au Gabon)* Edited by Raymond Mauny. Bissau. 226 pp.

Pageard, R. 1961. "Un mystérieux voyage au pays de Bambouc (1789)," *Notes africaines,* No. 89 (January), pp. 23–27.

Park, M. 1816–17. *Travels in the interior districts of Africa.* 2 vols. London. (Paris: Dentru-Carteret-Tavernier, An VIII (P t 1797) – 411.) 376 pp. 2 maps.

Pascal, S.L. 1860. "Voyage d'exploration dans le Bambouk, Haut-Sénégal," *Revue algérienne et coloniale,* 3: 137–64.

1861. "Voyage au Bambouk et retour à Bakel," *Le Tour du monde,* 3: pp. 39–48.

Pelletan, J.G. An. XI *Mémoire sur la colonie française du Sénégal avec quelques considérations historiques et politiques sur la traite des Nègres…* Edited by Marc-François Guillois. Paris: An XI.

Perrotet, M. 1833. "Voyage de Saint-Louis, chef-lieu du Sénégal à Podor fait en 1825." *Nouvelles Annales des Voyages et des Sciences Géographiques, 28,* January–June.

Prelong. 1793. "Mémoires sur les îles de Gorée et du Sénégal." *Annales de Chimie,* 18: 241–303.

Prevost d'Exiles, A.A.F. 1747–80. *Histoire générale des voyages.* New edition in 25 volumes. The Hague.

Pruneau de Pommegorge, A.E. 1789. *Description de la négritie.* Paris. 286 pp.

Raffenel, A. 1846. *Voyage dans l'Afrique occidentale exécuté en 1843 et 1844.* Paris: Bertrand. 512 pp.

1849. "Divers itinéraires de la Sénégambie et du Soudan." *Bulletin de la société de géographie de Paris,* 12 (3rd series): 303–30.

1849. "Second voyage d'exploration dans l'intérieur de l'Afrique, entreprise par M.A. Raffenel." *Revue coloniale,* 3 (2nd series): 217–76.

1849. "Le Haut-Sénégal et la Gambie en 1843 et 1844." *Revue coloniale*, 8: 309–40.

1849, 1850. "Second voyage d'exploration dans l'intérieur de l'Afrique." *Revue coloniale*, December (1849), pp. 217–305; June (1850), pp. 389–419.

1856. *Nouveau voyage au pays des nègres*. Paris: Chaix. 2 vols. 512 and 456 pp.

Rançon, A. 1894. "Le Boundou." *Bulletin de la Société de géographie de Bordeaux*.

1894. *Dans la Haute-Gambie: Voyage d'exploration scientifique 1891–1892*. Paris. 592 pp.

Roberts, G.P. 1726. *Four Years of Voyages of Captain George Roberts...* London.

Roger, M. le B. 1824. "Lettre de M. Roger, Gouverneur du Sénégal, à M. Jomard, membre de la Société de Géographie." *Bulletin de la société de géographie*, 2nd series, pp.176–8.

1825. "Résultats de questions adressées au nommé Mbouia, marabout maure, de Tischit, et à un nègre de Walet, qui l'accompagnait." *Recueil de mémoires*. Paris: Société de Géographie, pp. 51–62.

Rousseau, R. 1929. *Le Sénégal d'autrefois : étude sur le Oualo. Cahiers de Yoro Dyao. Bulletin du Comité d'Etudes Historiques et Scientifiques de l' Africque occidentale Française (B.C.E.H.S.A.O.F.)*, Vol. 2, Nos. 1–2: pp. 133–211.

1932. *Le Sénégal d'autrefois : étude sur le Toubé. Papier de Rawane Boy*. Paris: Cavose, 1932. Extract, B.C.E.H.S.A.O.F., Vol. 14, No. 3, 1931.

1933. *Le Sénégal d'autrefois: étude sur le Cayor. Cahier de Yoro Dyao*. B.C.E.H.S.A.O.F. Vol. 16, No. 2 (April–June), pp. 237–98.

1941. "Le Sénégal d'autrefois: seconde étude sur le Cayor (complèments tirés des manuscrits de Yoro Dyao)." *Bulletin de l'I.F.A.N.*, Nos. 1–4 (January–October), pp. 79–144.

Roux, E. 1893. *Notice historique sur le Boundou*. Saint-Louis: Imprimerie du Gouvernement. 15 pp.

Ruitiers, D., G.T., and J.P.R. 1969. "Le Flambeau de la Navigation de Dierrick Ruiters." *Bulletin de l'I.F.A.N.*, 31, Series B, No. 1, 106–19.

Saugnier. 1791. *Relations de plusieurs voyages à la côte d'Afrique au Maroc, au Sénégal, à Gorée, à Galam*. Paris. 341 pp.

Savigny, J.B.A.C. 1968. *Narrative of a voyage to Senegal in 1816*. London.

Semp, H. 1913. *La légende des griots Malinké*. Paris.

Smith, W. 1744. *A new voyage to Guinea*. London.

Soh, S.A. 1913. *Chroniques du Fouta Sénégalais*. Translated, with notes and an introduction, by Maurice Delafosse and Henri Gaden. Paris: Leroux. 328 pp.

Sow, A.I. 1968. *Chroniques et récits du Foûta Djalon*. Paris.

Stibbs, B., E., D., and R.H. 1738. "Journal of a voyage up the Gambia," in Francis Moore, *Travels into the Inland Parts of Africa*, London, pp. 235–97.

Stuckle, H. 1864. *Le commerce de la France avec le Soudan*. Paris.

Thilmans, G. and N.I. de Moraes. 1972. "La description de la côte de Guinée du père Balthasar Barreira 1606." *Bulletin de l'I.F.A.N.*, Vol. 34, Series B, No. 1 (January), pp. 1–50.

Tyam, M.A. 1935. *La vie d'el Hadj Omar*. Quacida en Poular. Transcription et Note de H. Gaden. Paris: Institut d'Ethnologie. 292 pp.

Van den Broek, P. 1725. "Voyage au Cap-vert," *Recueil des voyages qui servit à l'établissement et au progrès de la Compagnie des Indes Orientales*. 2nd edn, Amsterdam, pp. 289–93.

Vieillard, G.P. 1939. *Notes sur les Peuls au Fouta-Djallon.* Paris: Larose. 127 pp.
Villaut, N.S. de B. 1669. *Relations des côtes d'Afrique appelées Guinée.* Paris: Denys, Thierry.
Wade, A. 1966. "Chronique du Walo Sénégalais, 1186–1855." Translated from the Wolof by Bassirou Cissé. Published, with a commentary by Vincent Monteil, *Esquisses sénégalaises.* Dakar: I.F.A.N. *Bulletin de l'I.F.A.N.*, Vol. 26, Series B, Nos. 3–4, 1964. pp. 440–98.
Walckenaer, C.A. 1826–31. *Histoire générale des voyages.* 21 vols. Paris.
Winterbottom, T. 1969. *An account of the native African in the Neighbourhood of Sierra Leone.* 2 vols. 2nd edn. Frank Cass, London. 362 pp. and 283 pp.
Zeltner, F. de. 1913. *Contes du Sénégal et du Niger.*


ARTICLES

Alquier, P. 1922. "Saint-Louis du Sénégal pendant la Révolution et l'Empire (1789–1809)." *Bulletin C.E.H.S.A.O.F.,* 5, pp. 277, 320, 411–63.
Anonymous. 1828. "Afrique: Notice sur le Sénégal, la colonie française, ses dépe dances, les pays et les peuples environnants." *Journal des Voyages,* 37, pp. 5–27.
1916. "Un plan de colonisation du Sénégal en 1802." *Annuaire et mémoires du comité d'études historiques et scientifiques de l'AOF,* 1, pp. 130–214.
Bâ, T.O. 1957. "Essai historique sur le Rip (Sénégal)." *Bulletin de l'I.F.A.N.,* Series B, July–October, pp. 564–91.
Barry, B. 1978. "Crise politique et importance des révoltes populaires au Fuuta Jallon au XIXe siècle." *Africa Zamani, Revue d'Histoire Africaine (*Yaoundé), December, Nos. 8 and 9, pp. 51–61.
Bathily, A. 1972. "La conquête française du Haut-Fleuve (Sénégal) 1818–1887." *Bulletin de l'I.F.A.N.,* Vol. 34, Series B, No. 1, pp. 67–112.
Béart, C. 1947. "Sur les Bassari du cercle de Haute-Gambie (Sénégal)." *Notes africaines,* No. 34, pp. 24–6; No. 35, pp. 1–7.
Becker, C. and V. Martin. 1975. "Kajoor et Baol. Royaumes Sénégalais et traite des esclaves au XVIIIe siècle." *Revue Française d'Histoire d'Outre-mer,* Nos. 226–227, pp. 270–300.
1976. "Histoire sociale, économique, politique et religieuse du Kayor et du Baol (1695–1809)." Part II: *Recueil de documents historiques.* Kaolack. Mimeographed. 94 pp.
1977. "La Sénégambie à l'époque de la traite des esclaves." *Société Française d'Histoire d'Outre-mer,* No. 235, pp. 203–24.
Berdalle, J.B. 1917. "Monographie du Baol." *Bulletin de l'Enseignement de l'A.O.F,* No. 29, January, pp. 120–4.
Boulègue, J. 1966. "Contribution à la chronologie du royaume du Saloum." *Bulletin de l'I.F.A.N.* Vol. 28, Series B, Nos. 3–4, pp. 657–62.
1977. "Lat Sukabe Fal ou l'opiniâtreté d'un roi contre les échanges inégaux au Sénégal." *Collection Les Africains,* Vol. 9, pp. 167–93.
Boulègue, J. and B. Pinto Bull. 1966. "Les Relations du Cayor avec le Portugal dans la première moitié du XVIe siècle, d'aprè deux documents nouveaux." *Bulletin de l'I.F.A.N.* Series B, Nos. 3–4.
Brooks, G. 1980. 1975. "Peanuts and colonialism: consequences of the commercial-

ization of peanuts in West Africa 1830–1870." *Journal of African History,* Vol. 16, No. 1, pp. 29–54.

"Kola trade and state building in Upper Guinea Coast and Senegambia, XV-XVII Century." African Studies Center Working Papers, No. 38. Boston University.

1980. "Luso-African Commerce and Settlement in the Gambia and Guinea Bissau Region." African Studies Center Working Papers, Boston University.

Carreira, A. 1964. "Panaria Cabo-verdiano-Guinense : Aspectos historicos e socio-económicos." Lisbon.

1968. "Aspectos da influencia da cultura portugese na área comprendida entre o rio Senegal e o norte da Serra Leoa." *Boletim cultural da Guiné Portugese,* 20, pp. 373–416.

Charles, E.A. 1975. "Shaikh Amadu Ba and Jihad in Jolof." *The International Journal of African Historical Studies,* Vol. 8, No. 3, pp. 367–82.

Cissoko, S.M. 1967. "Civilisation Wolofo-Sérère au Xve siècle d'après les sources portugaises." *Présence Africaine,* No. 62, pp. 121–67.

1981. "L'impact de la Guerre sainte Umarienne dans les royaumes du Xaso 1850–1860." A collection in homage to Raymond Mauny. Paris: Société française d'histoire d'Outre-mer.

Colvin, L.J. 1974. "Islam and the State of Kajor: A Case of Successful Resistance to Jihad." *Journal of African History,* Vol. 15, No. 4. pp. 587–606.

1975. "International Relations in Precolonial Senegal." *Présence Africaine,* Vol. 93 (1st quarter), pp. 215–30.

1977. "Theoretical Issues in Historical International Politics: The Case of the Senegambia." *Journal of Interdisciplinary History,* Vol. 8, No.1 (Summer), pp. 23–44.

Curtin, P.D. 1968. "Epidemiology and the slave trade." *Political Science Quarterly,* Vol. 2, No. 83, pp. 190–216.

1971. "Jihad in West Africa. Early Phases and Interrelations in Mauritania and Senegal." *Journal of African History,* Vol. 12, No. 1.

Diop, A.B. 1968. "La tenure foncière en milieu rural Wolof." *Notes africaines,* No. 118, April, pp. 48–52.

Dodwell, H. 1916. "Le Sénégal sous la domination anglaise." R.H.C.F., Vol. 4, pp. 267–300.

Faure, C. 1919. "Le voyage d'exploration de Grout de Beaufort au Sénégal en 1824 et 1825." *Bulletin de la section de géographie, Comité des travaux historiques et scientifiques,* Vol. 34, pp. 146–204.

1920. "Le garnisson européenne du Sénégal (1779–1858)." R.H.C.F. Vol. 8, pp. 5–108.

1921. "Le premier séjour de Duranton au Sénégal (1819–1826)." R.H.C.F., Vol. 9, pp. 189–263.

Gaden, H. 1911. "Du régime des terres de la vallée du Sénégal au Fouta antérieure-ment à l'occupation française." *Renseignements coloniaux,* No. 10. pp. 246–50. Republished in C.E.H.S.A.O.F., Vol. 18, pp. 403–14. (1935).

1929. "La gomme en Mauritanie." *Annales de l'académie des sciences sociales,* Vol. 4, pp. 219–27.

Guèye, M. 1966. "La fin de l'esclavage à Saint-Louis et à Gorée en 1848." *Bulletin de l'I.F.A.N.,* Vol. 28, pp. 637–56.

Hardy, G. 1917. "L'affaire Duranton." *Annuaire et mémoires du comité d'études historiques et scientifiques de l'A.O.F.,* Vol. 2, pp. 413–36.

Hrbeck, I. 1976. "A Fighting Marabout. The Beginning of Mamadu Lamin's Struggle in Senegal." *Praha-Archiv. Oriental,* Vol. 44.

Idowu, H.A. 1917. "Café au lait: Sénégal's Mulatto Community in the Nineteenth Century." *Journal of the Historical Society of Nigeria,* Vol. 6, pp. 271–88.

Kane, A. 1916. "Histoire et origine des familles du Fouta Toro." *Annuaire du comité d'études historiques et scientifiques de l'A.O.F.,* Vol. 1, pp. 325–43.

Kane, A.S. 1935. "Du régime des terres chez les populations du Fouta sénégalais." *C.E.H.A.O.F.,* Vol. 18, pp. 449–61.

Kane, O. 1970. "Essai de Chronologie des satigis au XVIIIe siècle." *Bulletin de l'I.F.A.N.,* Vol. 32 (July), pp. 755–65.

—— 1970. "Samba Gelajo Jegi." *Bulletin de l'I.F.A.N.,* Vol. 32, Series B, No. 4, pp. 911–26.

—— 1973. "Les unités territoriales du Futa Toro." *Bulletin de l'I.F.A.N.,* Vol. 35, Series B, No. 3, pp. 614–33.

—— 1974. "Les Maures et le Futa Toro au XVIIIe siècle." *Cahier d'études africaines,* Vol. 14, No. 54, pp. 237–52.

Klein, M. 1972. "Social and Economic Factors in the Muslim Revolution in Senegambia." *Journal of African History,* Vol. 13, No. 3, pp. 419–41.

Knight-Baylac, M.H. 1970. "La vie à Gorée de 1677 à 1789." R.H.C.F., Vol. 58, pp. 377–420.

La Chapelle, F. de. 1935. "Esquisse d'une herbe du Sahara occidental." *Hespéris,* Vol. 2, pp. 35–95.

Lasserre, G. 1948. "L'or du Soudan." *Cahiers d'outre-mer,* Vol. 1, pp. 368–74.

Legrand, R. 1912. "Le Fouladou." *La géographie,* Vol. 24, pp. 241–53.

Lejean, G. 1859. "Le Sénégal en 1859 et les routes commerciales du Sahara." *Revue contemporaine,* Vol. 2, pp. 368–403.

Lespinot. 1828. "Sénégal. Saint-Louis. Esclavage des nègres dans l'établissement français." *Revue encyclopédique,* Vol. 37, pp. 549–51.

L'Orza R. de. 1892. "De Kayes au Bambouk." *Revue de géographie,* Vol. 30, pp. 101–71.

Ly, A. 1953. "Conséquences des cas Labat et Loyer." *Bulletin de l'I.F.A.N.,* Vol. 15, pp. 751–66.

Ly, D. 1938. "Coutumes et contes des Toucouleurs du Futa Toro." *B.C.E.H.S.A.O.F.,* Vol. 21, pp. 304–26.

Macklin, P. 1935. "Queens and Kings of Niumi." *Man.*

Makarius, L. 1969. "Observations sur la légende des griots malinké." *Cahiers d'Etudes Africaines (C.E.A.),* Vol. 9, pp. 626–40.

Mane, M. 1978. "Contribution à l'histoire du Kaabu, des origines au XIXe siècle." *Bulletin de l'I.F.A.N.,* Vol. 40, Series B, No. 1 (January), pp. 87–159.

Marty, P. 1927. "Les chroniques de Oualata et de Néma." *Revue des études islamiques,* Cahiers III et IV, pp. 305, 426, 531–75.

Masson, P. 1932. "Une double énigme : André Brue." *R.H.C.F.,* Vol. 25. pp. 9–34.

Mbaeyi, P.M. 1967. "The British–Barra War of 1831: A reconsideration of its origins and importance." *Journal of the Historical Society of Nigeria,* Vol. 3, (June), pp. 617–31.

McCall, D.F. 1971. "The Cultural Map and Time-Profile of the Mande-Speaking

Peoples," published in Carleton T. Hodge, ed., *Papers on the Mande-Manding.* Bloomington.

McGowan, W.F. 1981. "Fula Resistance to French Expansion into Futa Jallon, 1889–1896." *Journal of African History.*

Meillassoux, C. 1960. "Essai d'interpretation du phénomène économique dans les sociétés traditionnelles et d'autosubsistance." *C.E.A.,* Vol. 1, pp. 38–67.

1964. De l'économie d'autosubsistance à l'agriculture commerciale en pays gouro (Cote d'Ivoire). Paris-Hague.

Mere, G. 1911. "Les salines du Trarza." *Renseignements coloniaux,* Vol. 7, pp. 161–7.

Mettas, J. 1975. "La traite portugaise en Haute-Guinée, 1758–1797. Problèmes et Méthodes." *Journal of African History,* Vol. 16, No. 3, pp. 343–63.

Montheilhet, 1917. "Les finances et commerce du Sénégal pendant les guerres de la Révolution et de l'Empire." *B.C.E.H.S.A.O.F.,* Vol. 2, pp. 362–412.

J. 1920. "Le duc de Lauzun, gouverneur du Sénégal." *B.C.E.H.S.A.O.F.,* Vol. 3, pp. 193–237, 515–63.

Monteil, C. 1928. "Le site de Goundiourou." *B.C.E.H.S.A.O.F.,* Vol. 2, pp. 647–53.

1929. "Le Tékrour et la Guinée." *Outre-mer,* Vol. 1, pp. 387–405.

1950. "Réflexions sur le problème des Peuls." *Journal de la Société des Africanistes,* Vol. 20, pp. 153–92.

1966. "Fin de siècle à Médine (1898–1899)." *Bulletin de l'I.F.A.N.,* Vol. 28, pp. 84–171.

Monteil, V. 1941. "Goundiourou." *Notes africaines,* Vol. 12, pp. 63–4.

1966. "Le Djolof et Alburi Ndiaye." *Bulletin de l'I.F.A.N.,* Vol. 28, pp. 595–636.

Moraes, N.I. de. 1969. "Sur les prises de Gorée par les Portugais au XVIIe siècle." *Bulletin de l'I.F.A.N.,* Vol. 31, pp. 989–1013.

Moreira, J.M. 1964. "Os Fulas da Guiné portugesa na panoramica geral do mundo fula." *Boletim cultural da Guiné portugesa,* Vol. 19, pp. 289–327, 417–32.

Mouser, B.L. 1973. "Trade Coasters and Conflict in the Rio Pongo from 1790 to 1808." *Journal of African History.*

Ndiaye, L.O. 1966. "Le Djolof et ses bourbas." *Bulletin de l'I.F.A.N.,* Series B, Nos. 3–4, pp. 96–101.

Newbury, C.W., ed. 1966. "Northern African and Western Sudan Trade in the Nineteenth Century: A Re-evaluation." *Journal of African History,* Vol. 7, pp. 233–46.

Niane, D.T. 1960. "A Propos de Koli Tengella." *Recherches africaines,* Vol. 4, pp. 33–6.

Norris, H.T. 1969. "Znaga Islam during the Seventeenth and Eighteenth Centuries." *Bulletin of the School of Oriental and African Studies,* Vol. 32, pp. 496–526.

Pageard, R. 1962. "Contribution critique à la chronologie historique de l'Ouest africain." *Journal de la Société des Africanistes,* Vol. 32, pp. 91–117.

Pasquier, R. 1960. "Villes du Sénégal au XIXe siècle." *R.H.C.F.,* Vol. 47, pp. 387–425.

1968. "A propos de l'émancipation des esclaves au Sénégal en 1848." *R.H.C.F.,* Vol. 54, pp. 188–208.

Patenostre, Dr. 1930. "La captivité chez les peuples du Fouta-Djallon." *Outre-mer,* Vol. 2, pp. 241–54, 353–72.

Person, Y. 1963. "Les ancêtres de Samori." *C.E.A.*, Vol. 4, No. 13, pp. 125–56.

Quinn, C.A. 1968. "Niumi: A Nineteenth Century Mandingo Kingdom." *Africa*, Vol. 38, pp. 443–55.

Raybaud, L.P. 1968, 1969. "L'administration du Sénégal de 1781 à 1784 : L'affaire Dumonte." *Annales africaines*, 1968: pp. 113–72; 1969: pp. 173–210.

Robinson, D. 1973. "Abdul Qader and Shaykh Umar: A Continuing Tradition of Islam Leadership in Futa Toro." *International Journal of African Historical Studies*, Vol. 6, pp. 386–403.

Robinson, D., P.D. Curtin and J. Johnson. "Tentative Chronology of Fuuta Tooro from the Sixteenth Through the Nineteenth Century." *C.E.A.*, 48.

Rodney, W. 1965. "Portuguese Attempts at Monopoly on the Upper Guinea Coast, 1580–1650." *Journal of African History*, Vol. 6, pp. 307–22.

   1968. "Jihad and Social Revolution in Futa Djalon in the Eighteenth Century." *J.H.S.N.*, Vol. 4, pp. 269–84.

Sasoon, H. 1963. "Early Sources of Iron in Africa." *South African Archeological Bulletin*, Vol. 18, pp. 176–80.

Silla, O. 1969. "Essai historique sur Portudal." *Notes africaines, Vol.* 123, pp. 77–89.

Smith, H.F.C. 1961. "A Neglected Theme of West African History: The Islamic Revolutions of the nineteenth Century." *J.H.S.N.*, Vol. 2, pp. 169–85.

Smith, P. 1965. "3 notes sur l'organisation sociale des Diakhanké: Aspects particuliers à la région de Kédougou." *Bulletin et mémoires de la société d'anthropologie de Paris,* Vol. 5 (11th series), pp. 263–302.

   1968. "Les Diakhanké : Histoire d'une dispersion." *Bulletin et mémoires de la société d'anthropologie de Paris,* Vol. 8 (11th series), pp. 231–62.

Suret-Canale, J. 1970. "Touba in Guinea – Holy Place of Islam," in Christopher Allen and R.W. Johnson, eds., *African Perspectives: Papers in the History, Politics and Economics of Africa Presented to Thomas Hodgkin.* Cambridge, pp. 53–81.

   1977. "La Sénégambie à l'ère de la traite." *Revue canadienne des Etudes Africaines.*, Vol. 11, No. 1, pp. 125–34.

Sylla, A. 1955. "Une république africaine au XIXe siècle (1795–1857)." *Présence Africaine*, Nos. 1–2 (New Series), April–June, pp. 47–65.

Tautin, L. 1885. "Etudes critiques sur l'ethnologie et l'ethnographie des peuples du Bassin du Sénégal." *Revue ethnographique*, Vol. 4, pp. 61–80, 137–47, 256–68.

Techer, H. 1933. "Coutumes des Tendas. *B.C.E.H.S.A.O.F.*, Vol. 16: pp. 630–66.

Thilmans, G. 1968. "Sur l'existence, fin XVIe, de comptoirs néerlandais à Joal et Portugal (Sénégal)." *Notes africaines,* No. 2, pp. 17–18.

Thilmans, G. and I. de M. Nize. 1970. "Le routier de la côte de Guinée de Francisco Porez de Carvalho, 1635." *Bulletin de l'I.F.A.N.*, Vol. 32, pp. 23–369.

Vidal, M. 1935. "Etude sur la tenure des terres indigènes au Fouta." *B.C.E.H.S.A.O.F.*, Vol. 18, pp. 415–48.

Wane, Y. 1963. "Etat actuel de la documentation au sujet des Toucouleurs." *Bulletin de l'I.F.A.N.*, Vol. 25, pp. 459–77.

Wood, W.R. 1967. "An Archaeological Appraisal of Early European Settlements in the Senegambia." *Journal of African History*, Vol. 8, pp. 39–64.

Zuccarelli, F. 1962. "Le régime des engagés à temps au Sénégal, 1817–1848." *C.E.A.*, Vol. 7, pp. 420–61.

## GENERAL WORKS

Arcin, J. 1911. *Histoire de la Guinée française, Rivière du Sud, Fouta Djallon, région sud du Soudan.* Paris: Challamel. 752 pp.

Barry, B. 1972. *Le royaume du Walo, 1659–1859: Le Sénégal avant la conquête.* Paris, Maspero. 395 pp.

1976. *Bokar Biro – Le dernier Grand Almami du Fouta Djallon.* Paris, Editions ABC, 1978.

Boutillier, J. 1962. *La moyenne vallée du Sénégal – Etude socio-économique.* P.U.F.

Boutillier, J., P. Cantrelle, J. Causse, C. Lavrent, and T. Ndoye. 1962. *La moyenne vallée du Sénégal. A socio-economic study.* Paris.

Brooks, G. 1970. *Yankee Traders, Coasters and African Middlemen.* Boston: University Press. 370 pp.

Colvin, L.G. 1981. *Senegal.* African Historical Dictionary, No. 23. The Scarecrow Press.

Courtet, M. 1904. *Etude sur le Sénégal.* Paris: Challamel. 183 pp.

Crowder, M. 1968. *West Africa Under Colonial Rule.* Evanston: Northwestern University Press.

Curtin, P. 1967. *Africa Remembered. Narratives by West Africans from the Era of the slave trade.* Madison: University of Wisconsin Press. 383 pp.

1969. *The Atlantic slave trade: A Census.* Madison: University of Wisconsin Press. 338 pp.

1975. *Economic Change in Precolonial Africa· Senegambia in the Era of the slave trade.* Wisconsin. 2 vols.

Delafosse, M. 1912. *Haut-Sénégal-Niger (Soudan Français).* 3 vols. Paris: Larose. 428pp.

Delcourt, A. 1952. *La France et les établissements français au Sénégal entre 1713 et 1763.* Dakar. I.F.A.N. 432 pp.

Désiré-Vuillemin, G.M. 1962. *Essai sur le gommier et le commerce de gomme dans les escales du Sénégal.* Dakar: Clairafrique. 102 pp.

1964. *Histoire de la Mauritanie.* Nouakchott: Ministry of Youth and Education, Islamic Republic of Mauritania. Paris: Hatier. 144 pp.

Diagne, P. 1967. *Pouvoir politique traditionnel en Afrique occidentale.* Paris: Présence Africaine. 294 pp.

Diallo, T. 1972. *Les institutions politiques du Fouta Djallon au XIXe siècle.* Initiations et Etudes Africaines, No. XXVIII, Dakar: I.F.A.N. 277 pp.

Dieng, A.A. 1979. *Hegel, Marx, Engels et les problèmes de l'Afrique noire.* Dakar: Sankore. 152 pp.

Diop, A.B. 1981. *La Société Wolof: Tradition et changement. Les systèmes d'inégalité et de domination.* Paris: Karthala. 357 pp.

Diop, C.A. 1959. *L'unité culturelle de l'Afrique noire.* Paris: Présence Africaine. 203 pp.

1959. *L'Afrique précoloniale.* Paris: Présence Africaine. 203 pp.

Diop, M. 1971–2. *Histoire des classes sociales en Afrique de l'Ouest.* 2 vols. I. *Le Mali:* 1971; II. *Le Sénégal:* 1972. Paris: Maspero.

Godinho, V.M. 1969. *L'Economie de l'Empire portugais aux Xve et XVIe siècles.* Paris: S.E.V.P.E.N.

Grant, D. 1968. *The Fortunate Slave: An Illustration of African Slavery in the Early Eighteenth Century.* London: Oxford University Press. 231 pp.

Gray, J.M. 1966. *History of the Gambia.* Frank Cass. 508 pp.

Hardy, G. 1921. *La mise en valeur du Sénégal.* Paris: Larose. 376 pp.

Klein, M. 1968. *Islam and Imperialism in Senegal: Sine-Saloum, 1847–1914.* Stanford University Press. 285 pp.

Labouret, H., J. Canu, J. Fournier, and G. Bonmarchand. 1933. *Le commerce extra européen jusqu'au temps modernes.* Paris.

Lacroix, L. 1952. *Les derniers négriers.* Paris.

Lestrange, M. 1955. *Les Coniagui et les Bassari.* Paris: Presses Universitaires de France. 86 pp.

Levtzion, N. 1968. *Muslims and Chiefs in West Africa.* Oxford: Clarendon Press. 228 pp.

1975. *The Early Jihad Movements.* Cambridge History of Africa. Vol. IV. Edited by Richard Gay.

Ly, A. 1958. *La compagnie du Sénégal.* Paris: Présence Africaine. 310 pp.

Martin, E.C. 1927. *The British West African Settlements 1750–1821.* London.

Marty, P. n.d. *Etudes Sénégalaises.* Paris: Leroux.

1919. *L'Emirat des Trarzas.* Paris: Leroux. 483 pp.

1921. *L'Islam en Guinée, le Fouta Djallon.* Paris: Leroux. 588 pp.

1921. *Etudes sur l'Islam et les tribus Maures, les Brakna.* Paris: Leroux. 399 pp.

n.d. (post–1925) *Etudes sur l'Islam au Sénégal.* 2 vols. Paris: Leroux. Vol. I: 444 pp; Vol. II: 412 pp.

Mauny, R. 1961. *Tableau géographique de l'Ouest africain au Moyen Age.* Dakar. 588 pp.

Mauro, F. 1960. *Le Portugal et l'Atlantique au XVIIe siècle (1570–1670): Etude économique.* Paris.

Meillassoux, C. 1975. *Femmes, greniers et capitaux.* Paris: Maspero.

Méniaud, J. 1912. *Haut-Sénégal–Niger: Géographie économique.* 2 vols. Paris: Leroux. 396 pp.

Mercier, R. 1962. *L'Afrique noire dans la littérature française: les premiers images (XVIIe–XVIIIe siècles).* Dakar. 242 pp.

Mettas, J. 1978. *Répertoire des expéditions négrières françaises au XVIIIe siècle, édité par Serge Dages.* Nantes, Paris: Société Française d'Histoire d'Outre-mer. Vol. I. 795 pp.

Michel, P. 1973. *Les Bassins des Fleuves Sénégal et Gambie – Etudes de Géomorphologie.* O.R.S.T.O.M. Thesis No. 63, pp. 37–38. Paris: O.R.S.T.O.M. 2 volumes. 752 pp.

Mombeya, T.M.S. 1971. *Le filon du bonheur éternel,* edited by Alfa Ibrahima Sow. Classiques Africaines. Paris: Armand Colin. 204 pp.

Newbury, C. 1967. "Trade and Authority in West Africa from 1850 to 1900," in L.H. Gann and Peter Duignan, eds. *Colonialism in Africa.* 4 Vols. Cambridge.

Pelissier, P. 1966. *Les paysans du Sénégal : les civilisations agraires du Cayor à la Casamance.* Saint-Yrieux, Fabregue. 940 pp.

Polanyi, R. 1966. *Dahomey and the slave trade: An Analysis of an Archaic Economy.* Seattle.

Pollet, E. 1971. *La société Soninke (Dyahunu, Mali). Etudes ethnographiques.* Brussels: Institut de Sociologie. 566 pp.

Poole, T.E. 1850. *Life, Scenery and Customs in Sierra leone and Gambia.* 2 vols. London.

Quinn, C.A. 1972. *Mandingo Kingdoms of the Senegambia: Traditionalism, Islam and European Expansion.* Northwestern University Press. 211 pp.

Rinchon, D. 1938. *Le trafic négrier d'après les livres de commerce du capitaine gantois Pierre-Ignace-Liévin Van Alstein.* Vol. I. Paris.

1964. *Pierre-Ignace-Liévin Van Alstein, capitaine négrier – Gand 1733. Nantes 1793.* Dakar: I.F.A.N. 452 pp.

Roche, C. 1976. *Conquête et Résistance des Peuples de Casamance, 1850–1920.* Dakar: N.E.A.

Rodney, W. 1970. *A History of the Upper Guinea Coast 1545 to 1800.* Oxford: Clarendon Press. 283 pp.

Saint-Pierre, J.H. 1925. *Les Sarakollé du Guidimakha.* Paris. Larose. 188 pp.

Saunier, E. 1921. *Une compagnie à privilège au XIXe siècle: La Compagnie de Galam au Sénégal.* Paris: Larose. 199 pp.

Schnapper, B. 1961. *La politique et le commerce français dans le golfe de Guinée de 1838 à 1871.* Paris: Mouton et Cie. 286 pp.

Shefer, C. 1921. *Instructions générales données de 1763 à 1870 aux gouverneurs et ordonnateurs des établissements français en Afrique occidentale.* 2 vols. Paris.

Sow, A.I. 1968. *Chronique et récits du Fuuta Jallon.* Paris: Librairie Klienksiek.

Sundstrom, L. 1965. *The Trade of Guinea.* Uppsala.

Suret-Canale, J. 1970. *La République de Guinée.* Paris: Editions Sociales. 432 pp.

Suret-Canale and B. Barry. 1976. "The Western Atlantic Coast 1600–1800," in *History of West Africa,* edited by Ajayi Crowder. Vol. I. Longman.

Tauxier, L. 1942. *Histoire des Bambara.* Paris.

Teixeira da Mota, A. 1954. *Guiné portugesa.* Lisbon.

Villard, A. 1943. *Histoire du Sénégal.* Dakar: Viale. 265 pp.

Wane, Y. 1969. *Les Toucouleurs du Fouta Tooro (Sénégal) : Stratification sociale et structure familiale.* Dakar. 251 pp.

# Index

# Other books in the series

Please remember that this is a library book,
and that it belongs only temporarily to each
person who uses it. Be considerate. Do
not write in this, or any, library book.

WITHDRAWN